Reconstructing
Architecture

PEDAGOGY AND CULTURAL PRACTICE

Edited by Henry Giroux and Roger Simon

Recognizing that pedagogy begins with the affirmation of differences as a precondition for extending the possibilities of democratic life, the series analyzes the diverse democratic and ideological struggles of people across a wide range of economic, social, and political spheres.

RECONSTRUCTING ARCHITECTURE

CRITICAL DISCOURSES AND SOCIAL PRACTICES

THOMAS A. DUTTON AND
LIAN HURST MANN, EDITORS

PEDAGOGY AND CULTURAL PRACTICE
VOLUME 5

University of Minnesota Press
Minneapolis
London

Published by the University of Minnesota Press
111 Third Avenue South, Suite 290, Minneapolis, MN 55401-2520
Printed in the United States of America on acid-free paper

Library of Congress Cataloging-in-Publication Data

Reconstructing architecture : critical discourses and social practices
  / Thomas A. Dutton and Lian Hurst Mann, editors.
     p.   cm. — (Pedagogy and cultural practice ; v. 5)
  Includes bibliographical references and index.
  ISBN 0-8166-2808-4
  ISBN 0-8166-2809-2 (pbk.)
    1. Architectural practice — Decision making. 2. Architecture and
society — History — 20th century. 3. Architecture, Postmodern — Social
aspects. I. Dutton, Thomas A. II. Mann, Lian Hurst.   III. Series.
NA1996.R33   1996
720'.1'03 — dc20   96-22384

The University of Minnesota is an
equal-opportunity educator and employer.

This book has been with us for several years. No project of such duration can come to fruition without touching many friends and scholars. We are thus indebted to a wide orbit of folks, who, from conversation to editing drafts, have helped shape the final outcome.

Having read the manuscript in its proposed form, Jim Mayo and Stephen Haymes deserve special thanks for their insight and support. The whole project would not have moved forward without their critique.

People like Tony Schuman, Bill and Sue Stiles, Paul Clarke, and Richard Quantz have been constant sounding boards, critical and encouraging. We thank their patience and trust that our exchange has been fruitful for them, as it has been for us.

Many colleagues have read drafts of particular chapters, providing help and recommendations for making our analyses sharper: Robert Benson, Denise Bratton, Rita Burgos, Paul Clarke, Sam Hurst, Richard Quantz, Jesse Reichek, Kate Rousmaniere, Tony Schuman, David Sholle, Leslie Kanes Weisman, and Robert Zwirn.

Special appreciation is due the Department of Architecture at Miami University and the Labor Community Strategy Center for their extended institutional support. The project would never have been launched were it not for the time and attention we both were able to devote to conceptualizing the book because of Tom's sabbatical and Lian's postdoctoral scholar position in the Graduate School of Education at UCLA during the year 1992.

To our respective spouses, Janis and Eric, writers and editors both, who were there at every step, we offer our deepest gratitude for their time and heartfelt apologies for the disruption this project has caused within their own busy schedules, not to mention our family lives. This book would not have been possible without their unending support, intellectual as well as emotional.

Last, we wish to acknowledge the tremendous dedication and vitality of each of the contributors to *Reconstructing Architecture* in their commitment to conceive, write, struggle with, and revise their chapters over a period of three years. We owe them our deepest gratitude as colleagues and friends.

Modernism, Postmodernism, and Architecture's Social Project

Today, as the world teeters on the edge of a new millennium, saddled with unprecedented technological capability as well as untold human suffering, architects concerned with the global transformations of civil society wrestle with the problems of how to theorize and practice politically progressive architecture. Given that architecture — practice and discourse — is always social, the central questions we address in this book are these: What constitutes "the social project" of architecture in the current historical context? What critical discourses and social practices advance such a project? Can architecture be reconstituted in terms of a new social project? Addressing these questions, this book takes the stance that the dominant understanding of the relationship between architecture and society propagated throughout the institutions of architecture is long overdue for critical reassessment. How architects construct an understanding of the social world and how that construct affects possibilities for practice are pivotal concerns for architects who seek to challenge the status quo, construct new social formations and new identities, and help reconstruct a viable democratic public life in the face of inexorable forces driving economic growth, destroying global ecology, homogenizing culture, and privatizing the public realm. These questions frame our point of departure for reconstructing architecture in the current period.

The purpose of the book, then, is twofold: (1) to reformulate the role of architecture in society as well as the specific understanding of architecture's capacity to further a progressive social transformation and (2) to advance strategies for practice based on that reformulation. The making of architecture is a social practice; it is unavoidably an epistemological activity.[1] Much of what we know of institutions, the distribution of power, social relations, cultural values, and everyday life is mediated by the built environment. Thus, to make architecture is to construct knowledge, to build vision. To make architecture is to map the world in some way, to intervene, to signify: it is a *political act*. Architecture, then, as discourse, discipline, and form, operates at the intersection of power, relations of production, culture, and representation and is instrumental to the construction of our identities and our differences, to shaping how we know the world. Historically, this practice has constructed the environments that house the dominant culture and, as such, has acted — de facto or by intent — to construct consciousness through lived experience.

Critical practices in architecture that recognize their social character, attempt to alter relations of power, and pursue what we will continue to call "the social project" in architecture have a long history and are vital today. The social project adopted by the modern movement in architecture pledged generations of architects to the betterment of society. As a particular form of modernity's program of social progress, this social project had a distinct character: it broke with architecture's traditional service to the status quo and committed architectural practice to the emancipation of humankind. Its strategic power rested in the social potential of technological advancement. The potential of mass production to enable mass distribution called for the elevation of images to further consumption and the design of type-forms for industrial production. Architects embraced the imperatives for innovation brought forth by new materials, technologies, and production processes as well as Fordian and Marxian theories of progress.

During the past three decades, however, this progressive social imperative in the field of architecture has lost its moral authority and its momentum. The near annihilation of this emancipatory project follows numerous shifts in historical conditions. First, the historical period is radically different in terms of political economy, as the moment of European socialist revolution between the two world wars has seemingly overnight become the moment of global capitalism's greatest victory. Second, there is a widespread loss of faith in the Enlightenment promise of inevitable progress, as "truth" and "reason" fail to advance the human condition. Third, profound philosophical and political disorientation follows the collapse of the socialist experiments that transformed the relations of production, experiments that were of great interest to early modernists, many of whom were socialists. And fourth, varied antitotalitarian schemata, from poststructuralist philosophies to "free market" ideologies, proliferate across the globe by means of the culture industry. These shifts mark basic changes in political economy and culture, on the one hand, and in the nature of theory construction, on the other—in what are being distinguished as the postmodern condition and postmodernism theory, respectively.

As these changes correspond to a profound worsening of social life, the emancipatory social project of modernity—to the extent that it is critically transformed to seek radical societal change within the most advanced forms of modern capitalism—still orients the practice of many to envision a future that is not a past. From fights to gain worker rights for immigrants to campaigns that oppose environmental racism, from the defense of *Roe v. Wade* and affirmative action to the rejection of the Contract with America and the censorship of art, from demands for affordable housing to enactments of radical performance art, the struggle to advance the human condition—in full recognition of the failed experiments around us—persists. And the struggle on the part of politically progressive, "organic" intellectuals (from factory floors to university halls) to define the present historical period, to describe its characteristics, and to generate responsive social practices has spawned a multiplicity of discourses and accompanying strategies, each engendering a field of debate that itself includes a diverse set of voices.

The field of architecture is no exception. Indeed, the varieties of postmodern architectural practice and discourse—from historicism to deconstructivism—have come to emblematize postmodern culture at large. Having been among the first fields to critique the effects of its own aesthetic modernism and declare a break, architecture is now posited by various theoretical frameworks to offer, on the one hand, a prime expression of the fractured sensibilities produced by the contemporary postmodern condition and, on the other, an anticipatory vision of the reformed sensibilities of a perhaps better posthumanist future. Within the array of responses to the crises of modernity, and to the undisputed failures within modernism in architecture in particular, reside practices that specifically seek to change the political status quo of power relations in daily life. This book engages this historical situation—in the gaps within the modernism-postmodernism debates—by presenting contemporary oppositional approaches in architectural practice in order to clarify their frameworks of explanation and critiques of dominant approaches, to articulate their various "projects of possibility," and to explicate their attitudes with regard to ethics, cultural values, and societal change, as well as design strategy and professional practice. This is done with the firm belief that contributions to a renewed understanding of a social project for architecture are not only possible, but presently emerging.

THE LATE CAPITALIST CONDITION

What, then, of current societal directions? How might a renewed assessment of architecture's social project benefit from recent characterizations of the current social condition? Keeping in sight the dialectical relationship between culture and political economy, critics and theorists of all stripes have tried their hand at characterizing the contemporary condition. Some scholars, such as Cornel West in his important 1990 essay, "The New Cultural Politics of Difference," mark the global scale of the changes taking place before us, pointing to the decentering of Europe, the centering of the United States, and the decolonization of Asia and Africa.[2] In 1917, V. I. Lenin, in *Imperialism, the Highest Stage of Capitalism,* anticipated these transformations, not only the shift from competitive to monopoly capitalism, but the emerging imperialist phase of capitalist expansion, which by necessity viewed the globe as the marketplace.[3] By 1975, political economist Ernest Mandel described the "long waves" of capitalist development in his groundbreaking text *Late Capitalism,* identifying the most recent expansionary long wave as starting with the victory of European fascism and the growth of Anglo-American war economies in the 1940s.[4] By 1984, the American Marxist Fredric Jameson, in his critical foreword to Jean-François Lyotard's *The Postmodern Condition: A Report on Knowledge,* supported Mandel's thesis by critiquing the postmodern positions that proclaimed an end to capitalism:

All the features mobilized by [conservative intellectual Daniel] Bell to document the end of capitalism as such — in particular the new primacy of science and technological invention, and the technocracy generated by that privileged position, as well as the shift from the older industrial technologies to the newer information ones — can be accounted for... as indices of a new and powerful, original, global expansion of capitalism, which now specifically penetrates the hitherto precapitalist enclaves of Third World agriculture and of First World culture, in which in other words, capital more definitively secures *the colonization of Nature and the Unconscious.*[5]

Theorist Kwame Anthony Appiah observed in *Critical Inquiry* that the global capitalist economy "has turned every element of the real into a sign, and the sign reads 'for sale.'"[6] Such global shifts have created a new spatiality as well as new experiences of space and time. Marshall McLuhan's dictum about the world becoming a global village is now all too apparent: distinctions between the first and the third worlds are blurred, evidenced by the growing throngs of people who toil endlessly in modern-day sweat shops in the long shadows of corporate skyscrapers.

Many terms have come to characterize these shifting conditions: postindustrialism, postmodernism, and post-Fordism, to name three. In his incisive book *New Times,* cultural theorist Stuart Hall writes of New Times as interpreted by the nuances of these terms.[7] For Hall, New Times are not adequately captured by any of these terms taken singularly. But together, interrelationally, they reveal profound shifts in how life is lived economically and culturally. In the economic sphere, Hall characterizes change "in the technical organization of industrial capitalist production" and the creation of "new productive regimes" as exemplary of the shift from Fordism to post-Fordism. Fordism is that "era of mass production, with its standardised products, concentrations of capital and its 'Taylorist' forms of work organization and discipline." Post-Fordism refers to the shift to information technologies, mass communication, and electronically transmitted information that enables geographically dispersed production units to be integrated into a "more flexible, specialised, and decentralised form of work organization." This is an economy dominated by multinational corporations, whose playing field is now truly that — multinational — and thereby able, as economist John Urry says, to undermine "the coherence, wholeness, and unity of individual societies" by the "globalization of new economic, social, and political relationships."[8] Consequently, within first world countries white-collar and service work has come to displace "the manual working class" as big centralized plants follow the path of the dinosaur and off-shore production becomes the rule. All this conspires to thrust consumption into the driver's seat, reflected by "greater emphasis on choice and product differentiation, on marketing, packaging and design, on the 'targeting' of consumers by lifestyle, taste and culture rather than by... social class." All the while, the division widens between those whose income makes them viable consumers and those who, while displaced from the classic workforce, nonetheless constitute an impoverished international working class, a class made up largely of women and people of color. As planner Peter Marcuse asserted in his 1988 article "Neutralizing Homelessness," in the time since 1980, 44 percent of all new jobs created in the United States paid below poverty wages.[9] Conditions have only worsened since then.[10]

Sociologist Immanuel Wallerstein's 1990 conjectures on international relations are already revealing their grim actuality: post–cold–war power blocs are being led from the north with the United States dominating Canada and Latin America; Japan leading China to mutual benefit and together penetrating Siberia, Southeast Asia, and Australia; and the European Community, led by Germany, colonizing former Soviet nations and Eastern Europe. In such an evolving scenario, Wallerstein anticipates that the United States and Japan will likely ally in a bipolar opposition to Europe in a new cold war. With the recapitalization and expansion of newly reprivatized markets in the deteriorating socialist countries, much of the south, no longer viable as a market anyway, will be abandoned. No longer protected by socialist countries or colonial powers willing to maintain their bourgeois elites, southern countries will suffer a series of tribal wars and revolutions that will likely dismember and disintegrate nation-states, and an impoverished working class will cross any border in search of survival by means of work that will not exist.[11]

While the foregoing analysis is primarily economic, others have foregrounded the equally significant shifts within culture amplified by the economic and political centrality of communication technologies themselves in the present era. In 1984 Fredric Jameson in "Postmodernism, or, The Cultural Logic of Late Capitalism" and in 1989 David Harvey in *The Condition of Postmodernity: An Enquiry into the Origins of Cultural Change* analyzed postmodernity as a cultural expression of lived experience within the new conditions of capitalism.[12] In a lived experience that privileges "ephemerality, fragmentation, discontinuity, and the chaotic," it is difficult to make sense of things.[13] In *New Times* Hall elaborates,

"Post-Fordism" ... is as much a description of cultural as of economic change. Indeed, that distinction is now quite useless. Culture has ceased (if ever it was — which I doubt) to be a decorative addendum to the "hard world" of production and things, the icing on the cake of the material world. The word is now as "material" as the world. Through design, technology and styling, "aesthetics" has already penetrated the world of modern production. Through marketing, layout and style, the "image" provides the mode of representation and fictional narrativisation of the body on which so much of modern consumption depends. Modern culture is relentlessly material in its practices and modes of production. And the material world of commodities and technologies is profoundly cultural.[14]

Architecture is shamefully complicitous in these latter trends, in that image making and other modes of aesthetic differentiation are now key to general economic production. The pressure on architects to establish distinct forms, styles, and images is clearly felt.

Hence to state that the late capitalist age of postmodernism marks a time of upheaval and reorganization is now to state the obvious. Such sweeping restructuring confuses and bewilders human lived experience. Individuals experience an inability to explain their relationship of "self" to the social world. The question of identity reaches crisis proportions. Architectural critic Liane Lefaivre captures the experience of this crisis in her article "Constructing the Body, Gender, and Space":

> The Western world is undergoing one of the deepest cognitive crises in its history. Recategorization is occurring at all levels of life, from the most mundane to the most momentous. We are witnessing the questioning of centuries-old received truths, about childhood, family, rationality, race, sexuality, gender, architecture, and the built environment. Fundamental beliefs upon which we base not only our knowledge of the world but also our actions in it are being revised.[15]

More specifically, Cornel West describes "random nows" within black communities: "The collapse of meaning in life—the eclipse of hope and absence of love of self and others, the breakdown of family and neighborhood bonds"—has led to the "social deracination and cultural denudement of urban dwellers, especially children." West continues, "We have created rootless, dangling people with little link to the supportive networks—family, friends, school—that sustain some sense of purpose in life."[16] In a similar vein, Fredric Jameson, engaging Jacques Lacan, Gilles Deleuze, and Félix Guattari, describes the postmodern condition as a schizophrenic experience, where life is little more than a "series of pure and unrelated presents."[17] But for Jameson, and for us, this fracturing of lived experience is not in any way to be misunderstood as a disorganization of the social systems that remain our concern. "Postmodernism is not the cultural dominant of a wholly new social order..., but only the reflex and the concomitant of yet another systematic modification of capitalism itself."[18]

THE AFTER-MODERNISM DISCOURSE: POSTMODERNISM THEORY

Changing spatialities, the colonization of nature and psyche, the racialization and feminization of poverty, rootlessness, hopelessness, discontinuity, schizophrenia: these are indeed strange new times, a feature that is not only lived but reverberates through the state of theory and criticism. Discursive complexity now marks every discipline and professional field. While no discipline or field has ever been undifferentiated, the extent of heterogeneity within and among disciplines has never been so pronounced and celebrated. Propelled by new categories of experience, changes in sensibilities, new modes of representation, and an almost visceral fascination with the exotic and the Other, postmodern criticism and theory reveal what cultural practices articulate—the multiplicity of difference, the indeterminacy of language, the variety of subject positions, and the breakdown of boundaries. No wonder someone like Daniel Bell, a widely known conservative intellectual, can proclaim he is a "socialist in economics, a liberal in politics, and a conservative in culture."[19]

We use Daniel Bell to illustrate at least two features of the postmodern condition as they regard theory and criticism. First is the organization of disparate and contrary elements into a fractured heterogeneity and, second, an uncertainty about the clarity of intellectual domains, their boundaries, and their interrelations.

An entire industry has developed in order to retheorize and publish the work of intellectuals in light of these shifting conditions. It is not the task of this book to define modernism or postmodernism as theoretical movements or to trace their interrelationship within and across disparate discourses, but rather to develop strategies for a renewed social project with full consideration of these contending discourses. The various understandings of periodizations are so contradictory and so different within different fields that it would be desirable not to have to use the terms, if it were not for the fact that we want to discuss the phenomena to which they refer and draw lessons from those whose work presumes their distinction. Therefore, we must use the terms for shorthand, recognizing that their interrelationship is complex and contradictory.

The work of many authors in this book builds on practices that critiqued Enlightenment certainties long before the specific repudiation of modernism as a movement took place in the United States. Through the various Marxian, Freudian, and Nietzschian critiques of humanism, structuralism, and positivism, an inheritance of critical inquiry that already resided within so-called modernism became conflated in the 1960s and 1970s with this new assertion of a break from modernism. Within the Marxian framework, the primary distinctions made between modernism and postmodernism *as periods* are more satisfactorily explained as different fragments of historical production sliding against each other in any given time frame. As Ernst Bloch wrote in the 1920s, "Modernism must thus be seen as uniquely corresponding to an uneven moment of social development, the 'simultaneity of the nonsimultaneous,' the 'synchronicity of the non-synchronous': the coexistence of realities from radically different moments in history."[20] The Marxism that has come to be called "totalizing" and therefore "totalitarian" is the same philosophical tradition that initiated the critique of humanism and its idealist centrality of the transcendental subject, that is, it was among the first posthumanist discourses. Marxism, while maintaining many aspects of the humanism, idealism, and positivism that characterized Enlightment theory, nonetheless must be understood as standing squarely in opposition to their premises.

Additionally, posthumanist theories of cultural production had been developing in Europe among those who carried the legacy of Freud and Nietzsche, as well. Thus philosopher Jacques Derrida's *Of Grammatology* in 1968 challenged the logocentrism and false objectivity of the Enlightenment promise of progress in contradistinction to Ernest Mandel's political economy. And psychoanalyst Jacques Lacan, working within structuralism's contributions while critiquing it, conceived of the humanist subject as an unstable, socially constructed, but uniquely experienced entity.

Thus what may appear as "modern" in the stylist character of constructivism is already posthumanist in its rejection of human subjectivity, according to cultural theorist Peter Burger's interpretation in *Theory of the Avant-Garde*.[21] For us, the ambiguous and often conflicting attributes of modernism theory itself as evidence of a period in intellectual history may be understood as signaling the underlying social transformation of capitalism in the era of "modernity." Two concepts of modernity, which are well described by Hilde Heynen in *Assemblage* — that is, modernity as a programmatic emancipatory project and modernity as a transitory "fugitive" reality — coexist.[22] And theorization of these two dialectically related understandings continues throughout the shifting historical periods. Our contemporary approach to the critique and production of culture, thus, requires the acceptance, and indeed the incorporation, of these conflicting historical specificities.

While we tolerate, even embrace, this ambiguity, it is nonetheless true that the coalesence of certain "principles" of postmodernism theory is having its own historical effect, and thus this book must place itself in relation to this phenomenon. In significant ways, the postmodern principles of uncertainty, heterogeneity, and the lack of definite answers is positive. For example, it can empower subaltern groups in the struggle to gain voice and identity within and against the totalizing narratives of modernism. Writer and filmmaker Pratibha Parmar is particularly instructive here when she writes:

> In these postmodernist times the question of identity has taken on colossal weight particularly for those of us who are post-colonial migrants inhabiting histories of diaspora. Being cast into the role of the Other, marginalised, discriminated against and too often invisible, not only within everday discourses of affirmation but also within the "grand narratives" of European thought, black women in particular have fought to assert privately and publicly our sense of self: a self that is rooted in particular histories, cultures and languages.[23]

A distinction must be made here, however, between a postcolonial demand for self-determination such as Parmar's and its effective opposite, that is, a postmodern refusal of any common social project. While the struggle to shed the mantle of modernism's homogenizing force in order to affirm marginal identities is an essential contribution to new left theory, many who identify themselves as residing on the "postmodern Left" have failed to move beyond the pluralist notion of empowering disenfranchised groups or the metaphysical notion of rejecting master narratives in order to form a larger, collective counterhegemonic project. The result has been what cultural theorist Jonathan Rutherford has called "categorical politics": a recognition of the right and power of autonomy on the part of oppressed groups but not necessarily a recognition of the need for such groups to ally, in solidarity, in larger social movements.[24] For some this is precisely the problem with much of postmodern theory and criticism. As Marxists Steven Best and Douglas Kellner assert, "Postmodern theory splits capitalist society into separate and unmediated realms, analyzing culture in isolation from the economy, or politics apart from the conjuncture of business and government."[25] In addition to isolating subject areas, criticism, according to Jim Merod, "tends more than ever toward a rarefied self-interest, as if writing and the critical act were severed from the institutional practices that define a capitalist society."[26] Postmodernism theorist Christopher Norris says something similar: "We have reached a point where theory has effectively turned against itself, generating a form of extreme epistemological scepticism which reduces everything—philosophy, politics, criticism, and 'theory' alike—to a dead level of persuasive or rhetorical effect."[27] Refusal to advance progressive strategy (as opposed to rhetoric) does nothing to undermine the hegemony of the dominant capitalist culture.

Partly because of their refusal to undertake a thorough reevaluation of the contradictions inherent in the emancipatory social project and similarly because of their own problematic separation from contemporary left social movements, then, postmodern left theorists find themselves in a state of disarray, if not paralysis. Splintered into competing micropolitical entities, "political ghettoes of ideological purity," as Manning Marable calls them,[28] the preoccupation with fragmentation, indeterminacy, and disjunction is often handled in ways that beget a despairing nihilism which forecloses agency and the pursuit of any realm of possibility. Thus fearful of holistic theories, or even arbitrary closures, of capitalism because they smack of totalities or grand narratives, these professional intellectuals abandon the chance for a wider transformative social movement. One of the greatest contributions of both gender- and race-based theories is their challenge to the inherent totalizing power of "class" and the legitimacy of socialism itself. Those who have believed, based on analysis of the historical evolution of property relations, that sexism and racism both predate capitalism and have often been prevalent in state socialist models argue for the relative autonomy of male supremacy and white European chauvinism even within the bounds of capitalism—both in the ideological realm and the arena of actual practice. But at times, this belief has been used to evade understanding of the constitutive character that structural suppression and exploitation of women and peoples of color possess in capitalist economics, politics, and culture, as well as evading the undeniable rise of this phenomenon precisely as capitalism is moving to homogenize again an international working class. The task of disaggregating gender and race *temporarily* as a way to reintroduce them into a new configuration with class has never been more urgent than today. When the very character of the increasingly immiserated working class throughout the world is overwhelmingly female and multiethnic, efforts to segregate the theoretical pursuits of cultural studies, women's studies, and Black, Latino, Asian Pacific Islander, and Native American studies from the analysis of the increasingly ruthless nature of class-driven transnational capitalism and its drive to recolonize will only contribute to that very recolonialization. In other words, if we continue to swim in the fragmentary and bask in disaggregation, the universals of capitalism's requirement of expansion will relentlessly reorganize the world. Meanwhile, masking big sticks, big ideologies, and big economic maneuvers, the apparent atomization of the social successfully achieves *hegemony by disorientation*.[29]

Ironically, as left political leader Eric Mann says, "socialism is at a world-wide low exactly at a time when capitalism is performing at its worst"—and the absence of alternative social models, combined with widespread disillusionment with efforts to reform capitalism, has led to a cultural and political crisis of demoralization and despair throughout the international Left.[30] Compare the confusion fostered by postmodern theorizing on the Left to the success of intellectual work aligned with the political Right as it accounts for contemporary social conditions. Ironically, postmodern theorists—raising disorganization to a principle—are no match for the newly organized Right. One successful strategy of the Right is to explain social decay as the direct result of liberal policies: conjured up are such terms as "reverse discrimination," "welfare queens," "black rapists and murderers," "illegal aliens," "lazy workers," "shrewish women," and "political correctness" to embolden reactionary ideology.

Supplementing these successes is what cultural theorist Lawrence Grossberg critiques as the "depoliticization of politics" itself, where politics and issues are divorced from one another and positioned as affective investments, emptied of any political content. Grossberg argues convincingly that the project of the new conservatism in the United States is the attempt to refigure the ground of American life: all of the domains of people's lives, all of the practices and institutions of the social formation, and the very meaning of America and the vectors of its future.[31] What makes this attempted reconstitution so profound, however, has been the Right's ability to translate economic and ideological issues into affective sentiments — the mobilization of passion — whereby they are stripped of their complexity and reduced to mere slogans. Hence, social issues and concerns are voided of their complications ("Why Ask Why? Drink Bud Dry"); citizenship and equal rights are conflated to consumerism ("You've come a long way, baby"); the Gulf War was couched in empty signifiers ("Free Kuwait"); military missiles become the "Peace-keeper" and the "Patriot"; politics is displaced to the aesthetic and personal (the quest *To Renew America* [Newt Gingrich] becomes a simple matter of "virtues" [William Bennett] and a "contract"); and the experience of daily life is reduced to a series of unrelated "random nows" ("Don't Worry, Be Happy"). This highly successful ideological demagoguery is proliferated through the popular media while the postmodern Left is satisfied to "decenter the subject."

The mobilization and ascendancy of the Right has been successful not only politically and economically, but also culturally *and* pedagogically. At a time when cultural fragmentation and ideological disorientation reign, the Right, through the marshaling of conservative think tanks, the electronic media, the popular press, nationally syndicated columnists, and groups like Accuracy in Media and the National Association of Scholars as well as numerous grassroots movements, has realized big dividends in controlling the production of meaning around issues like schools, welfare, abortion, crime, the role of government, and urban and state policy. The scale and scope of this organization of knowledge is unprecedented. The quest is nothing less than the orchestration of consciousness to colonize subjectivity and to ensure ideological hegemony generally. The Right's consolidation of its hegemony has been devastatingly successful.

In the 1990s, after a decade that abandoned many of the constraints on capital that were won in the interwar period and that wreaked havoc with one-country socialist experiments around the world, U.S. capitalism spreads further in a grab at domination of the growing power of transnational capital. At the same time, the hegemony of bourgeois culture and its culture industry challenges early modernist strategies of resistance. Herein lies the value we ascribe to postmodernism theory: it challenges both the logo-Eurocentric constitution of Western bourgeois culture and the taken-for-granted emancipatory "promises" of radical and revolutionary social practices. Yet its challenge is insufficient — worse, disarming. Shifts in the dynamics of global capitalism unleashed with the collapse of the Soviet Union and the end of the cold war mark a qualitative leap in the complexity of capitalist operations, now functioning on a scale of plunder and development unimagined by Marx or Lenin. In this context, the quest for viable approaches to socially responsive architecture practice intensifies, and consideration of theories of cultural practice spawned by those who embrace this analysis of a postmodern cultural condition and offer postmodern theories, albeit highly problematic, seems worthwhile.

Architecture's Response

Statements of architecture's relation to society appear in written texts from the time of Vitruvius, based on the premise that architecture engages society and that a knowledge of society and its processes is basic to the education of architects. Architects have long since acted on the assumption that architecture participates in the formation of social order. The goal of that social formation has changed throughout the history of the profession. But the traditional approach has historically intended that its architecture serve (or build) society after the likeness of ruling power. This traditional social orientation has been periodically challenged by architects who professed social reform and sought an architecture responsive to the human condition of society in general.

In the early twentieth century, the modern movement in architecture—a loosely coalesced agglomeration of trends, styles, and political persuasions—upheld the basic premise that architecture had the power as a social force to engage society and actually transform it. These modernists were at once architects and social advocates. To the extent that they constituted an actual movement, they believed, in common, that architecture could cure social ills and prevent (or make) revolution. Art and technology united in mass production could bring increased social welfare as well as enlightened democratic consciousness to the downtrodden masses and contribute to the inevitable forward march of human progress. Concepts like "new objectivity" asserted that the universalizing, abstract qualities of technological reproduction could bring greater equality among peoples, not only greater access to shelter but broader access to common social values and collective experience, possibly resulting in a collective internationalist style. At a time when the Soviet Union and Germany's Weimar Republic were attempting socialist construction, and social revolution was either imminent or seemed so in many countries around the world, the concept of an objectified internationalist architecture in intent, content, and form dovetailed exactly with the institutionalized social movements led by the Communist and Socialist Internationals, which were striving for the betterment of humankind across all national barriers.

By midcentury—with the failure of the Weimar experiment in social democracy as well as the rejection of the avant-garde in the socialist construction of Eastern Europe—criticism of the negative social impact of modernism's objectified industrialized technological forms began to challenge beliefs about architecture's *positive* engagement with society. As modern architecture's postwar phase successfully engaged society in the United States as a corporate cog and in the Soviet Union as an instrument of a repressive state apparatus, disenchantment with the potential of an architecture for social change grew. In the 1960s, a surge of grassroots social criticism found its way into the fringes of architecture in the West. While still idealizing architecture's potential for social agency, grassroots reformers were particularly critical of the capitalist complicity of mature modernism.

By the early 1970s, evidence mounted that architecture was not the determinant progressive force that the early modern movement had hoped to unleash. But critics such as Robert Venturi, in his 1966 period-breaking book *Complexity and Contradiction,* granted just enough effectiveness to architectural determinism to blame the modern movement for the alienation of people from their physical environments. Belief in the redemptive power of modern architecture was ceremoniously exploded with the failed public housing project Pruitt-Igoe in Saint Louis. This explosion was named "the birth of postmodernism" in architecture by Charles Jencks in his 1977 book *The Language of Post-Modern Architecture,* and thus codified the critique of modernism's failed social agenda.

In the ensuing period a shift, comparable to that in other fields, occurred in the belief systems of architecture — from a pursuit of architecture as an agent of material social change to an exploration of architecture as a *language* related to society as a mode of cultural expression or as a system of signs, either affirmative of traditional bourgeois culture or resistant to it. As the dust settled over the rubble of Reaganomics, the stability of architectural meaning was being challenged in architectural offices and in the studios of architecture schools everywhere. As the rate of social change advances exponentially and the nature of architectural practice is challenged every day, questions about architecture's material and cultural roles in society persist.

Postmodern theoretical trends consistent with those previously described have been evident in architecture for some time. The manner by which architecture has shaped and been shaped by recent postmodern directions can be characterized as a *disengagement* from the modernist commitment to advance progressive projects. Indeed, a virtual army with multiple regiments aligned to critique modernism in architecture has organized to actually retreat from progressive social practice through their generation of new strategies that attempt to separate architecture from its social soul. With the growth of these regiments, the political valence of architectural theorizing has shifted from the development of strategies for architecture's progressive social agency to satisfaction with the crafting of tactical justifications for architecture's retreat from the crude and inhumane forces of modern social life, a nonetheless profoundly social act. The specific characters and institutional forces driving this retreat will appear throughout the chapters to follow, but their characteristics may be briefly outlined.

Retreat into Tradition

The regiment organized for the retreat into tradition sees architecture as a system of signs that can potentially recuperate lost meaning to a culturally deprived general population alienated (not by social or economic poverty but) by the poverty of cultural symbols that could make manifest for them a sense of continuity with past traditions. This regiment throws off the surface style of high modernism, seeing it as a vocabulary of failed elitist forms that are powerless against an increasingly fragmenting and alienating social order. To overcome the sense of loss, this return to humanism adopts popular cultural forms, or it "rediscovers" the neoclassical historicizing of cultural forms.

In either case, architecture is not understood as an agent for social change but as a language capable of signifying cultural meaning, a language that had been destroyed by modernism's severance with the past and capitalism's decentering of the humanist subject. In a period of recession in the building industry, the development of architectural language may be a constructive activity. However, unwittingly perhaps, in its retreat from modernism's progressive social agenda, this new traditionalism, this new classicism, this new universalism constructs new unities of language and art that act in full and unabashed service to the dominant bourgeois cultural industry, the traditional social role of architecture.

Retreat to a Strategy of Negation

In response to the traditionalist resurrection of meaning and the illusions of bourgeois subjectivity, this regiment promotes a counterinterpretation of the meaning of architecture as language. Revisiting the approaches of the late nineteenth and early twentieth centuries, when the artistic avant-garde opposed bourgeois art's affirmative character, the new antitraditionalist architectural designers subvert the comfort of universal language and the belief in common cultural referents by articulating *difference, rupture, fragmentation,* and radical *heterogeneity.* Architecture is "the new critical art of contemporary culture."[32] In its politically strong form, it carries forward the avant-garde strategies of the 1920s and 1930s, transformed into the 1980s and 1990s as the explicit pursuit of an *oppositional* attempt to disrupt the institutions of architecture. However, this contemporary strategy of negation is more characteristically a resistance not to bourgeois social relations by means of social praxis but to bourgeois philosophy by means of the formal subversion of architecture's language as a foundational metaphor for the bourgeois philosophical order. One leader of this movement, Peter Eisenman, explains, "Even as any architecture shelters, functions and conveys aesthetic meaning, a dislocating architecture must struggle against celebrating, or symbolizing, these activities; it must dislocate its own meaning."[33]

This regiment sees it as not only possible but also progressive to generate new forms that produce an estrangement or dialectical shock in the struggle to renew perception within a context of continual cultural commodification. Seeking to resist the construction of dominant unities, this group also resists alternatives. Its followers concentrate on the struggle within the aesthetic structures of the discipline and generate shocking negational metaphors removed from the struggle within society.

Looking to art once again to deliver us from the forces of social decay, these strategies of aesthetic disorientation do challenge received aesthetic beliefs and produce the subversion of aesthetic unity. But they do not offer a socially viable strategy of opposition. Perceptual renewal, or the continual realignment of structures for knowledge in order to expose their taken-for-granted character in the social world, has been a compelling strategy. But the historically progressive artistic strategies of the early-twentieth-century avant-garde — which struggled to undermine the artistic establishment, in light of the growing institutionalization and commodification of art, and to ally with social movements in their struggle for radical change — are not directly applicable today in the face of the culture industry's tremendous power of co-optation, as well as the separation of postmodern experimentalists from oppositional social movements. As Fredric Jameson articulates, the early avant-garde strategies for political art did not have to confront the absorption of the unconscious and the appropriation of perceptual renewal that have occurred with the postwar expansion into transnational capitalism, accompanied by its colonization of not only the precapitalist third world but also the unconscious human mind. New strategies of negation must incorporate knowledge of this co-optive operation and establish new links to active social movements. Otherwise, the political intent that motivates the search for novelty and the constant rejection of any *natural* status for form can turn into its opposite: a means of feeding the colonization of the mind. Whatever radicality previously existed for a strategy of defamiliarization, the constriction of the relative autonomy of culturally resistant work (in this case the cultural work of architecture), the explosion of cultural practice, and its now complete dependence on the social formation of capitalism deliver many experimental cultural practices directly into the pocket of late capitalism. Not only are inventive strategies of formal aesthetic subversion dubiously subversive, but they now actually supply the hegemonic commodity culture with sources of constant renewal at a time when fragmentation, not wholeness, is the lived experience, and when "difference and identity are the same" in a global hegemonic culture.[34]

Rapid stylist renewal is now no signal of opposition to the status quo, only a sign of the infinitesimal time within which newness is appropriated, within which shocking metaphors of resistance can be returned to construct dominating unities. Any relative autonomy that appears to exist is a momentary shift or rupture within the process of struggle and reconsolidation of the bourgeois global estate. And any truly oppositional strategy at this moment of rupture cannot be one that furthers *disorientation*. Under such conditions resistance to totalizing unities in the aesthetic realm displaces the actual site of social struggle.

It is important to recognize, additionally, the specificity of architecture as a social practice. Unlike modernist art that sought transcendence by attempting an autonomy from the contamination of social life, and unlike avant-garde art that advanced a resistant reengagement with society in the form of active negation of its rules and institutions, early-twentieth-century modern and avant-garde practices in *architecture* were defined by the constraint of architecture actually being an instrument of use, integral to daily life experience and the structures of society. Architecture is not only a compositional language. It is not a painting on the wall that critiques social fragmentation by creating it, that makes the familiar strange and thereby historicizes it. It is not a theatrical production that focuses attention and participation on a particular moment of critical consideration. Architecture is not even a commodity whose uncritical consumption can be resisted. Architecture is a multifaceted site of social formation that is subject to multiple and diverse forces. It is a means of capital expansion, dependent on land ownership. It is an omnipresent surround-sound environment for subjective lived experience. And consequently, it mediates the consolidating power of bourgeois hegemony that exceeds the fleeting stimulation and indoctrination that characterize the reception of most works of art. Thus, conscious withdrawal was never a strategy for modern architecture in its own time, and it offers no critical response to architecture's social dilemmas today. Given architecture's specific characteristics, as well as the power of appropriation that characterizes the current global culture industry, contemporary architectural strategies of negation, by attempting to resuscitate strategies that worked only to the extent they were linked to actual social movements and political struggles, continue to deliver architecture into the service of domination. Recent attempts to reorient this regiment in an "affirmative" direction — codified by the convening of the *Assemblage* editorial board at Tulane in the fall of 1994 — not surprisingly move to affirm the dynamic energy of a new global reorganization with what K. Michael Hays dubs "ideological smoothness," or a shift from "a Derridean to a Deleuzian framework."[35]

Retreat to Criticism as Closure

Critique of the role of architecture in the contemporary historic period is precisely the focus of the regiment of architectural criticism. Accordingly, architecture is bourgeois; architecture is hegemonic; architecture is oppressive; architecture is logocentric; architecture is fundamentally, irrevocably, bankrupt; and the constructive practice of architecture is both false and wrong.

Based on a powerful and welcome critique of the relations of architectural production, such critics see architectural discourse on the whole as "false consciousness" — a set of notions completely and irrevocably in the service of the overarching belief system developed by the dominant power structure of advanced capitalism. And they see architectural practice as socially destructive. Believing that architecture has no progressive transformative power, all contemporary "oppositional" strategies of practice are viewed as the subjective delusions of cultural radicals who unwittingly mobilize what formative power architecture has to invigorate the bourgeoisie. As architectural critic and historian Manfredo Tafuri asserts, "One cannot 'anticipate'... an architecture 'for a liberated society'; what is possible is the introduction of class criticism into architecture."[36] As Jameson responds, this perspective "rests on the conviction that nothing new can be done, no fundamental changes can be made, within the massive being of late capitalism."[37]

This trend of criticism helps to unmask the recurring illusion of architecture's own redemption and contributes the understanding that it is not only architecture that has produced alienation in late capitalism: "The principle task of ideological criticism is to do away with impotent and ineffectual myths, which so often serve as illusions that permit the survival of anachronistic 'hopes in design.'"[38] Yet this trend is structurally invested in the institutions of architecture it professes to critique. As professional architectural historians, professors of this regiment not only cannot lead us beyond the contradictions of architecture's relation to property development, they are the institutional gatekeepers whose very job in the academy is to reproduce architecture's purpose as a discipline and profession. Struggling against bourgeois hegemony by concentrating on the critique of architectural production in the social (rather than the aesthetic) domain, and convinced of the return to cultural domination of any professed "alternative" construction, this point of view produces a rhetorical closure on the entire project of architecture because there is no escape. Disallowing any vision of the future, slandering hope as a humanist lie, and seeing no possibility of struggle within the structures for knowledge of the field of architecture, this acceptance of *life-lived-within-the-critique* must realize the inevitability of its own socially constructive practice: only the critic is allowed to create, and then there is closure. However, we do not grant such a possibility of critical distance, of analysis from the outside. Critics *are* practitioners and cannot find comfort in the rejection of individual architects or "projects." Rejecting the pursuit of radical, oppositional, or anticipatory practices not only leaves critics in charge of architecture's future but also leaves social movements completely disarmed in the continual cultural-political struggle within the contradictions of capitalism.

Retreat into Socially Responsible Process

Any work grappling with architecture's social project must engage those battalions professing design consideration of user needs, social factors, and participatory strategies, in short, "social responsibility," precisely because it will be with such forces that this book will likely be positioned.

This regiment articulates useful goals and principles. For example, in March 1993 a worldwide show of student design projects was organized in New York by Pratt Institute in collaboration with Architects/Designers/Planners for Social Responsibility to examine the question, What is socially responsible design?— an effort requiring exhibit reviewers to engage one another about the project of social responsibility in order to make selections. After two exhausting days, the following consensus was reached:

> Socially responsible design celebrates social, cultural, ethnic, gender and sexuality differences; is critical of existing asymmetrical social structures and relationships of power and seeks to redistribute power and resources more equitably; changes society; continually calls into question its own social, cultural, and philosophical premises and, through a continuing dialectic, seeks to ensure that its ends are consistent with its means; seeks in its process, to develop strategies for public intervention and participatory democracy.
>
> Socially responsible design recognizes that only those people affected by an environment have any right to its determination; avoids the use of mystifying private or professional languages; takes as its frame of reference the collective meanings of empowerment; recognizes that the process of empowerment can only be a process of self-empowerment, and that designers must engage in a process of mutually empowering experiences with the disempowered; recognizes that the process of participatory self-empowerment is a never-ending, ongoing struggle—that there is no "ideal" or utopian state that can ever be attained.[39]

Within the regiment of social responsibility the position is clear that the built environment is a social, cultural, and political product, often reproducing the interests of dominant groups. As Professor Stephan Marc Klein writes in his introductory essay to the show's catalog, "Most often [architecture] is the product of the dominant culture and, as such, assists that culture in maintaining its hegemony. Designers, architects and planners often reinforce the existing order by shaping spaces and objects that support its interests of money and power and by creating its symbols. In this system style changes assume great importance." Given this assumption about the role of style, symbols, and aesthetics in securing hegemonic culture, it is troubling that Klein finds "many of the projects in the exhibition do not look out of the ordinary. Aesthetic issues, such as the role of aesthetics in reproducing the dominant order or multicultural alternatives to the dominant Eurocentric styles are for the most part absent.... [T]he salient stylistic characteristic of these projects is their lack of style."[40]

Failing to take up aesthetic production in the interests of counterhegemonic culture, this regiment retreats by privileging process over product, believing, for example, that "the true significance of participation lies in its effects on the participants, not on architecture," or similarly, "the paramount purpose of participation is not good buildings, but good citizens in a good society."[41] Aesthetics is relegated to inconsequential status, largely unimportant, rejected as if it is rejectable. Herein lies the contradiction with the advocates for social responsibility: they grant the political power of aesthetics to secure hegemony, but they do not take responsibility for their own aesthetic production. They understand how aesthetics can be used by formalists in alliance with dominant interests to reproduce the status quo, but they retreat from the potential of aesthetics as an apparatus of power to promote oppositional cultural production.[42]

CRITICAL CONSTRUCTIVE PRACTICE: REORIENTATION

The cultivation of a culture of resistance through retreat, which refuses to engage the struggle of social movements or proposes no constructive strategy, has no place in a struggle to define an antihegemonic social project for architecture. While it is fair to say that any constructive practice is always partially utopian and always co-optable, it must also be said that resistance through retreat is a more advanced path to commodification.

The wrenching of propriety from any knowledge construction is a critical strategic practice of construction in itself. And all these varieties of practice produce particular problems for knowledge construction. But the experimentation with formal processes of structuration without the engagement of social forces—the generative *form* without the professed *intent* or political *content*—produces a local view of self-referential formal autonomy that plays a strategic role in supporting the social status quo. And critical social practices of architecture that do not engage the interdependence of formal aesthetic articulation and social and cultural order—the professed *intent* without *form* and *content*—make statements in history but miss a major sphere of architecture's historical activity, that is, its power to affect culture through lived experience. Further, the analysis that satisfies itself with the detailed descriptive critique of this interdependence of architecture and society but refuses any constructive practice of design—the *form* and *content* without the profession of *intent*—makes its living within the discourse of the field by refusing any strategy of social practice that would seek intentionally to change it.

Resistance to the hegemony of bourgeois humanism through our suicide as socially produced subjects does not remove us from our historical practice as social agents. The problem of agency rises ever present.[43] Any critical practitioner of architectural design or discourse who does not locate himself or herself on the global social battlefield—as a strategist, that is, not *a map drawer* but *a drawer of lines of march,* a generator of structures for knowledge for social action—will be among the first intellectuals to serve the hegemonic class.

Any critical practitioner who deconstructs Western architecture and philosophy but refuses to see his or her own place in social reconstruction is doomed to return appropriated. All practices construct. The question cannot be how to resist construction of a project but rather how to understand the dynamic moments of struggle in the structuring of knowledge as a social, pedagogical practice with particular historical character and how to generate strategies that engage society and enable progressive social change. It is only by continual rearticulation or reorientation (even *re-placement*) of one's own social being and a constant *re-placing* of one's lived experience in relation to architecture and society that a conscious critical strategy of constructive antihegemony can develop.

In response to the modern strategies of "social engagement" that joined the dominant forces of capital, as well as to the postmodern strategies of social retreat that unwittingly advance bourgeois hegemony, a growing force of critics and practitioners seeks to reconstruct the critical social project of architecture. While our understanding of the complexity of human progress is much greater now than it was in the 1920s, and while many lessons may in time be learned from the history of the implementation of approaches such as "new objectivity," we must be clear when rewriting history from the present that we do not diminish the significance of these inadequately theorized, but also historically contingent, aspects of architecture's social practice. While this book is not another history of modernism, it does seek to reopen the question of architecture's social agenda, gather lessons from the struggle within society, and reformulate the problems of knowledge formation through the practice of architecture in a manner that resists bourgeois hegemony, poses alternative constructions, and recognizes the continual dynamic of struggle in any constructive social practice.

It may be then that in a historic period of bourgeois *hegemony-by-disorientation,* a pedagogical practice of *reorientation* would be a subversive act. How might this reorientation, this problem of generating new structures for knowledge of architecture in contemporary society, be formulated? The overarching unifying (although not unified) perspective of the authors included here embraces, on the one hand, the critiques of modernism's idealist and totalizing framework, while, on the other hand, rejecting the common postmodernist reduction of the diverse threads of modernism into a single dogma. Practicing in the space between modernism and postmodernism, these authors occupy an important position. Recognizing that the path forward cannot take us back to humanisms or modernisms already known (however "new" their attire) and acknowledging de facto "agency" through the practice of design, these theorists/architects accept professional and social responsibility for their practices. Variously, their approaches all carry the charge of a utopian impulse but struggle against reproducing an idealist utopian vision that universalizes experience and promises progress. Entering the debate about the ideological character of modernism and postmodernism through a critical appraisal of oppositional discourses and strategies that have surfaced in architecture, these authors engage and challenge contemporary mainstream notions of architecture with the intent to construct new knowledge and, accordingly, new social formations and identities that can lead to greater equality in the distribution of society's resources and greater democracy in public life.

In describing in 1973 the problems inherent in categorizing modern architecture as a "unified movement," Charles Jencks asserted that such a theoretical operation would only be initiated out of ignorance or political intent: "Those who [see modern architecture in unified fashion] are either unaware of the plurality of live architectural traditions, or else they hope to coalesce this plurality into some integrated movement."[44] We recognize and value highly the quite diverse perspectives of the authors presented here. At the same time we take responsibility for attempting to effect a project starting from necessary, but as yet insufficient, common premises.

Thus each chapter addresses a particular oppositional discourse that has been taken up within the field of architecture: feminism, social architecture, activist practice, environmentalism, cultural studies and critical pedagogy, racial studies, critical theory, and poststructuralism/deconstruction. Each chapter examines, from within the explanatory framework of its respective approach, how discursive formations, narratives, and spaces are articulated, constrained, and expanded by their position in relation to power and privilege. Each chapter examines the defining problematics, the theoretical premises, the design strategies, and the built work characteristic of that perspective, and each incorporates the author's critique. Based on this analysis, the authors propose ways that the perspective they advance can better address the problematic it has defined as well as chart new directions.

The chapters are interdependent. Thus, in its content and its process of production, the book both embodies and advances a dialogue: each chapter problematizes and advances an approach nurtured in its own specificity, but our desire is also present to create a larger collectivity, to propose a language of exchange and solidarity that is engendered by the interrelationships of the chapters without minimalizing or depoliticizing their specificity. By embracing diverse critiques of the modernist project of social change and its postmodern challenge, the book reconstructs architecture's social project. The book itself is a component of that project.

In this light we recognize several key elements of the reconstructed social project of architecture that we advocate: the desire to redeem the commitment of architects to progressive social agency that gave modernism its project, while we constructively learn from the critique of modernism's many immaturities, mistakes, and downright social abuses; the intent to recoup the social militance of the term "critical" in the face of its widespread co-optation; the commitment to develop strategies for practice that address their intent, form, and content to the contradictions of the contemporary historical context; the willingness to stand for a race, gender, and class politics in constructive resistance to many of the popular contemporary trends that define the political economy of the academy and architectural practice; and the commitment to link the practices of architecture with the activities of progressive social movements.

In chapter 1, "The Suppression of the Social in Design: Architecture as War," Anthony Ward explores and critiques the inheritance of the fine art and social science paradigms in the field of architecture. He traces the introduction of design methods, participatory processes, environmental psychology, social ecology, and behaviorist approaches, as well as the contributions of such organized groups as the Environmental Design Research Association (EDRA), in the history of postwar design theorizing. Somewhat autobiographically, Ward traces the history of these frameworks as they evolved in parallel with the movements for civil rights, women's rights, environmental activism, and the end of the Vietnam War. Having challenged the limits of rationalistic social science research in addressing the sociological problematics in architecture, Ward then turns his attention to the conservative postmodern realignment of the design disciplines with fine art and aesthetic avant-gardism. Tracing a line of architects from William Morris to Hannes Meyer to Christopher Alexander, he places the relations of production at the center of the practice of architecture in counterposition to the aesthetic strategies of architects like Robert Venturi and Peter Eisenman. Finally, Ward contrasts these two dominant paradigms with works of empowerment and cultural transformation from around the world, particularly in the complex social milieu of New Zealand.

Sherry Ahrentzen, in "The F Word in Architecture: Feminist Analyses in/of/for Architecture," investigates the genderization of architecture, focusing attention on how architecture is produced and evaluated from an analysis of masculinity. Based on an exhaustive documentation of the marginalization of female gender contributions to the field of architecture, Ahrentzen maps an extensively thorough variety of strategies for feminist design practice. These strategies are categorized into three feminist approaches: liberal feminism, cultural feminism, and contextual feminism. Analyzing the work of architects as diverse as Maya Lin, Jennifer Bloomer, the Matrix Architects Ltd. Feminist Co-operative, Joan Forrester Sprague, and Gail Dubrow, Ahrentzen explains the self-professed intentions, provides examples, and explicates their strengths and weaknesses.

Richard Ingersoll discusses the deleterious effect that buildings and settlement patterns are having on the global environment in his chapter, "Second Nature: On the Social Bond of Ecology and Architecture." Ingersoll gives a historical account of the attitude toward nature in Western architectural theory; discusses in detail the premises, achievements, and shortcomings of environmentalism in the 1970s;

and reshapes what tends to be a guilt-ridden, apocalypse-shaded present interest into something motivated by social justice and desire. Explicating the theories and projects of architects from Vitruvius and Alberti to Louis Sullivan, Rudolph Steiner, Frank Lloyd Wright, and Le Corbusier, then to Paolo Soleri, Sim van der Ryn, and Peter Calthorpe, Ingersoll argues that in the postapocalypse era ecology is being reconsidered as a social issue about organization and the maintenance of life.

In "*Cultural* Studies and Critical *Pedagogy: Cultural Pedagogy* and Architecture," Thomas A. Dutton presents the framework he has employed in his own teaching. Explaining the separate frameworks of British cultural studies and its importation into the United States through the works of Richard Hoggart, Raymond Williams, and Stuart Hall, and critical pedagogy through the work of Brazilian educational theorist Paulo Freire, Dutton presents architectural practices that attempt to convey progressive cultural-political meanings and work toward reviving agency — architecture as cultural pedagogy. The works specifically examined include Dolores Hayden's Power of Place project for Los Angeles, the participatory strategies of Lucien Kroll, and the "social formalism" of Günter Behnisch and Partner. Exploring the intersection between these two primarily academy-based movements, Dutton harnesses their critical power to interrogate recent architectural trends exemplified by the work of Bernard Tschumi, Lebbeus Woods, and Leon Krier.

In chapter 5, "Accommodation and Resistance: The Built Environment and the African American Experience," Bradford C. Grant studies American architecture and the planning of the built environment through the lens of race and its association with class and culture. He shows how race has been a powerful determinant in affecting architectural practice, design, and the spatiality of the built environment. Based on the work of Carl Anthony, Richard Dozier, Dell Upton, Harry Robinson III, and others, Grant provides a historical account of the contributions of African American designers, builders, and architects within the eras of slavery, Jim Crow, and civil rights. Through this history Grant critiques the structural racism of architectural practice and the building industry that makes architects of color "invisible," produces environmental racism, and spatializes race relations generally. Tracing the historical efforts on the part of African American critics and practitioners to be critical within the dialectical struggle between accommodation and resistance, Grant critiques strategies for a resistant racial-cultural practice of architecture — those strategies that attempt to resist appropriation, overcome invisibility, and alter racist spatialization. Critics and architects that Grant takes up specifically include Harvey Gantt, Jack Travis, Sharon Sutton, and J. Max Bond Jr.

Borrowing from the theoretical frameworks of structuralism, poststructuralism, and semiology, the design strategies discussed in Margaret Soltan's "Deconstruction and Architecture" take the "language" or "text" of architecture as the ground plane for theoretical work. These approaches originate primarily in the disciplines of linguistics and literature, shaped by the political experience of failing European social democracy and the rise of post-Marxist French new philosophy, and are intended to critique logocentric convention in architectural language. Primarily through the literary work of Jennifer Bloomer and Mark Wigley, Soltan critiques various philosophical strategies that derive in part from Jacques Derrida and literary theory and are currently being pursued in the field of architecture. Through the work of Peter Eisenman, Bernard Tschumi, Günter Behnisch and Partner, and Leon Krier, Soltan poses directly the question of what constitutes a critical architecture and the role that deconstruction may play in reconstructing progressive architectural building and theory.

And last, in "Subverting the Avant-Garde: Critical Theory's Real Strategy," Lian Hurst Mann explores a theoretical approach that proposes the making of architecture as a critical cultural practice. This approach borrows from the theoretical frameworks of Marxism and posthumanism originating in the disciplines of sociology, history, and art, as well as the political experience of Soviet socialism, the rise of Western European social democracy, and the post-Vietnam-era crisis of U.S. democracy. This direction for theoretical and practical work in architecture makes the problems of society (and the critique of culture) the ground plane from which a critical practice of architecture is theorized. A variety of strategic operations for critical cultural practice are presented and critiqued, manifested in the work of culture theorists Fredric Jameson and K. Michael Hays, contemporary architects Rodolfo Machado and Jorge Silvetti, Rem Koolhaas and the Office of Metropolitan Architecture (OMA), Diller + Scofidio, and activist artists such as Sheila de Bretteville, Social and Public Art Resource Center (SPARC), and Mann's own collaborative, AgitProps.

Notes

1. See Thomas A. Dutton, *Voices in Architectural Education: Cultural Politics and Pedagogy* (New York: Bergin and Garvey, 1991), and Lian Hurst Mann, "Architecture as Social Strategy: Structures for Knowledge for Change" (Ph.D. diss., University of California at Berkeley, 1990) for elaborations on this perspective that have formed the basis of this common work.
2. Cornel West, "The New Cultural Politics of Difference," *October* 53 (1990).
3. V. I. Lenin, *Imperialism: The Highest Stage of Capitalism* (1916; New York: International Publishers, 1971).
4. Ernst Mandel, *Late Capitalism* (London: New Left Books, 1975).
5. Fredric Jameson, foreword to *The Postmodern Condition: A Report on Knowledge,* by Jean-François Lyotard (Minneapolis: University of Minnesota Press, 1984), p. xiv.
6. Kwame Anthony Appiah, "Is the Post in Postmodernism the Post in Postcolonial?" *Critical Inquiry* 17 (Winter 1991).
7. Stuart Hall, "The Meaning of New Times" in Martin Jacques and Stuart Hall, eds., *New Times* (New York: Verso Press, 1990).
8. John Urry, "The End of Organized Capitalism," in Jacques and Hall, eds., *New Times.*

9. Peter Marcuse, "Neutralizing Homelessness," in *Socialist Review* 18, no. 1 (January–March 1988).

10. See Donald L. Barlett and James B. Steele, *America: What Went Wrong?* (Kansas City, Mo.: Andrews and McMeel, 1992), based upon their award-winning series of articles about the redistribution of income in the 1980s in the *Philadelphia Inquirer.*

11. Immanuel Wallerstein's 1990 paper for the Tokyo Colloquium, "The Transforming Socialist Systems—Their Future and Global Impact," October 11–12, 1990, was published as "Remarx: Post-America and the Collapse of Leninism," *Rethinking Marxism* 5, no. 1 (Spring 1992): 93–100.

12. Fredric Jameson, "Postmodernism, or, The Cultural Logic of Late Capitalism," in *New Left Review,* no. 146 (July/August 1984): 59–92; David Harvey, *The Condition of Postmodernity: An Enquiry into the Origins of Cultural Change* (Cambridge, Mass.: Blackwell, 1989).

13. Harvey, *Condition of Postmodernity,* p. 44.

14. Hall, "Meaning of New Times," p. 128.

15. Liane Lefaivre, "Constructing the Body, Gender, and Space," in *Design Book Review,* no. 25 (Summer 1992): 35.

16. Cornel West, "Learning to Talk of Race," *New York Times Magazine,* August 2, 1992, p. 26.

17. See Harvey, *Condition of Postmodernity,* p. 53.

18. Fredric Jameson, introduction to *Postmodernism: or, the Cultural Logic of Late Capitalism* (Durham: Duke University Press, 1991), p. xii.

19. Daniel Bell, quoted in Jonathan Arac, ed., *Postmodernism and Politics* (Minneapolis: University of Minnesota Press, 1986), p. xiii.

20. Ernst Bloch, "Nonsynchronism and Dialectics," *New German Critique* 11 (Spring 1977): 22–38.

21. Peter Burger, *Theory of the Avant-Garde,* trans. Michael Shaw (Minnesota: University of Minnesota Press, 1984).

22. Hilde Heynen, "Architecture between Modernity and Dwelling: Reflections on Adorno's *Aesthetic Theory,*" *Assemblage* 17 (April 1992): 78–91, esp. 80.

23. Pratibha Parmar, "Black Feminism: The Politics of Articulation," in Jonathan Rutherford, ed., *Identity, Community, Culture, Difference* (London: Lawrence and Wishart, 1990), p. 106.

24. Jonathan Rutherford, "A Place Called Home: Identity and the Cultural Politics of Difference," in Rutherford, ed., *Identity, Community, Culture, Difference.*

25. Steven Best and Douglas Kellner, *Postmodern Theory: Critical Investigations* (New York: Guilford Press, 1991), p. 289.

26. Jim Merod, *The Political Responsibility of the Critic* (Ithaca: Cornell University Press, 1987), p. 2.

27. Christopher Norris, *What's Wrong With Postmodernism?* (Baltimore: Johns Hopkins University Press, 1990), p. 4.

28. Manning Marable, *The Crisis of Color and Democracy: Essays on Race, Class, and Power* (Monroe, Me.: Common Courage Press, 1992).

29. Mann, *Architecture as Social Strategy.*

30. Eric Mann and Manning Marable, "The Future of the U.S. Left and Socialism," Working Papers Series (Los Angeles: Strategy Center Publications, 1992), p. 10.

31. Lawrence Grossberg, *We Gotta Get out of This Place: Popular Conservatism and Postmodern Culture* (New York and London: Routledge, 1992).

32. Irvine symposium, "Postmodernism and Beyond: Architecture as the Critical Art of Contemporary Culture," University of California at Irvine, 1989.

33. Peter Eisenman, *The House of Cards* (New York: Oxford University Press, 1988), p. 189.

34. Fredric Jameson, "Varieties of Historicism," talk given at the Conference of the Humanities Research Institute, University of California at Irvine (February 3, 1990).

35. K. Michael Hays, "Architecture Theory, Media, and the Question of Architecture," *Assemblage* 27 (August 1995): 42.

36. Manfredo Tafuri, *Theories and History of Architecture,* trans. Giorgio Verrecchia (New York: Harper and Row, 1980), p. iii.
37. Fredric Jameson, "Architecture and the Critique of Ideology," in Joan Ockman, ed., *Architecture, Criticism, Ideology* (Princeton, N.J.: Princeton University Press, 1985), p. 87.
38. Manfredo Tafuri, *Architecture and Utopia: Design and Capitalist Development* (Cambridge, Mass.: MIT Press, 1976), p. 182.
39. Stephan Marc Klein, Introduction to the catalog *What Is Socially Responsibly Design?* (New York: Pratt Institute and Architects/Designers/Planners for Social Responsibility, 1993).
40. Ibid.
41. C. Richard Hatch, ed., *The Scope of Social Architecture* (New York: Van Nostrand Reinhold, 1984), pp. 8, 9.
42. Much of the work of Tony Schuman is directly about this role of form and aesthetics in promoting culture in alternative directions. See Tony Schuman, "Forms of Resistance: Politics, Culture, and Architecture," in Dutton, ed., *Voices in Architectural Education.*
43. See Mann, *Architecture as Social Strategy,* for elaboration of this discussion.
44. Charles Jencks, *Modern Movements in Architecture* (New York: Anchor Books, 1973), p. 11.

THE SUPPRESSION OF THE SOCIAL IN DESIGN: ARCHITECTURE AS WAR

INTRODUCTION: ARCHITECTURE VERSUS SOCIAL ARCHITECTURE

Architecture is said to be "the Mother of the Arts," the quintessential social art, indeed as nothing *but* social—it is produced to shelter human activity and to express its significance; it is the backdrop against which the drama of everyday life is unavoidably played out, constraining and shaping possible social interactions. What is called *social* architecture is the practice of architecture as an instrument for progressive social change. It foregrounds the moral imperative to increase human dignity and reduce human suffering. The fact that architecture's very character is social has not meant historically that its specific social impact in particular moments has been to reduce suffering; in fact, architecture's social legacy has rather more often been one of producing, allowing, or celebrating the activity of those in power, often at the expense of large numbers of disadvantaged others. It has frequently played an integral role in the processes of disempowerment. Thus, architectural historians describe as "great" pyramids built with slave labor, arches of triumph celebrating military conquest, palaces that elevate the standing of despots, and cathedrals whose adornment celebrates the church's complicity in the conquest and pillage of foreign lands. More particularly, under the operations of capitalism, conditions of manufactured scarcity have ensured that competition for resources creates social conflict between competing groups of unequal power. The operation of professions under capitalism therefore frequently and perhaps essentially serves the values and needs of specific dominant classes at the expense of others. Architecture is still "nothing but social," yet its social practice has both supported and reinforced existing social hierarchies and has operated mostly as a mechanism of oppression and domination. "Social architecture," therefore, in seeking equality and dignity in the use and organization of built environment resources, challenges these structures of domination and, in the process, calls capitalism itself into question.

Any critical analysis of architecture must therefore take into account the political economy of environmental design production and its role in shaping social relations. Historically, Marxism has offered the most thorough analysis of the relationship between social and economic factors in Western philosophy, and although some of the precepts of orthodox Marxism are flawed (and have historically been used to silence the emergence of a more progressive Marxism), nevertheless, through its view, there is much that we can learn about the social and political role of architecture. Orthodox Marxism suggests that social relations are influenced by the ownership of the means of production and that no basic change in those social relationships can take place until this ownership is transferred to the producing classes themselves. While recent critiques of orthodox Marxism have cast doubt upon the simplicity of this analysis and have revealed the equal importance of cultural forces in the process of social change, nevertheless, access to and ownership of material resources is still acknowledged as a fundamental aspect of the power to transform the social world. For social architecture a corresponding theory asserts that only those directly affected by an environment should control its organization and fabrication.

C. Richard Hatch, in his foundational book *The Scope of Social Architecture,* treats architecture as primarily a social event, as a medium for the creation of community.[1] He illustrates projects of social architecture from around the world that are defined by the opportunities they create to help users reflect on their roles, on themselves, on their power of reflection, and on their ability to take control of their environment. Hatch asserts that "at its best, social architecture aims to create and develop critical consciousness."[2] This position stands ideologically opposed to mainstream or dominant theories of architecture, which increasingly place it in the category of high art—isolated from the social milieu of its time and supposedly transcending moral imperatives. That we accept a category of *social architecture,* as a separate and different category from *architecture,* is an indictment of the latter and a measurement of the success of neoconservatives to capture the center of theoretical discourse in design. In this chapter I hope not so much to define the limits or possibilities of social architecture as to question and subvert the socially constructed meaning of the category "architecture" itself. I will try to sketch a contemporary theory and practice of architecture that is transformative and to reconnect it with a moral and social imperative. To show how this imperative might operate I will first describe a brief alternative history of architectural theory.

PROFESSIONAL ORIGINS

Theories of design do not exist in isolation but shape and are shaped by the political circumstances in which they evolve.[3] Two competing yet paradoxically symbiotic theories of architectural design grew from the emergence of the modern professions in the seventeenth and eighteenth centuries during the Enlightenment, at a time of colonial expansion and the development of early capitalism. They were well expressed by T. L. Donaldson, the secretary of the RIBA, in 1841, on his inauguration as professor of architecture at University College London, when he delivered two lectures: "Architecture as an Art" and "Architecture as a Science."[4] Donaldson articulated an ideological dualism that already existed between two competing cultural groups—a culture of *taste* (representative of the old landed nobility) and a culture of *knowledge* (representative of the emerging and technologizing bourgeoisie). Taste became the badge of the dominant aristocracy in resistance to the emerging meritocracy, which originated in the early Renaissance and was fueled by the birth of capitalism and its attendant colonialism.[5] Art, no less than science and technology, was implicated in the colonization process. For all of its reputed artistic enlightenment, the supposed beauty of Brunelleschi's Florence was created from the sweat of slaves imported after the Plague of 1348,[6] and the foundations of the Renaissance architectural masterpieces of Michelangelo, Bernini, and Bramante are laid upon the bodies of a conservatively estimated ten million indigenous people of the Americas.[7] By 1600 the first peoples of the Americas had been rendered uniformly destitute. Under the cloak of the dual conceptions of civilization and progress, their natural resources—land, silver, and gold—were stolen and their (slave) labor used to further the geopolitical ambitions of Ferdinand and Isabella to unite Spain under one monarchy (which they did in 1512).

This plunder eventually found its way through the Fugger banking empire into the upper orders of European society, changing European countries themselves, driving the aspirations of the merchant classes, increasing their claims to an equal status with the traditional landed aristocracy, and precipitating a dramatic increase in building. Churches and church artifacts after the mid-1500s show a marked distinction from works only fifty years earlier, as the surplus capital was used to pay artisans to represent both ecclesiastical and secular power. Their previous simplicity is replaced by an explosion of rococo encrustations of gold, silver, and precious stones from Mexico and Peru. The war to capture the market of available souls being waged in Europe between the Protestant Reformists and the Counter-Reformists only succeeded in exaggerating this pornographic display predominantly by those consummate architectural propagandists, the Jesuits.[8]

Nor was colonization confined to the colonies. The theft of land and other resources was also inflicted on the peasants "at home." In Britain, the Enclosure Acts forced the peasants from the land, consolidating it into larger "holdings."[9] Britain was transformed from a traditional peasant culture to a displaced, socially fragmented pool of cheap urban industrial labor. Only the Enclosure Law–making landowners could vote, rendering the dispossessed peasants legally powerless to overturn their dispossession. Property ownership was the global linchpin of capitalist expansion, and it was to the old and new owners of the expropriated land that the emerging design professions paid allegiance, securing their place firmly within the ranks of the privileged (from which in any case they mostly originated), benefiting from the increased opportunities created through a plentiful supply of money for investment.[10] By the eighteenth century, the design and construction of large country houses provided a burgeoning market that nurtured their emergence.[11]

THE ARCHITECTURE-AS-AN-ART-OBJECT PARADIGM (1400–1945)

The category "fine art" played a fundamental role in this process of colonization. While it presumed to transcend social life, it proliferated as a commodity that manifested and augmented social power. By simultaneously masking and perpetuating relationships of power, art has always acted ideologically, paradoxically doing this by repudiating the ideological function itself and laying claim to being a transcendent autonomous practice. Until the Enlightenment, art, science, ethics, and politics had existed as an undifferentiated whole, structured around social traditions. One became what one was born to become. With the Enlightenment, each sphere of the social enterprise was split off and became an autonomous practice. Scientific knowledge (facts) was separated from ethical and aesthetic values, while art became a transcendent practice separated from politics and materialism—in the process providing the perfect vehicle for the aristocratic class to consolidate its power.[12] But the reproduction of this power required that art, science, ethics, and political economics remain forever separate. The tension in this post-Enlightenment opposition is therefore as integral to design theorizing as it is to the social hierarchies that they reproduce, and that in turn shape architectural professionalism.

The Enlightenment also created a distinction between mental and manual labor that paralleled an identical distinction between education and work. The transition from the guild system to the academies was congruent with an apparent need to distance art and architectural practice from their traditional craft base,[13] and in this process a shift occurred from "art" as *use value* to Art as *exchange value*.[14] An important component of the social power of art was that it be valued for itself and not as a livelihood.[15] The usefulness of an art product was far outweighed by the usefulness of its production — in this case the expression and consolidation of unremunerated class power and status. Great art was priceless, and its pricelessness flowed naturally from a labor that took place over time-consumed-without-payment.[16] Genteel women played an important part in this process, being most able to devote the (free) time necessary to the creation of a labor-intensive art commodity that was at the same time entirely without use.[17] They also consolidated the status of art (and by extension architecture) by establishing the academies, an education in which became a rite of passage to upper-class life. This conferred the respectability of peers and social superiors through the adoption of superior aesthetic (as opposed to commercial) cultural capital.[18] The socially engineered status of art and art education thus became part of the cultural power in the related field of architecture.

Not only was art valued for its uselessness, it was also a good investment, since it gave access to those levels of the social hierarchy that allowed for increased accumulation. It was commercially important precisely because it existed beyond commercialism. Its power lay in its simultaneously masking and perpetuating relationships of power by an ideology that excluded the ideological itself. This non-reflexive dialectic simultaneously established not only art's own legitimacy but also the public space of what might legitimately be considered ideological. Precisely those understandings that might challenge the mythology of nonideological art were the ones that were excluded and cast as inferior. In this way, the ideological became a negativity, concerned with issues of manipulation, coercion, and power, further discouraging reflexive critical analysis.[19]

What we mean by "design" or "architecture"—what these terms include and exclude—is not absolute. Their meanings change over time as they are contested by competing interest groups. The normative meanings that we attribute to these terms today have been successfully superimposed upon the practice and theory of architecture by specific social and economic interests at the expense of others. In this process, subordinate or competing theories of design have been marginalized or exteriorized from the history of the field. So it is with the qualifying term *social* architecture. When we revisit the history of the profession, we find that serious attempts to place the social at the center of design theory have been silenced and an attempt has been made to produce and maintain a seamless image of professional theory and practice associated with a depoliticized fine art. Yet this apparent seamlessness hides a series of internal contradictions that are expressed in the everyday world of education and practice. Challenge to these dualities has been systematically repressed, as we shall find in the lives of two important theorists, William Morris and Hannes Meyer, who both had their critical social theories misrepresented and their personalities publicly ridiculed by the dominant members of the design subculture.

WILLIAM MORRIS AND CLASS SUICIDE

William Morris, the nineteenth-century British designer who wrote about the symbiosis of power and aesthetics, politics and art, was a formidable design theorist whose struggle over the ideology of the aesthetic has been denied. We know Morris the poet; Morris the advocate of neo-Gothic revivalism; Morris the inspiration of the Arts and Crafts movement; Morris the designer of beautiful tapestries, carpets, paintings, glassware, and publications; and Morris the producer of exquisite commodities. But William Morris, the tireless advocate of revolutionary socialism, the ceaseless propagandist, street-corner agitator, writer, lecturer, socialist theorist, friend of Friedrich Engels, avowed communist, and much-loved servant of the working people—this William Morris is a different creature, strange, and barely believable. This aspect of his theories was rarely recorded in design history books. He has been mistakenly branded as an escapist, a Gothic revivalist longing for some unrecoverable medieval paradise. On the contrary, steeped as he was in the history of precapitalist society and the role of work in creative life, his aim in the 1850s was to create conditions of empowerment for the masses, and his strategy was to reawaken and popularize the lost crafts of an earlier era in order to put the workers once again in control of the means of building production. He was the first modern designer to recognize that design had a role to play in the movement for emancipation and to demystify the role of economics in shaping aesthetic values, noting that "it is impossible to exclude socio-political questions from the consideration of aesthetics."[20]

Moved by the disparities of wealth and poverty around him, Morris knew that he had no moral choice but to align himself with the oppressed. "How can we of the middle classes, we the capitalists, and our hangers-on help the workers? By renouncing our class, and on all occasions when antagonism rises up between the classes casting our lot with the victims. . . . There is no other way: and this way, I tell you plainly, will in the long run give us plenty of occasion for self-sacrifice."[21] He was able to risk and then suffer the inevitable rejection that resulted from his own repudiation of his class of origin because of his disgust that his services were available only to the wealthy who used his designs as symbols of social distinction by which to articulate their class superiority. Himself a member of that wealthy class which he was moved to criticize and by which he was later attacked, Morris took the step that the logic of his political analysis dictated, crossing "the river of fire" and committing what world-renowned pedagogue Paulo Freire would later call "class suicide."[22]

William Morris provides us with a radical alternative philosophy of social design committed to unifying mind and hand in an emancipated working class. Yet the William Morris who has come down to us through a hundred years of design history is a politically emasculated figure, his socialist voice silenced. His is not the only instance. Similar repression has taken place whenever a theory has emerged that reunited aesthetics and politics, that revealed the underlying class ideology inherent in the notion of a transcendent aesthetic. Another such figure is Hannes Meyer.

HANNES MEYER, THE FORGOTTEN BAUHAUSLER

As Magdalena Droste wrote in her 1990 monograph, "Hannes Meyer remains the 'unknown Bauhaus director' even today. Histories of the Bauhaus often condense his over three-year career at the Bauhaus—from April 1927 to August 1930—into just one sentence. In actual fact Meyer spent a few months longer at the Bauhaus than his more celebrated successor to the directorship, Ludwig Mies van der Rohe. Meyer's disappearance from the history books is explained not by his activities as architect or Bauhaus director, but by his political sympathies."[23]

The depoliticized aesthetic inherent in the architecture-as-an-art-object paradigm that Morris challenged in his own era remained dominant until the 1930s. Even the modernist manifestos after the Russian Revolution proclaimed architecture to be the sum of building plus art. The depoliticized art promulgated by an earlier era was reproduced uncritically by Walter Gropius, Le Corbusier, and so on, and in their theories the social was aestheticized. While the new ahistorical architecture contested the dead formalism of the classical orders, the paradigm of a transcendent aesthetic on which those orders were based was absorbed intact and survived along with a now well established belief in the social superiority of the designer. Calls for the reunifying of art and craft, later to become the guiding principle of the Bauhaus, presumed that a loose federation of artists and architects would gradually erode the institutionalizing power of the academies and transform the world through the medium of the aesthetic. Modernism itself became a style by virtue of being representative of something other than itself—not of classical antiquity, in this case, but of the new timelessness, of functionality.

At the Bauhaus, one voice stood out against this aestheticization of the social and in support of a scientific approach to design—the first director of the architecture course, Hannes Meyer. He came to the directorship at its most difficult time, when Gropius himself had left in the face of the political and economic difficulties attendant upon the mounting tide of repressive fascism. Meyer believed, like Morris, that the making of architecture was essentially a social process, involving not just one individualistic designer but the whole community, and this philosophy was anathema to those who believed in the sanctity of individual artistic genius.[24] Meyer held that

> architecture is a process of giving form and pattern to the social life of the
> community. Architecture is not an individual act performed by an artist-
> architect and charged with his emotions. Building is a collective action....
> The form of the building must have a social content, otherwise it is mere
> decoration and formalism. We condemn the exhibitionist as an antisocial
> element in society, and we should also condemn that type of architect for
> whom the building of a house is merely an opportunity to parade personal
> formal preferences for all the street to see.[25]

His first priority was to confront the needs of a community suffering in a disintegrating economy. He saw fascism prospering under conditions of social and economic deprivation, and he committed himself to addressing this issue through his teaching and design. But first he had to put the Bauhaus workshops on a more effective economic footing in order to achieve political independence from an increasingly critical and repressive city administration. He restructured the programs, making each of them self-administering, under a master of craft supported by paid student-assistants. This dramatically increased productivity. He then redirected this increased production to socially important projects. Where, under Gropius, the workshops had been a place to develop prototypes for industrial goods, Meyer decided that the products should match "the needs of the people," determining that the Bauhaus should produce "popular necessities before elitist luxuries."[26] This focused attention on social needs in an economically divided society, and Meyer introduced foundational courses in social science to address this problem, in the process downgrading the foundational courses in art and aesthetics and bringing him into direct confrontation with Wassily Kandinsky and others who were responsible for the iconographic Bauhaus aesthetic.

For Meyer, the "beautiful" objects that the Bauhaus was producing on his arrival, articulated in simple primary shapes and colors, were the epitome of bourgeois taste. He recognized that this "Bauhaus style" represented both a superficial legitimation of form over content and a perpetuation of a dominant cultural elite. He saw formalism as systematized elitism, the mystifying refuge of those who seek to perpetuate privilege while at the same time offering to abolish it. Like Morris before him, he was ridiculed by many of his professional colleagues who would not allow the sacred totem of art to be laid upon the altar of class struggle. During his three-year directorship, Meyer developed cooperative workshop units, vocational training on the job, and standardized products for manufacture; he successfully designed and built (with his students) a group of low-cost demonstration apartments, democratized the curriculum, and established closer working relationships with the workers' movement. He was dismissed from the Bauhaus not because he failed, but because he succeeded too well. Subsequently, his personal character was denigrated and his work misrepresented by Josef Albers, Kandinsky, and Gropius. It is only recently that the facts of his achievement have emerged.[27]

Meyer was replaced by Mies, who immediately initiated policies to appease the fascists, expelling socialist students who refused to sign a nonpoliticism pledge while at the same time doing little to discourage the increasingly open display of Nazi sympathies. He allowed a lecture on revolution from the Right by the right-wing sociologist Hans Freyer but simultaneously forbade socialist speakers.[28] Mies abandoned the integration of theory and practice as well as the foundational courses in social theory that Meyer had introduced. Instead, he concentrated almost exclusively on an aestheticized design theory, reintroducing the centrality of the foundational course in fine art as the basis of a new formalism. His aesthetic spoke so well to corporate interests that the future garb of transglobal capital, the International Style, would become the template for American modernism, in the process abandoning the moral basis of modernism — its liberatory social agenda. It is significant that Meyer's was the most conspicuous absence in Philip Johnson's and Henry Russell Hitchcock's Museum of Modern Art *International Style* New York exhibition of 1932. He was not invited to participate, presumably because he was a self-proclaimed socialist whose design theories were anathema to Johnson's corporate sponsors.

The Congrès Internationaux d' Architecture Moderne (CIAM) of 1929 (in which Meyer played a significant role) marked a turning point in modern design theorizing: in its manifesto science briefly replaced art as the dominant paradigm. The congress declared that modern architects were against formalism and aestheticism and suggested that social science could identify, analyze, and solve all social problems. However naive this may sound today, at that time it posed a serious challenge to the traditional architecture-as-an-art-object paradigm. In the context of mainstream theorizing, this paradigm had been an uneasy but necessary bed companion of its subordinated architecture-as-science counterpart. Art needed science for its social legitimacy; materialist science needed art for its spiritual legitimacy. This cozy relationship existed only as long as neither aligned itself with politics (which is to say with questions about the organization and distribution of power). Meyer's sin was that he introduced science into the debate not as depoliticized factual tool, but as a social process. The 1929 congress destabilized the old balance as this radical form of science was declared morally superior to a depoliticized art. Yet within four years, at CIAM IV (and following Meyer's public ostracism), conservative theoreticians, spearheaded by Le Corbusier, had reasserted their dominance, and the political and social imperatives of science had been replaced by an uncritical positivism as a once-again subordinated component of an overarching and depoliticized art. Modernist-style architecture once again occupied the center of the utopian vision, and architects were declared the new cognoscenti, the masters of taste, the leaders of the coming social transformation, realized through an aestheticized science. By 1933, the 1929 manifesto had been translated into a superficial post facto rationalization of Bauhaus aesthetics. An abstracted and aestheticized concept of rationality was used to justify an elitist aesthetic, the explicit purpose of which was the liberation of the masses (who were not in any case consulted), but the subtext of which was the creation of a market to serve the interests and reproduction of an elite corps of cultural gatekeepers: "The aspiring modern architect with a Beaux Arts training, wishing to obey Le Corbusier's exhortations, had no need to change his method, but only his formula.... Le Corbusier had no desire to be of the urban proletariat. It was his mission to house them as he diagnosed their needs. For himself, he was proudly of the intelligentsia. Art is essentially arrogant, he wrote, and performs its proper function when it addresses itself to the chosen few."[29]

The arrogance was not art's, but that of a cultural elite determined to advance their own social and economic interests by suppressing the architecture-as-social-process paradigm in favor of the normative architecture-as-art-object. The design community for its part was only too willing to accept the paradoxical premise that the social process of architecture could only be achieved through its suppression and that a politically neutralized formalism alone held the key to social change. Little wonder that this mystification found broad corporate support in postwar America.

ARCHITECTURE AS A SCIENCE (1945–1968)

The postwar reconstruction of Europe channeled the interests and resources of science away from contentious social issues and into the development of technologies that might better serve the interests of corporate capital. The devastation of war and the consequent economic expansion of the American economy provided the appropriate social and economic context for the development of modernism as an aesthetic style wedded to technology. The wartime triumph of technology and production lent credibility to the conceptions of a machine aesthetic evolving from improved efficiency and scientific analysis. Critical social analysis was temporarily sidelined.

To the conservative as well as the liberal mind, technology promised the opportunity to achieve general emancipation and at the same time bypass the specter of class conflict. Growth and production, aided by the sciences, would resolve the most glaring material disparities. In postwar America this translated into a particularly authoritarian brand of social science that appealed to anticommunism and supported a continual process of suburbanization, thus dispersing potential social discord through the mythology of the New Frontier. McCarthyism in all branches of intellectual discourse ensured that populist ideals of participatory democracy were expunged from social life. Participatory research and critical intellectualism were replaced by logical positivism, which supported the emergence of a new meritocracy.[30] This remained the undisputed approach of all research and theorizing for the next twenty years. In the face of such widespread intellectual repression in America, many European intellectuals and critical theorists who had fled the Holocaust returned home only to find that there, too, the chilly grip of cold war ideologies stifled creative critical thinking.

Only in Britain, which had recently elected a socialist government and embarked upon a massive policy of public spending on health, education, welfare, and housing, did critical theories of social life develop in a relatively open environment. For a brief time between 1950 and 1968, therefore, British social and design theorizing attained a position of unparalleled world dominance. It is pertinent that Gropius, widely regarded as a design champion of the masses, rejected an offer to remain in Britain at this time and moved instead to the rabidly anticommunist United States.

The Evolution of Postwar Design Theories

In design theorizing, the 1950s in Britain were mainly characterized by the gradual rejection of CIAM-initiated monumentality and the emergence of Team X, whose members included Giancarlo deCarlo, Alison and Peter Smithson, and (later) Aldo van Eyck. But the impact of science on postwar design was first seen in ergonomics, in the design of military operating systems. This research helped to reinforce a primitive belief in environmental determinism—the theory that environment determines behavior—which carried through until the late 1960s and early 1970s.[31] The earliest works were devoted to increasing efficiency in production. A particular interest in Taylorism with a penchant for measuring task performance became the sine qua non of early environmental design. A postwar Europe in need of a massive rebuilding program and hampered by an acute scarcity of human and material resources adopted standards of performativity that only a rational/scientific methodology seemed able to deliver.

The new discipline of systems analysis, also derived from wartime strategic research, emerged to promote the more efficient organization of production processes and was also used to shape building layouts to minimize circulation. Originally this work was concerned essentially with problems of material production. Symbolic issues concerning what an environment might mean were not regarded as pertinent. Some theorists even developed methods for the mathematical design of building layouts.[32] My own thesis at the Birmingham School of Architecture in 1965 involved the design of an electrical engineering building, in which the positioning in three-dimensional non-Euclidean space of all the building's activities was decided by a computer-generated optimization program.[33] All of this work saw a dramatic change in the role of the architect, as the economy moved toward a greater welfare state. By 1948 in Britain, no less than 40 percent of practicing architects worked for the government while most of the remainder acquired their work from government commissions. This huge centralization of design resources allowed for a substantial increase in the breadth of research, reinforcing the ascendancy of the social in British design theorizing.

By the mid-1960s a pressing need to establish minimum space standards so as to systematize design programming focused the attention of the large centralized research system toward user studies. These standards, together with the need for dignified housing, led to the creation of public housing standards, which resulted in some of the most successful public housing programs in Europe at that time. Similar research programs were developed in schools and were coupled with emerging prefabricated building systems to create prototypes that became renowned throughout the developed world for their simplicity and cost-effectiveness. Analysis of offices indicated that the efficiency of user movement and the depersonalization engendered in large offices were major factors in reducing production output.[34] A number of studies followed that attempted to humanize the office environment, culminating in what became known as the *Burolandschaft,* or office landscape. Office planning gained widespread support, since it enhanced the productivity of office workers and also generated spatial economies through the elimination of separately walled offices. Privacy was created through the use of low, sound-absorbing partitions and indoor planting. The required flexibility of interior space necessitated a greater transparency of the building skin than traditional masonry construction allowed. This dovetailed well with the increased use of curtain-wall construction and allowed for substantial increases in leasable space within the same building envelope for still less cost. It was from such attempts to achieve spatial economies that the environmental science of proxemics later developed.

Not surprisingly, research began to reflexively focus on the state system itself. In Lethbride, Alberta, psychologists discovered that there might be a direct relationship between the physical organization of mental hospitals and the mental health of their patients. And in Britain, studies tried to link the layout of prisons and mental hospitals to incidence of recidivism and therapeutic recovery. These studies marked the beginning of the field of "architectural psychology," later known more generically as environmental psychology.[35] They were based upon a theory of (social) design that concealed a subtext of economic conservatism. The actual motivation of the state was not the rehabilitation of inmates (as had been publicly proclaimed), but the need to have them work more efficiently and produce more profit in order to cover the cost of their institutionalized care.[36]

DESIGN PROGRAMMING AND THE EMERGENCE OF DIFFERENCE

Early social theorizing in design was premised upon the universalization of an essentially Eurocentric notion of human need. But it soon became clear that needs do not exist in an absolute way or in a social vacuum. Hence social context came to be recognized as an important design variable. Then the classical notion of an idealized internationalism connoting a superior and universalizing existence (as in Le Corbusier's utopian conception of city planning, Ville Radieuse) began to lose ground against an emerging environmental psychology that challenged the role of the expert and reinstated the dignity of the ordinary person. The first alarm was sounded by Jane Jacobs, whose *The Death and Life of Great American Cities* (1961) accurately predicted the terrible human consequences flowing from these universalizing (not to say totalitarian) conceptions of city planning.[37] She argued on behalf of the diversity and complexity of cities that insensitive "top-down" planning was erasing, suggesting in its place the importance of human context and involvement.

The chief professional theoretician of this contextualism was Christopher Alexander, whose notion that a building should "fit" its context was raised to the status of a scientific principle.[38] In his seminal *Notes on the Synthesis of Form* (1964), which was to dominate design theorizing for the next decade, Alexander referred to vernacular examples, suggesting that over time traditional societies had shaped their environments to provide a perfect "fit" for their own social needs, but in modern society the ability to achieve this fit had been lost through a greatly increased social complexity and pace of environmental change. His research became famous for its use of computers to apply mathematical set theory to interconnected issues in design problems. Others standardized the data collection process to facilitate the interchangeability of information across building types.[39]

Alexander later rejected design as information processing to consider the social phenomenon of *community*. In a 1966 award-winning paper he argued, echoing Jacobs, that the spatial hierarchies of cities created by architects and planners did violence to patterns of social relationships that occur "naturally."[40] The article was scathing of Le Corbusier's Ville Radieuse and his administrative capital of India at Chandigarh and Lúcio Costa and Oscar Niemeyer's similar capital city, Brasilia, as well as other modernist projects. Adopting a medical metaphor, it indicated a new interest in environmental diagnosis, seeking ways to define environmental problems objectively. Yet it still clung to the importance of the expert analyst, who alone was able to conduct the diagnosis and administer the treatment to a grateful and naive public.

In an important publication written with Barry Poyner, Alexander suggested the existence of environmental geometries—what they called *relations*—relating built form with human behavior and cultural practice.[41] Their work promoted the idea of a nonjudgmental attitude toward cultural practices, suggesting that all human behavior was faultless and that difficulties occurring between people actually resulted from inappropriate spatial organization. They believed that if all of the spatial arrangements in the world could be incrementally "corrected," then social conflict itself would eventually disappear. While aiming to place subordinated cultural practices on an equal footing, this theory glossed over real moral and political issues in a naive utopianism.[42] The political concept that the environment is a domain contested by *competing* social interests was ignored. Although the positivistic basis of this work was later criticized, it nevertheless initiated the field of *postoccupancy evaluation,* which continues to the present day to exercise considerable influence in environmental design research. Like other forms of analysis based on positivist principles, relational theory, as it was called, constructed the designer as a person without history, gender, ideological beliefs, or political affiliations. Consequently, the actual beliefs and ideologies of actual designers were rendered invisible. The role played by their values in shaping the world was overlooked, at the same time that the instrumental role of values per se was marginalized in the authenticating name of "science." These particular cultural values were thus granted an unseen centrality.

Not surprisingly, it was the values of the dominant culture that demanded objectification — which required that value itself be erased from the discourse. This allowed design theorists to reinforce their own authority and power, all in the name of social emancipation and egalitarianism. As with the architecture-as-an-art-object paradigm before it, this architecture-as-positivist-science paradigm was an important instrument in the quest for social dominance by the design professions. It appealed to professionals because it relieved them of the moral need to expose themselves reflexively to existential change in the course of their work. What was valuable was measurable, and, by extension, what was not measurable was not valuable. Personal factors, including unconscious factors of the designers or researchers themselves, were carefully excluded. But it was a self-referential ideology that ultimately could not avoid its own dialectic. Slowly the twin fields of environmental programming and environmental psychology converged, and their gaze turned inward toward the mental world of the designer himself.

AGENCY UNMASKED: DESIGN METHODS

As psychology superseded sociology as the dominant influence in social science, it was inevitable that attention would eventually turn toward a key component in the design system, the designer. Popular texts began to interrogate the creative process itself,[43] giving rise eventually to the subdiscipline of design methods, a new field that came into public awareness in 1962 at a conference at Imperial College, London.[44] As in positivist environment-behavior studies, the personal, social, and cultural histories of the designer were initially viewed as inconsequential to the determination of the design product, and issues of value and meaning were still ignored. The designer was seen as a "black box" — an impenetrable mystery whose inner life was unknowable but could be inferred by objective analysis of "design outputs." Such mechanistic conceptions of the design process were clearly naive, but it was not until 1967 that, in a watershed symposium at Portsmouth, Christopher Jones suggested that the designer might be neither a genius magician (as in Kantian terms) nor an objective (positivist) black box, but rather a self-monitoring and self-reflective human being with all of the existential and political responsibility that this might suggest.[45]

Such sentiments echoed the analytical work coming out of France, where Jean-Paul Sartre, reviewing the works of famous writers and sculptors, showed the influence of the creator's life experience upon the form of the creation.[46] In architecture, Amos Rapoport wrote about the effect of cultural experience upon the perception of the designer, as well as the relationship between culture and form.[47]

Others aligned themselves with the social phenomenologists and existentialists to question the legitimacy of social normativity itself and challenge the naive determinism of scientific design theories based solely upon principles of quantifiability.[48] They were supported by a growing body of literature in the social sciences, particularly those being popularized in the critical writings of Erich Fromm, Herbert Marcuse, Ronald Laing, Thomas Szasz, Paul Goodman, and others.[49]

Whereas prior to 1933 art had been the dominant design paradigm, after the war this had been almost entirely superseded by a depoliticized science. Yet there emerged in the years 1966 to 1968 a strong culture of resistance to the role of the "expert" in the architecture-as-positivist-science paradigm, presaging the arrival of what we now call "postmodernism." For the first time both art and science (indeed architecture itself) were beginning to be recognized as instruments of oppression. It was becoming clear that issues of design could not be separated from issues of power. The influence of power in design, often hiding behind bureaucratic state apparatuses, became topical. It followed that a design process that took seriously issues of power must also take seriously the participation of the powerless in the framing of design discourse. This led to advocacy of user participation in the design process, an idea that had been growing for some years, based upon an ideology of populist environmental control.[50]

DESIGN FOR A PARTICIPATORY DEMOCRACY

In 1961 John Habraken promoted the return of control of housing design and fabrication to the users.[51] Two years later, John Turner suggested that the self-help urban squatters of Peru and Venezuela were more effectively addressing housing issues than any of the institutional programs of professionals or aid programmers.[52] In 1964 these same sentiments were echoed by Bernard Rudofsky, whose celebration of the vernacular showed that architecture produced without architects exhibited a vitality and heterogeneity that modern systems of expertise were unable to match.[53] In 1965 Habraken created Stichting Architecten Research (SAR) at Eindhoven University to further developments in his own self-help building component system. Numerous designers adopted his principles to facilitate public participation in both the design and construction phases of building projects.[54] One of the most celebrated examples was Lucien Kroll's medical complex at the University of Louvain in Brussels in 1968 (see chapter 4 in this volume). One year later, Ralph Erskine was commissioned to work on the Byker participatory public housing project in Newcastle, England.

Toward the end of the 1960s, as social science became more assertive, it also became more reflexive, and the ideology of participatory democracy began to be felt in all fields, not least in design. By 1968 the dominance of positivism was seriously challenged even in the common press. Science and knowledge, far from being neutral, were now viewed as being used by private interests to propagate and maintain a system of capitalist exploitation.

While the theories of British designers predominated in the 1950s and 1960s, by 1970 several—Christopher Alexander, Reyner Banham, Kenneth Frampton, Charles Jencks, and many prominent artists and performers (including David Hockney and eventually John Lennon)—had moved down the "brain drain" to America. Dominance in design theorizing passed with them in a way most graphically demonstrated by the transference of the center of popular cultural style from Liverpool and London's swinging Carnaby Street to San Francisco's "Summer of Love" in the Haight-Ashbury district in 1967. Afterward America exerted an unmistakable hegemony over all Western cultural affairs, aided greatly by the expanded electronic media and communications industries of Los Angeles and New York and by the electronic revolution taking place in Silicon Valley (nourished by a geographically proximate aerospace industry heavily financed by cold war military budgets).

1968—A Cultural Turning Point

Throughout the 1960s the impetus toward social change had been growing stronger. Beginning in the United States with the Civil Rights movement in the 1950s and early 1960s, civil disobedience began to emerge as a strategic weapon in liberation struggles. The free speech movement at Berkeley in 1964 was the first of many similar actions across the nation, calling into question the role of the university as an instrument of capitalism.

While the 1965 assassination of Malcolm X presaged later tragic events, the brief hippie era held out the promise of peaceful revolution to a youth suddenly aware of itself as a cultural and political force. John Lennon's catchphrase "All you need is love" inspired a belief in community power among the youth that seemed almost palpable, were it not that the escalating war in Vietnam darkened the horizon. In April, events took a more sinister turn with the assassination of Martin Luther King Jr. This was seen by some as a failure of nonviolence, and the riots that followed marked the beginning of a drift toward civil insurrection that would herald the conservative backlash of the Thatcher-Reagan-Bush era. In June, the assassination of Robert Kennedy dispelled whatever lingering hope the youth culture of America may have had of real social change under the existing representative democratic system.

Questions about what is "normal" or "right" in philosophy and social theorizing do not stand in isolation, but are part of a wider field of relationships that support and reinforce existing asymmetrical distribution of power and resources throughout society. In this sense, they articulate a wider field of interest—the issue of *democracy* in a pluralist society. In 1968, the definition of democracy itself was at stake, as the system of carefully constructed normativities began to unravel under pressure from an articulate and increasingly militant youth. The year 1968 was the culmination of a rising tide of anger and resistance to modernism's belief that the good life was just around the corner and accessible to all. The transparent mythology of democratic pluralism could be seen in the glaring maldistribution of world resources and capitalism's neocolonialism, most vividly portrayed in images of burning Buddhist monks and napalmed children. The psychiatrist Ronald Laing and his colleagues, together with anarchist Paul Goodman and black activist Stokely Carmichael, pointed to the inherent racism behind the Vietnam War and the role of academic and social theories in supporting this oppression at a landmark international conference at the Chalk Farm in London.[55] It was in this social context that demands for participatory democracy took on greater insistence, creating a power vacuum in which society became unstable and old-order power structures seemed in imminent collapse.

This shift became dramatically apparent in France in May 1968, when workers and students combined to occupy the factories, offering university courses open to all and maintaining industrial production through elected student-worker councils. At the very moment when the transition to participatory socialism seemed won, the French Communist Party sided with the conservative government of Charles de Gaulle against the workers and students to crush the popular revolt. In August, Russian tanks moved into Czechoslovakia to similarly crush the "Prague Spring." It became clear that the dead weight of orthodox Marxism no longer spoke for universal emancipation. And when, in August, horrified middle America witnessed the reality of police brutality in the prime-time televised drama of the bloody Democratic convention in Chicago, it was equally apparent to a disillusioned youth that capitalism as well as communism spoke to systems of social repression, the primary aim of which was to prevent structural social change.

One cannot overstress the significance of the social and cultural repercussions of the political vacuum that events of mid-1968 created. From the point of view of the youth culture and the New Left, the developed world stood on the vertiginous brink of radical social change, while for the older mainstream of American society and for the Right it appeared that raw anarchy was afoot. The King and Kennedy assassinations, the crushing of democratic movements, and the naked brutality of the system when challenged demoralized the Left, which was unable to develop a coherent revolutionary strategy that could command public respect, factionalized as it was between its recent historical, nonviolent past and an emergent tendency to violent confrontation that could indeed prove deadly. Following King's assassination there were riots in 125 American cities, and in June 1969 the more militant elements of the student movement formed the armed Weathermen at the Chicago convention of the Students for a Democratic Society (SDS).

In November 1968, with the election of Richard Nixon, mainstream America stepped back from the brink of radical democracy and accepted the inexorable process of conservative retrenchment, which would last down to the present. Nixon immediately escalated the war in Vietnam. In the spring of 1969, Ronald Reagan, then governor of California, directed the National Guard to oust the Berkeley students and residents from People's Park, in the process killing one student, blinding another, and spraying the entire Berkeley campus by helicopter (including the hospital and the child care center) with nerve gas, which had been outlawed in war by the Geneva Convention. Reagan also vowed to sweep the liberals and Communist sympathizers out of their places of influence in academia.

With the end of the decade, the confrontation between the repressive conservative administration and the student movement became increasingly bitter as widespread opposition grew to the war in Vietnam and to racism at home. Thousands of progressive Americans demonstrated in the streets, as political groups such as the SDS and the Black Panthers captured the imagination of the nation's youth. Repression escalated beyond the catharsis of Nixon's "incursion" into Cambodia to the shooting of students at the Kent State University campus in Ohio in 1970 (an act that precipitated the last major student uprising of the era), the August 1971 murder of Soledad Brother George Jackson in San Quentin, followed by the fatal suppression by New York governor Nelson Rockefeller of the Attica Prison uprising that September, and the wholesale murder of the Black Panther leadership nationwide. Although the rising tide of conservatism was momentarily slowed with the end of the war and the imminent impeachment of Nixon following the Watergate hearings in 1974, a profound fatalism settled over the nascent democratic impulse in the face of growing reaction and repression.

Liberals were faced with the gradual backlash of conservatism that developed through 1969. White youth who had supported the civil rights movement began to seek reincorporation into the liberal and conservative mainstream, afraid of the potential cost of actual social change. The professions offered a refuge where what was left of the liberal Left would focus on separate, minority issues — migrant farm workers, women, gays, solo parents, and the panoply of emerging separate "subject groups." The movement fragmented. Women, disillusioned by the sexual politics of their "revolutionary" brothers, developed their own brand of political action — feminism — while the demoralized men moved into men's groups and the burgeoning human potential movement bent upon a process of "self-liberation" as the 1960s passed into the 1970s. The militant element of the movement was silenced as it lost the credibility it had possessed in the days when it could, from a position of moral superiority, accuse the establishment of violence. Groups like the New American Movement and the Black Workers' Congress began to rethink the potential for socialist and communist strategies for the United States and sought to build new Left political parties to replace the old Communist Party USA.

Meanwhile, middle America, overwhelmed by the spectacle of televised riots, shifted politically toward a law-and-order conservatism. Most middle-class youth, stunned at the ferocity of the repression and without an effective political strategy, abandoned confrontation and retreated to the safety and predictability of careerism.

ACTIVISM TO PARTICIPATION (1968–1980)

Design students had played prominent roles in this social drama. In the 1960s and early 1970s they were among the most vocal advocates of social change, critiquing corporate modernism as part of an oppressive capitalist political system. In 1968 students at MIT had reorganized their studio space into a live-in workshop; students at Columbia University School of Architecture, protesting the proposed demolition of a black neighborhood to make way for a university swimming pool, occupied their building and demanded sweeping curriculum changes and a greater social responsibility to the wider concerns of society at large. Reflecting upon these events thirteen years later, Tony Schuman noted, "The link between our concerns as architects and the social problems all around us was a natural step. During the student strike at Columbia in April of 1968, the School of Architecture was the only professional school on campus which was occupied predominantly by its own students. The impact of that experience was profound in many respects, from the intense communal environment at the school during the occupation itself, to proposals for curriculum reform and the establishment of a community service studio."[56]

In May 1969 at Berkeley, architectural staff and students had played a prominent role in attempting to resolve the fight over control of People's Park,[57] and in the same year students went on strike at Harvard and at Woluwé–Saint Lambert in Belgium. In the aftermath of the Kent State killings of 1970, it was once again the architecture students at Berkeley who were the first to strike and who lobbied successfully to close the entire University of California system—a precursor to a nationwide university strike. In England, France, Germany, and Italy, students in design schools participated actively in the social movements wrenching Western Europe. With the increasing repression of the 1970s and the realization of the disparity between student and mainstream ideologies, this militancy became absorbed into a growing ideology of participation.

In May 1968, many of the speakers from the previous year's symposium at Portsmouth gathered at MIT for the Design Methods Group Conference. At the end of that conference (and the day after the assassination of Robert Kennedy), the Environmental Design Research Association (EDRA) was inaugurated by a few remaining delegates. It became one of the most vocal advocates of "social" architecture, and its first chairperson, Henry Sanoff, became a leading advocate in the United States for participatory design processes that became popular in the

1970s.[58] In 1971, advocacy planner Robert Goodman, in describing the subservience to capitalism of the design professions (whom he referred to as "the soft police"), advocated the need to work directly with disenfranchised groups toward a decentralized "community socialism."[59] With such support, participatory design sustained itself for several years even in the face of increasing state conservatism.

In 1972 Rod Hackney, later the president of the Royal Institute of British Architects (RIBA), developed his self-help housing project in Macclesfield. In 1975 Christopher Alexander began his self-build housing project in Mexicali. In Britain, Walter Segal was commissioned by the Lewisham Borough Council to design a group of rationalized, timber-framed, self-build housing. In 1976, John Turner followed up his earlier work with his important book, *Housing by People.*[60] In 1977, together with Sara Ishikawa and Murray Silverstein (and numerous subauthors), Alexander published *A Pattern Language,* which followed from his earlier work and had been ten years in the making. The authors abandoned expert objectivism and instead formulated demystified design guidelines that nondesigners could understand and over which they might exercise control.[61] These theories enjoyed an extended life into the 1980s, through the patronage of the Prince of Wales and the election of Rod Hackney. But with the arrival of Margaret Thatcher and Ronald Reagan they were gradually silenced.

THE ARCHITECTURAL IMPACT OF CONSERVATIVE FISCAL POLICIES (1980–1990)

The conservative backlash of the late 1960s and 1970s carried enormous implications for design theory. The momentum for participatory democracy within the professions experienced a brief hiatus in the 1970s, as the new ideas trickled down to the level of professional practice. They diminished by the mid-1980s, as political conservatism and economic recession drove professionals to revert to traditional models of practice. Notions of equity and justice were expunged from the design theory discourse. Disparities of wealth increased dramatically, and the poor were pushed further beyond the range of professional assistance. Statistics show that the economic gap between the "developed" and the "developing" countries widened, while in all developed countries the gap between the rich and poor increased dramatically, with large numbers of the middle class falling below poverty levels.[62] This was due partly to changes in the world economy and partly to the policies of the Reagan and Thatcher administrations. Reagan's free-market ideology and overwhelming determination to raise the stakes on cold war spending to bankrupt the Soviet Union helped to reshape the world economic order. During his presidency, Reagan successfully inverted the differential public spending between housing and the military budgets.[63]

Reagan's policies also emptied the mental hospitals, as states, driven by reduced federal subsidies, balanced their budgets and turned their medicated inmates out of mental institutions onto the streets to the care of a nonexistent "community support." At the same time health, social welfare, and federal housing programs were decimated. The result was a marked reduction in federally funded housing, which, together with increased unemployment precipitated by capital flight, created a chronic condition of homelessness not witnessed since the 1930s. There was an 82 percent decline in the federal funding for housing between 1980 and 1988, and, while in 1981 the government provided funding assistance under Section 8 for 217,000 new households, by 1989 this had dropped to 85,000, creating a net loss of 1.2 million low-income housing units from 1980 to 1989. By 1989 the annual rate of loss was in the region of 300,000.[64] This downturn in public spending most affected those at the bottom end of the economic ladder. To this should be added the squandering of investor funds in the savings and loan scandal, caused largely by the 1982 deregulation of the banking industry. This created an increased tax burden on the already poor, who carried the full weight of corporate failure. On top of all this, the national tax revenue was used to support bailouts and payments of interest on an out-of-control national budget deficit.

When we take all of this into account, it becomes clear that the years from 1980 to 1990 constitute an unrelenting attack upon the lower and middle classes to the economic advantage of the most affluent although numerically small beneficiaries of corporate wealth.[65] Millions dropped out of the middle class below universally accepted poverty indices. During the era of fiscal cutbacks that followed the 1974 oil crisis, academia also became increasingly conservative as educational budgets were cut and jobs in outside industry became increasingly scarce. Through the Reagan years, EDRA increasingly avoided contentious political position-taking. This played a major role in the neutralization of radical design theory and in shifting design theorizing from a transformative to a conciliatory ideology. While individual acts of political activism were permissible, the organization as a whole increasingly espoused a supposed position of ideological neutrality in order to preserve a semblance of internal cohesion and external legitimacy with resource agencies. As research budgets were squeezed, theory was separated from practice and began to lose its critical edge. Theories of design research became more abstract and unrelated to the real problems of those most affected by governmental and economic policies. This refusal and that of similar professional organizations worldwide to embrace any official political or ideological position on poverty and homelessness has implicitly lent support to the savage cutbacks of the Reagan era that have so devastatingly affected the lives of the already powerless. It is perhaps for this reason that such organizations have continued to draw so few members from subordinated or minority cultures.

By the mid-1980s theories of participation were eventually overtaken by a further downturn in the building economy and by the need for a commodified, more marketable model of professional practice. In Britain, socialist local governments that had fostered participation came under ferocious attack from a conservative central government and, in the face of subsidy cuts, canceled further community programs. In America funding for community projects was similarly reduced. Numerous community design centers—havens for radical democratic theorizing— were shut down, and, in the name of challenging oppressive modernism, neoconservatives who had been silent throughout the 1960s (classical formalists like Philip Johnson in architecture) emerged to frame the "legitimate" discourse and to reconfigure the (post)modernist aesthetic in an expanding alignment with the interests of corporate capitalism. In the design disciplines this was accompanied by a return to formalism in which architecture, once again, reestablished its relationship to high art at the same time that social science as a generator of form was critically undermined by the reactionary postmodernism of the New Right.

In the process the legitimated field of inquiry shrank, and critical theorizing, which questioned social normativity and power and which had been such a powerful influence on design research, was now once again excluded from theoretical discourse. The mantle of critique in the English-speaking world passed to art historians with the published translation of Manfredo Tafuri's *Architecture and Utopia* in 1976. Changes in design publishing driven largely by the need to generate increased advertising revenues resulted in a loss of access to key journals that had previously championed social architecture.[66] Visual imagery began to predominate and in the process the critical definition of what properly constituted "critical" was transformed into a semantic game supporting and framing architecture as the practice of visual gymnastics.

The shrinking economy also had a direct influence on the design professions. By the 1980s architects had to compete more energetically for a reduced number of jobs. Major project roles in building design had been encroached on by others. Engineers, interior designers, project managers, facilities managers, landscape architects, economists, and investment consultants had all claimed significant areas of professional design territory.[67] While the number of architectural commissions in the United States increased significantly between 1972 and 1982, this increase was more than offset by a correspondingly greater increase in the number of architectural students in training. There was also an increase in the size and complexity of building projects necessitating specialized control of specific areas of the building design process. This all resulted in a consolidation of the building industry (indicated in the increasing amounts of work being undertaken by design/build contractors) and in increased competition from other professions.[68]

Competition for professional design services became extreme, and designers sought a "defensible professional space" to which they alone could claim exclusive right. Increasingly, this space confined itself to the applied visual aesthetic of the building envelope. At the same time that this erosion of professional space happened, an increasing amount of the work undertaken by designers was absorbed by much larger firms, thus reducing the scope of possible services for the aspiring graduate and consolidating the practice of design as a hierarchical, rather than a democratic, project in which design itself became a prize stake in the cultural capital competition of office practice. In addition, the burgeoning technologization of design through expensive CAD systems requiring major capital investment, coupled with the exponential increase in technical information, now threatens the survival of the small-scale practitioner, further consolidating the cultural capital of design into the hands of an increasingly few principals in large corporate firms and leading the "rank and file" workers to scramble for the decreasing number of jobs at increasingly low rates of wage labor.[69]

DESIGN AND CAPITAL ACCUMULATION

Another factor that led to the adoption of a conservative form of postmodernism in design had to do with changes in the role of building as a mechanism for the production of speculative profit. The exponential increase in speculative building after 1970 represented a significant shift in the circumstances of building production. Major corporations that have often preferred to lease space rather than tie up their capital in prestige buildings directed their capital into building production that promised a high rate of return—the speculative commercial building that could be quickly erected, leased, or sold. This change was driven by an increase in the global mobility of capital.[70] And it resulted in an increasing emphasis upon the built-in obsolescence of buildings—buildings designed specifically not to be permanent but to require frequent replacement. In speculative design these economic pressures largely determined the physical size, shape, proportion, and quality of construction. They left the architect little room other than to dress up the exterior as an object for desirable consumption. This transformation effectively limited the work of the architect to "designer" buildings for which they created an image—a task that bears more resemblance to Madison Avenue advertising than it does to the need to address serious social concerns.

As we have noted, professional design organizations remained mute about the cost of this shift for society's disadvantaged, making no commitment to lobby politically on behalf of the growing poor whom they had abandoned. The American Institute of Architects merely ran competitions to design "housing for the homeless" and thus lent professional weight to the illusion that the problem of homelessness was one of design, rather than a political problem of resource allocation in a military-based economy driven by enormous asymmetries of power. Such patterns are characteristic of a design theorizing that excludes progressive political considerations from its discourse, thereby once again framing architecture as a visual art. During the 1980s, professional design organizations colluded (by intent or benign neglect) with the political establishment and readopted the conservatism of the power status quo, and the issue of power itself was once again amputated from design theory.

DESIGN THEORY AS CONTESTED DOMAIN

In this brief and consciously partial history of design theorizing I have tried to show how transformative social practices have consistently been marginalized and/or expunged from the dominant discourse of the design professions in a way intended to mask conservative intentions. It should not surprise us to realize that the history of design theory should itself have been rendered so partial, since selective amnesia is such a key element in the process of social control: those who exercise control in the present also control the "official" history, our view of which informs and shapes our whole conception and practice of professionalism in the present and into the future.

One of the consequences of the elimination of "unofficial" histories from the "official" dominant-culture history is that history itself appears to be uncontested, assuming an aura of inevitability, of a "natural" evolutionary process without agency. This creates the impression that history literally just "happens"—that it is not created by actual living human beings but is the result of immutable historical forces that are beyond individual control. This has three consequences. First it hides the actions of members of the dominant culture who actually do control social, political, and economic circumstances, thus allowing these actions to continue invisible and uncontested. Secondly, it severs present experiences of oppression from those of the past. This creates the illusion that they are unique and personal and not part of a larger framework of the experience of "historical others" with whom we might forge a sense of solidarity and through whose stories we might confirm or authenticate our own experience. This then creates and perpetuates feelings of self-doubt and passivity among the subordinated, which further undermines their ability to resist dominant-culture versions of social reality.

In the 1960s, when society came to be viewed as consisting of separate cultures contesting the right to define the terms of wider social normativity, recognition of different levels of cultural power grew. Cultural dominance and subordination, beyond the Marxist conception of class, which until that time had commanded the center of social discourse, were accepted. These structures of cultural subordination exist not only in the "outside world" but within the professions themselves, where competing groups struggle to establish their hegemony. Key to this, as we have seen, are the limits applied to the history of theory itself, involving a war of position in which the major objective is the framing of the theoretical discourse.

This is particularly true recently, where the meaning attributed by designers to the term *postmodernism* is an important site of struggle. One must ask whose interests it serves to abandon the emancipatory impulse of modernism. The economic transformation that I have just outlined shows that the needs of continued capital accumulation crushed the social project, in the process transforming the profession and bringing into positions of dominance designers who embody and can most successfully further the needs of consumer capitalism in their work. The particular character of the profession's ideological shift into a struggle for the liberation of form rather than of people was crafted by design theorists like Charles Jencks, Robert Venturi, and Peter Eisenman, who currently dominate the industry of cultural reproduction and whose definitions of what properly constitutes "architecture" "design" hold sway with a whole new generation of designers. Their "postmodern" renditions of the theory and history of design as the creation of buildings viewed as depoliticized art objects have once again reasserted the cultural dominance of the status quo. The history that they proclaim as fact is self-serving. Once established, their history has made it easier to restrict design theorizing to issues of form, separated from content, and to reinstate the traditional paradigm of a depoliticized transcendental aesthetic. In what follows I will critically analyze the ways in which these more recent theories continue this process of cultural domination and colonization while promising social and cultural transformation.

POSTMODERN DESIGNERS OF THE NEW RIGHT

If modernism and emancipation are past, then what purpose can remain to the professional designer? Is the design of the built environment of no more consequence to humanity than the haute couture of the Paris fashion houses? In the process of relinquishing its moral grounding, architecture also relinquishes its legitimation and is forced to acknowledge itself as an instrument of privilege and power. In a would-be democracy, such a posture is extremely unstable and threatens to further undermine the profession. Shifting the "struggle for liberation" from the domain of social science to that of aesthetic philosophy enables architects to continue to package their services and to represent their products as connected to a different kind of liberation—one that, as in 1933, is (supposedly) nonpolitical, one that will unleash the essential transcendental character of architecture. The result of this is that notions of liberation are themselves detached from the social and economic reality of everyday life and drained of any moral or politically progressive significance: a process that works directly in the political and economic interests of the already powerful, whether landowners or architects.

Two major strategies follow this line. According to the first, put forward in the writings of Robert Venturi, Charles Jencks, and others, postmodernism replaces the stripped-bare modernist aesthetic with populist decorative images and meanings. The second strategy, critical of the first as well as of modernism, has been called *deconstructivism,* a term coined to conflate the style of the 1920s Russian constructivists with the poststructuralist theories of deconstruction in philosophy, emblematized by the work of architects such as Bernard Tschumi and Peter Eisenman. Both of these strategies embody the conservative ideology of the New Right, but they do so under the guise of theories that appear to speak to the philosophy of emancipation and equity previously attributed to the Left. A closer reading of the works of Venturi and Eisenman will show how this is done, as well as provide an insightful counterpoint to the lives and works of Morris and Meyer referred to earlier.

Robert Venturi: Champion of Common Culture?

Robert Venturi was one of the first postmodern architectural theorists. In the 1970s, he and his coauthors suggested that modern architecture had failed to capture the public imagination and that it ought to accept some of the lessons of the popular culture of the Las Vegas strip.[71] In choosing Las Vegas as the source of their study, Venturi et al. selected the least tasteful of American environments and attempted to show how its common popularity exposed a poverty of professional aesthetic values and taste. While this strategy at first seems to valorize elements of common American commercial culture, in fact it does so in a way that subverts them to the cultural dominance of professional values. Venturi and his colleagues are selective. They choose, from the infinite number of formal arrangements available, only those that are (to them) "culturally significant," and these choices are unavoidably circumscribed and determined by their own cultural backgrounds. Furthermore, to simply reproduce common cultural motifs would be to miss the opportunity for increasing their own cultural visibility and professional standing. In order to extract cultural capital from the appropriation, Venturi and his colleagues are required to transform the common cultural motifs they have appropriated. This transformation involves a process of abstraction and exaggeration that lifts them "above" the commonplace and establishes them as high-culture icons that carry increased consumer value—they are made "more ordinary," having cultural capital beyond that of everyday life. These transformed common cultural forms are then invested with a supposedly universal value, embodying meanings that are constant over time and culture, telling us, for instance, that the arched windows of the upper stories of the Guildhouse represent the stability associated with Roman classicism—a sixteenth-century Renaissance palace in the middle of Philadelphia—while at the same time evoking feelings of "dignity," "domesticity," suggesting the building as "palatial" as well as "commercial." Yet while proclaiming the parity of popular culture with high culture, Venturi and his colleagues stopped short of questioning the mechanisms of power through which such distinctions are created or their own role in the process of that creation.[72]

In presuming to know on behalf of its occupants what the building will mean, Venturi's universalizations inherently disempower the members of the common culture that they presume to celebrate. Mindful of the need to have a commodified professional identity easily recognizable and therefore more salable through the design of "signature buildings," he and his colleagues have opted for their own continued membership in the high culture elite, as gatekeepers of popular culture forms to be appropriated and recycled to the masses from a position of popularized authority. *Learning from Las Vegas* is a deceitful document. It promises to liberate us from theories of liberation. It offers to give voice to common culture, in the very act of silencing it. Venturi's real genius was to see that the decorated shed offered precisely that combination of separated form and content that would allow the spatial and structural economies of the International Style to be reproduced (even more economically) behind an inexpensive iconographic veneer. His postmodernism does even more with less. As critic Diane Ghirardo says, "Developers and real estate interests, in their wildest dreams, could not have come up with such an intellectually credible screen for their activities, an intellectually and academically respectable and viable means of diverting attention away from the toughest issues in land development and the building process, toward trivial matters of surface. But not only that: the work of the big name 'art' architect not only masks but legitimates the project by virtue of the power of art, rendering any other questions pointless."[73]

Venturi does not so much reproduce common meaning as create it. His success as an architect demands that he must give the appearance of serving the public good while simultaneously serving the interests of a corporate capitalism (which cannot operate other than on the basis of public disempowerment). His buildings are a picture of himself, struggling to maintain a benign public face while simultaneously engaging in cynical paternalism. The disempowerment inherent in his work operates by promoting the mystification of community power while simultaneously mystifying the social relations by which it might actually be brought about. Community, in this instance, is framed as a passivity. What is so alluring about such strategies is that they simultaneously give the impression of social transformation while preventing its occurrence, allowing for the appearance of change without the need to actually change, on the part of either the subject group or, more particularly, of the designer.

Peter Eisenman: The "Profit" of Mystification

Unlike Venturi, Peter Eisenman does not espouse a populist cultural position; rather he adopts a position that repudiates any cultural position. He is a proponent of deconstructivism in architecture, borrowing from deconstruction, the philosophy of Jacques Derrida. He challenges modernism, revealing its reliance upon misconceived notions of function and universal emancipation. He also implicitly accuses Venturi of merely substituting one form of representation (historicism) for another (function).[74] Eisenman's theory at first appears to offer the transformative potential to which Hatch earlier referred. It seems revolutionary, promising to undermine established aesthetic norms. Instead of replacing the architectural meanings of a privileged class with another set of classless meanings, as modernism tried to do, it attempts to define an architecture that is itself meaningless, or conversely, open to indefinite meanings. It seeks to avoid the trap awaiting most designers — of reproducing the circumstances of their own social and cultural conditioning.[75] Eisenman sees the process of design as a ritual cleansing of preestablished meaning, and therefore as an implicit critique of existing social structures.[76]

It is my belief that the crucial effect produced by deconstructivist theories is one of illusion, a masking of the role these theories play in the continuing reproduction of social structures of privilege and power, of which Eisenman and his colleagues are themselves the main beneficiaries.[77] In deconstructivism, the built environment is stripped of its emancipatory social power. Deconstructivism promotes architecture as the (individualistic) production of formalist icons, the effect of which is to perpetuate a star system of authorship, this in spite of a (postmodern) theoretical position that takes the problematization of authorship as one of its foundational premises.

To illustrate this operation, let's look at Eisenman's design for the Wexner Center for the Visual Arts at Ohio State University in Columbus, Ohio. Eisenman offers a quintessential example of the practical application of this strategic mystification. His fellow-traveler critics have insisted that the Wexner Center "liberates" the radical imperative of postmodernism from the naive eclecticism of Venturi and others.[78] Here, the building asserts its presence, distracts attention, demands an equality of status with the objects it is designed to house.[79] It asserts its equality, its congruence, with the paintings and sculptures as an object of desire. The glassed-in grids are said to throw direct sunlight and shadows onto the displays, calling into question the kinds of aesthetic objects that have been normatively taken to constitute art.

We are told that in this building, Eisenman reminds us that one of the primary functions of art is to shape our perception of reality, and he does this by undermining our certainty about the taken-for-granted conventions of our everyday experience of mass, structure, place, and time. His work of this period is said to address "decentering," the "death of the author," the "erasure of subjectivity." His intention is reputed to be to engage the displacement of subjectivity, the fragmentation of life, the loss of moral certainty, the relativity of values, the illusory aspect of history, and the unreliability of rationality. The Wexner Art Center is said to have an appearance that suggests the "irrational" and represents a repudiation of Enlightenment rationality and the veracity of science and logic. It is postmodern architecture become art, in contradistinction to a modern architecture embodying scientific rationality. Insofar as Eisenman's Wexner Art Center attempts to *be* art, it is also one of the clearest expressions of Eisenman *the artist*. He offers himself as an agent for social change, as a person who, he suggests, shifts public perception and transforms the way we collectively perceive ourselves as experiencing subjects by a variety of architectural devices, displacing our sense of verticality and horizontality.[80] In Eisenman's own words: "If you believe, as I do, that architecture can change culture, you don't make architecture to please a rich client"—and this from an architect whose oeuvre comprises hardly anything *but* houses for (pleased) rich clients.[81] Such strategies of mystification are integral to the reproduction of a language of mystique, which, as Cuff has reminded us, is a powerful "art defense" for architects in their relationship to critical clients.[82]

The suggestion that his formalist repudiation of rationalism represents a critically new artistic truth has a familiar ring. To pose art as a liberatory enterprise, resisting the dehumanizing effects of Enlightenment rationality, is, as we have seen, a strategy historically inscribed with the vectors and processes of power. Eisenman says he seeks a "dangerous" architecture, yet the real danger of Eisenman's work is that it appropriates the liberatory ideas of postmodern critique and uses them for conservative ends. What we are seeing is the depersonalization and commodification of difference. Difference is here transformed from an ontological condition into a commodity, serving directly the needs of designers looking for novelty in the pursuit of the next commission in a bitterly competitive consumer economy.

The twin concepts of voice and difference are not abstractions any more than is oppression. They are lived realities for those who are silenced, for those who are marginalized by virtue of their race, gender, or class, by a dominant culture blind and deaf to its own partiality. Difference, in fact, is one of the central elements in the marking of social and cultural boundaries, and as such is inseparably tied to cultural identity. In such a concept of difference, the cultural and social identity of groups whose autonomous existence is already under threat is erased, colluding with the tendency of the dominant culture toward cultural imperialism, visited now not upon remote "natives" but upon disempowered and invisible minorities within our society who have an equal if not greater stake in the definition of key conceptual terms. Furthermore, this vacuous formalist notion of difference is often used as a justification for the expression of a postmodern-day state of schizophrenia in which "stable categories of lived experiences are blurred, distinctions dissolve, and meaning itself seems to float, unanchored, adrift."[83]

As in the work of Venturi, such propositions universalize experience. For whom is the world fragmentary or adrift? Once again, a partiality is represented as a universality, and in the process, the voices of victims are silenced. Furthermore, to characterize the postmodern world as chaotic, fragmentary, schizophrenic, and meaningless is to place it conveniently beyond the range of meaning, to insulate it from the critical interrogation that might otherwise reveal its underlying structure of power and privilege. For if life itself is meaningless, why search for its meaning? In spite of Eisenman's attempt to render it meaningless, the Wexner is a monument to a particular meaning, reframing the social as neutral—as existing independent of relationships of power. It is strong in its capacity to convince that something can indeed be social without increasing the chances of social change. It is strong in its ability to gloss over the silences of its own exclusions and to convince those of the profession who wait to be convinced that all is well in the world and that social change can happen without personal sacrifice, without crossing William Morris's "river of fire."

INSTANCES OF RESISTANCE AND A POLITICS OF HOPE

It is important to recognize that such design theories as those promoted by Venturi and Eisenman are not exempt from ideological bias, even though that is their espoused intention. They are, on the contrary, the intensely ideological expressions of their membership in the dominant cultural elite. Architectural theorizing is a war that revolves around issues of empowerment and disempowerment. It is a war fought for the ideal of democracy—the right of individuals to directly and collectively determine the quality of their lives and their ultimate destiny. It is a war that has been waged since modern conceptions of architecture first emerged, as the histories of William Morris and Hannes Meyer indicate. It is important to record the history of this war in order to maintain a sense of solidarity and continuity with the past so as to establish a resistance to the tendency to strip "official" history of its political content, and in so doing to reinfuse future work with democratic hope.

What to do? Where to turn? As I mentioned at the beginning of this chapter, C. Richard Hatch's book contains many examples of successful resistances to culturally colonizing architecture. They depict communities in the process of creating and sustaining their cultural identities by designing and often building their own world. But they were collected before the worst of Thatcher-Reagan-Bush. Of the fifty-six community design centers he lists, only the Pratt Institute Center for Community and Environmental Development (PICCED) appears to have survived with any vitality, doing remarkable urban rehabilitation work in the South Bronx and other blighted areas of New York. A sister organization, the City College Architectural Center (CCAC), is also doing exemplary work in Harlem.

Despite this, notable theoretical and practical work in community (or social) design is beginning to rise from the ashes of the 1980s. In March 1993, the Pratt Institute, along with the New York Chapter of Architects, Designers and Planners for Social Responsibility (ADPSR), sponsored an exhibition on socially responsible design in education, which attracted 196 entries from around the world.[84] Since that exhibition, other chapters of ADPSR have formed elsewhere, offering hope of a renewal of professional concern for a renaissance of the social in design.

In the literature of design theory, there has been a noticeable resurgence of scholarship based upon the liberatory aspects of postmodernism. This book represents an addition to that literature, building upon the critical theorizing of Tom Dutton's earlier work, as well as the works of Mike Davis, Dolores Hayden, Diane Ghirardo, and others.[85]

Tony Schuman, a founder of ADPSR New York and tireless advocate of social architecture, has also made notable contributions to the field in both Ghirardo's and Dutton's books. What distinguishes his writing is his ability to take seriously the formalist theories of design in their own terms and to subject them to rigorous social and political analysis. In his chapter for Ghirardo he compares historical utopian precedents with Ricardo Bofill's Abraxas apartments at Marne-la-Vallée, examining the hierarchies of social space and the implicit role of the family vis-à-vis the social life of the community. He finds in Bofill's designs an inherent cynicism belied by the architect's public utterances. In his chapter for Dutton he moves beyond critique to uncover, in the work of Lucien Kroll (in the French town of Alençon), an example of utopian practice in which the formation of community successfully plays a key role. He also explores the work of the Belgian firm AUISA at Alma-Gare. What Schuman discloses is that Kroll, particularly, has been quite successful in engaging participatory design strategies that embody the words of French theorist Michel Foucault: "(Architecture) can and does produce positive effects when the liberating intentions of the architect coincide with the real practice of people in the exercise of their freedom."[86]

Schuman perceptively notes that "an architecture that takes seriously its social vocation must be based on direct contact with the public it serves." This represents the cornerstone of Kroll's philosophy and constitutes the core principle of the social. It implies a very different role for the architect—seen now as a part of rather than separate from the community he or she serves. This carries substantial implications for practice, suggesting that the focus of architecture should shift from image making to community creation.

Some community design practices have accomplished significant work even in these economically depressed times. These practices, often working within specific cultural groups and under circumstances of extreme economic constraint, have maintained a very high standard of community empowerment. The work of

Asian Neighborhood Design in San Francisco's Chinatown and the courtyard housing at Valencia Street in San Francisco by the now defunct Community Design Collaborative of Oakland are both models of dignified public housing in a high-density urban context. Perhaps the most prolific community designer in housing is Michael Pyatok, whose numerous award-winning designs bear witness to a remarkable skill as well as a deep commitment to community. Pyatok combines a lucid analysis of the regimes of economic domination and exploitation in public housing in the United States with a steadfast compassion for its victims. Comparing housing design competitions with housing design realities, he notes that the provision of housing, while important, represents only one small component of the difficulties of disadvantaged groups, whose participation at every level of the process is crucial to the achievement of an empowered and dignified life:

> The aggressive utilization of participatory development strategies never seems to be an important judgment criterion in housing design competitions, but it is the *sine qua non* of most nonprofit housing work in practice. These participatory strategies construe the development sequence—land acquisition and financing, political organizing, choosing contractors and professional consultants, designing and building the project, owning and managing it afterwards—as components in the larger process of community building. Each step along the way provides jobs and learning experiences for lower-income people. Their active involvement improves their ability to survive within the system, expands their awareness of the strengths and weaknesses of the institutional framework, increases their skills in working the political system, and generates a sense of pride and accomplishment as they witness the emergence of a cultural enterprise they helped shape with their own hands and ideas.[87]

(Interestingly, support systems like those described by Pyatok are an integral part of the work and programs of PICCED in the South Bronx).

Pyatok also notes that design competitions are product oriented and do not recognize housing design as an opportunity for empowerment. We have seen how the category "architecture" has itself been socially constructed throughout history to exclude any potential for actual social transformation or empowerment. It should not come as any surprise, therefore, that it should also be absent from public housing processes. In the United States particularly, public housing design is seen as something outside of architecture proper.[88] We see here, once again, divergent models of what constitutes architecture: architecture as finite material product, as formal image, as object, rather than architecture as community-building process. The war of position between these two ideologies permeates every tentacle of the professional process because it is "wired into" conceptions of architecture and design that occupy positions of centrality in design education.

Toward a Transformative Design Education

Pyatok's comments about the role of competitions could be equally applied to the architectural studio, through which the architecture-as-art-object paradigm is transmitted through succeeding generations of designers. The "hidden curriculum" of the design studio, which similarly tends to be product-oriented, overly influenced with image making, and often involving a pedagogy that is highly competitive, hierarchical, and disempowering, is an important ingredient in this transmission process, if only because it operates at the unconscious levels of learning. Yet even within architectural education, pedagogies of resistance are beginning to emerge. Not surprisingly, these also usually involve direct contact with disempowered community groups, and involve students in attempts to address and resolve real-world problems and issues. Such projects place great emphasis on process along with product.

The work of Jacqueline Leavitt at UCLA, particularly her work at Nickerson Gardens, in which students engaged with low-income housing tenants in helping them to bring dignity to their otherwise bleak environment, is worthy of note. The so-called Mad Housers project at the University of Illinois in Chicago is also worth noting. Similar, if less confrontational, is the work of Gary Greenan at the University of Miami in Florida in developing, with his students, a dignified short-term shelter program for the proliferating homeless. All of these projects were included in the Pratt Institute exhibition already noted.[89]

Finally, my colleagues and students at the University of Auckland in New Zealand in the Community Design Studio, have joined me in attempting to address design issues in the framework of a cooperative pedagogy.[90] Working in the context of a culturally diverse and contested landscape, the studio is openly, politically progressive in order to produce a critical reflexive consciousness in students, staff, the university community, and the wider public about the role played by the physical environment in expressing and reproducing the social and economic structures of late capitalism, as well as the European cultural hegemony that continues to dominate this former British colony in the South Pacific. The experience of the studio becomes framed within a society divided by classed, gendered, and racist practices. Projects have spoken to these issues directly: the design of an alternative one-hundred-million-dollar performing arts center, the development of town plans for the cities of Hamilton (population 100,000) and Whakatane (population 35,000), a major urban design analysis of the politics and revitalization potential of Auckland's (population 1 million) waterfront, and the unrealized design of New Zealand's first Maori University.[91] These are just a few of the numerous projects that have been completed in Community Design Studio in the last ten years. Some have been described elsewhere. For me, the most significant and rewarding aspects of this work have been those projects that have involved working

Figure 1.1. The Hamilton Town Plan on public display. (Photo by Anthony Ward.)

directly with the Maori and the Pacific Island communities. One recent and successful example has been the design of Te Kura Tuarua o Hoani Waititi Marae—New Zealand's first Kaupapa Maori (Maori pedagogy) secondary school. Another has been the revitalization of the Otara Town Center—a poor and largely Polynesian community in South Auckland.

The secondary school was commissioned by the Ministry of Education and coincided with the establishment by Maori architecture students of the university's first professional Maori student support group, Whaihanga (meaning "in pursuit of the built form," and pronounced "fiehanga"). The group also includes staff and

Figure 1.2. The mayor and senior executives of Auckland City visit the Waterfront project display. (Photo by Anthony Ward.)

students from the other university departments as well as Maori architects in practice. Whaihanga has been very successful in making a place for Maori students to explore the implications of traditional Maori pedagogy and traditions for today's professional practitioner. In effect it has enabled them to explore in a protected environment their own identities as the subjects of a real, not imaginary, cultural difference as emerging Maori architects, and to develop an architectural voice distinct from that of non-Maori.

Te Kura Tuarua o Hoani Waititi Marae

We were fortunate to be able to link Whaihanga's inception to an event in New Zealand educational and social history. The Kura Tuarua project marked the latest episode in the successful Maori educational renaissance after one hundred and fifty years of colonizing, assimilationist education policies. The Maori community of New Zealand is finally succeeding in gaining control over its own educational resources and developing a distinct education system designed to cater specifically to the needs of its own children. Maori design students participated in this process and in so doing made for themselves a space in which to develop their distinct voice. During the project most of the studio discussion was conducted in the Maori language. Meetings were conducted using Maori protocols, and decisions were made about the design of the school in very close consultation with the Maori client group, the board of trustees of Hoani Waititi Marae, on a traditional Maori consensus basis. Consensus decision processes, often marked by strongly held and opposing viewpoints, represent a powerful aspect of traditional Maori relationships. That these processes can be adopted to facilitate community design — not only for the rather mundane design of facilities for preexistent communities, but as the actual formation of community through a shared design experience — furthers a wider arena of participatory democracy. Working cooperatively, students were responsible for the conceptual design and developed design stages, with some assistance provided by Ministry of Education consultants. The project ran for ten weeks and construction was scheduled to begin in November 1995 with occupation to be completed by mid-1996.

The Otara Town Center Project

More recently, the Community Design Studio was involved in a design project to revitalize the Otara Town Center. Otara is the setting for the internationally acclaimed New Zealand film *Once Were Warriors*. It is the largest Polynesian habitat on the planet, with people from a wide variety of cultural groups — Maori, Samoan, Tongan, Samoan, Nueian, and so on. It is a very poor community in which statistics for crime, unemployment, and truancy are disproportionately high. Gangs proliferate and their territorial "tagging" adorns most building surfaces.

Working with community leaders in 1994, the Community Design Studio undertook a project to redesign the social hub of the community, the 1950s shopping center. The intention was to "turn around" the poor image and economy of Otara by building upon the exuberant but socially unacknowledged creativity of its people. In line with the studio's integrated philosophy of praxis, the goals of the project were conceptualized to be realized as part of the design process itself. Thus, for instance, since one of the goals of the finished town center was to be the creation of employment opportunities, this criterion was also essential to the actual design process. To realize this, eight long-term (minimum one year) unemployed youth from the community were employed through government work-scheme subsidies as integral and equal members of the design team. All were the same age as the architecture students. None had any previous training in design or drafting.

Since cultural harmony was also an important design goal (that is, designing a town center that would promote cultural and racial harmony) this might be demonstrated and realized *in process* by the high visibility of youth from many cultures working harmoniously together for the benefit of the whole community. The team

Figure 1.3. The Otara Town Center Project with the Otaran members of the team. (Photo used by permission of the *New Zealand Herald*.)

thus acquired a store-front office in the heart of the shopping center and for twenty-four weeks conducted an open-door policy of consultation with the people of the community. This consultation took place in the diverse languages of the community in both formal surveys and informal conversations. As the project progressed, there emerged not only a comprehensive design for the town center with a unique Polynesian flavor (embodied in a twenty-by-eight-foot scale model), but also a renewed sense of excitement and civic pride in and around the community as a whole.

The project was an outstanding success as a process and as a product. Funding studies are now underway to implement the first stages of the development. By the end of the project, the once shy and reticent Otaran members of the team were both verbally and graphically articulate. Over the course of the project, their drawings progressed from "tag"-captioned cartoon images of lightly clad, large-breasted women and muscle-bound supermen to exquisitely crafted and colored perspective drawings of building designs indistinguishable from those produced by architecture students with three or four years of architectural education.

For their part, the university students developed an intimacy with and respect for their colleagues that all admitted would have been previously considered un-attainable. By the project's end the town center had already begun a process of transformation—colorful and culturally appropriate Polynesian graphics replacing culturally alien gang insignias (imported from the Cripps and Bloods of Los Angeles). Of the eight Otaran youth who originally joined the project, three have since been accepted into tertiary education and two are permanently employed as consultant graphic artists with the city, directing and executing large-scale murals and cultural events.

The integration of academic and practical components that is important to this studio reflexively enhances the empowering potential of both. Students engaged in democratic design processes experience firsthand the process of community formation, not just "out there" in the subject community, but in the internal social dynamics of the studio itself. As they facilitate the emergence of the client community, so also do they experience the process of their own collective self-empowerment, often developing close personal ties for the first time in their professional careers. Thus the intention, the product, and the studio process become integrated into an experiential whole.

Accordingly, students are exposed to the lived realities of actual as opposed to cosmetic difference and witness directly the ways in which the dominant culture maintains its hegemony through the shaping of public life. The design studio thus keeps as its primary goal a self-critical understanding of the ways in which power shapes the creation of the physical world and the potential collusion of design education in that process. A concrete relationship with the poor or disempowered members of the community is thus crucial to the maintenance of a socially self-emancipatory perspective. This ensures that formal goals are situated in the real histories, cultural traditions, and experiences that make up communities of people.

CONCLUSION

This solidarity is often omitted from typical design theories and practices, and partly accounts for the professional license to universalize others' needs. The irony is that it was the tendency of modernist theories to universalize that prompted the inception of postmodernism itself. Postmodernism, like modernism before it, has been appropriated by neoconservatism and transformed into a style, stripped of emancipatory potential and commodified as a new kind of formalism that preserves the status quo, while simultaneously offering the illusion of actual social change.

While accepting the failure of modernism as a style, a critical postmodern design theory such as that suggested here interrogates the use of culture and power to mystify the ways dominant social groups shape meaning to their own ends — the ways in which meaning is created. It recognizes architecture itself as the site of continual struggle for a particular kind of meaning, between the dominant culture of the power status quo and the demands of subordinate cultures for voice and progressive political valence. The trajectory of this struggle reveals the ways in which subjectivism (architecture-as-art) and objectivism (architecture-as-science) are equally used by members of the dominant culture to continually reinforce their power and authority. It shows the ways in which the privileged reproduce their hegemony, promoting a mythology of universal values to mask their own ideology.

Against this, I echo Henry Giroux's "radical provisional morality" in which utopian visions may be created not as an end in themselves but as a way of establishing community participation in the movement toward greater solidarity. Its purpose is the creation of a decentralized community socialism in which the primary goal is the elimination of human suffering and the augmentation of human dignity.

Critics will say that socialism has already failed and that capitalism has survived triumphant. I will remind them that socialism, in the sense intended here not as universalizing totalitarian ideology, but as a springboard toward creative cultural pluralism, remains untried — most particularly in the former Soviet Union. I point to the widening social and economic divisions, to burgeoning unemployment, to the increasing social unrest, not just in the Balkans or South Africa, but in Los Angeles and London. I point to the depletion of global resources and to the degradation of the global environment that have resulted in our futile attempt to conquer it (and each other), and simply say that, in the end, there may be no alternative to radical change if human dignity is to survive.

Notes

1. C. Richard Hatch, ed., *The Scope of Social Architecture* (New York: Van Nostrand Reinhold, 1984).
2. Ibid., p. 7.
3. Dana Cuff, *Architecture: The Story of Practice* (Cambridge, Mass.: MIT Press, 1992), esp. pp. 11–34.
4. J. Wilton-Ely, "The Rise of the Professional Architect in England," in Spiro Kostoff, ed., *The Architect* (New York: Oxford University Press, 1977), p. 198.
5. Roger Taylor, *Art, an Enemy of the People* (Hassocks, England: Harvester Press, 1978), p. 44.
6. Giuseppe Martinelli, ed., *The World of Renaissance Florence* (London: Macdonald, 1968), pp. 93–94.
7. Howard Zinn, *A People's History of the United States* (New York: Harper and Row, 1980), pp. 7, 18.
8. Michael Raeburn, ed., *Architecture of the Western World* (London: Orbis, 1980), pp. 161–79.
9. Edward P. Thompson, *The Making of the English Working Class* (London: Penguin Books, 1980), pp. 237–38.
10. Cuff, *Architecture*, pp. 24–26.
11. Bill Risebero, *Modern Architecture and Design* (Boston: MIT Press, 1982), pp. 32–34.
12. Terry Eagleton, *The Ideology of the Aesthetic* (London: Blackwell, 1990), p. 366.
13. Cuff, *Architecture*, pp. 28–31.
14. "Art" is set in quotation marks here to emphasize that until the fourteenth century it was un-differentiated from "craft" and to distinguish it from the commodified art of the later period.
15. According to Kant, appreciation of beauty required a condition of perceptual *disinterestedness,* that is, an awareness unclouded by the possibility of material gain, thus setting aside art appreciation as a special and unique form of experience, unrelated to the process of cognition, and outside of and superior to the rationalism of emerging scientific culture.
16. Germain Greer, *The Obstacle Race* (London: Picador, 1981), p. 280.
17. Harold Osborne, *Aesthetics and Art History* (New York: Dutton, 1968), p. 43.
18. Greer, *Obstacle Race,* p. 309. For a definition of cultural capital, see Pierre Bourdieu, *Outline of a Theory of Practice* (Cambridge: Cambridge University Press, 1977).
19. The dictionary defines *ideology* as follows: 1. A body of ideas that reflects the beliefs of a nation, political system, etc. 2. (In philosophy) an idea that is false or held for the wrong reasons, but is believed with such conviction as to be irrefutable. 3. Speculation that is imaginary or visionary. 4. The study of the nature and origin of ideas (William T. McLeod, ed., *The Collins Dictionary and Thesaurus* [London: Collins, 1989], p. 494). I am using the term in the first sense, as a system of beliefs. In public life, the negativity associated with ideology also extends to politics; see David Nyberg, *Power over Power* (Ithaca: Cornell University Press, 1981), p. 32.
20. William Morris, "The Revival of Handicraft" (1880), cited in Edward P. Thompson, *William Morris: Romantic to Revolutionary* (Palo Alto, Calif.: Stanford University Press, 1976), p. 783.
21. William Morris, "Art and Socialism," in May Morris, ed., *Collected Works of William Morris* (London: Longmans Green, 1910–15), vol. 23, p. 213.
22. Paulo Freire, *Pedagogy in Process* (New York: Seabury Press, 1973).
23. M. Magdalena Droste, *Bauhaus 1919–1933* (Berlin: Bauhaus-Archiv Museum für Gestaltung, 1990), p. 166.
24. The notion that art was the exclusive production of individual genius originated with Kant as a corollary to his theory of art-as-transcendence, that is, beyond the rational. It was capitalism-driven, coinciding with emerging conceptions of (intellectual and creative) property rights while speaking simultaneously to a domain of spiritual superiority. See: Immanuel Kant, "Beautiful Art Is the Art of Genius," in *Critique of Judgement,* book 2, *The Analytic of the Sublime,* trans. J. C. Meredith (Oxford: Clarendon Press, 1952), section 46.

ANTHONY WARD

25. Hannes Meyer, "Education of the Architect," lecture to San Carlos Academy, Mexico, September 30, 1938, cited in Claude Schnaidt, *Hannes Meyer* (Teufen, Switzerland: Verlag Arthur Niggli, 1965), pp. 53–55. Schnaidt notes that in this lecture, Meyer has moved from his hard-line antiart philosophies of the late 1920s.

26. Droste, *Bauhaus 1919–1933*, p. 174.

27. Ibid., p. 166.

28. Ibid., p. 209.

29. Anthony Jackson, *The Politics of Architecture* (London: Architectural Press, 1970), pp. 20–38.

30. Michael Young, *The Rise of the Meritocracy, 1870–2033* (Baltimore, Md.: Pelican Books, 1965); Daniel Bell, "On Meritocracy and Equality," in Jerome Karabel and A. H. Halsey, eds., *Power and Ideology in Education* (Oxford: Oxford University Press, 1977), pp. 607–35.

31. Donald Broadbent, *Perception and Communication* (New York: Pergamon, 1958); Donald Broadbent, *Behaviour* (London: Methuen, 1964).

32. Lynn Moseley, "A Rational Design Theory for Planning Buildings Based on the Analysis and Solution of Circulation Problems," *Architects Journal*, September 11, 1963; B. Whitehead and M. Z. Elders, "An Approach to the Optimum Layout of Single Storey Buildings," *Architects Journal*, June 17, 1964, pp. 1373–80; Peter H. Levin, "The Use of Graphs to Decide the Optimum Layout of Buildings," *Architects Journal*, October 7, 1964, pp. 809–14.

33. Anthony Ward, "Right and Wrong," *Architectural Design*, July 1969, pp. 384–89.

34. Peter Manning, ed., *Office Design: A Study of Environment* (Liverpool: Department of Building Science, 1965).

35. William H. Ittelson, Harold M. Proshansky, and Lee G. Rivlin, eds., *Environmental Psychology* (New York: Holt, Rinehart and Winston, 1970). See also Terence R. Lee, "The Optimum Provision and Siting of Social Clubs," in *Durham Research Review* 14 (1963): 53–61; Terence R. Lee, "Urban Neighborhood as a Social and Spatial Schema," in *Human Relations*, no. 21 (1968): 241–67; Terence R. Lee, *Psychology and the Environment* (London: Methuen, 1976).

36. This author worked at that time for what was then the Ministry of Public Building and Works, researching the design of prison workshops. I produced a report, *Prison Workshops*, which was highly critical of Home Office policy toward the prison work. It also laid out detailed design proposals for more therapeutic prison working environments, and was unanimously endorsed by Home Office prison psychologists. It was withdrawn from circulation within twenty-four hours.

37. Jane Jacobs, *The Death and Life of Great American Cities* (New York: Vintage Books, 1961).

38. Christopher Alexander, *Notes on the Synthesis of Form* (Cambridge: Harvard University Press, 1964).

39. Ian Moore and Barry Poyner, *Activity Data Method* (London: Ministry of Public Building and Works, 1965).

40. Christopher Alexander, "A City Is Not a Tree but a Semi-Lattice," *Architectural Design*, no. 206 (February 1966): 46–55.

41. Christopher Alexander and Barry Poyner, *The Atoms of Environmental Structure* (London: Ministry of Public Building and Works, 1966).

42. Janet Daley, "A Philosophical Critique of Behaviourism in Architectural Design" in Geoffrey Broadbent and Anthony Ward, eds., *Design Methods in Architecture* (London: Lund Humphries, 1969), pp.71–75.

43. Brewster Ghiselin, *The Creative Process* (Berkeley: University of California Press, 1952); Arthur Koestler, *The Act of Creation* (New York: Macmillan, 1964).

44. J. Christopher Jones and Derek C. Thornley, eds., *Conference on Design Methods* (Oxford: Pergamon, 1963); Christopher Alexander, *Notes on the Synthesis of Form*; Sydney Gregory, ed., *The Design Method* (London: Butterworth, 1966); Geoffrey Broadbent and Anthony Ward, *Design Methods in Architecture* (London: Lund Humphries, 1989); J. Christopher Jones, *Design Methods* (New York: Wiley, 1980); J. Christopher Jones, *Essays in Design* (Chichester: Wiley, 1984).

45. J. Christopher Jones, "The State-of-the-Art in Design Methods," in Broadbent and Ward, eds., *Design Methods in Architecture,* pp. 193–97.
46. Jean-Paul Sartre, *Essays in Aesthetics* (New York: Washington Square Press, 1966), pp. 77–95.
47. Amos Rapoport, "Facts and Models," in Broadbent and Ward, eds., *Design Methods in Architecture,* pp. 136–46; Amos Rapoport, *House Form and Culture* (Englewood Cliffs, N. J.: Prentice-Hall, 1969).
48. Janet Daley, "A Philosophical Critique of Behaviourism in Architectural Design," in Broadbent and Ward, eds., *Design Methods in Architecture,* pp. 71–75.
49. Thomas S. Szasz, *The Myth of Mental Illness* (London: Secker and Warburg, 1962); Paul Goodman, *Growing Up Absurd* (New York: Vintage Books, 1960); Paul Goodman, *Compulsory Miseducation and The Community of Scholars* (New York: Vintage Books, 1964).
50. Anthony Ward, "Rightness and Wrongness in the Physical Environment," in Broadbent and Ward, eds., *Design Methods in Architecture,* pp. 166–78.
51. N. John Habraken, *Supports: An Alternative to Mass Housing* (London: Architectural Press, 1972).
52. John F. C. Turner, "Dwelling Resources in South America," *Architectural Design,* August 1963, pp. 360–69.
53. Bernard Rudofsky, *Architecture without Architects* (New York: Museum of Modern Art, 1964). This was followed by numerous similar publications: Bernard Rudofsky, *The Prodigious Builders* (New York: Harcourt Brace Jovanovich, 1977); Paul Oliver, ed., *Shelter and Society* (London: Barrie and Jenkins, 1969); Paul Oliver, ed., *Shelter in Africa* (London: Barrie and Jenkins, 1971); Art Boerike and Barry Shapiro, *Handmade Houses: The Woodbutcher's Art* (San Francisco: Scrimshaw, 1973); Jan Wampler, *All Their Own: People and the Places They Build* (New York: Oxford University Press, 1977).
54. N. John Habraken, *Variations* (Cambridge, Mass.: MIT Press, 1976).
55. David Cooper, ed., *The Dialectics of Liberation* (London: Pelican, 1968).
56. Tony Schuman, "Form and Counterform: Architecture in a Non-Heroic Age," *Journal of Architectural Education* 35, no. 1 (Fall 1981): 2–5. Schuman goes on to catalog the radical professional groups that were formed in the wake of the 1960s uprising: The Architects Resistance (TAR), Radical Environmental Designers (REDS), both in the United States; Architecture Radicals, Students, and Educators (ARSE) in the United Kingdom; UP6 at the Ecole des Beaux Arts in Paris; and the French group Utopie. He also cites several field study and community design advocacy organizations that were created.
57. William James McGill, *The Year of the Monkey: Revolt on Campus, 1968–69* (New York: McGraw-Hill, 1982), p. 196.
58. This author was one of the founding members at that meeting.
59. Robert Goodman, *After the Planners* (New York: Simon and Schuster, 1971), p. 178.
60. John F. C. Turner, *Housing by People* (London and New York: Marion Boyars, 1976).
61. Christopher Alexander, Sara Ishikawa, and Murray Silverstein, *A Pattern Language* (New York: Oxford University Press, 1977).
62. Donald L. Barlett and James B. Steele, *America: What Went Wrong?* (Kansas City: Andrews and McMeel, 1992); Teresa Hayter, *The Creation of World Poverty* (London: Pluto Press 1982), pp. 16–17; Michael Parenti, *Democracy for the Few* (New York: St. Martin's Press, 1988), pp. 10–11; Michael Harrington, *The Other America: Poverty in the United States* (New York: Penguin, 1981), p. 88; Michael Harrington, *The New American Poverty* (New York: Penguin Books, 1984).
63. Kevin Phillips, *The Politics of Rich and Poor* (New York: Random House, 1990), pp. 87–88.
64. Robert C. Coates, *A Street Is Not a Home* (Buffalo: Prometheus Books, 1990), p. 130.
65. Barlett and Steele, *America.*
66. Terrance Goode, "Typological Theory in the United States: The Consumption of Architectural 'Authenticity,'" *Journal of Architectural Education* 46, no. 1 (September 1992): 3–4.

67. M. S. Larson, "Emblem and Exception: The Historical Definition of the Architect's Professional Role," in Judith R. Blau, Mark LaGory, and John S. Pipkin, eds., *Professionals and Urban Form* (Albany: State University of New York Press, 1983).

68. Robert Gutman, *Architectural Practice: A Critical View* (Princeton, N.J.: Princeton Architectural Press, 1988).

69. Cuff, *Architecture,* pp. 49–52.

70. Fredric Jameson, "The Ideological Analysis of Space," *Critical Exchange,* no. 14 (Fall 1983); David Harvey and Neil Smith, "Geography: From Capitals to Capital," in Bertell Ollman and Edward Vernoff, eds., *The Left Academy: Marxist Scholarship on American Campuses* (New York: Praeger, 1984), 2:99–121; David Harvey, *The Condition of Postmodernity* (Cambridge, Mass.: Blackwell, 1989); Neil Smith, *Uneven Development* (Oxford: Blackwell, 1990); Henri Lefebvre, *The Production of Space* (Oxford: Blackwell, 1991).

71. Robert Venturi, Denise Scott Brown, and Steven Izenour, *Learning from Las Vegas: The Forgotten Symbolism of Architectural Form* (Cambridge: MIT Press, 1977).

72. Alan Lipman and Peter Parkes, "The Engineering of Meaning: Lessons from Las Vegas Recalled . . . and Declined," *Design Studies* 7, no. 1 (January 1986): 31–39.

73. Diane Ghirardo, "Introduction," *Out of Site: A Social Criticism of Architecture* (Seattle: Bay Press, 1991), p. 15.

74. Peter Eisenman, "The End of the Classical," *Perspecta,* no. 21 (Summer 1984): 158.

75. Mark Wigley, *Deconstructivist Architecture* (New York: Museum of Modern Art, 1988), p. 20. In a bizarre logical twist, this is precisely the aim of the design theories of modernism, based, albeit falsely, on notions of objectivity that Eisenman sets out to repudiate.

76. Peter Eisenman, *House X* (New York: Rizzoli, 1982), pp. 40–42.

77. This argument is supported by Ghirardo, *Out of Site;* see also Diane Ghirardo, "Eisenman's Bogus Avant-Garde," *Progressive Architecture,* November 1994.

78. R. E. Somol, "o-O," *Progressive Architecture,* October 1989a, p. 88.

79. R. E. Somol, "Between the Sphere and the Labyrinth," *Architectural Design* 59, no. 11/12 (1989): 45.

80. Somol, "o-O," p. 88.

81. Douglas Davis and Mary Rourke, "Real Dream Houses," *Newsweek,* October 4, 1976, pp. 66–69.

82. Ibid., p. 37.

83. Thomas A. Dutton, "Introduction: Architectural Education, Postmodernism, and Critical Pedagogy," in Thomas A. Dutton, ed., *Voices in Architectural Education: Cultural Politics and Pedagogy* (New York: Bergin and Garvey, 1991), p. xxii.

84. Stephan Mark Klein and Eleanor Moretta, *What Is Socially Responsible Design?* (Brooklyn: Pratt Institute, 1993).

85. Dutton, *Voices in Architectural Education;* Thomas A. Dutton, "Cultural Politics and Education," *Journal of Architectural Education* 44, no. 2 (February 1991): 67–68; Thomas A. Dutton, "Design Studio and Pedagogy," *Journal of Architectural Education* 41, no. 1 (Fall 1987): 16–25; Mike Davis, *City of Quartz: Excavating the Future of Los Angeles* (London: Verso, 1990); Dolores Hayden, *The Power of Place* (Cambridge, Mass.: MIT Press, 1995); Dolores Hayden, "Placemaking, Preservation and Urban History,"*Journal of Architectural Education* 41, no. 3 (Spring 1988): 45–51; Ghirardo, *Out of Site.*

86. Michel Foucault, cited in Tony Schuman, "Forms of Resistance," in Dutton, ed., *Voices in Architectural Education,* p. 23.

87. Michael Pyatok, "Housing as a Social Enterprise: The Ambivalent Role of Design Competitions," *Journal of Architectural Education* 46, no. 3 (February 1993): 159.

88. Tony Schuman and Thomas A. Dutton, "Housing and Architecture," *Journal of Architectural Education* 46, no. 3 (February 1993): 130.

89. Klein and Moretta, *What Is Socially Responsible Design?*

90. Anthony Ward, "Design Archetypes from Group Processes," *Design Studies* 8, no. 3 (1987): 157–69.

91. Anthony Ward and John Hunt, "The Alternative Aotea Centre Project," *Journal of Architectural Education* 41, no. 1 (Fall 1987): 34–45; Anthony Ward, "Biculturalism and Community: A Transformative Model for Design Education," *Journal of Architectural Education* 44, no. 2 (February 1991): 90–110; Anthony Ward and Wong Liu Shueng, "Equity, Education and Design in New Zealand: The Whare Wananga Project," *Journal of Architectural Education* 49, no. 3 (February 1996).

THE F WORD IN ARCHITECTURE: FEMINIST ANALYSES IN/OF/FOR ARCHITECTURE

The F word in architecture.

If that word is "Frank," it's glorified, debated, canonized, and meticulously studied. Constantly. There are more than one hundred publications on Frank Lloyd Wright alone.[1]

But there's another F word in architecture, one that is rarely spoken, sometimes whispered or snickered, and that word is "feminism." As Edward Ball notes, "Architecture imagines itself to be the most asexual of occupations. What could gender have to do with decorated sheds and *grands projets*?"[2]

Why the overt neglect or naive attitude of feminism in the profession, practice, and discipline of architecture? Certainly the male-dominated canon and population has much to do with it. But other fields, such as the natural and physical sciences, literature, history, film, medicine, and law, also have a male-dominated foundation yet have more flourishing feminist endeavors.[3] I cannot here answer why, by and large, architecture has neglected feminism. But ignorance and naïveté will be architecture's loss as the practice and concept of feminism becomes one of the more transformative movements of this century, paving new directions for the twenty-first.

Feminism is not one set of tenets. It is more accurate to speak of feminism*s* than of feminism as a singular orientation. Nonetheless there are certain premises shared among various feminist thinkers and doers. In contemporary American society feminism usually signifies commitments to gender as a category of analysis *and* to sex equality and the betterment of women's conditions as social goals. While the choice of means to actualize these commitments engender considerable debate and acrimony, feminism's commitment to social justice distances it from much postmodernist rhetoric.

Because the initial stage of effecting this social justice is to reveal the masculinity inherent in the notion of the universal or generic human, I first present in this chapter my arguments that architecture is a gendered field. I show evidence of this in how we label and define architecture, the criteria established for judging and evaluating it, and who gets to establish those criteria; who is legitimized as an architect; how we train and socialize people into the profession; what architecture is produced; and how we practice the craft. Viewing architecture—practice, product, actors—as it presently exists as a gendered discipline and practice helps us to understand the covert yet pervasive control of certain individuals and institutions over the production, representation, myth-making, and standard-setting in architecture. The gendered nature of the field was rarely acknowledged until challenged by feminist scholars in the 1970s and early 1980s.[4] But from their efforts we now recognize the often unspoken social and cultural beliefs of gender that shape landscapes and how those landscapes conversely set the contexts within which men and women act, reproduce, and challenge gender.

In the last section of this chapter, I describe architectural premises, practices, and products reflecting three different feminist postures. The first, a liberal feminist stance, claims that differences between sexes should not occur and maintains that women should have the same opportunities and rights as men. The second stance, variously called cultural feminism or feminist standpoint, acknowledges sex differences and celebrates rather than discounts or marginalizes women's experiences. Contextual feminism, the last type, attempts to dislodge the centrality of the sex difference argument, but does not deny the social existence of difference. Rather its focus is on recognizing those social conditions that make difference matter and on creating new spaces, relationships, and identities emanating from altered contexts.

GENDERING ARCHITECTURE

> We inhabit male outcomes.
> —Norman Rush, *Mating* (1991)

More and more, talk and language in feminist scholarship has turned to the "G word"—gender.[5] Gender is *not* sex, that is, biological differences, and should not be construed as the property of individuals. Rather, gender reflects and represents how social expectations, beliefs, and positions treat the biological characteristics of sex to form a system of values and identities. The construction of gender happens in the media, the economy, private and public schools, playgrounds, courts, families, the academy, intellectual communities, religious institutions and practices, avant-garde artistic practice, radical theories, and in feminism itself. As Simone de Beauvoir observed, one is not born a woman, one becomes one. But one does so differently depending on whether one is rich or poor, Muslim or Christian, black or white, and so on.[6] It is important to recognize that our social constructions of masculine and feminine are fluid: from one culture to another, within any culture over time, over the course of one's life, and between and among different groups of men and women depending upon class, race, color, ethnicity, geographic region, age, physicality, sexuality, and other social differences. Genderization also dichotomizes and consequently homogenizes, although sexual construction is actually much more complex than simply male and female. Sexual identities are not finished products but are constantly produced and changing within histories, cultures, language, community, and class.[7]

Genderization also deals with issues of power: who wields it, how they receive that power, in what forms, and who decides what actions, attitudes, and products are labeled male or female and subsequently dominant, normative, subordinate, or marginal. The power to dominate, dictate, or obscure is not power held by individuals per se, but by means of organization. The power of gender is exerted in economies, industries, institutions, political parties, law, and families. Power has more than one face, and the powerful exercise their power in many different sets of interactions—through persuasion, representation, socialization, social customs, and silencing, for example. Power and control in today's world are often reflected in mundane, everyday actions.

While "masculinity" is variously defined, a certain form of masculinity has come to define the universal or the superior in many industrialized societies and in many nonindustrialized ones, as well.[8] Ironically, the power of this masculinity is often invisible to those men holding such. Michael Kimmel talks about one day "seeing" his gender: "For when I looked in the mirror, I thought I saw a 'human being,' a generic person, universally generalizable. What had been concealed—race, and gender, and class—was suddenly visible. As a middle-class white man, I was able to not think about the ways in which class and race and gender had shaped my existence. Marginality is visible, and painfully visceral. Privilege is invisible, and painlessly pleasant."[9]

Gender is often invisible to men because it serves them. Men in Western society benefit, to varying degrees, from the sex-role definitions of one form of masculinity which I call the "Marlboro man myth": individualism, competitiveness, control, mastery, rationality, and emotional distance. These qualities specify a normative masculinity, a version (albeit white, middle-class, and heterosexual) that is often used as the standard against which other masculinities are compared and other social groups suppressed.

In architecture, gender operates when we attach to our concept of an architect or architecture our cultural constructs of a certain form of masculinity, and conversely exclude from the realm of architecture those attitudes, actions, and persons associated with feminine or female attributes. Masculinity is manifested in our architecture in various ways. With power, social position, and money, men overwhelmingly control environmental decision making and often base this decision making on male-experience-as-norm. Leslie Kanes Weisman shows, for example, that while giving birth was the ultimate in femaleness, controlling and supervising it was masculine, expressed in the spaces and technology of birthing.[10] Elizabeth Grosz exposes the implicitly phallocentric coding of the body politic, which, while claiming to model itself on the human body, uses the male to represent the human:[11] in architectural imagery, Vitruvian man and Le Corbusier's universal man come quickly to mind. Phallocentrism in architecture is not so much the dominance of the phallus as the pervasive, unacknowledged use of the male or masculine to represent the human and the physical environment.

I have given considerable thought to those attributes of the architectural field that make the field expressly masculine. (See accompanying chart.) One attribute, most visible, is the overwhelming male representation in the practice and profession. Men have dominated and continue to dominate in numbers, leadership, and gatekeeping roles as critics, publishers, historians, design jurors, and press editors. Architecture today, while changing, remains very much a white, male-dominated profession. Unfortunately, national labor statistics of this profession are not entirely reliable since federal labor statistics define architecture very broadly, but such statistics show that nearly 85 percent of practitioners are men.[12] Consistent with this pattern is the composition of the regular membership of the American Institute of Architects (AIA): 93 percent white, 92 percent male, and 85 percent white male members. Of the emeritus members of the AIA, 95 percent are white males. And of the associate members—those individuals not registered in the United States but affiliated with an architectural practice or school here—62 percent are white males.[13] The principals of the large firms—those that control a large portion of the architectural work done in this country—are predominately male and white.[14] Things are not much different in the schools: 91 percent of tenured architectural faculty are males.[15]

Masculine Attributes of Architecture

Overwhelming male representation in the profession

An emphasis on individualism and group isolationism in architectural training and education

The notion of the sanctity of the individual creator and an elusive knowledge base, founded on an art legacy of male practices and standards

Reference groups of highly paid male professionals

But it is not solely the male population of architecture that gives this particular profession a masculine orientation. A second attribute lies in its training and enculturation of individuals into the field. As Dana Cuff notes, schools highlight the importance of pure design by removing from its study key *social* aspects of professional practice: client, patron, user, the coordinated group process of design, and economic and power relations. Architects are not educated to see the social milieu that structures their world and their decisions by means of social relations, economic distribution, power, group decision making processes, and the like. Art historian William E. Wallace demolishes the myth of the solitary architect-creator in his book *Michelangelo at San Lorenzo: The Genius as Entrepreneur.*

SHERRY AHRENTZEN

The romantic myth that Michelangelo worked by himself fits our notion of the lonely, self-sacrificing genius — conditions that presumably are necessary for creating art. Actually, he was never alone. He lived with two male assistants and always had a female housekeeper. Thirteen people helped him paint the Sistine ceiling; about 20 helped carve the marble tombs in the Medici Chapel in Florence. . . . And to build the Laurentian Library in Florence, he supervised a crew of at least 200. . . . Michelangelo's workers sometimes disappointed him but he never fired them. "One must have patience," he wrote. . . . The workshop's organization was more horizontal than pyramidal: Michelangelo was at the center, not the top. And while not efficient by today's standards, it did promote versatility and the Renaissance equivalent of Total Quality Management.[16]

The principal social relation in school is that between instructor and student, portrayed and carried out as a relationship between unique individuals. The primacy of the individual becomes the basis for explaining everyday occurrences (such as the quality of the design) as matters of personality, talent, creativity, or convictions.[17] The studio, being a closed system, becomes an incubator in reproducing these beliefs.

A third masculine attribute of the profession lies with promoting its Arts legacy — as opposed to craft, or popular, vernacular, or native art. This legacy is distinct among the professions: medicine may be an art, but it is not Art. The Horatian definition of the purpose of art is to teach and to delight. However, art has a political dimension also. Many feminist scholars have exposed the relativity of aesthetic claims, often established on male and upper-class standards.[18] Pierre Bourdieu shows that dominant groups retain their positions of power and enhance their status by specific mechanisms, one of which is to invent the "aesthetic" category as a universal entity.[19] Certain premises of art assumed by the discipline of architecture that promote this exclusionary posture are the sanctity of the individual designer (a myth in architectural practice, but a myth too often perpetuated in schools and the media) and an elusive knowledge base. Standards of excellence are persistently set by critics (I include here design awards committees) and the "star designers" often designated as such by these critics.[20] However, in art and architecture, such critics have been male and have used male practices as the basis for their standards and criteria.[21] As Denise Scott Brown contends:

Faced with unmeasurables, people steer their way by magic. . . .
[A]rchitects, grappling with the intangibles of design, select a guru whose work gives them personal help in areas where there are few rules to follow. The guru, as architectural father figure, is subject to intense hate and love; either way, the relationship is personal, it can only be a one-to-one affair. . . .

I suspect . . . that for male architects the guru must be male. There can be no Mom and Pop gurus in architecture. The architectural prima donnas are all male.[22]

But, the idea of architecture-as-art must coexist with the also prevalent ideas of architecture-as-technology and architecture-as-service. Within this tangle of competing conceptualizations, architecture remains befuddled as to whom to serve — clients, users, financiers, regulatory bodies, public agencies, society at large, historical posterity, architectural award panels, or themselves.[23] Further, this tension operates within a capitalist building and land-use industry, a system not favoring art or service in lieu of profit. The expense of building production inevitably binds architects to the dictates of the sources of finance and power, making it almost impossible to achieve an autonomy of practice they wish they could enjoy as artists — unless it pays to do so.

The final attribute to consider in the masculinization of architecture is the profession's reference groups, usually medicine and law, two other male-dominated, licensed-professional fields. But compared with these two, architects make a lot less money, experience more unemployment, and maintain less powerful positions in their respective industry (developers, bankers, contractors, most clients, and even building codes and regulations play more prominent roles than architects in building production). Curiously, other licensed professionals who earn salaries equivalent to architects are nurses, social work professionals, and public school teachers — all female-dominated fields.[24] But such professions are never used as reference groups to architects. Not surprisingly, sociologist Robert Gutman claims that architecture is populated by a higher proportion of alienated and disappointed men and women than any other major profession.[25] Such low self-esteem in times of economic and social turmoil often results in backlashes against groups trying to enter the field or achieve equity, such as people of color and women.

These four attributes of the field, I believe, contribute to the gendering of architecture by means of how we label and define architecture, who is legitimized as an architect, how we socialize people into the profession, what architecture is produced, and how we practice the craft.

The Gendering of the Definition of Architecture

> In the end it all depends on who is allowed to define and manage it.
> — Richard Ingersoll, "Never Lose Sight of the Primitive
> (Menstrual) Hut," *Design Book Review* (Summer 1992)

What is architecture? Architectural critics and practitioners are quick to point out that not any built structure represents architecture. *Architecture* is not only different from *building,* but superior to it. Hence, labeling an object as architecture is conferring legitimacy and status.

Defining what is architecture is the purview of those who have the power, clout, and marketability to label. Architecture historically has largely been defined by men, and men in rather insular, exclusionary, and privileged (by race, class, and education) positions. While the definitions, questions posed, and parameters change over time, as Gwendolyn Wright adroitly shows in her history of architectural history,[26] the history of defining and describing architecture has been established primarily by Western white men. Western values regarding architecture similarly prevail in many non-Western contexts, as Sanjoy Mazumdar demonstrates in his autoethnography of architectural education in India.[27]

Challenges to or shifts within architecture are legitimated if proposed by sanctioned men. For example, in response to a question from editor Lian Hurst Mann of *Architecture California,* Peter Eisenman lamented the absence of young architects and women speakers at a recent ANYone conference that was intended to provoke "changes in the possibilities of architecture."[28] He claims that the risks of engaging in such challenge are too great for women who still have not become established or have not been accepted by the profession. Thus, he is suggesting (unknowingly?) that one must be part of a club before one can challenge it. In this interview, Eisenman derides women architects, saying they are reactionary in their attempts to emulate the "great hero figures of architecture," referring to I. M. Pei, Cesar Pelli, and Philip Johnson in this regard. But when he mentions theorists Ann Bergren, Jennifer Bloomer, and Catherine Ingraham and architect Zaha Hadid as potential ANYone participants, he does not consider any similar emulation on their part. But is it an affinity to the ANYone's men's crowd (rather than to those "great hero figures") that allows Eisenman to consider them? To this conference intended to provoke change, he only invited those speakers who take up a "radical ideology of undecidability," that is, a predefined, legitimated challenge represented by Frank Gehry, Rem Koolhaas, Rafael Moneo, himself, and other men — clearly prominent and powerful male figures (but not "great hero figures"!) in the discourse of architecture, as Mann points out to Eisenman. As Diane Ghirardo clearly suggests, "Dissent is inscribed in such a narrow circle of formal choices that it loses any capacity to challenge all but the most banal of issues."[29]

Exclusion may be *determined* by those with power, but also may be *chosen* by those not wishing to participate in a system that affords them lesser status. Many women and people of color have been silent in theoretical debates of deconstructivism, for example, for reasons other than their alleged attempts to emulate prominent white male architects or because of a lack of invitations to conferences. As Mary McLeod considers, they may choose to remain silent in this discourse because of the elitist atmosphere brought about by hermetic forms and an obscure discourse, a rhetoric of subversion that ironically rings of a new machismo, and probably the most fundamental reason of all—the denial of real institutional transformation,[30] the foundation of many feminist agendas. Their silence may reflect a refusal to enter a "discourse" that is really a monologue.

An example of a feminist challenge to redefine architecture is found in Pauline Fowler's critique of Kenneth Frampton's definitions of architecture and building.[31] In two essays, Frampton contends that philosopher Hannah Arendt's descriptions of "labour" and "work" parallel the dual definitions of "architecture" in the *Oxford Dictionary*: (1) the art or science of constructing edifices for human use, and (2) the action and process of building.[32] "For human use" refers to the creation of a specifically human world, whereas "action and process of building" alludes to a continuous, never-ending act, comparable to domestic labor. Frampton argues that domestic buildings are not architecture because, he believes, they have nothing to do with the traditionally representative role of architecture. "Only a very small part of architecture belongs to art.... [E]verything which serves a purpose should be excluded from the realms of art." Architecture of the public realm assumes a position that is clearly superior to building (the private realm). Frampton laments that this hierarchical relationship has been lost in the twentieth century, provoking a crisis of identity within the discipline of architecture (although his lament of identity crisis could also be interpreted as a concern for legitimacy). He contends that "social concerns" are private interests at a public scale, and hence have no place in public life. This is certainly contrary to the feminist premise that "the personal is the political." He believes "we shall need to distinguish carefully both culturally and operationally between acts of 'architecture' and acts of 'building' and to discretely express both 'labour' and 'work' within each building entity irrespective of its scale. Only in this way perhaps can we hope to eventually evolve and impart to the society a coherent structured language of the environment that is both operationally appropriate and a true reflection of our human consciousness."

Whose consciousness?

Fowler contends that the phrase "our human consciousness" in Frampton's statement refers to the concept of *polis,* in which citizenship in ancient Greece was barred to all but a particular class of Greek men. Women, slaves, underclasses, and *barbaroi* were excluded from the *polis.* But this strategy is used in Frampton's analysis to legitimate certain forms of building by couching them in terms of "human" representation. Such contentions of legitimacy are common in architecture. The male bias or phallocentrism that pervades such thinking and labeling results not from a conscious exhortation of "I am male; I shall construct a theory or building or space that only a man could create," but instead from the habit of deriving ostensibly universal truths from their particular—namely, privileged male—viewpoint.

Who Gets to Be Architects, Then?

In *Women in American Architecture: A Historic and Contemporary Perspective,* Susana Torre asks, "Why have there been so few women architects?"[33] Architects, legally defined, are licensed by states.[34] Hence, the official exclusion of women in architecture schools and by licensing boards in the 1800s and early to mid-1900s partly caused the historical dearth of women architects.

But legitimacy has also a nonlegal counterpart—that is, being professionally recognized or honored as an architect by demonstrating a certain type of skill, producing a certain type of style or object, and/or being a certain type of person. While such recognition may take the form of commissions, another form of recognition is the status and attention received from architectural publications, design competition invitations, and peer awards. Drawing upon architecture's arts legacy and its peer-group isolationism developed in architecture schools, such peer recognition is highly prized.

As Kathryn Anthony and I contend, female absence in architectural history and precedence results from the definitions of "architecture" and "architect" established by the gatekeepers of this discipline and practice.[35] But falling outside these definitions, however, are many, many women who have designed and developed our built landscapes.[36] Recent historical investigations of women in architecture "document the discrimination that has kept women out of the architecture schools and offices. They show, however, that despite overt discrimination and cultural prejudice women have become architects and that they designed not only houses but commercial and civic buildings.... They have been contractors, builders, and engineers. These professional women challenged the cultural assumptions about women's role."[37]

Is it simply a body of work that establishes whether or not a professional is honored by one's peers? The insidiousness of gender in shaping the definitions of "architecture" and "architect" poses perplexing, even disturbing, answers to this question. For, if E. Fay Jones had been Ms. E. Fay Jones of Fayetteville, Arkansas, would she have received an AIA Gold Medal and have been so honored by her peers? Is a "soft," small-scale, self-effacing, environmentally sensitive (read "feminine") approach honored only when done by a male architect, and not a female one? Do certain (or all?) forms or styles of architecture gain greater acceptance when the designer is a man rather than a woman?

The star system is entrenched in the architectural profession. And in architecture as in art, stars are defined in part by their sex. But what about those countless number of architects who are quite capable but are not "stars"? Ellen Perry Berkeley recounts a story of a midwestern architecture school that told its students that it could find no "outstanding women" to serve as visiting critics. But does this school ask all its men critics to be "outstanding"?[38] The double standard that Rosabeth Moss Kanter noted in her study of women and men corporate managers also likely operates in architecture—men are expected to be at least competent while women must be outstanding.[39]

Karen Kingsley believes that another reason for women's relative absence in architecture is that collaboration has not been a defining characteristic of "good" architecture even though it lies at the very foundation of design, development, and construction.[40] In American society, girls and women are often socialized to collaborate, and hence they come to value collaboration as a means to achieve desired ends.[41] But collaboration contradicts a belief of personal initiative, autonomy, and becoming a success on one's own merits—essentials in a star system as well as in the "Marlboro man myth." When collaborative efforts are acknowledged, historians and critics appear to value certain roles over others. When women collaborate with male architects, their roles have been deemed marginal to the finished product, or even worse, their efforts have been inappropriately attributed to their male collaborators: Denise Scott Brown, Anne Griswold Tyng, and Truus Schröder are only a few cases in point. Ironically, male architects collaborate (for example, Robert Venturi, Louis Kahn, and Gerrit Rietveld), but the professional press often attributes their contributions as totalizing.

Becoming Architects

Gendering in architecture schools occurs in three arenas: collective identification, social relations, and substance—that is, what is taught, how it is framed, who decides what is taught and evaluated, and on what basis.[42] Much of this occurs within a climate that might be considered patriarchal and fratriarchal. While patriarchy means the primacy of the father in kinship and by extension an authoritarian and paternalistic form of control and rule, fratriarchy is based simply on the self-interest of the association of men itself. It reflects the demands of a group of men to have the freedom to do as they please. Sociologist Heinrich Schurtz stresses the autonomous character of the age-set of such fratriarchies.[43] Women's groups do not represent the same sort of power enclave.

John Remy stresses the importance of the "men's hut" in developing a sense of fraternity.[44] The characterization of this milieu is strikingly similar to that of many design studios. Clannishness is one of the more obvious hallmarks of the "culture of architecture." This is reinforced by the studio's physical setting, where students work hours on end, isolated from the rest of the university and often from family and friends. Donald Schön and Chris Argryis speak of the studio's mastery-mystery method, in which the instructor acts as master to apprentices who model appropriate behaviors, values, design strategies, talk, and thinking.[45] The role models are predominantly male: only 14 percent of full-time architectural faculty are women, and only 6 percent of tenured instructors teaching in design studios are women.[46]

In such arenas, sexual harassment is not uncommon and may even be exacerbated by the characteristics of the studio milieu. The common "all-nighter" atmosphere, where self-esteem is fragile and bodies are unhealthy and fatigued, emotions intense, and instructors absent, makes it opportune for harassment to develop. While the majority of women disapprove of sexually harassing behaviors, many find the situation unavoidable. Some students as well as some school administrators take the attitude that "boys will be boys" or advocate that "women should give it right back," simply reinforcing fratriarchal conditions. But coping with sexual harassment in the studio can prevent many women from achieving their best work. If a woman avoids going to studio charrettes late at night, when the instructor is not present and harassment is more likely to occur, she may not be in a situation to produce her best work, unlike her male peers. Hence, rewards may be unevenly distributed based on harassment and the attempts to cope with or avoid it.[47]

But sexual harassment is not the only sexist practice in studios. While architectural schools no longer exclude women, they often continue to exclude certain ways of thinking, speaking, and doing—a common practice in establishing a profession, in defining the outsider from the insider. But recent research suggests that many women have been socialized to think and structure experience in ways different from men: for example, many women prefer or use "connected" rather than "separate" learning.[48] Separate learning—the foundation of our college environments—is isolated and emphasizes doubt and competition; connected learning occurs in a community and stresses empathy and believing before making judgments.

In their schooling, architectural students are taught to use the spatial language of domination, hierarchy, and power. Design studios and juries generally prize abstraction, competition, and separation. But these types of learning environments may not be geared to many women's and men's experiences or abilities. Thus, as Eleni Bastéa points out, correcting the imbalance of gender numbers gives the appearance of maintaining equity, but it does not rectify thought and spatial-translation control.[49] Hence constructing a collective identity by circumscribing ways of thinking discourages and disassociates those who do not easily follow the prescribed practice.

Gendering Space

I will not dwell here on the nature of our gendered landscape, since much has already been written on the subject.[50] As Leslie Kanes Weisman points out in her book *Discrimination by Design*, social, political, and economic values are embodied in architectural forms themselves, the processes through which they are built, and the manner in which they are used.[51] Thus, spatial arrangements of our buildings and communities reflect and reinforce the nature of gender, race, and class relations in society.

Feminist architectural criticism reveals the sexual control, stereotypes, and masculine domination embedded in our built environment. Beatriz Colomina, for example, analyzes Adolph Loos's design of the Moller, Müller, and Josephine Baker houses as a feminist, reading space in terms of power and control. Loos, she claims, presents the house as a theater box, an enclosure of a family of actors.[52] The boxes in the Moller and Müller houses are marked as female, but they become spaces that protect and draw attention to the occupant of these intimate spaces. But the Baker house excludes family life. It celebrates a female object as the focus of a particular gaze, the looking subject—a gaze that augments the body as an object of pleasure. As she claims,

> The Baker house represents a shift in the sexual status of the female body. This shift involves determinations of race and class more than gender. The theater box of the domestic interiors places the occupant against the light. She appears as a silhouette, mysterious and desirable, but the backlighting also draws attention to her as a physical volume, a bodily presence within the house with its own interior. She controls the interior, yet she is trapped within it. In the Baker house, the body is produced as spectacle, the object of an erotic gaze, an erotic system of looks. The exterior of the house cannot be read as a silent mask designed to conceal its interior; it is a tattooed surface which does not refer to the interior, it neither conceals nor reveals it. This fetishization of the surface is repeated in the "interior." In the passages, the visitors consume Baker's body as a surface adhering to the windows. Like the body, the house is all surface; it does not simply have an interior.[53]

Ways of Doing

> Aesthetics is more than a philosophy or theory of art and beauty; it is a way of inhabiting space, a particular location, a way of looking and becoming.
> —bell hooks, *Yearning* (1990)

Architecture is a process—a social and material one. Architecture proceeds in a world of cultural and social forms. In talking about the cultural determinants of architectural form, we must question who or what culture has the power to control the production and subsequent use of built form, and how they do so.

SHERRY AHRENTZEN

Political economic analyses of urban spatial form highlight the distribution of economic power within society and how it affects the nature of the material world and the formation of human consciousness. Much of this work is of limited value to feminism, being highly abstract and treating human action and subjectivity rather passively.[54] Few scholars incorporate gender, ethnicity, culture, or sexuality in their interpretations.

But suffice it to say, in the massive speculative building process begun in the mid–nineteenth century, real estate developers largely determine the decisions about American space. And built space is directed as a commodity. Dolores Hayden denounces urban designers and critics for neglecting the role of developers in place production and meaning:

> Many American postmodern designers have not analyzed the concept of "vernacular" but romanticized it. Many architects, students, and critics have approached the "vernacular" of America in a spirit of deference to speculative tracts and commercial strips. This is one kind of romance that exalts Las Vegas and Levittown, but ignores the fusion of Mafia and Mormon financial clout in Las Vegas, or the absorption of merchant builders into multinational corporations. Describing such places as products of American working-class taste is simply a mistake. The tastemakers are Bugsy Siegal and Bill Levitt.[55]

There has been increasing speculation about the role women will play in building production as more women enter the paid labor force and claim management and leadership positions. But it is organizations that direct such production. And as Joan Acker shows, organizational structures are not gender neutral.[56] The absence of sexuality, emotionality, and procreation in organizational logic and theory obscures yet helps to replicate the underlying gender relations. The concept of the "disembodied job" symbolizes this separation of work and sexuality. However, as Acker argues, the abstract worker associated with the job is actually a man (phallocentrism appearing again), and it is the man's body—its sexuality, minimal responsibility in procreation, and conventional control of emotions—that pervades work and organizational processes.

Still, some critics argue that as more women enter large corporations, organizational structures will change because women have a different way of working and relating to work. This theory gained widespread attention in a 1990 article in the *Harvard Business Review* by Judy Rosener entitled "Ways Women Lead."[57] Rosener argued that women are more likely than men to manage in an interactive style—that is, they encourage participation, share power and information, and enhance the self-worth of others. Rosener claims that women use "transformational" leadership, motivating others by transforming their self-interest into the goals of the organization, while men use "transactional" leadership, doling out rewards for good work and punishment for bad.[58] Her findings sparked a controversy, and the letters in response filled nine pages in a later issue of the *Harvard Business Review.* But Alice H. Eagly and Blair T. Johnson reviewed the research and found that women practiced more democratic or participatory leadership styles, and men, more autocratic or directive. However, such differences may be partially explained by organizational recruitment or by the organizational context itself. Rosener claims transformational styles work best in organizational contexts that are medium sized, have higher numbers of professionals, and have experienced fast growth and change, not yet characteristics of the building industry, financial institutions, or architectural firms.

Nonetheless, several speculations and anecdotal accounts suggest that women practice architecture differently—not that they design differently, but they practice the social art of architecture differently.[59] While no evidence for this has been sought, there is some compelling empirical evidence in another field—politics— that does suggest that an influx of women in power brings about changed values and perspectives within organizations. The research on leadership and decision-making patterns of politicians documents different driving forces that affect the ways in which men and women, within and across political parties, practice their craft (here, their voting records and legislative proposals) when in positions of legislative power. But the generalizability to architecture from politics is still questionable, given the relative power-deficient position of architects within the building industries and political domains.

ARCHITECTURE FROM FEMINIST PERSPECTIVES

What would architecture look like if it were driven by purposes and problematics informed by feminism? Feminist efforts have expanded our way of thinking of and doing architecture. Here I discuss architectural premises, practices, and products founded on three different feminist perspectives:[60] (1) liberal feminism, (2) cultural feminism, and (3) contextual feminism. My intention here is to highlight these three general types, conceding that they represent "ideal types" and are for heuristic purposes only. They are not exclusive: clearly, work that some women and men consider feminist might fall in two types or even in-between the cracks. Further, while I have ordered the types in this chapter, I do not intend to imply a hierarchy. This is made clear in the last section of the chapter.

An Equal Rights Architecture

The liberal feminist position is likely the most widely known feminist position in Western countries. This stance claims that difference between sexes should occur *and* affirms that women should have the same opportunities and rights as men. In architecture women who hold this position seek to match men's achievements in the profession by filling long-established and accepted roles that in the past have been held almost exclusively by men. Their goals are to increase the number of women in the profession at all levels of practice, to promote comparable opportunity, and to achieve equitable pay and recognition. The question of whether or not women and men "do architecture" differently is not a viable one here. Design decisions are made by individuals, groups, or by negotiation, but should be untouched by the sex of those making the decisions. A female sensibility has no place in the shaping of architecture. An example of this position is the national exhibition on the history of women in architecture sponsored by the AIA, "That Exceptional One: Women in American Architecture, 1888–1988," and by the AIA's Archive on Women in Architecture, in which forgotten names of women in architectural history are recovered.[61]

This feminist approach presents how it wishes things were—women and men equal, that is, the same—when, first, they are not; second, if they were, there would be little social inequality to address; and third, some women and men have higher aspirations than what is provided in this approach. As Sandra Harding claims: "A woman who could say 'I've never been discriminated against as a woman' has not taken the risks that patriarchy finds so threatening—an unsettling thought for the token woman that so many of us professional-class women are."[62] As such, this approach is consequently problematic to many feminists. To assert that "women are as good as men" is a paradox because *man* is the referent in that statement; it reaffirms male actions as the standard against which all actions are judged. But as Catherine MacKinnon asks, why should one have to be the same as a man to get what a man gets simply because he is one?[63]

Some liberal feminists claim they want to be "as good as a human," offering androgyny as the proper paradigm for gender. But as I have previously proposed in this chapter, our profession and society are phallocentric, and we do not know what form this nonmale human takes. As MacKinnon maintains:

> Men's physiology defines most sports, their health needs largely define insurance coverage, their socially designed biographies define workplace expectations and successful career patterns, their perspectives and concerns define quality in scholarship, their experiences and obsessions define merit, their military service defines citizenship, their presence defines family, their inability to get along with each other—their wars and rulerships—define history, their image defines god, and their genitals define sex."[64]

Further, by seeking to replace male and female with "human," the androgyny paradigm is guilty of rendering race and gender difference invisible at a time when such social differences do exist and structure our lives and efforts.

Nonetheless, this liberal feminist position is possibly the most prominent feminist posture among architects. And advantageous lessons appeared for those in architecture. In taking another look at the book *The Fountainhead*, Ellen Perry Berkeley does not ask women and men to mimic Howard Roark, but she does encourage us to reexamine the qualities we think of as "macho," such as independence, creativity, and integrity, before we discredit them from a feminist architectural vocabulary. One of Roark's qualities is his ability to survive without others' approval. Until recently, women architects also had to be loners and fighters. Being strangers in a strange land, they learned to survive by relying on their own self-assessments. Berkeley certainly does not accept all the premises of *The Fountainhead*, but she does ask us to ponder whether the fully "liberated" woman will be as liberated from feminist dogma (constructed in patriarchal societies) as she will be from any prefeminist dogma. Instead of emulating men or emulating women, she asks us to consider which masculine attributes of the field might be important to retain.[65]

Architecture of the "Other"

> If you think equality is the goal, your standards are too low.
> —T-shirt slogan

A cultural feminist position seeks a transformation of current professions, institutions, and practices to those based on values historically and culturally attributed to women. This position has a long heritage in the United States, but it has gained considerable prominence in recent years because of object-relations feminist scholarship.

The epistemological grounds for this position lie with the belief that knowledge is grounded in experiences made possible by historically specific social relations. Class, race, and gender structure the individual's understanding of reality and hence direct the constructs of knowledge. Views are not only partial but also distorted. The view from the perspective of the powerful is far more partial and distorted than that from the perspective of the dominated because the powerful have much more interest in obscuring the injustice of their privileges and authority. But the positions of those "controlled" can deconstruct dominating ideologies and reconstruct a truer understanding of the world. Importantly, this position maintains that knowledge is always of a particular social group: I always see the world through my culture's eyes, I think within its assumptions. As bell hooks maintains in *Feminist Theory: From Margin to Center*: "Living as we did—on the edge—we developed a particular way of seeing reality. We looked both from the outside in and from the inside out. We focused our attention on the center as well as on the margin. We understood both. This mode of seeing reminded us of the existence of a whole universe, a mainbody made up of both margin and center."[66]

Some scholars claim that the views and knowledge of women are founded in part on the woman's body, the historic division of labor, and/or parenting and psychological development. For example, Nancy Chodorow contends that men and women develop differently constructed selves and different experiences of their gender and gender identity.[67] Through their early relationships with their mothers, women develop a sense of self in relation with others and a richly constructed inner self-object world that continuously engages unconscious and conscious activity. Women grow up with relational capacities and needs and psychological definition of self-in-relationship, which commit them to mothering. By contrast, men develop a self based more on denial of relations and on a more fixed, firmly split, and repressed inner self-object world. The basic masculine sense of self is separate.[68]

These perspectives are not completely new; they echo some of the assertions of Sigmund Freud and Erik Erikson. But these positions, unlike Freud's, are valorized. In fact, many feminists believe such female-based qualities should form the basis for societal change. Suzanne Gordon, in *Prisoners of Men's Dreams,* laments that women's participation in the corporate world of men has been driven by liberal feminism, or what she calls equal-opportunity feminism.[69] Women have molded their lives with greater or lesser eagerness to a male corporate culture contemptuous of time and concern for caring, whether for family, friends, or colleagues. What Gordon would prefer to see is a radical transformation of contemporary society in which caring would be an integral part of life and corporate culture. She conceptualizes caring not as limited to particular kinds of work but rather as a more diffuse and pervasive relational quality expressed through work relationships and tasks. It is not a feminized, sentimentalized, privatized care, nor is it care as self-sacrifice. It is one that draws upon but transcends women's traditional practice.

In architecture, Karen A. Franck has perhaps expressed the cultural feminist stance most articulately.[70] Citing the psychoanalytic and object-relations literature as a basis for her analysis,[71] she identifies seven qualities of women's architectural work that characterize women's ways of knowing and creating: connection to others, to objects of knowledge, and to the world and a sensitivity to the connection of categories; a desire for inclusiveness and a desire to overcome opposing dualities; a responsibility to respond to the needs of others, represented by an ethic of care; an acknowledgment of the value of everyday life and experience; an acceptance of subjectivity as a strategy for knowing and of feelings as part of knowing; acceptance of and desire for complexity; and an acceptance of change and a desire for flexibility. She does not claim that these characteristics are manifest in all women's architecture work but that they variously appear in social-architectural research by women, in alternative communities proposed by women, and in projects designed by women. Her purpose is not only to exalt these qualities but also to propose them as a basis for a transformed profession more hospitable to people's needs and to feminist practitioners.

Franck describes several architectural projects and architects whose work reflect these characteristics. For example, Dolores Hayden proposed reorganizing the typical suburban block of autonomous houses to a community with the provision of on-site jobs, good public transport, and shared services and facilities. Both Eileen Gray and Lilly Reich designed furniture and spaces specifically sensitive to mundane needs and human comfort. While still working within the modern genre, Gray was especially critical of modernism's lack of emotion and intimacy: "Modern designers have exaggerated the technological side.... Intimacy is gone, atmosphere is gone.... Formulas are nothing, life is everything. And life is mind and heart at the same time." Other work of this genre not discussed by Franck includes Susana Torre's 1977 installation of the *Women in Architecture* exhibit, set up to be nonhierarchical. Likewise Torre's design for a fire station in Columbus, Indiana, carefully considered the spatial integration of women firefighters in the building. A leading issue was to use the design to support the goals of the institution, such as encouraging equal opportunities for women firefighters and promoting teamwork. The living quarters were organized into separate wings so that the women firefighters might develop their own bonding and sense of autonomy.[72]

Maya Ying Lin's design of the national Vietnam Veterans Memorial resulted in a memorial space connecting visitors with memories of the people of the war. As she herself claimed: "I didn't want a static object that people would just look at, but something they could relate to as on a journey, or passage, that would bring each to his own conclusion."[73]

This memorial arguably generated more controversy than any other work of architecture in recent time, not surprising given the highly emotional reactions and divided feelings about the Vietnam War, the country's military conduct, and the wisdom and purpose of our involvement in it. The contrast between the design of Lin's V-shaped memorial wall and the Frederick Hart sculpture — both memorials at the same site — is an interesting lesson about gendered spatial representations of commemoration. Streams of visitors interact with the names on the wall. Its shape, scale, and texture invite them not simply to reflect but to touch, embrace, kiss, take rubbings of the names, and leave behind mementos. The wall sometimes has a healing, cathartic effect. So pronounced is this phenomenon that psychologists who specialize in Vietnam-stress-syndrome cases regularly bring groups of patients to the memorial to help them come to terms with their grief, anger, and suppressed feelings. Many fewer people visit the statue, and their interaction with it is much more distant, less emotional and kinetic, and predominantly visual.

SHERRY AHRENTZEN

An example of cultural feminist efforts in the history of architecture is provided by Mimi Lobell. Drawing upon archaeological evidence, Lobell shows a women's cultural heritage in architecture dating to 25,000 B.C. in which to some degree the work is the product of a culture that revered the archetypal feminine principle; women enjoyed equality, independence, and respect; and the work is gynecomorphic, that is, shaped like the female body or symbolizing it in some way.[74] Some examples she gives are the pueblos and cliff-dwellings in the southwest United States. The round, subterranean sacred kiva is a womb-cavern where spiritual birth occurs. Lobell asks us to recognize these structures as models of culture, consciousness, and gender.

All of these examples reflect the qualities and characteristics associated with this cultural feminist position (whether or not the designer perceived it as "feminist"): an architecture and treatment of space that enhances cooperation or social connection among residents or visitors, nonhierarchy and equity between women and men, connection to the space and the symbolic and social embodiments of that space, and an ethic of care and responsiveness to the needs of others.

But while there are many more examples of an architecture informed by cultural feminism, many feminists are wary of uncritical acceptance of this position. Assumptions of differential experience often fall victim to a certain social slippage, in which the original premise, "Women are this way because of different experience," becomes "Women are this way because they are women." Cultural feminism, while providing "new and improved" ways of looking at the contributions of women to architecture, has neglected to stress the *basis* for such differences — how they come to be — and the *consequences* in maintaining this "special quality" perspective. Differences in knowing, learning, designing, or working with clients may be related to sex, but not simply because of biological or psychological reasons, but also because of the different socialization and social positions of boys and girls, men and women. Such valorization without concomitant social transformation can result in stigmatization, discrimination, and additional burdens unless the understanding for the development of such diversity is critically assessed and appreciated. Increasing attention to women's special qualities without an accompanying critical examination of such social development may lead to stereotyping and further marginalizing of women in architecture. Women will be expected to excel in certain types of architectural practices or building types. For example, a 1989 poll of architects conducted by *Progressive Architecture* magazine found that almost 40 percent of women and men architects believed there was a difference in architectural design done by women and men.[75] They believed women are better at design related to "caring" — housing and schools — and men better in design related to power and commerce.

Another problem with this position is that the characteristics it valorizes can also be detrimental ones. Nancy Chodorow argues that women's relational self can be a strength and a pitfall.[76] It enables empathy, nurturance, and intimacy, but it also threatens to undermine autonomy and to dissolve the self into others. She further argues that women's empathetic, relational self rests on the repression of selves bound up with autonomy, aggression, intellectual and interpersonal mastery, and active sexual desire.

A most important challenge to the cultural feminist position is one advanced by Catherine MacKinnon—that we do not know what "woman" is.[77] The feminine sensibilities and experiences valorized today are those developed within a patriarchal system, shaped directly or in defiance of oppressive conditions. So far we only know what being a woman is as constructed and socialized within a patriarchal society. As she claims:

> Women have done good things, and it is a good thing to affirm them. I think quilts are art. I think women have a history. I think we create culture. I also know that we have not only been excluded from making what has been considered art; our artifacts have been excluded from setting the standards by which art is art. Women have a history all right, but it is a history both of what was and of what was not allowed to be. So I am critical of affirming what we have been.... Women value care because men have valued us according to the care we have given them, and we could probably use some. Women think in relational terms because our existence is defined in relation to men.[78]

Further, the cultural feminist position implies an ahistorical, essentialist notion of women. Homogenizing women, this position reflects race, class, and sexuality biases. Such biases have a long history in both feminist and patriarchal polemics. For black and white women, gendered identity has been reconstructed and represented in very different, indeed antagonistic, racialized contexts.[79]

But these arguments also pose a further problem—how to strengthen, not dilute, the voices of women. While over the last decade feminists have increasingly realized the necessity to focus on differences among women along the lines of class, race, ethnicity, age, and sexual orientation, there has also been concern that such differentiation will eventually result in the negation of any women's experiences. In context, nondifferentiation may be beneficial in giving initial visibility to many women's concerns. For example, Patricia Hill Collins has been accused of homogenizing the thought and experiences of black women in her book *Black Feminist Thought*.[80] She replies to these charges by claiming that her deliberate efforts to minimize the obvious heterogeneity among African American women were shaped by the political context in which she was writing.[81] Prematurely claiming heterogeneity among African American women could become a "divide-and-conquer" tool, allowing the differences among black women to be used to discredit the notion that any worthwhile community of black women existed.

Her claims reflect a conundrum for writing and theory in the arena of difference, including gender difference. How do we address the diversity and dynamism of difference within a political context that can disable or subvert any social justice by converting such diversity into fragmentation? In response to such potential annihilation, some critics suggest that community and connection become political tools. As Collins keenly reveals, it is within communities of resistance — extended families, communities, churches, the blues tradition — that self-empowerment and the self-expression of many African American women took hold and flourished.

An Architecture of Context

> Context is all.
> — Margaret Atwood, *The Handmaid's Tale* (1985)

> *Thelma*: I guess I've always been a little crazy, huh?
> *Louise*: You've always been crazy. This is just the first chance
> you've ever had to really express yourself.
> — *Thelma and Louise*

The structure of the built environment can be understood only within the economic, judicial, social, and political systems in which it is embedded. Since the power of architects and place production are shaped by these forces, any significant change to establish gender equity in the environment must involve redefining and restructuring the social context of the practice and discipline of architecture. This feminist position goes beyond valuing or reshaping architecture according to female experiences, recognizing that "female" today is socially constructed within a patriarchal, racist, and classist society.

This feminist perspective involves contextually situated analysis and praxis in which gender is context as well as other social constructions such as class, race, and sexuality. Not always recognized in feminist polemics is the fact that people have identities other than gender. A person is a member of many social groups at any one time, and all groups have the capacity to act in ways that oppress, dominate, and wound. For instance, there is a racial element in much feminist theory and writing resulting from lack of efforts to "see" race. Adrienne Rich contends that color blindness is really white solipsism in which whites would look at a black woman and see her as white.[82] Elizabeth Spelman suggests that white solipsism can be overcome by acknowledging in any analysis just which women we are talking about and just which women we are.[83]

This feminist strategy thus attempts to challenge the rigidity and narrowness of dualistic thinking, common in architecture. For example, Charles Jencks establishes major architectural styles in terms of three dichotomies, one of which is a gender dichotomy.[84] Buildings or building details that are large, solid, massive, linear, or vertical are labeled as masculine; delicate and curved forms constitute the feminine. This conceptualization appeals to the Western (white male) social construction of body ideals of men and women. But the dichotomy is insensitive to the interplay of gender with class, status, ethnicity, religion, and time. As Liz Bondi notes, buildings of the Baroque—those solid, massive, *male* structures—were also the settings of exorbitant wealth, corruption, and power on the brink of collapse.[85] Such meanings are lost in a simplistic gender dichotomy.

Formulating problems and contentions only in terms of male-female polemics obscures much of the social relationships we seek to understand, deflects focus from gender as a social construct, and clouds the processes that amplify or mute its significance. To see female only in comparison with male also diverts attention from women's relations to each other and to power distributions that cut across sex-based categories. Class privilege, for example, strongly informs social behavior, setting standards that govern gender interactions. The goal of contextual feminism is to interpret all social relations through the lens of multiple power, including gender, relations.[86]

Within architecture, I see two strands of the contextual feminist posture. While both emphasize context and specificity, and acknowledge that gender is a context in which architecture operates, one strand does so in a textual manner, the other strand embraces a transformative agenda. I refer to these two strands as the *textual* and *transformative* strands of contextual feminism.

Textual/Contextual. The textual strand has been roundly criticized for its method, not so much for its message. As Margaret Crawford notes, engagement is primarily formal and philosophical, and as such it becomes apolitical, detached from the specific mechanisms of power and exclusion that maintain women's marginality.[87] Here the text itself and the textual devices of etymology, linguistic conundrums, and semiotic meanings often preclude sociopolitical and personal actions. Ironically, among the writings of this strand, the constructed work of women architects is seldom acknowledged. Evidence is often provided in the form of word meanings and fiction (text and film), not narratives of actual people's lives and lived experiences. It is representational rather than corporeal persons who are referenced. The symbolic is disrupted from the sociological.

Criticism here is a self-justifying end. Change called for by these feminists is change within a certain architectural discourse, and theory supersedes engagement with political realities or the landscapes that hold the problems and experiences of everyday life. But, as philosopher Richard Rorty maintains, no critique of ideology can effectively destroy ideology, no matter how perceptive or devastating that critique.[88] Only an alternative paradigm, or vision with political means to reach it, is sufficiently robust to replace existing ideologies.

SHERRY AHRENTZEN

Nonetheless, such feminists do provide fodder for others to contemplate, and they advance the thinking of their male theoretical counterparts by attending to the gender context. For example in a chapter titled "Big Jugs," Jennifer Bloomer draws upon various devices—the hatchery, the hatch to Dorothy's house, the Statue of Liberty, and other metaphors and objects—and looks at the male gaze of these devices through a feminist gaze of the male gaze, as it were. The Statue of Liberty is woman as presentation, woman as currency, and woman as fetish construction for the imagination (whose?). In a restructuring of the Statue of Liberty for a competition for the design of cultural artifacts commemorating the French Revolution bicentennial, Bloomer and her colleagues Durham Crout and Robert Segrest dissect and mutilate a drawing of the statue, and in so doing return the gaze: "To return not merely in a sense of the conventional female acquiescence in sexual discourse, but also to re-turn, to deflect the power of the male gaze through a return of the repressed, through the exorbitance of the female gaze. There is then in the project something of a reversal of the mechanics of the fascinus, a phallus-shaped amulet for warding off the 'evil eye' of the fascinating woman. The evil eye, and to whom it belongs, is called into question."[89]

Curiously, the textual strand continues certain thematic concerns of Western patriarchal philosophy and cultures, such as separateness and control through abstraction, strikingly visible in the text. It distinguishes itself by a language that is so "coded" that it becomes allusive and alienating to many architects.[90] Bell hooks points out the irony of a discourse obsessed with the decentered subject and "Otherness" yet still directed to a specialized audience that shares a language (or a "coded familiarity," as she calls it) rooted in the very master narratives it claims to challenge.[91] Marilyn French suggests that one principle of feminist art—which not all feminists subscribe to—is accessibility, that is, a language and style that aims at comprehensibility.[92] And one, as Patti Lather would suggest, that allows for people to transform their selves and their surrounding environment by encouraging self-reflection and a deeper understanding of their particular situations.[93] This is unlikely here except to a very few of the cognoscenti. However, Lois Nesbitt acknowledges that the erudition of these textual feminists is intimidating and that the texts are oppressively allusive. But, she claims, obscurity is the price to pay to disrupt old ways of thinking.[94] I disagree. Clarity and accessibility are not the enemies of intelligence or social justice. As Audre Lorde called to our attention: "The master's tools can never dismantle the master's house. They may allow us to beat him at his own game, but they will never enable us to bring about genuine change."[95] But then again, genuine change is not the motive here.

Transformative/Contextual. The transformative strand of contextual feminism is not devoid of criticism (although there is less of a textual, etymological focus), but it emphasizes praxis and a struggle to change ourselves as well as social structures.[96] Looking at the social context shifts analysis from abstract and binary differences to the social relations and contexts in which multiple differences are constructed and given meaning. Transformative contextual feminism's focus is on dislodging or altering those social and political conditions that make sex difference matter. Such feminists seek the production of a better set of social constructs than the ones presently available, and thus the creation of new and better sorts of people and places. As Adrienne Rich points out, such a feminist position may have little to do with sexual preference or with civil rights, and a lot to do with making things easier for women of the future to define themselves in terms not presently available.[97]

From where will this emanate? Bell hooks speaks of such reconstructions emanating from *communities of resistance*.[98] Likewise Richard Rorty sees roles requiring a community, a web of social expectations and habits that define the role in question.[99] He suggests that we see the contemporary feminist movement as playing the same role in intellectual and moral progress as was played, for example, by Plato's Academy, the early Christians meeting in the catacombs, the groups of workingmen gathering to discuss Tom Paine's pamphlets, and those other "clubs" that came into being in order to try out new ways of speaking and to gather the moral strength to change the world. Such communities have been invented and used also by women in the recent past, something Rorty neglects to mention. In the consciousness-raising group—that small-scale, democratic, collective enterprise of renaming the world that appeared and spread in the late 1960s and early-to-mid-1970s—many feminist redescriptions were gestated (for example, sexism, sexual harassment, marital rape, date rape, the double shift) and new social movements and collectivities mobilized. They were not the products of individual fashioning or poetizing, but rather of the collective practice of consciousness-raising.

But such communities are means to an end. In the final analysis it is *institutions* that establish what are considered correct and incorrect patterns of thought, doing their work through what we experience as our own individual judgments. As anthropologist Mary Douglas suggests, "When the institutions make classifications for us, we seem to lose some independence that we might conceivably have otherwise had.... This is indeed how we build the institutions, squeezing each other's ideas into a common shape so that we can prove rightness by sheer numbers of independent assent.... The high triumph of institutional thinking is to make the institutions completely invisible."[100]

If her assessment is correct, then challenging gender assumptions will require more than fresh thinking and talk, since dialogue can be curbed or stymied by institutionalized patterns of thought. *Hence, for transformative feminism, the bottom line is changing those institutions that structure the gendered contexts in which we live.* When context—not object—becomes central, the position of architecture expands, to analyze and redesign the legal foundations of building production and land use; the economic distribution systems of the building industry, of communities, and of families; education as well as indoctrination of the professional and nonprofessional involved in placemaking; patronage or the process of "getting commissions"; and the list continues. While efforts at such contextual restructuring are embryonic and often frustrated by firmly entrenched patriarchal institutions, I will describe here a few examples of the ways in which transformative contextual feminism has directed the manner in which architecture—as process and product—has been conceived and created.

Architecture as an Advocacy Profession

All too often architects end up supporting the status quo while they continue to lament their role as pawns to developers, banks, and clients. Robert Goodman calls planners and architects "soft cops," enforcing the ruling class's codes through design.[101]

But the idea of architects as social advocates also has a history—albeit not a central one—in the canons of architectural practice.[102] However, as Kenneth Frampton claims, "No new architecture can emerge without a new kind of relation between designer and user, without new kinds of programs."[103] Architecture as an advocacy profession for social justice would not only seek new programs but, more important, would also restructure the social relationships of those involved in placemaking.

Such advocacy work does appear today among many feminist architects and planners. One faction of feminist advocacy planning argues that planning must do more than merely identify women as beneficiaries of planning and design efforts or increase jobs or housing for women and nonprivileged groups. Instead it must transform the economic and patriarchal systems underlying planning and land use decisions. Charlotte Bunch proposes five criteria to assess the transformational nature of planning proposals: (1) Does this reform materially improve the lives of women, and if so, which women, and how many? (2) Does it build an individual woman's self-respect, strength, and confidence? (3) Does it give women a sense of power, strength, and imagination as a group and help build structures for further change? (4) Does it educate women politically, enhancing their ability to criticize and challenge the system in the future? (5) Does it weaken patriarchal control of society's institutions and help women gain power over them?[104]

Under such criteria, planning efforts assume different actions and decisions, argues Jacqueline Leavitt. Instead of simply looking at physical data or even incorporating cultural data, a planner would also consider issues arising from the division of labor within the household. Issues about accessibility to commercial and public facilities, for example, might then reveal whether the site location facilitates or exacerbates the domestic labor of women.[105]

The fifth criterion that Bunch mentions—helping women gain control over society's institutions—has a history of support among social critics and planners such as Paul Davidoff and Barbara Bryant Solomon, who discuss the need to develop a professional practice that aims to release the powerment potential in every person.[106] Elisheva Sadan and Arza Churchman argue that empowerment is not granting power to someone else. A professional is neither meant to, nor able to, endow people with power. The professional is responsible, in his or her field, for the creation of the environmental conditions that facilitate the realization of the empowerment potential within the individual and the community. In their article "Empowerment and Professional Practice," Sadan and Churchman provide various approaches, principles, and ideas to remold professional practice to be appropriate to the development of empowerment.[107]

In *Making Space,* Francis Bradshaw reports on her experiences as a feminist architectural advocate. Realizing that the tools of the architectural trade were insufficient for working with women in developing new types of spaces, she learned how to function as a facilitator rather than as a decisive expert, and developed new ways to talk about the qualities of space, using language that was accessible rather than abstract. She developed new drawing techniques to present design schemes. She found ways the group could get a feel for manipulating the spaces and take an active part in the process. Once a design was achieved, women remained involved in the building process. Bradshaw concludes that the ways in which women are involved in the building process affect the final result as much as their involvement in the design.[108]

Matrix Architects Ltd. Feminist Co-operative is a women-only architectural practice based in London, organized on the egalitarian principles of the cooperative common ownership movement. Its roots lie in the feminist and community politics of the 1970s, when groups like the New Architecture Movement in England took a radical socialist perspective on the public's disillusionment with modern architecture. Its aim of empowering women to take control over their own lives and its belief that the personal is political directed its organizational structure and relationship with clients. They prioritize working with women's groups and groups that benefit women, since women traditionally have had little access to and have been excluded from the building process. They have developed a consultative approach and have become involved not only in the conventional areas of building design and supervision, but also in education, training, and publishing. The Jagonari Educational Resource Centre for Asian Women is one project that illustrates their approach of reshaping the power relationship between the "expert" and the "layperson" in the design of buildings.[109]

Working with a group of Asian women in East London, Matrix avoided cultural assumptions by involving the women in discussions about spatial arrangements, resulting in a blend of contemporary and non-European cultural elements and

SHERRY AHRENTZEN

conditions in the design. When Jagonari originally met with Matrix, they wanted a low-key, unobtrusive building. But their participation in the programming, design, and development process heightened their confidence in themselves. They could make a mark, take space, in the world. They gradually moved toward a more emphatic building statement: a four-story main building that fronts the main road with an enclosed courtyard, and a two-story crèche building behind. In recognizing their multiple lives, the kitchen was designed with a high Western sink as well as a shallow, low-level Asian sink.

In the past, feminists have been absent in the leadership of the world's major industrial and real estate corporations. But feminism is slowly entering the development realm, in which design and planning decisions are ultimately made. A number of groups that put women in charge of developing land and investing capital have sprung up in the last fifteen years. Loosely called "women's economic development," these groups are quite varied, encompassing loan funds, housing corporations, self-employment programs, worker-owned cooperatives, and business development programs. Women today involved in development come from many different venues: the for-profit business or banking sector, women's crisis services, "traditional" economic development, and community organizing. Some see the development of housing or enterprises as the key to women gaining access to a world of opportunity; others want to create alternative models of economic activity as a step toward changing the larger economic and political system; while others focus on the value of redistributing resources and know-how into the hands of women or women's organizations.[110]

A stellar example of a feminist architect-developer is Joan Forrester Sprague, who has dedicated her career to creating architecture by and for women. She has founded several nonprofit corporations to develop comprehensive housing for single-mother households. In her book *More Than Housing: Lifeboats for Women and Children,* Sprague argues that affordable housing requires not only effective building design, but the architect's understanding and perhaps involvement in all of housing's aspects: real estate development, design, social and economic development services, and facilitation of residents' participation in creating and maintaining their own housing. She demonstrates this in her own considerable efforts in providing affordable housing for women throughout New England.[111]

Reexaming and Rewriting Our Past

> Choosing a past helps us to construct a future.
> —Kevin Lynch, *What Time Is This Place?* (1972)

Abigail A. Van Slyck claims that women architects are often evaluated according to masculinist criteria, and hence fall short or do not even achieve recognition in architectural texts and publications, because such biographies and perspectives do not consider how gender affects designs, accomplishments, recognition, legitimacy, and patronage.[112] Peer recognition and most historical theses do not take into account a person's ability and accomplishments within the social worlds in which he or she operates.

Van Slyck further claims that the growing sophistication of feminist theory requires a serious reassessment of the usefulness of the standard architect's biography as a tool for reintroducing women into architectural history. It is not simply "add women and stir." As Elizabeth Kamarck Minnich maintains, we have "to consider not just what was already known and how women could be added to it, but how knowledge was constructed and what kind of thinking the dominant tradition has privileged. . . . I believe that the effort to find out why and how our thinking carries the past within it is part of an on-going philosophical critique essential to freedom, and to democracy."[113]

One suggestion for reexamining the past is to look at the individual designer in relation to other professionals of her or his time. In looking at the work of artists Mary Cassatt and Berthe Morisot, for instance, Griselda Pollock demonstrates that men and women experienced the modern city differently.[114] Men moved freely and independently through all strata of urban society, while female painters were constrained by social expectations and norms. This affected what they painted and how they translated their experience of the modern world into art.

But another venue for reexamining the past is to interpret the lives of architects within the social context — including gender — of their times. While in the 1970s, Gwendolyn Wright portrayed architect Julia Morgan as one of the exceptional women of her time, following the dominant male paradigm, later historians and critics have tried to frame Morgan with a female-oriented style based on her architectural practice, in which she treated her staff as an extended family — financing the education of some employees, sharing profits, and giving gifts to workers' children.[115] Diane Favro, however, in her analysis of Julia Morgan, goes beyond both the liberal and cultural feminist interpretations to braid together the social facets that shaped Morgan's practice, influence, and posterity. Favro's perceptive analysis is worth recounting as an example of a new way of thinking about our architectural heritage.[116]

An analysis of Morgan's work reveals a sensitivity to the needs of all users. For example, her concern for the needs of minimum-wage girls was atypical for designers of the early twentieth century. From an upper-middle-class background herself, she presumably had little experience with female workers. She likely drew upon the Arts and Crafts model, which was less preoccupied with the image of the structure and more with needs of the building users. Such an emphasis of user needs was also in line with the proclaimed goals of the women's institutions that commissioned her. Julia Morgan entered architectural practice at a time of emerging feminism within American society. While she labored to present the image of a genderless architect, a number of her early commissions came from female clients eager to support women's efforts. Arts and Crafts philosophy, the nature and objectives of her clients, and gender training, Favro claims, made Morgan more interested in process than product.

Responsiveness to clients and users has been touted by cultural feminists as a female attribution. But Morgan's work at the Ecole des Beaux Arts was as object-oriented and style-conscious as that of her peers there. What she lacked was the opportunity to express this approach after she left the Ecole. What she received were commissions based on preconceptions about female sensitivity. In response to existing preconceptions and to her desire to develop her own practice, Morgan fashioned a nonthreatening professional image and a work philosophy of accommodation. As a marginalized professional, being a woman in a male-dominated field, Morgan relied heavily on satisfied customers to bring in more work. But the cultivation of client satisfaction further marginalized her position in the profession: user or client satisfaction does not earn the architect peer recognition. Giving William Randolph Hearst exactly what he wanted at San Simeon instead of developing a unique personal style or recognizable aesthetic theory diminished her stature within the architectural community.

While such a contextually oriented analysis adds considerable insight into the life and work of this architect, some feminist art and architectural critics advocate the more radical idea of dispensing with biographies altogether.[117] Griselda Pollock argues that biography reinforces the myth of bourgeois individualism and deliberately obscures the structural inequalities of Western society that maintain a hierarchy based on gender, class, and race. To her, biographies of female artists flourish because they rarely challenge the biases of the scholarly field.[118]

A suggestion for rewriting our history is offered by Dell Upton.[119] He proposes that the *unit of analysis* for a reconstituted architectural history be the entire cultural landscape. This history would take into account builders and buildings, but it would be concerned with construction only on the way to construing. Its focus is the human experience of its own landscape, rather than the relationship of maker and object. It attempts to encompass as many modes of perception as possible and, equally important, the mental categories through which perception is interpreted. Thus, a working definition of *cultural landscape* emphasizes the fusion of the physical with the imaginative structures that all inhabitants of the landscape use in constructing and construing it. An example of such work is provided by architectural historian Barbara Allen. Using feminist and nonwhite discourses of the built environment, her analysis of the Franco-African plantation in antebellum Louisiana builds connections between personal histories and situated knowledge, and as such builds openings for affinities to emerge. For example, she finds several stories in one plantation house:

It speaks of the assimilation of an African woman's family into French manners and customs prevalent in the region. It illuminates the hybridity of culture always/already present at any point in the construction of people's lived lives. It is a comparative tale of the freedom and dignity allowed by the laws and acceptable practices of certain nations (France) and points to the oppression and suffering caused by the rules and social mores of other nations (England, U.S.). Lastly the house is a rather somber reminder of the totalizing influence of capitalism (with its accompanying traits of domination and patriarchy), a homogenizing force blending the Cane River creoles of color in with their white neighbors into the consuming logic of the market economy. And this is where the final story is uncovered.[120]

Such transformation of architectural history and criticism calls into account the myriad social contexts. Similarly, Alice Friedman advocates an approach that shifts the focus away from individual architects and the notion of singular heroic actions, and instead recognizes that built form is generated through a process that takes place over time and is the product of decisions made by a wide variety of practitioners and interest groups.[121]

In her analysis of Hollyhock House, for example, Friedman demonstrates the central roles played by the client Aline Barnsdall, her class background, her family status as a single parent during this era, the theater culture of the time, the culture of health, the feminist postures held by Barnsdall and Frank Lloyd Wright, and the interaction between client and architect (Wright), in the evolution of the house. As Friedman summarizes:

> Barnsdall's feminism and her unwillingness to conform to convention are key factors both in the history of Olive Hill and in the design of Hollyhock House. This is true at three levels. At the level of the program, her household was neither a conventional family nor could its activities be fitted into a conventional home. At the symbolic and artistic level, because Wright's interpretation of Barnsdall's commission was colored by his response to her personality and values and by her relationship with him. At the level of gender politics, it deeply affected the response of artists, theater people, and others in the community, including public officials, to her ideas and to projects in which she sought to provide leadership. Wright understood that Barnsdall had substituted the bonds of her project theatrical community for that of the conventional family.[122]

As Friedman demonstrates, the Olive Hill project is an example in which one woman brought together feminism, socialism, experimental theater, and new American architecture in a single far-reaching project intended not for her own private enjoyment but for the public good.[123]

A further contextually oriented possibility in rewriting our history is identifying "sites of resistance" of communities and groups typically excluded from the map. Gail Lee Dubrow and Dolores Hayden have made heroic efforts in identifying such places in Los Angeles and Boston. The Power of Place project directed by them and Carolyn Flynn is discussed elsewhere in this book (see chapter 4 in this volume).

Legislating the Designed Environment— and Our Place In It

Another arena for contextual consideration is land use policy—that is, the legal environment that establishes what gets built where. In several articles, Marsha Ritzdorf has explored the linkage between regulatory land use and women's lives.[124] She reveals the power of municipal zoning ordinances to spatially direct family lives, the location of support systems, and the composition of household arrangements. While in theory the purpose of zoning is to protect the health, safety, and general welfare of the community by separating incompatible uses, Ritzdorf shows how such actually enforces social agendas, impacting the lives of many women.

Ritzdorf believes there has been no major public outcry against the social injustices of zoning because of the complexities that race, class, and gender play in our society. She contends that the family ethic reinforced the growing industrial expansion and provided a way to translate the growing separation between middle-class and working-class lives into a spatial reality. This separation was keenly important to middle-class women and men who participated, and still participate, in its enforcement. The importance of living in a single-class, residential-only neighborhood so fundamentally defines the collective identity of the middle class that it supersedes the importance of gender-role considerations for the vast majority of middle-class women. Ritzdorf contends that even though a body of research shows that contemporary women are less happy with the suburbs than are their male counterparts, there is little evidence to show that they are doing anything to change their neighborhoods into more economically, socially, and physically mixed environments. Class consciousness and racism are not merely the province of men, Ritzdorf shows.

But Ritzdorf believes that it is possible to accept the eventuality of the single-family detached home as an American society norm and still restructure zoning to allow the changing lives of women to be met with changing neighborhood availability of needed goods and services. With the goal of gender-sensitive land use reform in mind, she confronts communities and educates policymakers who use their zoning and land-use power to discriminate. Reform is enacted when communities make more conducive living environments by providing opportunities to site child-care homes, group homes for the handicapped, and home-based work.

Rethinking Whom to Educate

Architectural education does not train students to be advocates of their ideas. In school, architectural initiates generally present their design ideas to other architects, who frequently dodge or fudge questions of how money, legislation, politics, and sociology will shape implementation of their proposals. When architectural students then enter the commercial realm and discover their lowly status, they do not have the skills or experience to initiate their ideas. Too often they join the fray and become "hired guns." Many authors in Thomas Dutton's collection *Voices in Architectural Education* discuss ways that architectural students can reappropriate architectural education for advancing both critical consciousness and social justice within the field.[125] Others outside of architecture, such as Jane Roland Martin, even call for redefining what it means to become educated.[126]

But education for creating our built environment becomes more encompassing than simply studio education when the contextual dimension is considered. Sharon Sutton has sought broader educational change in architecture by focusing on the development of environmental values among young children.[127] In developing the Urban Network, a national urban design program that helps children gain a sense of control over the urban environment, Sutton has also been instrumental in having children develop the collective identity that is essential to growing up as compassionate, responsible citizens. She quotes Martin Luther King: "When an individual is no longer a true participant, when he no longer feels a sense of responsibility to society, the content of democracy is emptied."

The Urban Network is more than a curriculum to increase environmental awareness; it aspires to help children learn to live together by generating an exchange of ideas. Students make a critical analysis of their school-community environment, create idealistic visions, select an area of need, develop a plan, and then raise money to implement the plan. This critical, participatory process helps children to understand problems in the larger environment, to imagine a better world, and to create practical solutions to problems in their immediate purview.

The Urban Network took shape in 1988 and has served more than one hundred schools and community organizations in the United States and Canada. The program challenges young people first to be critical of their physical surroundings and then to take action to improve those surroundings. Believing we need to rethink what it means to learn from and live in a menacing environment, Sutton suggests that images of self and place are connected. She also believes that collaborative art activities have the power to create tightly-knit and purposeful social groups. By making some place or thing, children learn to "construct" their own individual and collective lives, improving the environment and empowering themselves at the same time. Her work centers around a variety of cooperative endeavors and team- and community-building techniques. In comparison to traditional

SHERRY AHRENTZEN

classroom practices, this kind of effort advances children's social skills. Sutton has also developed a program in which environmental learning promotes respect for cultural differences. She developed an urban studies curriculum to make children aware of the advantages and disadvantages that come with living in a specific place, and conveyed it via Spanish and English to fourth-grade teachers and students living in New York City, Chicago, and Mexico City. The Urban Network earned the American Planning Association's Education Award in 1991.[128]

Other educators have similarly focused on educating young people in the ways of environmental and social change. A team of women professionals (notably Joanne Yoshida, Janet Sygar, Susan Fleminger, and Ann deVere) from New York City Public School 110 and Henry Street Settlement's Arts in Education program have been using the Lower East Side as a stage upon which to encourage environmental activism. The program is aimed at developing students' awareness of their surroundings, but it also emphasizes their capacity to improve those surroundings. Jan Culbertson, a partner in Culbertson Jacobs & Milling Architects, has developed a consensus-building methodology that enables students, parents, teachers, and staff to participate in the planning of their school buildings. The strategy was used in designing additions for three schools in Ann Arbor, Michigan.[129]

An Architecture of Mind and Body

Philosopher and educator John Dewey spent his life combating the tendency of educators to divorce mind from body and reason from emotion. But this separation tendency is part of a larger contemporary Western pattern of separation of mind and body in various institutions and settings. While architectural theorists today are abuzz with talk of architecture and body invaders, or bodybuildings, some architects are making efforts to not simply anthropomorphize, but to create an architecture that more richly provides for the bodies *and* minds of people.

Perhaps this is best illustrated in places of birth. Birthing began to change from a social to a technical-medical event at the end of the nineteenth century, both in hospital and home settings.[130] In her analysis of the landscape of middle-class pregnancy and childbirth between 1870 and 1900, Annmarie Adams shows that the medical profession tried to dissolve the boundaries between the outside and the inside of women's bodies in order to see, explain, and control reproduction.[131] This breakdown did not happen simply in the medically controlled hospital, but also in the lying-in room of the middle-class house. More than an innovation of architectural convenience, this special room was both a symbolic and visible extension of the mother's body, and provided observable space through which doctors could expand the conceptual limitations of the body.

Much has been written about modern-day medical practices to technologize, isolate, and control birth through equipment, lighting, posture, furnishings, space allocation, movement-control, and other physical measures.[132] The routine pattern dictated by a medicalized conception of birth implies a fixation of roles imposed upon each woman by the obstetric theorization of a generalized process of birth. The medical interpretation of birth as potential pathology has created hospital wards of control and intervention, characterized by simplified rectilinear paths connecting a variety of specialty rooms where women wait for "intervention." As architect Bianca Lepori contends, this linear succession of rooms expresses a factory pattern that "the product to be" undergoes.[133] This sequence promotes the competence and identity of the operators in charge of a successful production of healthy births—the medical staff. Each phase is extracted from the whole process of birth, thus from the total subjective experience of it. The continuity of personal timing is dependent upon an established schedule, while the psychobiological process of the individual woman is reduced to mechanical episodes concerning separate and specific parts of one's body.

Lepori has reenvisioned new spaces for birth allowing women control of their bodies and minds during birthing. She finds that each woman, given the freedom to give birth as she wishes, locates a territory in which she progresses toward a center of action and concentration, almost toward the creation of a microenvironment or microcosm, a circumscribed area similar to the one other mammals circumscribe for themselves. Individual births as unique experiences, as private experiences of intimacy and freedom, require a space of hospitality and home rather than hospitalization. For a birthing woman, "home" means freedom of movement, comfort and ease, the possibility to choose and control, and the provision of fittings created to support bodily needs. It means having her own power to choose, no matter what she chooses. The territory of birth that women choose is not programmed, not defined by external authorities, seldom prearranged, and always spontaneously determined during birthing as a focus of action and concentration. The path is a spiral leading toward the center of woman's concentration and ability to listen, therefore expressing her control and choice.

In the birth center in Milan that Lepori has designed, a receptacle was created to enhance the whole process of birth from the woman's point of view and to guarantee the security provided by technology without negating the woman's freedom of expression. Since birthing women need room to move, the design of the space was made flexible. Lepori removed the bed from its dominant position, allowing the layout to become more relaxed and open to varied design solutions and experiences, and used a large single platform where women can sit, rest, lie down, lean, or kneel on the floor with their elbows over it.

Even water was renamed. In hospitals, water is considered unclean because of its bacterial content, and thus is often expelled from surgical contexts. Since water can relieve pain, accelerate dilation, and also facilitate the medium for birth from the child's point of view, Lepori introduced a pool into the birthing space.

The location of the pool is not far from the fittings for rest or from the free patches of floor where birth suddenly happens.

The overall composition of the birth setting aims to provide a sequence of interconnected contexts related by visual and tactile continuity, to support the birth event in its own rhythms and specific mutations. The plurality of performances within this room is meant to enhance the relationship of individuals with the place, with each other, and with themselves.

CONCLUDING THOUGHTS ON MULTIPLICITIES

> Only if somebody has a dream, and a voice to describe that
> dream, does what looked like nature begin to look like culture,
> what looked like fate begin to look like a moral abomination. For
> until then only the language of the oppressor is available, and
> most oppressors have had the wit to teach the oppressed a
> language in which the oppressed will sound crazy—even to
> themselves—if they describe themselves as oppressed.
> — Richard Rorty, "Feminism and Pragmatism,"
> *Michigan Quarterly Review* (1991)

There is no way to determine the numbers of women and men within the architectural profession who are committed to feminism and are directing their work accordingly. There are those women who do not want to set themselves apart, but rather seek to match men's achievements in the field, looking to fill long-established and accepted roles that have been held almost exclusively by men. Other women in the profession engage in and even create distinctive roles in the profession that diversify the performances of their male counterparts.[134]

This chapter has attempted to show the various—sometimes conflicting—ways feminist efforts can shape the practice and discipline of architecture. This diversity of voices and actions should dispel the notion and value of one female point of view. Some feminist critics maintain that such diversity is of strategic importance in struggling against those in control. By not collapsing their differences, women refuse to become one pole—the weaker pole—in a force field dominated by "the Marlboro man." Adumbrated by Gilles Deleuze and Félix Guattari, "nomad thought" similarly implies a resistance to settling into any one theoretical position, a willingness to challenge and revise one's own critical positions and practices.[135] Men's differences similarly need to be emphasized—so that together the possibility of stretching the field of debate beyond polarized oppositions is furthered.

Many women assume this multiplicity approach not for political reasons, but because it more truly reflects their nature and experiences. As Maxine Hong Kingston says in *The Woman Warrior*, "I learned to make my mind large, as the universe is large, so that there is room for paradoxes."[136]

The dilemma exists in finding the courage to speak this "nomad thought," these paradoxes in a world that labels persons or groups with divided opinions as "schizophrenic" or, even worse, as "hysterical women." Luce Irigaray reminds us that "we haven't been taught, nor allowed, to express multiplicity....Of course, we might—we were supposed to?—exhibit one 'truth' while sensing, withholding, muffling another. Truth's other side—its complement? its remainder?—stayed hidden."[137] Healthy self-identity as established by patriarchal Western cultures is unified and consistent. But, as Karen A. Franck contends, there are many "healthy" women who assume a "rational maximizing aspect" of self that seeks equality with men; an incorporative aspect that prizes nurturance and intimate relations with others; and a visionary, utopian rebel, also.[138] Walt Whitman perhaps said it best: "I am large. I contain multitudes."[139]

This paradoxical state is also brought on by the complexity of world problems today. For example, former surgeon general Dr. Antonia C. Novello announced to Congress in 1991, "The home is actually a more dangerous place for American women than the city streets."[140] While building crisis shelters for battered women does not ameliorate the economic, political, and social conditions and institutions that lead to the violence of battering in the first place, escape from domestic violence depends upon the existence of places of safety outside the home. But while such shelters are necessary for getting individual women out of the immediate crisis situation, the creation of such shelters is simply a reactionary, albeit necessary, measure. A contextual feminist position would take a proactive stance to subvert the problem itself—the home as a site of violence. It would not simply build shelters as way stations for women fleeing violent homes, but would restructure the gender appropriation of homeplace.[141]

Such restructuring, however, may take years, even decades, while many women's lives are in imminent danger in their homes. In today's complex world we have to embrace both practical and strategic gender needs, a model posed by Caroline O. N. Moser. Practical gender needs arise from the concrete conditions of women's positioning within the sexual division of labor. Such needs for battered women may be the existence of safe shelters. By contrast, strategic gender needs are those needs identified from the analysis of women's subordination, and deriving out of this, the formulation of an alternative, more satisfactory organization of society in terms of the structure and nature of relationships between women and men. Such needs may include the economic enhancement of women's lives, the removal of social and institutional forms of violence against women, and the empowerment of women's place inside and outside the home. The distinction between practical and strategic gender needs is useful to correct the assumption that meeting women's practical needs automatically furthers women's strategic needs. What Moser considers in the particular case of housing could be extrapolated to other built environment concerns:

Thus the specific circumstances by which conventional assumptions can be challenged and restructured may be dependent on the development of consciousness at two levels. It may depend as much on the "bottom-up" emergence of women's consciousness through the experience of participation in human settlement, as it does on the "top-down" opening up of political space. Ultimately it may be the conjuncture of the two that is necessary for any fundamental change in the nature of gender relations and housing to occur.[142]

Many men and women find themselves drifting or frantically hustling between different, often conflicting, responses to create a world of social justice and gender equity. Lynda Schneekloth believes that an agenda that advocates instability actually creates a space in which to consider the many different relationships and connections confronting us, to focus on the spaces between the categories, and to bring forward formerly subjugated knowledge.[143] Donna Haraway even argues "for *pleasure* in the confusion of boundaries and for *responsibility* in their construction."[144] To Schneekloth "this sounds like coyote work, demanding that we give up our position as knower and expert, creating the space to make mistakes, to be wrong, to make fools of ourselves, and to continue practicing."[145] She advocates that we use the image and intent of the coyote, an irreverent mythic commentator, trickster and teacher, wise one and fool, of Native American heritage. "This is coyote work—the tricky work of staying in-between, of being in more than one place."[146]

I believe a feminist community must acknowledge both positions of this dilemma, embracing a short-term determination to reform existing society and a long-term desire to transform it. By becoming more self-conscious about our strategic choices about when to deny, celebrate, represent, or dislodge difference, we may come closer to minimizing the inequalities difference has traditionally entailed. As Alison M. Jaggar says, "Sometimes equality in outcome may be served best by sex-blindness, sometimes by sex-responsiveness—and sometimes by attention to factors additional to or other than sex."[147] Our thinking must be simultaneously pragmatic and utopian to mutually strengthen. And it should be constantly played at the level of "everyday rebellions and outrageous acts."[148]

The "empowerment of multiplicity" that bell hooks calls for is the construction of interconnected communities of resistance as opposed to competitively fragmented and separate ones.[149] Such spaces of these multifaceted communities can be seen at the recent conferences and symposia focusing on women in architecture held across the country. For example, the symposium "Women in Architecture: Fitting In or Making a Difference," held in January 1991 at the Graham Foundation in Chicago, utilized two types of forums: guest speakers and—what can be labeled an outgrowth of feminist consciousness-raising—group discussions. The format itself for the conference spoke to the plurality of approaches, and the speakers themselves expressed this diversity.

Finally, this search must take place within a moral milieu or else it risks traveling the cul-de-sac that postmodernism discovers itself in. In *Architecture, Ethics, and Technology,* Alberto Pérez-Gómez laments that much too often ethics is seen as external to architecture. But, he contends,

> if architects are to play a role in the complex world of the twenty-first century — a world more conscious of environmental limits and cultural differences while civilization continues to embrace the goal of technological globalization — they must ponder strategies to disclose their discipline's potential for embodying an ethical intentionality. . . . The potential integration of ethic and aesthetic concerns has profound consequences for architectural practice. Indeed, it confronts the issue of form generation at its inception.[150]

How do we proceed? Building upon the pragmatic heritage in American philosophical thought, cultural critic Cornel West proposes the distinctive hallmarks of prophetic pragmatism: a consciousness that promotes an all-embracing democratic and libertarian moral vision, a historical consciousness that acknowledges human finitude and conditionedness, and a critical consciousness that encourages relentless critique and self-criticism for the aims of social change and personal humility.[151] Like Foucault, prophetic pragmatists criticize and resist forms of subjection, as well as types of economic exploitation, state repression, and bureaucratic domination. But unlike Foucault, these critiques and resistances are guided by moral ideals of creative democracy and individuality.

While architectural rhetoric has long given lip service to architecture's role in enhancing the common good, too often a commercial imperative usurps the ethical one, reducing the architect to rationalizing projects whose form and use have already been determined by real-estate speculators and financial backers. Creativity and morality are uneasy bedfellows. As geographer Yi-Fu Tuan contends, "As we study the human use of the earth, moral issues emerge at every point if only because, to make any change at all, force must be used and the use of force raises questions of right and wrong, good and bad."[152] Any slash upon the earth — constructing a residence, siting a subdivision — is an ethical decision, not simply a design one.

Complex and difficult challenges unfold today that cannot be met by the status quo of the profession. But giving birth to something new involves labor and pain. The culture of architecture must redefine and reshape itself to address these challenges that "emerge from a greater and more universal human compassion, from an increasing awareness of the limits that make human life possible, and from a new sense of human identity that respects cultural distinctiveness."[153] Major revolutions in architecture coincide with major societal movements and changes in the power structure of society, new beliefs about the nature of natural and social worlds, the emergence of new societal and professional organizations, new types of clients, a revision in values, and thus changes in the perceived purposes of the built environment and of architects. Perhaps this is the time for a new culture of architecture.

Notes

1. None look at him through the prism of gender: as a midwestern-bred white male working in a world privileging whiteness and masculinity. In a brief chapter, architectural historian David Van Zanten initiates a gender analysis of Wright's early life and work. Sociologist Michael Kimmel refers to an upcoming biography of Frank Lloyd Wright from the perspective of masculinity. See David van Zanten, "Frank Lloyd Wright's Kindergarten: Professional Practice and Sexual Roles," in Ellen Perry Berkeley and Matilda McQuaid, eds., *Architecture: A Place for Women* (Washington, D.C.: Smithsonian Institution Press, 1989), pp. 55–61; Michael Kimmel, "Reading Men: Men, Masculinity, and Publishing," *Feminist Collections* 13, no. 1 (1991): 11–17.
2. Edward Ball, "Building to a Climax: Or, Sex Is in the Details," *Village Voice Literary Supplement* 111 (1992): 27.
3. For example, there are organizations and journals devoted exclusively to women's and feminist issues in these areas. Law, for example, has *Yale Journal of Law and Feminism* (started in 1989), *Harvard Women's Law Journal* (1978), *Berkeley Women's Law Journal* (1986), *Columbia Journal of Gender and Law* (1990), and *Wisconsin Women's Law Journal* (1985), among others. Architecture has no such journals, although there is the geography journal *Gender, Place and Culture* and the more general *Women and Environments*.
4. Some of these early writings include Doris Cole, *From Tipi to Skyscraper: A History of Women in Architecture* (Boston: I Press Incorporated, 1973); Dolores Hayden, *The Grand Domestic Revolution: A History of Feminist Designs for American Homes, Neighborhoods, and Cities* (Cambridge, Mass.: MIT Press, 1981); Catherine Stimpson, Elsa Dixler, Martha Nelson, and Kathryn Yatrakis, eds., *Women and the American City* (Chicago: University of Chicago Press, 1981); Susana Torre, ed., *Women in American Architecture: A Historic and Contemporary Perspective* (New York: Whitney Library of Design, 1977); Gerda Wekerle, Rebecca Peterson, and David Morley, eds., *New Space for Women* (Boulder, Colo.: Westview Press, 1980).
5. Interestingly, the use of gender as an analytic tool has coincided with the emerging scholarship on masculinity (I am *not* considering here the popular mythopoetic strand of masculinity study that laments the powerlessness of men, for example, books by Robert Bly and Sam Keen). In a review of fifteen books on masculinity, Michael Kimmel notes that men have finally figured out that they have a gender and that gender matters and affects them (positively and negatively) as well as women and society at large. See Kimmel, "Reading Men."
6. Simone de Beauvoir, *The Second Sex,* trans. H. M. Parshly (New York: Bantam, 1960).
7. The history of homosexuality, for example, shows us how masculinity is constantly being constructed within the history of an evolving social structure of sexual power relations. See Sallie Westwood, "Racism, Black Masculinity and the Politics of Space," in Jeff Hearn and David Morgan, eds., *Men, Masculinities and Social Theory* (London: Unwin Hyman, 1990), pp. 55–71. Another historical example that questions and expands the social construction of gender is the *berdache* of certain Native American tribes, a gender not considered a special type of man or woman but rather a third type of person. See Suzanne J. Kessler and Wendy McKenna, *Gender: An Ethnomethodological Approach* (Chicago: University of Chicago Press, 1978).

8. I must stress that masculinity is variously defined (for example, the masculinity of pro football, the masculinity of Asian Americans, the masculinity of retired men) and that this chapter speaks about a particular construction of masculinity (described in more detail in the text). As Shane Phelan points out, most men do not represent the "men" of much white feminist polemics — typically white, middle-class men. White women seeking sex equity, for example, did not seek equality with nonwhite men. This blindness not only contributed to inadequate theorizing about the positions and problems of women, but also contributed to the naïveté and racism of much feminist rhetoric. Shane Phelan, "Specificity: Beyond Equality and Difference," *Differences: A Journal of Feminist Cultural Studies* 3, no. 1 (1991): 128–43.

9. Michael Kimmel, "After Fifteen Years: The Impact of the Sociology of Masculinity on the Masculinity of Sociology," in Hearn and Morgan, eds., *Men, Masculinities and Social Theory*, pp. 93–109.

10. Leslie Kanes Weisman, *Discrimination by Design: A Feminist Critique of the Man-Made Environment* (Urbana: University of Illinois Press, 1992).

11. Elizabeth Grosz, "Bodies-Cities," in Beatriz Colomina, ed., *Sexuality and Space* (New York: Princeton Architectural Press, 1992), pp. 241–54.

12. The Department of Labor lists architects as those people who describe their occupation as such. The term "architect" here does not necessarily indicate whether or not the person is legally registered as an architect.

13. John Dixon, "A White Gentleman's Profession?" *Progressive Architecture,* November 1994, pp. 55–61.

14. While there are more than 12,000 architectural firms in the country today, 250 of them (or 2 percent) collect 30 percent of the fees for architectural services, hence illustrating the political clout of the few. Robert Gutman, *Architectural Practice: A Critical View* (Princeton, N.J.: Princeton Architectural Press, 1988).

15. AIA figures are from Jean Barber, American Institute of Architects, in Washington, D.C. Also see "School Statistics," *ACSA News* 24, no. 3 (1994): 8–9; Michael Kaplan, "Statistics on Tenured Faculty," *ACSA News* 23, no. 5 (1993). These figures, of course, reflect the power situation of white males in American society in general. While white males compose 39 percent of the American population, they account for 83 percent of Forbes 400 (people worth at least $265 million), 77 percent of Congress, 92 percent of state governors, 70 percent of tenured college faculty, 90 percent of daily newspaper editors, and 77 percent of television directors. David Gates, "White Male Paranoia," *Newsweek* 131, no. 13 (1993): 48–53.

16. William E. Wallace, "Michelangelo, C.E.O.," *New York Times,* April 16, 1994, p. A11; William E. Wallace, *Michelangelo at San Lorenzo: The Genius as Entrepreneur* (New York: Cambridge University Press, 1994).

17. Dana Cuff, *Architecture: The Story of Practice* (Cambridge, Mass.: MIT Press, 1991).

18. Martha Vicinus, *The Industrial Muse* (New York: Barnes and Noble, 1974); Judith Newton and Deborah Rosenfelt, eds., *Feminist Criticism and Social Change: Sex, Class and Race in Literature and Culture* (New York: Methuen, 1985).

19. Pierre Bourdieu, "The Aristocracy of Culture," *Media, Culture and Society* 2 (1980): 225–54.

20. Sharon E. Sutton, "Practice: Architects and Power," *Progressive Architecture,* May 1992, pp. 65–68.

21. Christine Battersby, *Gender and Genius: Towards a Feminist Aesthetics* (Bloomington: Indiana University Press, 1989); Griselda Pollock, *Vision and Difference: Femininity, Feminism and Histories of Art* (London: Routledge, 1988).

22. Denise Scott Brown, "Room at the Top? Sexism and the Star System in Architecture," in Berkeley and McQuaid, eds., *Architecture: A Place for Women,* p. 241.

23. For interesting accounts of whom architects see themselves as "serving," see Russell Ellis and Dana Cuff, eds., *Architects' People* (New York: Oxford University Press, 1989), esp. Dana Cuff, "Through the Looking Glass: Seven New York Architects and Their People," pp. 64–102.

24. According to statistics compiled by the Washington, D.C., and New York chapters of the AIA, the National Council of Registration Boards, and a survey of architects' salaries conducted in 1988 by D. Dietrich Associates, the salary range for a senior designer is $22,000–45,000, and for a project manager, $28,000–56,000. A licensed architect with eight years' experience earns a median of $37,000 (1990 dollars). Compare these figures with those from other licensed professionals. A *beginning* lawyer earns on average a $47,000 annual salary (experienced lawyers earn an average $120,000). Physicians on average earn $155,800 (1989 dollars), with the lowest-paid specialist—the general or family practitioner—still earning on average more than an experienced architect, at $94,900. A physician under the age of thirty-six earns an average $113,300. But a licensed social worker employed by the federal government earns an annual average salary of $38,200 (1991 dollars). A certified public elementary school teacher earns $32,400 (1990); a licensed occupational therapist, $30,400 (1990); and registered nurses earn on average $16.20 an hour, translating to an average salary of $33,700 for a full-time RN. While salaries vary considerably by region, city, years of experience, and sex, these data suggest that architects' salaries are more in line with the licensed fields of nursing, teaching, social work, and other health care specialists (excluding physicians) than they are with law and medicine. However, it is also the case that the highest-earning architects make more than the highest-earning nurses, for example. Architecture—compared with the female-dominated fields mentioned—does provide some opportunities for high salaries. It may be that the image of the "top dogs" rather than the typical or more common architect is what directs perceptions of architects as being within the same economic realm of law and medicine. However, I would argue that the basis for such a perception also reflects a masculinist thinking—using the highest earners to represent "the field," to the exclusion of the range or the typical. Data from John W. Wright, *The American Almanac of Jobs and Salaries, 1987–88* (New York: Avon, 1987); U.S. Department of Commerce, Bureau of Labor, *Occupational Outlook Handbook, 1992–93,* Bulletin 2400 (Washington, D.C.: U.S. Government Printing Office, 1992).

25. However, Gutman does not cite the source of this evidence; Robert Gutman, *Architectural Practice: A Critical View* (Princeton N.J.: Princeton Architectural Press, 1988), p. 110. However, a study conducted by the Association of Collegiate Schools of Architecture (ACSA) indicates that 70 percent of architectural graduates are "satisfied," 25 percent "somewhat satisfied," and 4 percent "very dissatisfied" with their current work activity. However, only 39 percent were "somewhat satisfied" with their present earnings, 45 percent were "somewhat dissatisfied," and 15 percent were "very dissatisfied." Cited in Wright, *American Almanac.*

26. Gwendolyn Wright, "History for Architects," in Gwendolyn Wright and J. Parks, eds., *The History of History in American Schools of Architecture, 1865–1979* (New York: Temple Hoyne Buell Center for the Study of American Architecture, 1990), pp. 13–52.

27. Sanjoy Mazumdar, "Cultural Values in Architectural Education: An Example from India." *Journal of Architectural Education* 46, no. 4 (1993): 230–38.

28. Lian Hurst Mann, "Why ANYone Writes Such Good Books: Lian Hurst Mann Talks with Peter Eisenman," LA *Architect,* July/August 1991, p. 4. The ANYone multidisciplinary conference was one in a series sponsored by the ANYone Corporation in New York City to examine the condition of architecture at the end of the millenium.

29. Diane Ghirardo, "Eisenman's Bogus Avant-Garde," *Progressive Architecture,* November 1994, p. 73.

30. Mary McLeod, "Architecture and Politics in the Reagan Era: From Postmodernism to Deconstructivism," *Assemblage* 8 (1989): 23–60.

31. Pauline Fowler, "Shaking the Foundations: Feminist Analysis in the World of Architecture," *Fuse* (Toronto) 7, no. 5 (1984): 199–204.

32. Kenneth Frampton, "Labour Work and Architecture," in Charles Jencks and George Baird, eds., *Meaning in Architecture* (London: Barrie and Rockliff, Cresset Press, 1969); Ken-

neth Frampton, "The Status of Man and the Status of His Objects," *Architectural Design* 52, special issue, *Modern Architecture and the Critical Present* (1982): 6–19.

33. Torre, *Women in American Architecture.*
34. This is not an international practice. In some countries, completion of an architectural education qualifies one as an architect.
35. Sherry Ahrentzen and Kathryn Anthony, "Sex, Stars, and Studios: A Look at Gendered Educational Practices in Architecture," *Journal of Architectural Education* 47, no. 1 (1993): 11–29.
36. For reviews of such, see Sally McMurray, "Women in the American Vernacular Landscape," *Material Culture* 21, no. 1 (1989): 33–46; also Hayden, *Grand Domestic Revolution*; Cole, *From Tipi to Skyscraper*; Gwendolyn Wright, "Women in American Architecture," in Spiro Kostof, ed., *The Architect: Chapters in the History of the Profession* (New York: Oxford University Press, 1977); Torre, *Women in American Architecture*. For a growing number of biographical accounts, see Abigail A. Van Slyck, "Women in Architecture and the Problems of Biography," *Design Book Review* 25 (1992): 19–22.
37. Natalie Kampen and Elizabeth Grossman, *Feminism and Methodology: Dynamics of Change in the History of Art and Architecture* (Report of Center for Research on Women) (Wellesley, Mass.: Wellesley College, 1983), p. 14.
38. Ellen Perry Berkeley, Introduction to Berkeley and McQuaid, eds., *Architecture: A Place for Women.*
39. Rosabeth Moss Kanter, *Men and Women of the Corporation* (New York: Basic, 1977).
40. Karen Kingsley, "Rethinking Architectural History from a Gender Perspective," in Thomas A. Dutton, ed., *Voices in Architectural Education: Cultural Politics and Pedagogy* (New York: Bergin and Garvey, 1991).
41. For example, see Nancy Chodorow, *The Reproduction of Mothering: Psychoanalysis and the Sociology of Gender* (Berkeley: University of California Press, 1978); Nel Noddings, *Caring: A Feminine Approach to Ethics and Moral Education* (Berkeley: University of California Press, 1984).
42. Ahrentzen and Anthony, "Sex, Stars, and Studios"; Sherry Ahrentzen, "De-gendering by Engendering: Reconstructing Social Dynamics in the Design Studio," in Michael Fazio and Jeanna Lombard, eds., *Proceedings of the 81st Annual Meeting of the Association of Collegiate Schools of Architecture* (Washington, D.C.: ACSA, 1993).
43. Cited in John Remy, "Patriarchy and Fratriarchy as Forms of Androcracy," in Jeff Hearn and David Morgan, eds., *Men, Masculinities and Social Theory* (London: Unwin Hyman, 1990).
44. Ibid.
45. Donald A. Schön, *The Reflective Practitioner* (New York: Basic, 1983); Chris Argyris, "Teaching and Learning in Design Settings," in Consortium of East Coast Schools of Architecture, ed., *Architecture Education Study, volume 1, The Papers* (New York: Mellon Foundation, 1981).
46. ACSA Task Force on the Status of Women in Architecture Schools (Sherry Ahrentzen and Linda Groat, authors), *Status of Faculty Women in Architecture Schools: Survey Results and Recommendations,* report of the Association of Collegiate Schools of Architecture, Washington, D. C., 1990; Kaplan, "Statistics on Tenured Faculty."
47. I thank James Mayo for suggesting this point to me.
48. For example, Mary Fiske Belenky, Blythe McVicker McClinchy, Nancy Ruld Goldberger, and Jill Mattuck Tarule, *Women's Ways of Knowing: The Development of Self, Voice and Mind* (New York: Basic, 1986). This research has primarily focused on white, middle-class women. There is mixed evidence that this holds for other groups of women, particularly in moral orientations. See Carol B. Stack, "Different Voices, Different Visions: Gender, Culture, and Moral Reasoning," in Ginsburg Faye and Anna Lowenhaupt Tsing, eds., *Uncertain Terms: Negotiating Gender in American Culture* (Boston: Beacon Press, 1990), pp. 19–27. However, Patricia Hill Collins suggests that concrete experience, use of dia-

logue, an ethic of caring, and personal accountability represent four Afrocentric criteria for assessing the truth claims of Black women's standpoint and feminist thought. These characteristics closely resemble what Belenky et al. and other feminists call women's modes of knowing (Particia Hill Collins, *Black Feminist Thought: Knowledge, Consciousness, and the Politics of Empowerment* [Boston: Unwin Hyman, 1990]). However, no matter the conclusions of any of these studies, it should be remembered that research focuses on general trends among members of a group, not on exclusive behavior of each individual within a group.

49. Eleni Bastéa, "Inherited Space/Created Space: Language, Gender and Architecture," in *Socio-Environmental Metamorphoses: Builtscape Landscape Ethnoscape Euroscape,* proceedings of the Twelfth International Association for People-Environment Studies Conference, Marmaras, Chalkidiki, Greece, July 11–14, 1992 (Thessaloníki: Aristotle University of Thessaloníki, Greece, 1992), vol. 5, 148–52.

50. For monographs reviewing the material, as well as providing each author's analysis, see Dolores Hayden, *Redesigning the American Dream* (New York: Norton, 1984); Daphne Spain, *Gendered Spaces* (Chapel Hill: University of North Carolina Press, 1992); Weisman, *Discrimination by Design.*

51. Weisman, *Discrimination by Design.*

52. Beatriz Colomina, "Intimacy and Spectacle: The Interior of Loos," in John Whiteman, Jeffrey Kipnis, and Richard Burdett, eds., *Strategies in Architectural Thinking* (Cambridge, Mass.: MIT Press, 1992).

53. Beatriz Colomina, "The Split Wall: Domestic Voyeurism," in Beatriz Colomina, ed., *Sexuality and Space* (Princeton, N.J.: Princeton Architectural Press, 1992), p. 98.

54. Doreen Massey criticizes Edward Soja's *Postmodern Geographies* (London: Verso, 1989) and Harvey's *The Condition of Postmodernity* (Cambridge, Mass.: Blackwell, 1989) for their exclusionary, undemocratic style and construction, the assumption of universals that are in fact particulars, and a politics that assumes the only enemy is capitalism. Doreen Massey, "Flexible Sexism," *Environment and Planning D: Society and Space* 9 (1991).

55. Dolores Hayden, "The American Sense of Place and the Politics of Space," in David G. DeLong, Helen Searing, and Robert A. M. Stern, eds., *American Architecture: Innovation and Tradition* (New York: Rizzoli, 1986), p. 187.

56. Joan Acker, "Hierarchies, Jobs, Bodies: A Theory of Gendered Organizations," *Gender and Society* 4, no. 2 (1990).

57. Judy B. Rosener, "Ways Women Lead," *Harvard Business Review* 68, no. 6 (1990).

58. While the reasons for this difference have not been explored (recruitment, selection bias, self confirming prophecies, socialization, and so on), a lot of women embrace the theory. But some feminist critics warn that women may be embracing this position because it recognizes that they have something of value. Conversely men may also embrace this position because it offers an easy way of dealing with women without having to surrender any of their power or privilege.

59. See Ahrentzen and Anthony, "Sex, Stars, and Studios." By and large these speculations are assuming white, middle-class women, reflecting the demographics of the architectural profession. In 1984, of the AIA's 42,000 members only 7 were black women! Ten years later there was not much change: 361, or .64 percent, of the regular AIA 43,219 members are women of color; 3,494, or 8 percent, are white women. Data from Renee Kemp-Rotan, "Being a Black, Female Architect in a White, Male Profession," *Progressive Architecture,* February 1984, p. 11; Jean Barber, American Institute of Architects, Washington, D.C., January 1995 figures.

60. A number of other scholars have developed typological schemes for designating different feminist positions. For readings summarizing a variety of feminist perspectives (and using their own typological schemes), see Rosemarie Tong, *Feminist Thought: A Comprehensive Introduction* (Boulder, Colo.: Westview Press, 1989); Josephine Donovan, *Feminist Theory: The Intellectual Traditions of American Feminism* (New York: Continuum,

1991); Deborah L. Rhode, "Theoretical Perspectives on Sexual Difference," in Deborah L. Rhode, ed., *Theoretical Perspectives on Sexual Difference* (New Haven, Conn.: Yale University Press, 1990); Alison M. Jaggar and Paul Rotherberg Struhl, *Feminist Frameworks* (New York: McGraw-Hill, 1978); Sandra Harding, *The Science Question in Feminism* (Ithaca, N.Y.: Cornell University Press). While I have spent considerably more space in this chapter providing examples of the contextual feminist position than the other two, it is in part because there are fewer reviews of this position in the feminist architectural literature. It is also a "newer" position than the others.

61. American Architectural Foundation, *That Exceptional One: Women in American Architecture, 1888–1988* (Washington, D.C.: American Architectural Foundation, American Institute of Architects, 1988); Matilda McQuaid, "Educating for the Future: A Growing Archive on Women in Architecture," in Berkeley and McQuaid, eds., *Architecture: A Place for Women.*

62. Sandra Harding, "How the Women's Movement Benefits Science: Two Views," *Women's Studies International Forum* 12, no. 3 (1989): 280.

63. Catherine A. MacKinnon, "Legal Perspectives on Sexual Difference," in Rhode, ed., *Theoretical Perspectives on Sexual Difference.*

64. Ibid., p. 219.

65. Ellen Perry Berkeley, personal communication, 1992.

66. Bell hooks, Preface to *Feminist Theory: From Margin to Center* (Boston: South End Press, 1984).

67. Nancy J. Chodorow, "What Is the Relation between Psychoanalytic Feminism and the Psychoanalytic Psychology of Women?" in Rhode, ed., *Theoretical Perspectives of Sexual Difference.*

68. The "validity" of such research is still controversial and subject to methodological and sample selection limitations that restrict the generalizability of the claims. But some research does show that women are more concerned than men with human relationships, that professional women may have greater sensitivity for moral issues than their male counterparts, that many women express leadership and management skills that are more egalitarian and less authoritarian, and that women are more likely than men to be politically concerned with issues of war and poverty. For a review, see Nel Noddings, "Ethics from the Standpoint of Women," in Rhode, ed., *Theoretical Perspectives of Sexual Difference.*

69. Suzanne Gordon, *Prisoners of Men's Dreams* (Boston: Little, Brown, 1991).

70. Karen A. Franck, "A Feminist Approach to Architecture: Acknowledging Women's Ways of Knowing," in Berkeley and McQuaid, eds., *Architecture: A Place for Women.* Weisman in *Discrimination by Design* also suggests a cultural feminist orientation in architecture. Her contention that women and men design differently is anchored in the different ways women and men develop psychologically and morally, referring to those psychological theories that explain male gender identity as being critically tied to separation from the mother, while female gender identity depends upon a continuing identification with the mother. She contends that these different frames of reference are not necessarily manifest in the use of different spatial forms and building technologies, but rather in the different social and ethical contexts in which women and men are likely to conceptualize and design buildings and spaces. She exemplifies this with Eileen Gray's work.

71. Franck acknowledges that the evidence for such object-relations assertions is suggestive, but asks readers to test these assertions with their own experiences rather than by the lacking scientific evidence.

72. Eileen Gray, quoted in Weisman, *Discrimination by Design,* p. 30; Ellen Shoshes, *The Design Process* (New York: Whitney Library of Design, 1991).

73. Cited in Adrienne Gans, "The War and Peace of the Vietnam Memorials," *American Image* 44, no. 4 (1985): 316–17.

74. Mimi Lobell, "The Buried Treasure: Women's Ancient Architectural Heritage," in Berkeley and McQuaid, eds., *Architecture: A Place for Women.*

75. Susan Doubilet, "P/A Reader Poll: Women in Architecture," *Progressive Architecture*, 1989, pp. 15–17.

76. Chodorow, "What Is the Relation?"

77. Catherine MacKinnon, *Feminism Unmodified: Discourses on Life and Law* (Cambridge, Mass: Harvard University Press, 1987).

78. Ibid., p. 77.

79. Evelyn Brooks Higginbotham, "African-American Women's History and the Metalanguage of Race," *Signs* 17, no. 2 (1992).

80. Collins, *Black Feminist Thought.*

81. Collins, "Reply," *Gender and Society* 6, no. 3 (1992).

82. Adrienne Rich, *On Lies, Secrets, and Silence: Selected Prose, 1966–1978* (New York: Norton, 1979).

83. Elizabeth V. Spelman, *Inessential Woman: Problems of Exclusion in Feminist Thought* (Boston: Beacon, 1988).

84. Charles A. Jencks, *The Language of Post-Modern Architecture* (London: Academy Editions, 1978).

85. Liz Bondi, "Gender Symbols and Urban Landscapes," *Progress in Human Geography* 16, no. 2 (1992).

86. My labeling of this feminist orientation as contextual has no prior feminist reference. The labeling does *not* reference the term "contextual" as used in architectural discourse to refer to physical compatibility of styles or to regional contextualism. *The label contextual here derives from social, not architectural, theory.* This feminist position incorporates the thinking of many feminists (sometimes qualified as radical, gender schema, sociological, pragmatist, postcolonial, or poststructuralist), particularly Teresa Lauretis, Catherine MacKinnon, Cynthia Fuchs Epstein, bell hooks, Charlene Haddock Seigfried, Martha Minow, and Deborah Rhode, as well as theoretical orientations of social constructionism, structuration, and pragmatism. At first glance, the contextual feminist position may appear to be a gender-flavored postmodernism. Postmodernism is inclusionary, allowing multiple interpretations of every social phenomenon. Postmodernism celebrates the particular. But, as discussed later, the transformative strand of contextual feminism takes a position. A commitment to plural and provisional accounts does not necessarily commit one to agnosticism toward the accounts offered. Although all understandings may be partial, some are more incomplete than others. Further, not all theories are respectful of evidence or empowering.

87. Margaret Crawford, "In Favor of the Fringe," *Progressive Architecture,* March 1993.

88. Richard Rorty, quoted in Haddock Seigfried, "Shared Communities of Interest: Feminism and Pragmatism," *Hypatia* 8, no. 2 (1993).

89. Jennifer Bloomer, "Big Jugs," in Arthur and Marielouise Kroker, eds., *The Hysterical Male* (New York: St. Martin's Press, 1991), p. 22.

90. Margaret Crawford claims that the discourse dismisses or silences women who do not speak in the same dense, difficult language. Edward Ball calls it a game of decipherment. Robert Sargent sees that the complex, narrowly academic theory they use risks alienation. While argument by etymological analysis can be irritating, Sargent also notes that women's involvement in this discourse—predominately male-dominated and male-devised—staves off the sexual dichotomy of women doing practical criticism and men doing theoretical criticism. However, if this be the case, then I believe it is certainly an appeasement to liberal feminism, a contradiction of cultural feminism, and an exasperation to transformational feminists who advocate social structural change. Crawford, "In Favor of the Fringe."

91. Bell hooks, "Feminism: A Transformational Politic," in Rhode, ed., *Theoretical Perspectives of Sexual Difference.*

92. Marilyn French, "Is There a Feminist Aesthetic?" in Hilda Hein and Carolyn Korsmeyer, eds., *Aesthetics in Feminist Perspective* (Bloomington: Indiana University Press, 1993).

93. Patti Lather, "Research as Praxis," *Harvard Educational Review* 56, no. 3 (1986).
94. Lois Nesbitt, "Postscript," in Andrea Kahn, ed., *Drawing/Building/Text* (New York: Princeton Architectural Press, 1991).
95. Audre Lorde, *Sister Outsider* (Freedom, Calif.: Crossing Press, 1984), p. 112.
96. Bell hooks, *Yearning: Race, Gender, and Cultural Politics* (Boston: South End Press, 1990). Many premises expressed in transformative feminism are linked with American strands of pragmatism. The pragmatists aimed at democratic inclusiveness and fought the development of a specialized disciplinary jargon inaccessible except to a specialist elite. Further, pragmatism is not simply a descriptive stance, nor only a critical one, but it also assumes reconstructive positions. Thus it ties in well with the purposes of many transformative/contextual feminist efforts and other environmental designers seeking social change and justice. It also ties theory with method and application, because it claims that theory without application/praxis is useless.
97. Rich, *On Lies, Secrets, and Silence.*
98. Hooks, "Feminism."
99. Richard Rorty, "Feminism and Pragmatism," *Michigan Quarterly Review* 30, no. 2 (1991).
100. Mary Douglas, *How Institutions Think* (Syracuse, N.Y.: Syracuse University Press, 1986), p. 91.
101. Robert Goodman, *After the Planners* (New York: Touchstone, 1971).
102. For description and analyses of architects as social change advocates, see C. Richard Hatch, *The Scope of Social Architecture* (New York: Van Nostrand Reinhold, 1984); Tony Schuman, "Forms of Resistance: Politics, Culture, and Architecture," in Dutton, ed., *Voices in Architectural Education.*
103. Kenneth Frampton, "Toward a Critical Regionalism: Six Points for an Architecture of Resistance," in Hal Foster, ed., *The Anti-Aesthetic: Essays on Postmodern Culture* (Seattle: Bay Press, 1983), p. 25.
104. Charlotte Bunch, "The Reform Tool Kit," in Charlotte Bunch, Jane Flax, Alexa Freeman, Nancy Hartsock, and Mary-Helen Mautner, eds., *Building Feminist Theory: Essays from QUEST* (New York: Longman, 1981).
105. Jacqueline Leavitt, "Feminist Advocacy Planning in the 1980s," in B. Checkoway, ed., *Strategic Perspectives on Planning Practice* (Lexington, Mass.: Lexington Books, 1986). Another example of feminist advocacy planning is the National Congress of Neighborhood Women (NCNW), a community-based women's organization with a central office in Brooklyn, New York. Since 1974, this nationwide grassroots women's group has dealt with housing, education, economic development, and employment at the local level. Neighborhood women are given space in which to ask questions and overcome intimidation by professional jargon. The very act of organizing a dialogue in the form of a national institute begins to give women a sense of power and strength. The institute provides a vehicle for discussing and formulating ways to challenge economic and patriarchal aspects of current or proposed policy.
106. Paul Davidoff, "Advocacy and Pluralism in Planning," *Journal of the American Institute of Planners* 31 (1965); Barbara Bryant Solomon, *Black Empowerment: Social Work in Oppressed Communities* (New York: Columbia University Press, 1976); J. Rappoport, "In Praise of Paradox: A Social Policy of Empowerment over Prevention," *American Journal of Community Psychology* 9, no. 1 (1981).
107. Elisheva Sadan and Arza Churchman, "Empowerment and Professional Practice," paper presented at the twenty-fourth annual conference of the Environmental Design Research Association, Chicago, March 1993.
108. Frances Bradshaw, "Working with Women," in Matrix, ed., *Making Space: Women and the Man-Made Environment* (London: Pluto Press, 1984).
109. Janie Grote, "Matrix: A Radical Approach to Architecture," *Journal of Architectural and Planning Research* 9, no. 2 (1992).

SHERRY AHRENTZEN

110. Women's Institute for Housing and Economic Development, *Making It Ourselves: A Primer on Women's Housing and Business Development* (Boston: Women's Institute for Housing and Economic Development, 1992).

111. Joan Forrester Sprague, *More than Housing: Lifeboats for Women and Children* (Boston: Butterworth, 1991).

112. Van Slyck, "Women in Architecture."

113. Elizabeth Kamarch Minnich, *Transforming Knowledge* (Philadelphia: Temple University Press, 1990), pp. 28–29.

114. Pollock, *Vision and Difference.*

115. Wright, "Women in American Architecture."

116. Diane Favro, "Sincere and Good: The Architectural Practice of Julia Morgan," *Journal of Architectural and Planning Research* 9, no. 2 (1992).

117. Van Slyck, "Women in Architecture."

118. Pollock, *Vision and Difference.*

119. Dell Upton, "Architectural History or Landscape History?" *Journal of Architectural Education* 44, no. 4 (1991).

120. Barbara L. Allen, "Reconstituting the Vanished: A Black Feminist Critique of a Franco-African Plantation in Antebellum Louisiana," in John Edwards, ed., *A Community of Diverse Interests: Proceedings of the Eighty-second Annual Meeting of Association of Collegiate Schools of Architecture* (Washington, D.C.: ACSA Press, 1994), p. 80.

121. Alice Friedman, "A Feminist Practice in Architectural History," *Design Book Review* 25 (1992).

122. Alice Friedman, "A House Is Not a Home: Hollyhock House as 'Art-Theater-Garden,'" *Journal of the Society of Architectural Historians* 60, no. 3 (1992): 246–47.

123. Friedman has another provocative investigation into the role of a woman patron, Bess of Hardwick, in Alice Friedman, "Architecture, Authority, and the Female Gaze: Planning and Representation in the Early Modern Country House," *Assemblage* 18 (1992).

124. Marsha Ritzdorf, "A Feminist Analysis of Gender and Residential Zoning in the United States," in Irwin Altman and Arza Churchman, eds., *Women and the Environment* (New York: Plenum Press, 1994); Marsha Ritzdorf, "Women and the City: Land Use and Zoning Issues," *Urban Resources* 3, no. 2 (1986).

125. Thomas A. Dutton, ed., *Voices in Architectural Education: Cultural Politics and Pedagogy* (New York: Bergin and Garvey, 1991).

126. Jane Roland Martin, "Becoming Educated: A Journey of Alienation or Integration?" *Journal of Education* 167, no. 3 (1985).

127. Sharon Sutton, "Creating a Safe Space in Which to Grow," in Association of Collegiate Schools of Architecture, ed., *Architecture: Back . . . to . . . Life* (Washington, D.C.: ACSA, 1991); Sharon Sutton, "Year(s) of Women's Leadership in K-12 Design Education," *Network News (of the Urban Network)* 4, no. 1 (1993).

128. Sutton, "Year(s) of Women's Leadership."

129. Ibid.

130. Sherry Boland Ahrentzen, "Birth Settings: A Perspective on Our Progress," *Women and Environments* 8, no. 1 (1986).

131. Annmarie Adams, *Architecture and Reproduction: The Landscape of Middle-Class Pregnancy and Childbirth, 1870–1900* (Report of the Center for Environmental Design Research, University of California, Berkeley, n.d).

132. For example, Ahrentzen, "Birth Settings"; P. E. Sumner and C. R. Phillips, eds. *Birthing Rooms: Concept and Reality* (St. Louis: Mosby, 1981); R. W. Wertz and D. C. Wertz, *Lying-In: A History of Childbirth in America* (New York: Schocken, 1977); S. Kitzinger and J. A. Davis, *The Place of Birth* (New York: Oxford University Press, 1978).

133. Bianca Lepori, *La nascita e i suoi luoghi* (Como, Italy: Red Studio Adazionale, 1992).

134. Roberta Feldman, "Women in Architecture: Fitting in or Making a Difference," *Chicago Architecture* 9 (1991).

135. Gilles Deleuze and Félix Guattari, *A Thousand Plateaus: Capitalism and Schizophrenia* (Minneapolis: University of Minnesota Press, 1987).
136. Maxine Hong Kingston, *The Woman Warrier* (New York: Knopf, 1976).
137. Luce Irigaray, *This Sex Which Is Not One* (Ithaca, N.Y.: Cornell University Press, 1985).
138. Karen A. Franck, "Deconstructing, Reconstructing Self and Environment," in *Socio-Environmental Metamorphoses: Builtscape Landscape Ethnoscape Euroscape,* pp. 263–72 (see n. 49).
139. From Walt Whitman, "Song of Myself," in *Leaves of Grass* (New York: Viking Press, 1855).
140. "Physicians Begin a Program to Combat Family Violence," *New York Times,* October 17, 1991, p. A16.
141. Appropriation of space is not a solitary process; the individual actions and meanings always are realized within the broader society. While space appropriation is typically seen in terms of the individual dwelling, other researchers studying working-class and lower-income communities have challenged this view. Actions and experiences indicative of the appropriation of homeplace extend well beyond the confines of the dwelling into the neighborhood environs. Work by Roberta Feldman and Susan Stall and Jacqueline Leavitt and Susan Saegert demonstrates public housing residents' appropriation of homeplace, focusing on the struggles of households *against* extra-household institutions, organizations, or individuals. Roberta Feldman and Susan Stall, "The Politics of Space Appropriation: A Case Study of Women's Struggles for Homeplace in Chicago Public Housing," in Altman and Churchman, eds., *Women and the Environment*; Jacqueline Leavitt and Susan Saegert, *From Abandonment to Hope: Community Households in Harlem* (New York: Columbia University Press, 1990).
142. Caroline O. N. Moser, "Women, Human Settlements, and Housing: A Conceptual Framework for Analysis and Policy-Making," in Caroline O. N. Moser and Linda Peake, eds., *Women, Human Settlements, and Housing* (London: Tavistock, 1987), pp. 30–31.
143. Lynda H. Schneekloth, "Partial Utopian Visions: Feminist Reflections on the Field," in Altman and Churchman, eds., *Women and the Environment.*
144. Donna Haraway, "Situated Knowledges: The Science Questions in Feminism and the Privilege of Partial Perspective," *Feminist Studies* 14, no. 3 (1988): 575–600.
145. Schneekloth, "Partial Utopian Visions," p. 17.
146. Ibid., p. 19.
147. Alison M. Jaggar, "Sexual Differences and Sexual Equality," in Rhode, ed., *Theoretical Perspectives of Sexual Difference,* p. 253.
148. Gloria Steinem, *Outrageous Acts and Everyday Rebellions* (New York: Holt, Rinehart and Winston, 1983).
149. Hooks, *Yearning.*
150. Alberto Pérez-Gómez, Introduction to Louise Pelletier and Alberto Pérez-Gómez, eds., *Architecture, Ethics, and Technology* (Montreal: McGill–Queen's University Press, 1994), pp. 4–5.
151. Cornel West, *The American Evasion of Philosophy: A Genealogy of Pragmatism* (Madison: University of Wisconsin Press, 1989).
152. Yi-Fu Tuan, *Segmented Worlds and Self* (Minneapolis: University of Minnesota Press, 1982).
153. Pérez-Gómez, "Introduction," pp. 13–14.

SECOND NATURE: ON THE SOCIAL BOND OF ECOLOGY AND ARCHITECTURE

ANTIECOLOGY

Ecology and architecture make strange, but star-crossed, bedfellows. The former is the study of how all things in the natural world are related to each other, while the latter is in its essentials the reaction of the human imagination to nature's inhospitality to dwelling. By extension, the production of buildings, cities, and regional infrastructures has directly and indirectly provided the impetus for technological and industrial transformations that have thoroughly transformed the natural world. Because the impact of human interventions during the last two centuries has been so pervasive, it is difficult to claim that such a thing as "nature" still exists.[1]

The appeal to ecology within the discourse of architecture arouses a historic paradox, since every act of building is inherently antiecological to the degree it induces a displacement of "natural" relationships. At its most confident, architecture is portrayed as a second nature. As Louis I. Kahn so succinctly put it, "Architecture is what nature cannot make."[2] Among the various intellectual tactics that attempt to mitigate architecture's antiecological position are the symbolic representation of nature in architecture, the use of built form to imitate or enhance natural features, or the recourse to theories of nature as analogues in design methods. Leaky roofs, cracking foundations, spalling surfaces, infestations of insects, mold formations, fires, floods, earthquakes, and the like are nature's rebuttal to any architectural position.

Since the social movements of the 1960s, ecology has become an ineluctable political issue and has been admitted as an awkward guest in architectural theory. The alarm over industrial pollution, the disgust with consumer culture's wastefulness, and the overall recognition that human technology has accelerated entropy to the point of endangering the survival of the species are part of the social concerns that have inspired a mandate for "ecological architecture." Entropy, also known as the second law of thermodynamics, a theory according to which all matter and energy, once expended, are dissipated, has become the basis of a collective sense of guilt.[3] Although entropy is theoretically irreversible, there are various conservationist strategies for agriculture, industry, and urbanism—the three major human sources of environmental depletion—to lower entropy and encourage a "sustainable" environment.[4] The attempt to curtail accelerated entropy is both an ethical and a technological matter. Ethically the ecological position argues for the rights of nature against the onslaught of development; technologically, the waste and inefficiency of high-entropy design is faulted as a misappropriation of resources. It is in this frequently contentious betrothal, between *moral impera-tives* and the *desire for material well-being,* that the most important critical positions on ecology and architecture emerge.

Like other aspects of building that require pragmatic solutions, the question of sustainability in architecture is usually breached through technical rather than historical or social criteria. Yet like any other strain of theoretical reasoning, it is caught in a skein of precedents, some to be explicated from written documents, others from built fabric. That passive solar principles, for example, were intuitively practiced since the time of the most ancient cultures until the advent of artificial climate control, yet were not formulated into a conspicuous body of written testimony, is an obvious instance where a theory of ecological architecture must be interpolated retroactively from the measurable built remains.[5] In many preindustrial cultures natural forces were (and still are) commonly treated in a mythopoeic, animistic way. Theories of building from around the world, including those described in the Chinese manual, the *Chou-li,* dating from the first century B.C., or the similarly ancient Sanskrit treatise, the *Manasara,* as well as the principles discernible in the practice of the ancient Greeks, call for the planning of buildings as a sacred act that will be respectful of these forces.[6] The survival of *Feng shui* in parts of China and the ritual placement of a growing tree on the top of a new building during its construction in northern European countries are evocative reminders of this traditional reverence for the transcending power of nature. Industrialism and the more competitive aspects of capitalist production have tended to deny architecture its sacred and metaphoric value, which has been an instrumental phase in the transition to high-entropy building practices.

Previous to the widespread reproduction of Isaac Watt's steam engine in the late eighteenth century, societies generally built in a much more sustainable manner, and the per capita consumption of energy was minuscule compared with that of modernized populations. Currently the combined impact of buildings and urban organization in industrialized societies plays *the* major role in the budgeting of resources. This aspect of development, which seems at once uncontrollable and yet is the essence of modern policymaking, infuses the question of ecology with social and political imperatives.

Disenchantment with the environmental profligacy of the industrial present has led one strain of ecologically inclined architects to a willfully naive idealization of the low-entropy past. The presumed autarky of the preindustrial village has been optimistically rehabilitated as a mythical alternative to the irresponsible waste of the metropolis. Included in this contingent would be architectural theorists such as Christopher Alexander and Leon Krier, who, while quite different in their approaches — the former advocating a neovernacular architecture, the latter a neo-

RICHARD INGERSOLL

classical — both embrace a systematic noncooperation with the forces of modernity.[7] Nostalgic incantations of this sort, as much as they may pamper a collective guilty conscience about development, always involve a selective and mystifying use of the past that precludes the dynamic social processes of history, which are inextricably engaged with those of nature. The static historic model set in the fluid multidimensional reality of time severely limits it as a sufficient basis for dealing with the complex problems of the present.

While many important lessons can be gathered from the past on how to build and how to conserve resources, it should not be forgotten that preindustrial societies, despite their lower entropy, have been responsible for cycles of ecological calamities, such as the salinization during the first millenium B.C. of the Tigris and Euphrates Delta due to overintensive settlement and agriculture,[8] the deforestation of the Dalmatian coast to furnish the piles for Venetian palaces, and the recurrence of bubonic plague and cholera facilitated by crowding and inefficient waste management in most European cities until the nineteenth century. A return to the preindustrial past might aspire to redeem the future from high entropy, but it is doubtful that such a move would be made without bringing the baggage of the scientific and industrial revolutions. The infrastructure needed for the latter necessarily relegates the nostalgic models to an epidermal or aesthetic solution.

Probably the greatest factor inhibiting ecology from becoming more than a marginal element of architectural discourse is the endemic utopianism attached to it. Utopian solutions, as first criticized by Marx and Engels, are counterproductive to real social progress because they evade the political process it would necessitate to achieve social goals. The sociological naïveté of most utopian models invariably implies some sort of totalitarian subtext about how to achieve and maintain the new system, and this new system is less likely to permit change than the one it proposes to replace. In the case of ecological utopias, the matter of how to effect a transition to sustainability within the constraints of late-twentieth-century capitalism without betraying citizens' rights is immensely complex.

Ecology movements have secured legislative victories and influenced changes in lifestyles. In practice, however, local advances in environmental regulation are often made to the detriment of environmental quality elsewhere because of the flexibility and dissimulating tactics available to multinational corporations. The banning of a substance like DDT, or more recently chloroflourocarbons, in one society, with the subsequent unloading of the substance in an unmonitored country, has been standard procedure. E. F. Schumacher's well-intended slogan for environmentalism to "act local, think global" has in a nefarious way been co-opted during the last two decades by the forces of development in its process of "globalization."[9]

A project for sustainability thus requires global strategies that can keep pace with the globalization of capital. But considering the demise of planned economies during the 1980s, which have been mostly abandoned to the unpredictable consequences of deregularization, it is small wonder that ecologists are prone to utopian solutions. Architecture in the name of ecology has attracted more than its share of utopians. If the neovillages proposed by the aforementioned Alexander and Krier can be offered as examples of nostalgic utopianism, there are at least two other strains of utopian efforts that avoid historical precedents in favor of a functionalist model. In one case building technology is limited to the lowest expenditure of resources possible—for example, in works such as Michael Reynolds's "Earthships" (mud-covered houses that use old tires and cans as primary building materials) or in the fantastic, labor-intensive concrete shell constructions of Paolo Soleri at Arcosanti.[10] This trend, which involves a righteous retreat from industrial and metropolitan civilization to sparsely settled desert environs, belongs to the world-weary tradition of monasticism. The constraints on the conventions of social life and the possibilities of construction only in remote desert areas, however, make such environmentally attractive solutions unfeasible under other conditions.

The other functionalist approach is the pursuit of maximum efficiency through the highest use of available resources, a path predicated by R. Buckminster Fuller and practiced by, among others, Sir Norman Foster. This leads to the project of a technocratic utopia. Fuller was responsible for one of the most unifying metaphors of the ecology movement, "Spaceship Earth," for which the technocratic implications are obvious.[11] His theory is lodged in the belief that it is not technology that is at fault, but the incumbent inefficiencies of up to 95 percent wasted energy that need to be resolved. The industrial and managerial organization necessary for Fuller's models, however, implies a world where technological means would probably become more important than social ends.

The utopian solutions for the reduction of entropy, from nostalgic retreats to high-tech assertions, have led to many spectacular architectural hybrids, such as the mud-covered earthships or Fuller's dymaxion house, a lightweight prototype for mass production, but thus far they have only related to the rest of the built environment as intriguing exceptions. Utopian responses to the environmental crisis such as these, in which a new kind of architectural technique is offered as the solution to problems of great social and political complexity, subscribe to a form of *architectural determinism,* the belief that architecture controls social relations or behavior. They remain economically unrealistic on a large scale because they are conceived outside of the general economic systems of production and cannot be integrated easily without rupturing the system, nor do they account for a strategy of systematic transformation.

While populist attempts to assuage the antiecological condition of architecture usually rely on a preindustrial ethos that precludes the social and cultural complexities of metropolitan life, high-tech alternatives require the intercession of a technological elite that will bypass the decision-making process of the *polis.* Both extremes, while they offer attractive models, are delusional and anathema to the

RICHARD INGERSOLL

ideals of the liberal city. Until the problem of high entropy is inscribed in the social and political language of cities, a task in which utopian architectural thinking
can have some influence, it will be difficult to forecast strategies involving architecture that are accountable, responsible, or consistent with the ethic of the public realm. Which is to say that unless an ecology-conscious architecture is rooted
in social practices, it will have little chance for making a significant impact on the
production of the built environment, because, to paraphrase Fernand Braudel,
technology alone is never the cause of social change, it is always implemented by
social forces.[12]

ARCHITECTURE AS A SECOND NATURE

Although preindustrial architecture generally performed with a greater responsibility to the natural environment, the twentieth-century notion of *ecological* relationships, let alone references to nature, is conspicuously absent from earlier architectural theory. As Françoise Choay concludes in her study of Renaissance
architectural theory, unlike any other early culture it "assigned to the organization of built space an autonomous discursive formation."[13] Aspects of nature, such
as growth, proportionality, symmetry, and patterns of fluidity, were generally recognized as analogues to be emulated rather than systems to conserve or to integrate.
Architecture and the city became constituent elements of a socially constructed
"second nature" distinct from the world as found.

   The theoretical autonomy of architecture can be traced to Vitruvius (circa 25 B.C.),
whose treatise, while probably not widely followed in its own day, became the basis
of the Western canon that developed since the fifteenth century. Vitruvius was
primarily concerned with establishing the rules of architecture, describing building types, and explaining proportional relationships, in particular those of the
columns. The propriety of the classical orders became the theoretical obsession
in the Vitruvian revival, which set architecture in an ever greater realm of autonomy. Vitruvius, when he writes of nature, invests it with a mythological respect,
associating the initial act of entropy, the discovery of fire, with the origins of architecture. This Promethean scenario that combined building a fire with building a
house was reelaborated frequently during the Renaissance and might be considered as architecture's original sin in terms of ecology.[14] Although the practice of
architecture in Hellenistic times was demonstrably attentive to solar orientation,
drainage, and use of natural materials, these were negligible issues on a discursive
level. Vitruvius offers advice about site and wind conditions for founding cities
and mentions divination rituals, such as examining the entrails of animals that
have grazed on a site being prepared for a settlement, but the majority of his treatise isolates architecture as an autonomous event involving geometry, typology,
stereotomy, and artifice.

Leon Battista Alberti, the greatest fifteenth-century interpreter of Vitruvius, was not much more concerned with natural processes in *De re aedificatoria* (1451). Alberti clarified the Vitruvian principles of architecture and opened up the theory by demonstrating the options that can exist for every design problem. He only slightly addresses what could be considered ecological matters, however, when he writes on the siting of cities, always qualifying his judgments with erudite references to ancient authors and rarely providing direct observations of nature. "And so the foremost authors of antiquity," he explains, intimating Plato and Aristotle's models of autarky, "...considered the ideal location for a city to be one that provided for all its requirements from its own territory and would not need to import anything."[15] In Alberti's treatise, the autonomy of architecture is heightened by his avoidance of natural metaphors: he compares the city first to a house and vice versa, and later to a ship, confining design to geometric and technical analogues. When he compares a building to the body, a famous trope derived from Vitruvius (Book III, 1), later immortalized in Leonardo's drawing of the "Vitruvian man," whose body is inscribed in a circle and a square, he treats it in terms of proportionality. Alberti concludes "that the building appears a single, integral, and well-composed body, rather than a collection of extraneous parts."[16] Architecture is *analogous* to nature: as a second nature it remains conceptually distinct as the product of human reason. Alberti's chief criterion for architecture is essentially an abstraction of nature, found in his theory of *concinnitas,* concerning appropriate proportions and the fitness of parts to the whole.[17]

Alberti's theory of *concinnitas* argued for a type of architectural order that can be understood as "organic," in that the ordering principles of a single building can be projected onto the expansion of an entire city. But his organic order of building is separate from the organic order of nature. In this vein he writes in reference to the merits of round temples, "Nature delights primarily in the circle, need I mention the earth, the stars, the animals, their nests and so on, all of which she has made circular?"[18] Through this type of analogy, rules for architecture could be extrapolated to validate it as an abstract, second nature. It is characteristic of Alberti, who had complex interests, that in some of his nonarchitectural texts he will allude to an entropy-like problem that is not included in his architectural treatise. In *Theogenius,* for instance, he alludes to the vanity of human enterprise: "While the other animals are content with what is given them, man is always investigating new things to infest his world."[19]

There were other writers during the Renaissance who seemed more attuned to nature, but they had much less influence than Alberti. The eccentric treatise of Filarete, the architectural notes of Leonardo da Vinci, and the enigmatic novel *Hypnerotomachia Polyfili* all communicate a greater sensitivity to the integration of natural processes in relation to building.[20] Leonardo, in particular, was an astute observer of natural phenomena. In his diaries he conceived of multileveled buildings and cities with water rushing through them the way that bodily fluids circulate through living organisms. When considering how to replan plague-ridden Milan in the 1490s, Leonardo arrived at a proleptic scheme of regional scale that was likewise more akin to the organization of organisms than of the traditions of city making. He proposed the decentralization of the city into ten generously distributed satellite towns of five thousand dwellings, each served by an efficient system of canals to drain off sewage and facilitate transportation.[21]

Filarete, writing a decade earlier, begins his treatise with an anthropomorphic analogy: "I will show you how a building is exactly like a living man." His radially planned ideal city of Sforzinda alternated streets with canals for efficient transportation and sewerage, although it lacked the sectional complexity of Leonardo's schemes.[22] The models of Leonardo and Filarete would have reduced densities and improved hygienic and transportational infrastructures, but they had little direct impact on the planning of European cities or the theoretical consideration of nature in respect to architecture, as neither was published until the twentieth century. The *Hypnerotomachia Polyfili*, printed in 1500, had a wide diffusion as one of the first novels ever published, and some would claim the first printed architectural illustrations, but the message of the book, which involves a kind of initiation to the natural world, was and remains a mystery. Even Alberti's treatise, published in printed form in 1485, had only a limited influence on the more formally oriented canon, which developed in the sixteenth century with Serlio, Palladio, and Vignola, of a rational and rhetorically correct organization of inert materials disengaged from the realm of nature.

A different agenda for the city, treating it almost exclusively according to military concerns, emerged during the mid–sixteenth century both because of changes in the structure of the state from self-governing city-states to national monarchies and because of the convulsive innovations in ballistic technology. Francesco de Marchi's treatise on fortifications is exemplary of a trend that treats the city as a military machine, a hovering and perfectly geometrical figure determined by mechanical responses to lines of fire and the rapid circulation of troops.[23] The competitive demands of the military agenda from this point on encouraged the growing alienation between the natural world and mechanical processes.

Considering the aforementioned tendency toward utopianism of ecologically inclined architects in the twentieth century, it seems appropriate that the first Renaissance treatise to propose a reintegration of urban culture with natural processes should be Thomas More's *Utopia*. Published in Latin in 1516, *Utopia* describes an ideal social organization of a city and its territory. More wrote his fictional dialogue in response to the peasant evictions from the land caused by Henry VIII's rural policies. In his narrative he attempts to imagine a complete alternative to the misappropriation of agricultural lands and the inhumane conditions of crowded cities. His rational solutions envisioned a new egalitarian order in which certain forms of injustice, contingent on greed, poverty, and ignorance, could not survive. The way of life imposed on Utopia, however, presents such severe limits on basic personal freedoms that the book has often been read as a satire. The contradictions of the original Utopia establish a perennial flaw that can be recognized in most utopian projects.

In the protocommunistic society of the island of Utopia the problems of the distribution of wealth, division of labor, and the management of growth are solved comprehensively. When the optimal size of a city is reached, that is, six thousand families (from sixty thousand to a hundred thousand people), a new town is founded on the island, and if the island fills up, colonies are to be founded elsewhere, using military force, if necessary. The island of Utopia was imagined to reach a point of homeostasis with fifty-four cities, no city different from another.[24] Each town was to be located a minimum of twenty-four miles, or a maximum of a day's walk, from any other. All the houses in Utopia are identical, all the towns have the same plan, all the people wear the same clothes — the only changes that will occur in Utopian cities are the obligatory change of house every ten years so that residents will not become possessive about their houses as personal property. Utopian society was predicated on the maintenance of agriculture, and each inhabitant was obliged to serve for two years on a farm before taking up a craft occupation in the city. The city dwellers would also be inducted for agricultural chores at various times of the year when extra labor was needed on the farms.[25] Each neighborhood of a city was organized on a straight street, twenty feet wide, with fifteen houses on either side and ample backyard gardens. A communal house was placed in the middle, where a matron from one of the thirty households was put in charge of cooking for the whole community once a month. There was no private property or need for money in Utopia, where the welfare of each citizen was universally guaranteed. All religious beliefs were tolerated, but the most prevalent belief was Mythraism, which considered the supreme being to be synonymous with nature.

Despite Utopia's sensible alternative to the crowded European city and its attempt to eliminate the social inequities bred by religious and aristocratic privilege, and despite its reference to nature as the ultimate source of reason, the rigidity of its planning was unwittingly intolerant of the diversity and mutability of nature. The lack of accommodation to either the natural or social processes of change lent a frightening, dystopian quality to *Utopia* that was acknowledged by More himself in the many ironies embedded in his text, such as the name of Utopia itself, meaning "nowhere." The work was no doubt intended as a vehicle of critique (at a time when direct criticism was not possible) rather than as an applicable model.

Alberti's flexible rules for design and More's inflexible model for society represent opposing positions in a retroactive debate on how to treat nature: the former alienates nature but allows for adjustments according to circumstance; the latter seeks to preserve a natural balance but does not account for nature's most essential characteristic, that of change. The two positions survived into the nineteenth century with such examples as the rational rules for design proposed by J. N. L. Durand and the formulation of a new communal social order projected by Charles Fourier. Durand's "graphic method" plots standard dimensions of form on a grid with no reference to the natural world; Fourier, in his proposal of the Phalanstery, puts his sixteen-hundred member phalanx of liberated society into a single, Versailles-like building, where individual freedom can be exercised while collective needs are supplied. Durand justified his expedient solutions in architecture in terms of social responsibility as being formally appropriate and respectful of economy; Fourier proposed an architectural solution to contain his new unit of social justice.[26]

Most environmental historians consider the Western humanist tradition, which had its roots in the researches of Renaissance writers like Alberti and More, as the intellectual source of the calamitous path of modern development.[27] The projected conquest of nature through modern science acquired at this time a Faustian subplot involving the redeeming concern for the welfare of humanity, what Marshall Berman so astutely identifies as "the tragedy of development."[28] In this line Francis Bacon's *New Atlantis* (1624) proposed a world made plentiful through a regime of scientists who would institute ways of asserting greater power over nature and eliminating scarcity.[29] The eventual displacement of religious authority by rationalism during the Enlightenment and the application of science to technology established a new ethical frame in which to pursue the exploitation of nature in the name of social justice. The demand for social progress was usually hinged upon material progress and rarely acknowledged the environmental consequences. One of the major ideological tasks of current environmentalism should be to correct this historic rift and resituate the idea of social justice in a dependency on the preservation of nature.

Nature, from the time of Jean-Jacques Rousseau in the mid–eighteenth century, acquired a metaphysical role as the ultimate measure of what is right in the world. If, as Joseph Rykwert has pointed out, Abbé Laugier's primitive hut, the "natural" foundation of his architectural theory, was sited on Rousseau's riverbank (where "natural," preurban man lived happily), Laugier's treatment of nature is nonetheless metaphoric. Natural relationships are used to justify preconceived formal relationships: a thicket of trees can be ordained as the typological progenitor of the peripteral Doric temple, but it is by no means presented as part of an ecosystem.[30] Nature in this paragon is used as a reconfirmation of formal models. The symbolic use of nature reached its climax in the eighteenth-century formulation of the picturesque English garden, such as Stowe or Stourhead, where nature was made to look more "natural" in order to create emotional effects.[31]

In retrospect it seems that the chief reason for the absense of a theory that would integrate architecture with natural processes in the West can be attributed to the prevalence of anthropocentrism in the dominant philosophical and scientific trends. Nature was in this way kept conceptually alien and separate from culture, often in the name of social progress. Architecture as a second nature did not evolve in response to the forces of nature but according to the rational practices of development in a man-centered understanding of the universe.

ECOLOGY BECOMES IMMANENT

The terms "entropy" and "ecology" were both coined in the 1860s, one hundred years after the introduction of Watt's steam engine, and about this time a new sensitivity to nature in architectural theory occurs. The motivations to bring architecture closer to nature derived, on the one hand, from transcendentalist attitudes celebrating the oneness of nature and, on the other, from a moral imperative to find palliatives to the effects of industrialism. The horrific accounts of Manchester in the 1830s and 1840s by Alexis de Tocqueville and Friedrich Engels were indictments both of the extent of environmental degradation and of the inhumane exploitation of the working class.[32] This denunciation of the twin injustices wrought by industrial capitalism established a criterion for a contingency that current environmentalists often prefer to leave obscured: although the crisis of natural conditions can be assessed through scientific means and policies and technologies can be proposed to mitigate its effects, the management of the environment is ultimately a social problem requiring political solutions.

While the interrelatedness of the natural world is a common line of reasoning in most non-Western cosmologies, the reigning positivist mentality of the West could not entertain such a concept until nature had been adequately defined in scientific terms. Although Karl Linnaeus's great work, *Species Plantarum* (1753), is limited to the taxonomy of the realm of plants, it was determinant of a method for future studies in all areas of natural history. His essay "The Economy of Nature" set the coordinates for the future study of ecology. Johann Wolfgang von Goethe, the great poet, naturalist, and connoisseur of architecture, helped to popularize an idea of organicism and holism at the end of the eighteenth century with dictums such as "In organic life nothing is unconnected with the whole."[33] He revived the tragedy of Dr. Faustus for his greatest narrative, *Faust,* which revolves around the question of the use of resources and its relationship to human welfare.[34]

Another key contribution to the development of a theory of ecology was *An Essay on the Principle of Population* by Thomas Malthus, perhaps the first work grounded in scientific method in a distinguished line of apocalyptic prognoses of human development. Malthus's analysis, although not his chiliastic conclusions, served as the source for both Alfred Russell Wallace's and Charles Darwin's independently arrived at theories of natural selection.[35]

With the publication of Darwin's theory of evolution in 1859, the concept of holism in the natural world became canonical.[36] It has not only affected the paradigms of scientific thought in related fields, but has had important repercussions

RICHARD INGERSOLL

on economic and political theories as well, since *The Origin of Species* illustrates the dynamic patterns of natural processes that seem to explain, or in some cases justify, those involving human negotiation.[37] The crucial postulate affecting the social sciences has been whether natural selection occurs more through the agency of "mutual aid" or more through competition for resources in which only the strong survive, the latter leading to what is generally referred to as Social Darwinism.

Elaborating on Darwin's theory of the interrelatedness of species in nature, the German naturalist Ernst Haeckel in 1866 invented for his own analysis of contextual biology the proper name of "ecology." Derived from the Greek word for house, the neologism had important metaphoric implications for architecture: the relationships in the natural world being like the organization of a household and vice versa. This use of an architectural metaphor for a scientific study, however, did not automatically stimulate an ethic of ecology in the discourse of architecture. It is the enduring characteristic of metaphors to keep meanings from ever becoming synonyms. If Haeckel's research ever had a direct influence on design it was in the inspirational capacity of his elaborate drawings of natural morphologies, later used to justify principles of balance and proportionality in architectural form.[38]

Haeckel was fascinated with the compensations among species in the natural world and was one of the first intellectuals to advocate the application of natural principles to the human political realm. He believed that obedience of biological laws would result in an equitable, efficient, and peaceful state.[39] Unfortunately this line of reasoning often has been used by Social Darwinists to support racist theories of political order.[40]

Organicism, as it was coming to be understood by naturalists, had a special appeal to Americans. Henry David Thoreau, in his narrative about life at Walden Pond, popularized a radical awareness of organic relationships and natural correspondences. He offered the construction of his cabin, built with borrowed tools and recycled boards for $28.12, as a polemical alternative to the vain and unnatural inclinations of architecture in the 1850s.[41] The American transcendentalist position was transposed definitively to the realm of architectural theory by Louis Sullivan in his celebrated dictum "Form ever follows function," which consecrated the teleological conclusions of the natural historians. His skyscrapers of the late nineteenth century are designed according to the logic of efficient structures, while the decorative skin laid over the surfaces carried foliated patterns generated by abstracting the forces of growth in plant life.[42]

The shock of the size, speed, and alienation of the nineteenth-century metropolis encouraged various returns to nature. While London and then Paris were being substantially eviscerated and rebuilt during the mid–nineteenth century with new sanitary and transportation infrastructures, the two most influential writers on architecture, John Ruskin and Eugène-Emmanuel Viollet-le-Duc, pursued parallel interests in premetropolitan social organization, medieval architecture, and observations of the natural world. A comparison of their drawings illustrates their theoretical differences. Ruskin's depictions of medieval Venice and of alpine rock formations are emotional and atmospheric, beautifully rendered in chiaroscuro, and almost always unfinished; Viollet-le-Duc's renditions of the same phenomena are graphic, with clean lines, and reveal the precise structural relationship between the parts.[43] Ruskin (his early pseudonym was "Kata Phusin," Sanskrit for "according to nature") in the 1850s and 1860s became a leading critic of the industrial metropolis, condemning with equal vigor the immoral use of industrial materials for constructions such as the Crystal Palace and the unsavory environmental conditions of big cities. As a step toward interrupting the alienating and polluting methods of industrial capitalism, Ruskin founded Saint George's Guild in 1871, a neomedieval arts and crafts organization that inspired William Morris, C. R. Ashbee, William Lethaby, and others to create similar guilds.[44] Out of this intellectual milieu of medievalizing socialism and "arts and crafts" came the most articulated alternative to the high-entropy path of industrial development: the Garden City.

A very different, although in some ways compatible, reaction to Viollet-le-Duc's architectural and naturalistic interests developed into the various national strains of Art Nouveau. The construction of the Eiffel Tower (1885–89) stimulated such socialist architects as Frantz Jourdain, Victor Horta, and Henry van de Velde to seek a radical art form that utilized industrial processes while taking its structural and morphological inspiration (and usually its iconography) from nature.[45] Jugendstil in Vienna and Munich, Modernisme in Barcelona, and the Glasgow circle of Mackintosh and Art Nouveau in Paris, Nancy, and Brussels all broke dramatically with historically bound styles to produce a sensual, transgressive style based on natural imagery — but it is clear that works such as Hector Guimard's Paris Metro stations or Victor Horta's Maison du Peuple in Brussels (both 1900), were designed to represent rather than interact with natural forces. The socially progressive brief of the latter institution was typically unconcerned with the question of high entropy in its efforts to advance socialist consciousness.

Art Nouveau mutated into subsequent strains of expressionist architecture, such as Bruno Taut's crystalline Glass Pavilion at the Werkbund Exhibition in Cologne (1914), van de Velde's theater for the same event (1914), or Erich Mendelsohn's Einsteinsturm in Potsdam (1917–21), each of which are suggestive of natural forms but, like their Art Nouveau forebears, are not contingent on a reintegration of architecture with natural process. Taut as an exponent of both Garden Cities and expressionism came closest to an organic theory of environmental design, charted in his utopian manifestos of *Alpine Architecture,* the Crystal Chain, and the *Dissolution of Cities.* Architecture was proposed as a spiritual catalyst that would help engender the new synthesis of society and nature.[46]

The naturalistic treatment of form did not necessarily perform more ecologically but nonetheless was important in influencing consciousness toward a theory of holism. This ideal reached its fullest manifestation in the buildings designed by Rudolph Steiner for his anthroposophical community in Dornach, Switzerland (1908–27). Steiner, an Austrian philosopher, was the leading authority in his day of the work of Goethe, and wrote extensively on Hegel, Nietzsche, and, most important in this context, Ernst Haeckel. From Goethe's theories he would elaborate that "a product of art is no less nature than a product of nature, only the lawfulness of nature has already been poured into the product of art in the way this lawfulness appeared to the human spirit."[47]

In 1913, Steiner seceded from the German Theosophical Society to found his own Anthroposophical Society, a movement that has been fundamental to many environmental activists. Steiner was adamant that buildings express organicism in order to achieve harmony with nature and with the human spirit. Of the First Goetheanum (1913–22), the double-domed central meeting hall of his community, he wrote: "The entire building is conceived out of the whole. Every single form in this organically conceived building..., in that it represents a part of the whole, must make evident in its own form that it is indispensable... as manifestly indispensable as the lobe of the ear, or an arm or a head is to the human organism."[48] Such a claim approaches Alberti's analogue yet attempts to invest it with a new holistic understanding of nature. Steiner theorized such architectural elements as a "living wall," which would demonstrate the characteristics of the earth's surface, a theory that led him to the design of double curved planes to show the counterbalancing forces operating in nature. Right angles were almost completely eliminated in his designs. The Second Goetheanum was executed in fireproof reinforced concrete upon the same principles with very different formal results, resembling alpine rock formations.[49] The architectural solutions of Steiner's so-called spiritual functionalism were unmatched in originality, but whether or not the organic forms had a beneficial influence on the human pysche, as was claimed, did not hinge on their being closer to natural process. Steiner's greater legacy to ecology, it must be admitted, was in the realm of education and horticulture, the latter following the most radical ecological position of biodynamic farming. His buildings theoretically respond to the ecological imperative that was developing from biological theories, but they still conformed to the analogical tradition in architecture, representing natural processes rather than sustaining them.

UTOPIAN EFFORTS TO REDEEM INDUSTRIAL SOCIETY

The difference between the stylistic developments of Art Nouveau and the theory of Garden Cities put forth by Ebenezer Howard in his tract *To-morrrow, a Peaceful Path to Real Reform* (1898) during the same period is tantamount to the difference of genotype to phenotype — that is, the organic process of growth versus the appearance of its full-grown product. Although Howard's Garden Cities program is often misconstrued as one of the sources of the sprawling American suburb, and thus inimicable to sustainable strategies, it was in its origins the most completely detailed alternative to suburban developments from social, economic, and infrastructural points of view. In his diagram of the three magnets, Howard depicts a new synthesis of town and country, where the high level of culture of a large city can be maintained with a commitment to preserving natural processes in a managed working landscape.[50]

The Garden Cities goal was to plan an entire region with regularly spaced towns. In each town the buildings would be clustered in an area of roughly a thousand acres for a population of thirty thousand residents, and would be surrounded by about five times that amount of land for agricultural and industrial functions. Local industrial and agricultural production were meant to supply this small region with most of its consumer needs, thus circumventing the centralizing tendencies of the chain of command of the metropolis. The hint found in Leonardo's scheme for Milan and More's organization of Utopia as a system of rationally planned settlements that preserved the proper balance between working lands, production spaces, and housing was fully developed into a modern vision that theoretically would greatly reduce wasteful urban development.

The experience of Letchworth, the first Garden City planned by Raymond Unwin and Barry Parker in 1904, demonstrates at once the formal success of low-density neighborhood planning and the difficulties of adhering to principles of cooperative ownership. To avoid speculation, the land was originally to be collectively owned so that the coherence of the plan could be guaranteed by the lack of competing land ownership. Located on 3,800 acres thirty-five miles south of London, Letchworth attracted about 8,500 people by 1914, and included Ebenezer Howard himself as one of its residents. Due to the diverging aspirations of reform movement residents, who lived there with a certain righteous agenda, and working-class residents, who did not share the same ideals, the town never coalesced into a community.[51] The aesthetic of winding streets and neo–cottage style architecture derived from the Arts and Crafts movement, however, added another dimension to Letchworth that was easier to export than its cooperatively based plan. Subsequent suburbs, including those designed by Unwin, borrowed heavily from the formal ideas without including the social, economic, and environmental premises of Howard's Garden City. Without the structuring benefits of protected green belts and regional infrastructure, and without the development of a local economy and cultural base, the compromised garden city became a hapless agent of sprawl, which in its dependency on center city institutions and polluting transportation devices, reversed its potential for lowering entropy.[52]

The theory of bioregionalism, which is still much debated among environmentalists, influenced Howard and was transmitted by him to others. Bioregionalism was formulated in the 1880s by utopian land reformers, such as the Russian anarchist Peter Kropotkin, as the project of human settlement according to a more natural distribution of resources in a complex biological system that shunned arbitrary political and ethnic boundaries in favor of natural units.[53] Bioregionalism was expanded upon by the Scottish biologist and city planner Patrick Geddes in the first two decades of this century and was championed by the American critic Lewis Mumford as the path of redemption from the ills of the sprawling conurbations.[54] While the attendant theories of urban decentralization had a large impact on the planned economies of the Soviet Union and other socialist states, the parallel path of intensive industrial development usually overcompensated the ecological advantages of such planning with ruinous results.

Perhaps the only instance of coordinated regional planning to approximate the bioregional and Garden Cities ideal occured in the Jewish settlements in British-ruled Palestine, which after 1948 became the state of Israel. Patrick Geddes was in fact involved in the planning of Tel Aviv, Jerusalem, and Haifa during the first years of the 1920s. In successive years there would be greater influences coming from the radical culture of Germany and Eastern Europe.[55] Although it is now difficult to dissociate the colonial immigration of Russian, Polish, and German Jews to the Middle East from the major international conflicts in that region, the initial dream of Zionism, set forth in the utopian novel by Theodor Herzl, *Altneuland,* was based on a benign insertion of collectivism, stewardship of agricultural lands, and high technology. The kibbutz movement, which was generated by mostly Russian and Polish socialists around 1910 and formally institutionalized in 1920, projected the settlement of communistic villages, with characteristics not unlike the towns of Utopia. The size of each commune was initially set at about a hundred members, but soon debates opened for communes with a thousand members to allow for a greater division of labor. The distribution and planning of these democratically managed, collective agricultural (and later light industrial) settlements was decided first by the Jewish Agency, which owned all the potential sites, and after statehood by the state planning bureaucracies. That the placement of these villages was determined as much by strategic defense as by biological considerations is due to the historic political situation of the region, and it offers a good example of why bioregionalism can never be fully implemented in a world governed by political and military priorities.[56]

The kibbutzim, of which there are currently over 270 (housing less than 3 percent of the population of Israel), are enduring examples of collective living and landscape preservation.[57] Automobiles are left at the edges of the settlements and not used internally; the inner core is laced with bike paths, reducing most paving and producing a remarkable atmosphere of tranquility in a space where a diversity of activities, almost as complex as those of a city, occur. The kibbutzim, although they are mostly secular, would never have lasted as collectivized environments without a highly motivated and ethnically based sense of purpose. This makes the kibbutz a limited model for replication. The rest of Israel, which was generally not developed with the same criteria as the kibbutz (as much as the early planners of the state, who mostly came from kibbutzim, desired), demonstrates the typical imbalance of development due to Westernization, modernization, and advanced capitalism, as found elsewhere on the planet.

The efforts of utopian settlements to resist the effects of industrialism have been relatively ineffective in curtailing the rampant waste of human and material resources. While the modern movement in architecture is usually associated with the ideal of mass industrialization and is often too easily dismissed as ecologically insensitive, several issues dear to present-day environmentalists, in fact, were central to the architectural agenda of most modernists. In particular, the preservation of green spaces and the analysis of solar orientation became canonic. Victor Olgyay's treatise, based on research begun in the 1920s, is a compendium of modernist knowledge on solar orientation.[58] In addition, the modernists promoted an ideal of fair housing, rarely separating the social from the environmental. In Weimar Germany the garden city concept evolved away from the bourgeois estate of individualized villas into the movement for social housing estates and allotment subsistence gardens for the workers. During the mid-1920s the planning of long strips of apartments, the *Zeilenbau,* put into practice by Ernst May in Frankfurt and Bruno Taut, Martin Wagner, Walter Gropius, and others in Berlin, were geared to solar orientation and collective services, such as laundries, and were always provided with allotment gardens. German Social Democratic planners usually established these estates on cooperatively owned land to avoid speculation.[59] Lembrecht Migge's theories of intensive horticulture for increased densities were well known, and his concept of the "growing house," which predicated a basic plot for growing food with a two-room unit that could be expanded in several directions, was widely copied.[60] These Social Democratic planning efforts went toward the reorganization of the industrial city into a "green city," but unfortunately the green zones were not defended by successive administrations of planners, and today these housing estates have become almost indistinguishable from sprawl. The functionalist architecture of this period, best represented by the *Zeilenbau* projects, was obsessive about the issue of solar access, to the point of being heliotropic. In the name of function the architects would often reduce the concept of architecture to one of solving a single problem, such as solar orientation, without addressing other traditional functions such as circulation, the street, or scale. The most common urban approach called for a scraped site, or tabula rasa, which eliminated the contextual factors of the environment, wiping out with one hand what was trying to be conserved with the other.

The functionalist approach was pursued on an urban scale and developed into wedge-shaped enclaves by Ludwig Hilberseimer, one of the ideologues of the German Social Democratic housing movement, in *The New City,* a book he published in reference to American cities in the mid-1940s. A basic L-shaped house unit with its own garden was plotted on a cul-de-sac which was joined to a series of fish spines radiating from a major transportation node. Parkland and space for public institutions such as schools were tucked between the spines in the green swards. The wedge was located upwind from polluting industries placed in an opposite quadrant, with farming protected in the remaining two quadrants.[61] The new towns movement in social democratic administrations after World War II in England, Sweden, and Holland, in particular, resulted in many comprehensively planned towns, such as Harlow or Vallingby or Almere, where transportation has been intelligently organized, the pedestrian well provided for, and working landscapes safeguarded. A fairly universal critique of these places is that while they are more ecologically organized to sustain life, they are socially and culturally sterile. New towns have a difficult time, even after a large population has settled in them, creating enough cultural initiative or human diversity to generate and sustain an interesting urban culture.

Utopian planning has contributed formally and ideologically to the debate on how to organize human life and should not be automatically discredited as a source for obtaining principles. It is the inability of utopias to cross from the imaginary into the real that makes them useful for discussion but suspect as actual places. More's paradoxical etymology for the name Utopia — "no place" — is fundamental to its didactic function.

MASTERS OF THE ORGANIC

Probably the two greatest influences on architectural theory during the first half of the twentieth century, Frank Lloyd Wright and Le Corbusier, each had a more than casual interest in natural factors. Luis Fernández Galiano attributes this not solely to the moral imperative of environmentalism but to the transcendent metaphysical function of *energy* in the conception of architecture that had particular appeal to the mythopoeic methods of both architects.[62] Despite their mutual interest in Ruskin, neither of these architects rejected industrialism — Frank Lloyd Wright in his 1901 essay, "The Art and Craft of the Machine," advocates a new synthesis with the machine, and Le Corbusier from 1920 until World War II posed as an evangelist of technocracy — but both had visions of the structural reorganization of society that would be less wasteful and provide better protection of the natural environment.[63] While it can be quite successfully argued that the application of their automobile-based models of urban organization — one the sprawling Broadacre City, the other the highrise-based Radiant City — have resulted in higher entropy, that was not the intention. Le Corbusier advocated greater density than in the traditional city; Wright demanded an end to that density and the spread across the landscape of single-family Usonian houses, each on an acre of productive land.[64] The fatal flaw in both their visions was what in retrospect seems to be the inevitable privileging of the automobile. The traditional street, and with it the preservation of human scale, was eliminated to favor the mechanical space of transportation.

The Corbusian model, although it looks much more alienating, and certainly the many derivatives of it have proved aesthetically awkward and functionally incomplete, was theoretically more ecological, since it wasted less land and concentrated services. Broadacre City proposed that most of its inhabitants participate in some form of agriculture, as Wright himself did at Taliesin East, in order to contribute to the autonomy of the family unit and reduce demands on centralizing economic structures, which, because of the incompetency of large-scale bureaucracies, are wasteful.

Aside from their utopian visions, both architects also produced buildings that actually integrated natural processes in their designs. Le Corbusier, disenchanted with his own attempts at artificial climate control, developed the *brise-soleil* (sunbreaker) in the 1930s as a means of naturally shading and ventilating buildings in a Mediterranean climate. He built several houses with sod roofs, one of the best bioclimatic solutions for retaining thermal comfort. His mother's house on Lake Léman (1924), the houses for the Jaoul family in Neuilly (1952–56), and the Sarabhai House in Ahmadabad (1956) all have this feature. While many of the buildings Le Corbusier designed in India are inappropriate for the climate, unable to deal with the hot winds of the fall season, he usually attempted to mediate the climate with innovative forms that were poetic reactions to traditional forms. The concrete screens shading the front of the Justice Palace at Chandigarh, for instance, are gigantic extrapolations of wooden *masharabiyya* screens used to shield windows in many Middle Eastern countries. The Mill Owners Association in Ahmadabad, a building that has proven to be uninhabitable for three months of the year because of its failure to keep out warm winds, was planned to have a water-filled pool in the scoop of its umbrella-like roof to act as a natural cooling device.[65] During the last two decades of his life Le Corbusier shifted his metaphors from machine age to biological; the "machine for living in" was replaced in his rhetoric by "the biology of the house." The free-form shapes found in his last buildings, such as the lobes on the Carpenter Center in Cambridge, are biomorphic expressions, and many of the features, such as the "aeratur" slit windows designed to breath in cool air, are meant to make the structure behave according to biological processes.[66]

Frank Lloyd Wright, who for much of his career specifically used the term "organic architecture" as a catchall for his theory of architecture, was generally more successful in the energy performance of his buildings. The Robie House of 1910 was not only interesting for its innovative pinwheel plan, but also for its astute solar orientation, a feature that became programmatic in all of his later work.[67] The Usonian house was Wright's answer to affordable housing during the Great

Depression, and it was supplied with many energy-efficient features. The first proto-type, constructed in 1936 for Herbert Jacobs in Madison, Wisconsin, was a model of solar orientation. The L-shaped plan situated the major windows to the south, with mass elements and clerestories on the north. Most of the Usonian houses were proposed as partially mounded houses with good southern orientation and carefully calculated shading.[68] In particular, Wright's Second Jacobs House (1943–48), for the same client as the first Usonian house, is a textbook example of pas-sive solar heating and cooling. It is a two-story structure built into a mound on the north that rises to the second level to provide thermal mass. The hemicycle plan is oriented to the south, with a roof overhang that keeps the summer sun out and lets the winter sun in. Air circulates freely from room to room, each room be-ing open to the south. Air also circulates between floors, as a gap has been left be-tween the glazed south wall and the floor separation.[69]

Like Ruskin, Wright founded his own utopian community of Taliesin for absorb-ing eager young apprentices into a communal existence. The summers were spent in Wisconsin, the winters in Arizona. Taliesin was an architectural office in which the job tasks could include milking cows, tending the vegetable garden, and can-ning fruit. The members of Taliesin lived according to the rural ideals expounded for Broadacre City. Taliesin West, near Scottsdale, Arizona, built in the late 1940s, was meant to passively mediate the winter climate of the desert; it is partially sub-merged, and the pitched wooden rafters originally supported a canvas roof, in prin-ciple a tent, that provided natural illumination and good climate control (except in the rare case of rain).[70]

While their urban models are seriously flawed, the explicit concern for reduc-ing entropy in the late works of both Wright and Le Corbusier heightens the com-plexity of these works. That ecology is not the most evident determinant of the design of these works has allowed them to be considered according to the con-ventional aesthetic criteria of the anonymous discourse of architecture; however, as the terms of valuation shift, they may gain new status as prototypes for a sus-tainable environment.

THE SOLAR STIGMATA OF THE ECOLOGY MOVEMENT

There is an ironic serendipity in the proliferation of solar collectors, attached to buildings with functionalist conviction in the 1970s, and the deconstructivist taste for fragmentation in the 1980s, when an aesthetic based on dismembered bits of metal trusses that could have carried solar panels but didn't was widely admired. (A synthesis finally occured when the Benisch & Partner office hired a designer from Coop Himmelblau to work on the Hysolar Institute in Stuttgart in 1988 and placed solar collectors on the extruded parts of the building.) Solar buildings produced during the 1970s caused a certain embarassed revulsion because the awkward solar technology overpowered the architectural program and form, reducing design to something less than the sum of its parts. Ecological architecture built since the energy crisis carries the stigma of solar collectors and generally suffers from the same positivist logic of functionalist modernism, by which the complexity of architecture as an aesthetic, urban, and structural system is reduced to solving prioritized functions.

Although there had been a thriving industry producing solar water heaters before World War II, their poor efficiency (ten-year life expectancy) and the low price of postwar electricity made them economically obsolete. The resurgence of solar heaters during the 1970s energy crisis was thus an unacknowledged revival. There had been an earlier generation of solar architecture, proposed initially between 1938 and 1958, when scientists and architects at MIT collaborated on four experimental solar houses that used active equipment for gathering and storing solar radiation. The principles of these systems were developed from Horace de Saussure's heat trap, or "hot box," introduced in 1767. He based the design on observing glass-walled conservatories. An insulated box with three layers of glass when left in the sun could reach a temperature of 230°F. The MIT group perfected the copper-coiled mechanism invented by Edward Morse in the 1880s for rooftop solar collectors and added innovative storage tanks, a feature that proved to be uneconomic. In 1947, Dr. Maria Telkes and the architect Eleanor Raymond collaborated on a house, the Dover House, that used glauber salts, which could absorb seven times as much heat as water or crushed rock, as a means of improving heat storage.[71] But until the development of photovoltaic panels in the 1970s, it was impossible to guarantee complete heating needs through solar devices in northern climates. The expense of solar houses could not compete with those heated by fossil fuels, and the research program was discontinued.

During the 1960s a significant change of consciousness occurred, and the subsequent demand for solar energy was championed not from an economic perspective but from one of social responsibility. Most important in this shift in mindset were the jeremiads of Rachel Carson, who in *The Silent Spring* (1962) exposed the extent to which the pesticide DDT had penetrated the world's ecosystems and launched the general challenge to think of pollution as a global problem. Tangential to this were the Civil Rights movement and the movement to ban nuclear weapons. Ecology became an ethical position at that moment, and it was one of several political issues that shook the established ideology of progress based on the expansion of military and industrial technologies.

The reactions to the first wave of environmentalism were multifarious, ranging from reforms within the profession to anarchic utopian experiments. Ecology, although it had been used in science for several generations, was not explicitly appropriated by architecture until the 1950s, when Richard Neutra made it the cen-

RICHARD INGERSOLL

tral focus of his writings on architecture. Neutra built a series of desert houses in California that use architectural and landscape features to naturally mediate the climate.[72] Lewis Mumford had been preparing a critical terrain for the ecology movement since the 1920s with his steady stream of attacks on urban policies and machine civilization. His most devastating critiques of the military industrial complex were published in the late 1960s in the two-volume *Myth of the Machine.* Serge Chermayeff allied his studies of the relationship of community formation to Mumford's environmentalism at this time. His thinking was influenced by gestalt research in cognitive theory and aspired to an architectural theory of holism. *The Shape of Community,* written with Alexander Tzonis in 1971, was one of the first academic attempts to promote a theory of architecture based on multidimensional environmental considerations.[73]

Two projects by Roche and Dinkeloo, the Oakland Museum (1963) and the Ford Foundation (New York, 1967), serve as emblematic responses by official culture to the environmental movement. In each case a symbolic garden is integrated into the building's program and offered as a public landscape. The Ford Foundation, which has an immense atrium garden, is, in fact, energy inefficient, since the garden necessitates extra climate control machinery. Such practices are a form of ecological tokenism, and once again natural conditions are represented rather than sustained.

Chermayeff's most famous student, Christopher Alexander, first devised a systems theory of decision making for architectural form that was close to cybernetic theory before converting his holistic method to more subjective, quasi-mystical criteria. *A Pattern Language,* written with six colleagues and published in 1977, is a veritable treatise on ecologically responsible design. It prescribes 253 rules, ranging from the scale of the region to that of the inglenook. As a theory it is intricate and ingenious in guiding the complex interrelationship of various design factors, but is seriously flawed by the insistence on universals that generally have been deduced from an ethnocentric analysis of the built form of traditional cultures. Alexander's attempt to generate a system of building procedures that is analogous to natural processes, where everything is connected to everything else, is, nevertheless, a conceptual breakthrough that seriously challenges the role of authorship in architectural design while questioning the validity of industrialized methods of production of the environment. Like the theories of Ruskin, Taut, or Steiner, his theory has a metaphysical platform that advocates the isomorphism between the human spirit and architectural form. It is not possible to properly construct buildings according to Alexander's pattern language until the overall system of production changes. The theory is thus unrealizable in its anticipation of redemptive circumstances, and has a latent suggestion of cultist control in the insularity of its logic. Although the rules of the pattern language are meant to insure variety, their application infers an authoritarian mandate.[74]

Probably the most widely used ecology-inspired text of this period was Ian McHarg's treatise on landscape, *Design with Nature* (1969), which created an awareness of geographic and natural features as elements of conservation. One of the largest applications of McHarg's methods was partly implemented at The Woodlands, a 25,000-acre new town on the edge of Houston, Texas, developed in 1971. McHarg advised the planners to avoid clear-cutting of trees and to enhance the paths of natural drainage, locating golf courses and other recreation facilities on the flood plain land. The first residents left a completely natural landscape around their houses, without front or back lawns, but this practice has been discontinued. While such an approach can be seen as relatively benign at the level of microclimate, the spread-out design of The Woodlands forces residents to drive for all their basic needs—school, work, and shopping—and thus does little to reduce daily contributions to high entropy. Saving a tree may not in the end be as environmentally astute as saving a trip.[75]

Paolo Soleri, an Italian student of Frank Lloyd Wright, produced a visually stunning utopian theory called "arcologies" in the 1960s. He proposed a synthesis of architecture and ecology. His argument, illustrated with preposterous megastructural projects for urbanizations in the air, below ground, and in the sea, each with a glorious Old Testament–sounding title, such as Noahbabel, is similar to Le Corbusier's desire to raise buildings off the ground and have people live in denser settlements so that services can be concentrated. Like a prophet, Soleri fled to the desert to construct Arcosanti, a demonstration community near Phoenix, which has been built mostly through the volunteer labor of architecture students since 1970. Arcosanti, which has immense concrete exedra hugging the cliffs of its site, is true to much of the formal promise of the arcologies models but does not make a convincing model of ecological or community organization because it is based upon geographical, economic, and social marginalization. Like all generalizing utopias, it is a victim of its own specificity.

At the other end of the spectrum, such mainstream architects as Richard Stein tried to reform the conventions of practice. Long a member of the Sierra Club, Stein formed a study committee on environmental issues within the American Institute of Architects (AIA) in the late 1960s that led to the publishing of *Architecture and Energy* (1978), a thorough examination of how energy performance can be analyzed and improved. The Department of Energy was established in 1971, and standards for energy efficiency were developed during the decade that greatly reduced energy waste. Funded research and sponsored competitions during the 1970s led to computer programs to analyze the performance of buildings and improved thermal devices, such as double-paned windows filled with argon gas.[76]

In California, Governor Jerry Brown appointed Sim van der Ryn as state architect to develop a series of programs that would popularize ecology-conscious building practices. Van der Ryn had been one of the founders of the Farallones Institute, which produced the Integral Urban House in 1974, a lived-in exhibition of sustainable dwelling techniques fit into a conventional Victorian house on an urban site in Berkeley. During his tenure six energy-efficient state office buildings were constructed to demonstrate the advantages in comfort and cost of maintenance of passive systems. The Bateson Building in Sacramento is an attractive alternative to bureaucratic office buildings. It relies on vernacular solutions, such as planted trellises and shaded courtyards, as well as technologically innovative passive devices, such as suffusing screens to augment the distribution of light. Since their design, other issues such as indoor air pollution have altered even further the standards for environmentally sound office buildings.[77]

The oil embargo of 1973 created a frenzied demand for alternative energy solutions. Solar collectors became a symbol of environmental righteousness; President Jimmy Carter had some solar collectors installed to heat the White House swimming pool almost as soon as he took office to show a personal commitment to the movement. Hugh Stubbins's Citycorp skyscraper in New York City (1977) was designed with a dramatically sliced, solar-oriented top to demonstrate corporate support, but this was in fact a bluff since the solar panels were never installed, making it an empty symbolic gesture.

As part of the solar movement, Judy and Michael Corbett developed and designed a solar subdivision called Village Homes on seventy acres in Davis, California. Using some of McHarg's precepts, they reduced the width of the streets, exploited natural ground swales for drainage, and sited all the houses with southern exposures. The landscape needs a third less watering, and the solar features account for 50 to 75 percent of the heating. The success of the development did not lead to others like it, because short-term costs have remained a much higher priority than lowering entropy. The satisfaction of Village Homes is in the realm of energy consciousness and community values (very few of the original owners have moved), but not in architectural quality. The "wood butcher" ethic that set itself as the ecological subversion of architecture did as much to prevent a change in consciousness as the profession's own reluctance to accept reform.[78]

Recent buildings that have been designed to perform environmentally are usually uninspiring from a formal point of view. Most of the examples illustrated in Brenda and Robert Vale's *Green Architecture* (1991), for example, are either frightful neo-Steinerian excursions into resisting urban order, such as Alberts and Huut's grotesque NMB Bank in Amsterdam (1983–87), allegedly the most energy-efficient office building in Europe, or are well-meaning but awkwardly detailed retreats such as Amory and Hunter Lovins's Rocky Mountain Institute (1983, Aspen, Colorado). Only a few works, such as Glenn Murcott's Kempsey Museum in New South Wales, or Clark and Menafee's Middleton Inn near Charleston, or the Carraro House by Lake Flato in San Antonio, promise to combine ecology-conscious design with a synthesis of good details, expert proportional relationships, and a spatial order that would demand one to consider it culturally. Such works address the autonomous aspects of architecture while functioning well with thermal and fluvial conditions.

There are, of course, many more buildings that behave in a converse manner, where poor environmental performance is masked by inspiring form. Helmut Jahn's Illinois Center in Chicago or Richard Meier's High Museum in Atlanta are two of the more egregious examples: because of overexposed glazing they provide a preview of the greenhouse effect.

One of the few environmentalist-oriented projects where the design communicates more than just its teleological relationship to place and climate is Sea Ranch, a ten-mile stretch of Northern California coast, planned by Lawrence Halprin in 1964. The natural features of the rugged landscape were preserved by clustering the buildings at the edge of the clearings and leaving large meadows and undisturbed sea cliffs in between. The architects Moore, Turnbull, Lyndon, and Whitaker, who designed the initial condominium complex, and Joseph Esherick, who did several houses, played with a limited palette of materials and single-slope shapes to create a recombinatory vernacular derived from the wood-slat demeanor of local barns. A code for the rest of the buildings at Sea Ranch was developed from their initial designs, but the dwellings constructed over the past twenty-five years have not maintained exactly the same sense of harmony with the natural surroundings and with the original buildings.[79] For all its excellence as an example of how to build with nature, Sea Ranch, it must be remembered, is a vacation resort, an indication that most conscientious approaches to the environment happen best in marginal spaces of luxury and are often motivated by a desire for atonement for the polluting circumstances that created the surplus needed to finance such places.

The first wave of ecology consciousness in architecture led to reforms in building codes, utopian fantasies, and the proliferation of solar panels that stigmatized it as trivial in reference to the larger discourse of design. The emphasis on functional criteria limited the understanding of ecology as a primarily technical matter. In the reduction of entropy through the use of appropriate technology, in the contribution to urban life, and in the maintenance of a community's equilibrium with the land, ecological values have the potential to transfuse new meaning to Le Corbusier's lyrical definition of architecture as the "masterful, correct, and magnificent play of forms in light." The energy of that light can only strengthen the greatest game of civilization, the art of architecture.

THE ECOLOGY QUESTION

Despite the technical and biological issues concerning architecture and ecology, the attempt to restore the ecological balance of the biosphere can be viewed as having profound social relevance. In effect the very means for exploiting and controlling the natural environment are no different from those that have been used to exploit and control the social one. The "Ecology Question" in current architectural discourse is analogous to "The Housing Question" formulated by Engels during the nineteenth century. The Housing Question, an issue that arose in regard to the demand for fair and healthy housing for all, served as one of the most powerful critiques of capitalism and was instrumental in mobilizing a consciousness of social responsibility among designers and architects. Most modernists felt a certain unity of purpose, a naive belief in the good intentions of their various attempts to resolve the housing question through architectural means.[80]

In terms of a socialist revolutionary strategy, Engels had great reservations about a struggle waged through housing reform, since the supply of good housing once achieved would placate the revolutionary momentum; it thus was criticized as a tactic of the liberal reform of capitalism, like treating the symptoms without changing the system. A project such as Karl Marx Hof in Vienna, which is expressly ideological in its name and iconography, must be seen as an attempt to respond to Engels's critique: it was proposed as good housing that would also perpetuate the revolutionary rhetoric of the working class, and even become a literal bastion of class struggle against the state.[81]

Ecologists, who call for a transition from the dominant Western mentality of anthropocentrism to one of biocentrism, rarely take into account the immediate social injustices that also demand solidarity. The neo-Malthusians are thus able to interpret starvation in remote quarters as a natural process not to be interfered with, while never doubting the primacy of their own well-fed being. One of the major issues articulated at the Earth Summit in 1992 was the matter of environmental justice, whether in reference to poor countries receiving the toxic waste of wealthier ones or poor neighborhoods suffering the same.

The Ecology Question has the potential for generating one of the deepest critiques of late-twentieth-century capitalism, especially since the demise of official Marxism. But just as the social housing created in the name of the Housing Question has led to some of the more egregious failures of modern architecture — it became the crucible of the functionalist fallacy — the architectural response to the Ecology Question runs the same risk. A green functionalism promises to lead to a similar treatment of symptoms and an unrealistic retreat from a system that has not been changed. The attempt to restore the ecological balance of the biosphere has profound social relevance. If urban planning and architectural policies are reduced to mechanical solutions based on cause and effect rather than being grounded in a social conception of ecology, they will not easily adhere to a frame of social justice.

Such a consideration is programmatic rather than projectual. The effectiveness of an architecture that emerges from the Ecology Question will depend on the handling of two other factors: (1) the social and political nature of cities in which buildings are built; and (2) an acknowledgment of the rhetorical nature of architecture. The functionalist fallacy that was present in the planning and architecture projected in response to the Housing Question failed regularly on those two accounts, in particular.

The infamous social failures of public housing during the past three decades are blamed on functionalist fallacies and help detract attention from the fact that the demand for social housing still exists. The ever-worsening environmental crisis will probably supersede matters such as housing, and in the near future the housing question will be subsumed into a greater ecology question. As with the old functionalism, it will have benign intentions but will probably mask the potential for a new code of repression. The higher sense of responsibility toward the environment lies not in the solutions but in the formation of the question. Can there be such a thing as ecological balance if it is not socially determined? Is not human consciousness the major component both of the cause of the imbalance and of its possible rectification?

The Ecology Question, if it is not proposed as a question of justice among humans, will in the short term risk continuing to be submerged, and thus in the long term will require drastic, and probably inhumane, palliatives. Designers and planners should recognize that each act of design not only plays a part in the balance of the environment but also is dependent upon policy, and that a strategy at both levels that does not include the self-determination of communities and the social reintegration of life functions will most likely contribute to repressive consequences analogous to those engendered by so many of the functionalist public housing projects. The Ecology Question as a socially based priority asks that design and planning conceive of sustainability and social justice as reciprocal conditions— that saving the planet and saving the community become inseparable.

POSTAPOCALYPSE DESIGN

The forecast of a green apocalypse has been used as a scare tactic that forces an interpretation of all uses of energy in apodictic terms. Malthusian anxiety about population explosions and alarmist predictions of heat death provide external pressures that cannot be easily translated into architectural terms. Perhaps the anxiety and paranoia that have served as key inducements to support the ecology movement could be replaced by more life-enhancing values if it were admitted that the green apocalypse has already occurred and that it is no longer a question of saving humanity from extinction and the planet from heat death but rather of slowing down that eventuality. Reform through volunteerist example and propaganda and reform through democratic process have succeeded in lowering the emission of air pollutants only 18 percent during the last fifteen years.[82] While statistically it can be shown that because of the environmental policies of the 1970s great progress was made in saving energy, the same statistics will also reveal that *no progress has been made in reducing net entropy,* because development has increased exponentially. For every BTU of energy saved through better insulation and proper solar orientation, the same amount has been squandered in other forms of consumption, mostly related to the Western way of life. While the circumstances seem dire, the most extreme reactions to the green apocalypse, those in which the rights of biotic communities are placed above those of humans, often verge on dictatorial conclusions and run the risk of advocating ecofascism.[83]

In the postapocalypse era, ecology is already being reconsidered as a social issue about the organization and maintenance of life. Technology is no longer anathematized, but is seen as something that must be artfully mediated and used more efficiently in order to regain a better equilibrium with natural processes, an attitude that has been adopted by hard-line ecologists through the spread of computer use. Instead of cultivating the paranoia of self-sufficient ecological correctness, the second wave of environmentalism, which emerged in Europe in the mid-1980s, is much less prone to utopian experiments and more to direct political engagement. The issue of ecology is being shifted from the realm of individual buildings and individual consumer choices to collective choices, since it is the performance of cities and urban organization that has the largest impact. There is no single solution for cities, which are complex interactive environments; solar collectors or conscientious recycling will not save people from driving to work. In postapocalypse times there can only be transitional strategies in urban situations, and these are as much political as they are technological.

While high entropy is a relatively recent, quick-breeding phenomenon in the history of human settlement, the struggle for sustainability will take much longer to effect. In some ways the fact that nature is no longer pure has helped to root ecology into architectural discourse. Even cynical theorists, such as Peter Eisenman, who has made a career of denying that architecture is a socially benign activity, have incorporated interpretations of natural phenomena such as chaos theory and rhyzome analogues because of the consensus of a merging of inorganic and organic.[84] Ecology, or what could be called today "the interrelationships of things in a natural world that has been altered by humans," is closer to the center of architectural discourse than the built results would testify. It has penetrated the autonomy of architectural theory by way of contextualism, appropriate technology, urban conservation, energy conservation, and community organization.

In the critique of modernist tabula rasa, planning principles carried out in the mid-1960s, diverse architectural theorists ranging from Robert Venturi to Aldo Rossi to Colin Rowe to Leon Krier pleaded in varying degrees for contextualism: the defense of the scale and morphologies of an organism's habitat. While only Krier has since pronounced himself an ecologist, and none of them would agree upon a definition of "habitat," the postmodernist mission of emphasizing the city as the nondeterministic generator of architecture has become a major element of architectural theory that bonds easily with a new ecological agenda. That most of the postmodernist generation of architects were absorbed into a cultural network based on the promotion of authorial images, however, seems to have inhibited their further potential for integrating ecological principles into discourse.

The major attempt to divert the co-optation of the critique of modernism into such commercial exploitation came from Kenneth Frampton in his proposition for critical regionalism. Without using the term "ecology," Frampton's theory is ecologically inspired. Misunderstood by many as a nostalgia for regionalism, Frampton proposed an architecture that resisted the wasteful regime of mass culture by specifying the materials and climate-mediating devices derived from local priorities. One of the main points he emphasizes is that it not be dependent on universal technologies such as air conditioners. Critical regionalism thrives on the marginality and difference already present in any geographic situation. It should appeal to the haptic rather than the merely visual, the tectonic rather than the scenographic; it should be connected to its site rather than hovering. Instead of simulating vernacular solutions, however, it must also be critical, addressing itself to something more universal through its refinement of the particular.[85] Exactly how a building behaves critically while staying within the dictates of the region is not always clear, however, and does not lend an air of unity among projects that might qualify.

The question of what a building looks like, what other buildings or natural things it reminds you of, and what it represents is still of primary importance. This is why the rhetorical function of architecture is so important. A good building must convince one that it is good — it must have appeal as a cultural product as well as a phenomenal, sheltering device.

The transitional strategies for lowering entropy and improving urban organization can be found in many recent works. In the Montrouge district of Paris, Renzo Piano's firm has produced an office complex for the Schlumberger Corporation that has conserved a working-class district in a beautiful way. Instead of relocating to a far-off suburb where land is cheaper, the company decided to reuse the factory and warehouse buildings already on the site as offices. This kept jobs in the neighborhood and helped the district to retain its scale. The site was opened up by the removal of a few buildings, and a new parking structure was located under planted berms. A high-tech Teflon tent structure stretches over a gap in the berm to create a naturally lit, well-insulated social space for the company's coffee shop and other collective services. The old buildings were gutted and rehabilitated with exposed ducts and office spaces to obtain better circulation and access to natural light. The Schlumberger office complex enhances the environment through a beautiful garden by Alexandre Chemetov, while conserving buildings and neighborhood relations, including employment.[86]

The Croxton Collaborative's two rehabilitations in New York City, one for the Natural Resources Defense Foundation and the other for the National Audubon Society, do similar things in an even more conscientious manner. In the Audubon offices, located in the formidable Shermerhorn Buildings (1910), almost everything that was thrown away from the original building was recycled, 79 percent of the materials that come through the offices are recycled in separated chutes, and energy use has been reduced 60 percent through natural lighting. All the elements used were available off the shelf, making the technology appropriate rather than based on further development. Through the conservation of a significant building and continued energy conservation techniques, urban values have been maintained and a high level of comfort and beauty have been achieved.[87]

New technologies and materials are working their way into a transitional approach to building, in particular the photovoltaic panel. Advanced Photovoltaic Systems Manufacturing Facility in Fairfield, California (1993), by Kiss Cathcart Anders, uses the items it produces as integral components and as a demonstration of easy adaptation to current mass building methods: photovoltaic panels provide an energizing wrapper.

In non-Western settings, where the question of natural and economic resources is doubly important, the theory of appropriate technology geared to time and place has emerged as a transitional strategy. In the new districts of Bombay, India, Charles Correa has designed the Belpur project for one hundred subsidized housing units with minimal resources. The scheme provides basic service cores that can be added to in two directions to accommodate growing needs. Rather than employ technologies that depend on energy-intensive resources that are not available locally, the construction is of modest, easy-to-assemble masonry blocks and tiles produced locally. The plan proceeds according to a game pattern of expansion clusters, with some protected areas for public space. The spatial patterns retain traditional relationships without mimicking traditional forms.[88]

A transitional strategy for controlling metropolitan sprawl without scaring away the existing modes of development is currently being proposed as the key to reducing entropy. Peter Calthorpe is perhaps the most audible spokesman. In his book *The Next American Metropolis* (1993), he outlines a way to attract the same developers who are building suburban America and get them to build village-scale environments tied to good transportation networks. The scheme is self-consciously close to Ebenezer Howard's Garden Cities, without the utopian aspects of requiring cooperative ownership of the land and an altered way of life. The "pedestrian pocket" allows for various options of transportation and housing. In a hypothetical pedestrian pocket, all buildings, which include a mix of apartments, single-family homes, offices, and retail space, are within a five-minute walk of a transit station. What distinguishes Calthorpe's model from other suburban developments is that the land surrounding this enclave is protected by a regional plan for agri-

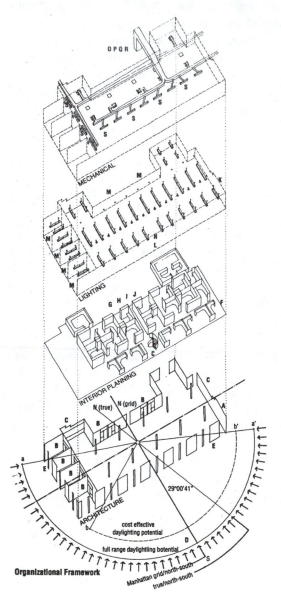

Mechanical Components

O High efficiency gas-fired absorption heater/chiller serves air handler at each floor.

P Separate, mandated outside air system delivers 24 cfm per person.

Q Number of air changes (recirculated and filtered air) is 6.2 per hour.

R Moisture carry-through in system is minimized by low velocity (less than 500 fpm) as well as cooling coil configuration.

S Variable volume units at each perimeter office assure individual control and their arrangement in open office assures full "mixing" of air.

Lighting Components

K Daylighting photocell controls outer bay of lighting (full range dimming)

L All lighting is high efficiency, high color rendition fluorescent with electronic ballast (one ballast for two fixtures).

M Sensors at offices, conference room, etc., turn off lights when room is unoccupied (zone sensors for open area).

N Pendant arrangement of single tube fixtures with up/down components achieves 30 fc ambient light level with low glare characteristics overall.

Interior Planning Components

F Perimeter work stations are held to 3 ft. 6 in. to maximize daylight to interior.

G Open office area is organized east/west to take maximum advantage of daylighting.

H Colors for systems furniture and interior surfaces are in high reflectance range to maximize both natural and artificial light.

I Task lighting is incorporated as part of high efficiency task/ambient system.

J All work stations meet test method and criteria for offgassing of formaldehyde, volatile organic compounds, particulates, etc.

Architectural Components

A Full-height ceiling maintained at building perimeter to maximize daylight effect.

B Enclosed office grouped north and west with clerestory glass.

C Core elements (elevators, fire stairs, pantry and mechanical rooms) on north and east solid exterior walls.

D High thermal performance windows with high transmissivity of natural light.

E Exterior wall thermal upgrade (insulation) approximately three times code requirement (applies to all exterior walls)

Figure 3.1. Croxton Collaborative, National Audubon Society (1990), New York City.

Figure 3.2. Kiss Cathcart Anders, Advanced Photovoltaic Systems (1993), Fairfield, California. (Photo by Richard Barnes.)

cultural uses, and the automobile, although still a possible component, is no longer indispensable.[89] Calthorpe's concept was applied to the development of the Laguna Ranch subdivision in Sacramento, which is frankly indistinguishable from other developments nearby, but perhaps when it is integrated into the planning of larger parts of the city it will become part of a transportation strategy.

Figure 3.3. Charles Correa, Belpur Project (1983), Bombay, India.

There are dozens of similar settlements designed by Andreas Duany and Eliza-beth Plater Zyberk that return the order of the suburb to that of a village, the most famous being Seaside, Florida.[90] The major difference in these latter examples is that they do not stress transportation links. A reversal of sorts has been envi-sioned for inner cities by Richard Register in his theory of ecocities, which pre-dicts the de-development of the existing modern city, with a similar morphologi-cal outcome to the pedestrian pocket. He has projected a scenario for the city of Berkeley according to a 125-year span, from a spread-out grid system that denies most of the natural features, such as shorelines and creeks, to a series of dense urban clusters, where buildings are built taller and closer together than in the ex-isting sprawl. The natural features are allowed to reemerge and urban agricul-tural zones are interspersed between the clusters. The automobile becomes less necessary as diversity of functions are brought into proximity in each cluster.[91] Such a vision is less pragmatic than the pedestrian pocket because it is more con-fined by existing real estate values. If it were proposed for downtown Detroit it might sound more realistic.

These exponents of what is being called the "New Urbanism," in their interest to proceed pragmatically, may be solving technical questions with their models but are ultimately contributing to the chauvinism of the American suburb, where good things happen to white, middle-class people. Such models unselfconsciously help reinforce the injustices of environmental discrimination and trivialize ecological

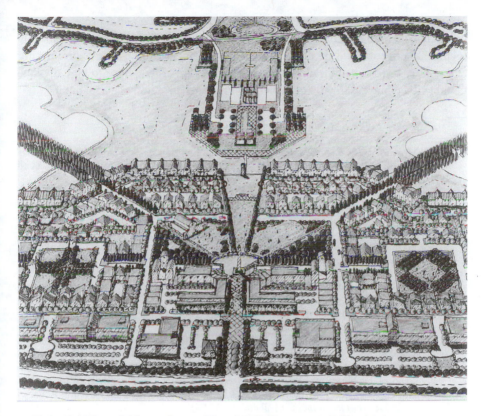

Figure 3.4. Peter Calthorpe, Laguna West (1990), Sacramento, California.

planning as a luxury item, analogous to organically grown produce in the grocery store. There are other contexts where the free market of real estate has been coerced through a political process and the intervention of visionaries to include a more comprehensive social agenda, resulting in more equitable urbanizations. Both in Almere, a new town for 150,000 inhabitants thirty miles northeast of Amsterdam, and in Curitiba, a replanned city of 500,000 in the south of Brazil, remarkable transportation planning and fair housing programs have been combined into urban formations that reduce automobile dependency and preserve urban green spaces.[92] Urbanization, although it is mostly under the control of developers and politicians, also requires the imagination of architects, planners, and designers to move beyond the technical and social givens to encourage a better and more equitable quality of life.

The attitude to urbanization is ultimately what will determine to what degree architecture can contribute to the reduction of entropy. The day may already be here when the notion of a good building is not only one that includes good proportions, clever details, sensible structure, and a sensitive interpretation of program, but also one that comprehends energy performance and a project's capacity to contribute to the public realm through its siting. To be ecological in a merely technical sense will not be enough to be good, but it can no longer be missing from the criteria of goodness. But most of all, for an architecture to be truly sustainable it will necessarily be inscribed in a new urban vision of social justice.

Notes

1. Bill McKibben, *The End of Nature* (New York: Random House, 1989). McKibben's popular thesis is that industrial and chemical processes have altered the habitat and genetics of all living things. The term "Oekologie" was first coined in 1866 by Ernst Haeckel as "the science of relations between organisms and their environment." See Anna Bramwell, *Ecology in the Twentieth Century: A History* (New Haven: Yale University Press, 1989), p. 40.
2. Alessandra Latour, *Louis I. Kahn: Writings, Lectures, Interviews* (New York: Rizzoli, 1991), p. 195.
3. Jeremy Rifkin and Ted Howard, *Entropy: Into the Greenhouse World* (New York: Bantam Books, 1989). Entropy was introduced as a scientific phenomenon having metaphysical connotations by Rudolf Clausius in the 1860s.
4. See, for instance, Edward Goldsmith et al., *Imperiled Planet: Restoring Our Endangered Ecosystem* (Cambridge: MIT Press, 1990).
5. Ken Butti and John Perlin, *A Golden Thread: 2500 Years of Solar Architecture and Technology* (Palo Alto, Calif.: Cheshire Books, 1980).
6. Françoise Choay, *La regola e il modello: Sulla teoria dell'architettura e dell'urbanistica*, ed. Ernesto d'Alfonso (Rome: Officina, 1986), pp. 35–37. Choay does not consider texts such as the *Chou-li* and the *Manasara* to be treatises, as they are uncritical compendia of traditions and religious practices. She cites Joseph Needham ("Building Science in Chinese Literature," vol. 4, in *Science and Civilisation in China* [Cambridge, 1971]) and P. Acharya (*The Architecture of the Manasara* [Allahabad, 1933]).
7. Christopher Alexander et al., *A New Theory of Urban Design* (New York: Oxford University Press, 1987). This book, based on many of the notions of the earlier tract *A Pattern Language* (1978), mentions casually in passing that "the process we have outlined is incompatible with present day city planning, zoning, urban real estate, urban economy, and urban law"; see Richard Ingersoll, "Postmodern Urbanism: Forward into the Past," *Design Book Review* 18 (Winter 1990). Leon Krier, in his essay "The Reconstruction of the European City, 1978–1984," in *Leon Krier: Architecture and Urban Design, 1967–1992* (London: Academy Editions, 1992), calls for the kind of regulations that require a stricter application than liberal society has generally been able to enforce.
8. Daniel Hillel, *Out of the Earth: Civilization and the Life of the Soil* (New York: Free Press, 1990).
9. David Harvey, *The Conditions of Postmodernity: An Enquiry into the Origins of Cultural Change* (Oxford: Blackwell, 1990), pp. 147–97. Harvey calls the new capacity of markets to involve an international division of labor "flexible accumulation."
10. Michael Reynolds, *Earthships: How to Build Your Own*, vol. 1 (Taos, N.M.: Solar Survival Architecture, 1990); Paolo Soleri, *Arcology: The City in the Image of Man* (Cambridge: MIT Press, 1969).
11. Martin Pawley, *Buckminster Fuller* (London: Trefoil, 1990), p. 116. Fuller's great concept of "dymaxion" (the term was coined by a journalist) conflates "dynamic," "maximum," and "ions" to express a philosophy of "more for less" whereby progressive technology can yield greater potential from fewer resources, thus lowering entropy.
12. Fernand Braudel, *Civilization and Capitalism, 15th–18th Century*, vol. 1, *The Structures of Everyday Life: The Limits of the Possible*, trans. M. Kochan, revised by Sian Reynolds (New

York: Harper and Row, 1981). Braudel writes: "No innovation has any value except in relation to the social pressure which maintains and imposes it" (p. 431).

13. Choay, *La regola,* p. 20.
14. Luis Fernández Galiano, *El fuego y la memoria: Sobre arquitectura y energia* (Madrid: Blume, 1991), offers an excellent reflection on this fatal alliance of building and energy.
15. Leon Battista Alberti, *On the Art of Building in Ten Books,* trans. J. Rykwert, N. Leach, and R. Tavernor (Cambridge: MIT Press, 1988), p. 96. A few pages later (p. 99) he observes: "Any river flowing either to eastward or westward will not be all that unwelcome, because the breezes that arise with the sun will either disperse any harmful fumes passing through the city, or with their arrival, do little to increase them." This sort of comment is about as naturalistic as Alberti will allow.
16. Alberti, *Art of Building,* p. 23: "If (as the philosophers maintain) the city is like some large house, and the house is in turn like some small city, cannot the various parts of the house ... be considered miniature buildings?" For Alberti's analogue of a ship, see p. 100.
17. Hans-Karl Lücke, "Alberti, Vitruvio e Cicerone," in J. Rykwert and A. Engel, eds., *Leon Battista Alberti* (Milan: Electa, 1994), pp. 81–82. *Concinnitas* was a well-fit combination of *numerus* (proportions), *finitio* (dimensions), and *collocatio* (the disposition of elements).
18. Alberti, *Art of Building,* p. 196. The argument is used to sustain circular temple plans. "Nature also delights in the hexagon," he adds. The reasoning is close to Plato's *Timaeus,* which introduced the canonical geometrical figures.
19. Manfredo Tafuri, *Ricerca del Rinascimento* (Torino: Einaudi, 1992), p. 53. The *Theogenius,* written circa 1440, was a commentary on Cicero's *De natura deorum.*
20. On Filarete, see Choay, *La regola,* pp. 230–32. Filarete made a curious natural analogy of the building process to the patron impregnating the architect, who then gives birth to the building after nine months.
21. Serge Bramly, *Leonardo: Discovering the Life of Leonardo da Vinci* (New York: Harper Collins, 1991), pp. 194–96. See also Carlo Pedretti, *Leonardo Architect,* trans. Sue Brill (New York: Rizzoli, 1980), p. 55.
22. John Spencer, *Being the Treatise on Architecture by Antonio di Piero Averlino, Known as Filarete* (New Haven: Yale University Press, 1965).
23. Simon Pepper and Nicholas Adams, *Firearms and Fortifications* (Cambridge: MIT Press, 1986). De Marchi's was one of several mid-sixteenth-century treatises, including Pietro Cattaneo and Girolamo Maggi, that proposed geometrically composed city plans for efficient military defense.
24. Rosario Pavia, *L'idea di città: Teorie urbanistiche della città tradizionale* (Milan: FrancoAngeli, 1994), pp. 66–72. More served as the vice-sheriff of London and thus had practical knowledge of urban problems. His choice of fifty-four cities parallels the division of England into fifty-four counties.
25. Thomas More, *Utopia,* trans. Paul Turner (London: Penguin, 1965). One of More's purposes was to demonstrate the devastating effect that the enclosure movement had on the land and the economy of peasants.
26. Werner Szambien, *Jean-Nicolas-Louis Durand, 1760–1834, de l'initiation à la norme* (Paris: Picard, 1984); Anthony Vidler, "Scenes of the Street: Transformations in Ideal and Reality, 1750–1871," in Stanford Anderson, ed., *On Streets* (Cambridge: MIT Press, 1978), pp. 50–54.
27. Caroline Merchant, *The Death of Nature: Nature, Women, Ecology, and the Scientific Revolution* (San Francisco: Harper and Row, 1980), pp. 74–80.
28. Marshall Berman, *All That Is Solid Melts into Air: The Experience of Modernity* (New York: Penguin, 1982), pp. 37–86. The tale of the alchemist Dr. Faustus was published by Johann Spiess in 1587 and by Christopher Marlowe the following year.
29. Merchant, *Death of Nature,* pp. 236–40. The course of science, however, was by no means monolithic or without concern about the effects of entropy: John Evelyn, better known as Christopher Wren's rival for the new, postfire plan of London in 1667, published a thesis on the problem of deforestation in 1662, one of the first appeals for a scientifically man-

aged forest in order to protect a vanishing natural resource; it led to a temporary program of reforestation in 1668. John Evelyn's treatise was called *Sylva, a Discourse of Forest Trees and the Propagation of Timber in His Majesty's Dominions.*

30. Joseph Rykwert, *On Adam's House in Paradise: The Idea of the Primitive Hut in Architectural History* (Cambridge: MIT Press, 1989). Goethe in fact reserved severe criticism for Laugier in his brief passages on architecture in regard to this betrayal of nature. Carlo Lodoli, the Venetian monk and architectural theorist, was perhaps closer to the essence of a natural paradigm. In his teachings he allegedly referred to a set of teleological phenomena in natural morphologies and proposed that buildings follow above all the logic of statics and materials. On Lodoli, see Joseph Rykwert, *The First Moderns* (Cambridge: MIT Press, 1980).

31. John Dixon Hunt, *The Figure in the Landscape* (Baltimore: Johns Hopkins Press, 1976).

32. Steven Marcus, *Engels, Manchester, and the Working Class* (New York: Random House, 1974). Tocqueville in 1835 described it thus: "From this foul drain the greatest stream of human industry flows out to fertilize the whole world, from this filthy sewer pure gold flows. Here humanity attains its most complete development and its most brutish; here civilization works its miracles, and civilized man is turned back almost into a savage." Quoted in Marcus, p. 66.

33. Donald Worster, *Nature's Economy: A History of Ecological Ideas* (Cambridge: Cambridge University Press, 1977), p. 82.

34. Berman, *All That Is Solid Melts into Air,* p. 40. The "tragedy of development," as Berman calls it, is the tragedy of modernity, since "the only way for modern man to transform himself... is by radically transforming the whole physical and social and moral world."

35. Worster, *Nature's Economy,* pp. 147–52.

36. Charles Darwin, *The Illustrated Origin of Species,* ed. R. Leakey (London, 1986). Worster, *Nature's Economy,* says Darwin is "the single most important figure in the history of ecology over the past two or three centuries" (p. 113).

37. Worster, *Nature's Economy,* pp. 174–82, on Social Darwinism.

38. Ernst Haeckel, *Kunstformen der Natur: 1000 Illustrationstafeln mit beschreibendem Text* (Leipzig: Verlag des Bibliographischen Instituts, 1899–1904).

39. Bramwell, *Ecology,* pp. 42–53; such thoughts on the political nature of biology were expounded in Haeckel's *The Wonders of Life* (1905). In this same generation of scientific thought, Rudolf Clausius proclaimed the dominance of entropy over energy in 1865. Fernández Galiano, *El fuego* (p. 67), cites Clausius's formulation: "Die Energie der Welt is Konstant. Die Entropie der Welt strebt einem Maximum zu" (The energy of the world is constant. The entropy of the world strives to overcome it).

40. Daniel Gasman, *The Scientific Origins of National Socialism: Social Darwinism in Ernst Haeckel and the German Monist League* (London: Macdonald, 1971). Gasman finds Haeckel to be a key source for justifications of racism, imperialism, and authoritarianism, but Bramwell, *Ecology,* refutes the evidence, sustaining that Haeckel was a pacifist (p. 50).

41. Henry David Thoreau, *The Variorum Walden,* ed. W. Harding (1854; New York: Twayne, 1962), pp. 42–60. Thoreau's "functionalist" position is sounded in this statement: "What I know of architectural beauty I now see, I know has gradually grown from within outward, out of the necessities and character of the indweller, who is the only builder, — out of some unconscious truthfulness, and nobleness, without ever a thought for the appearance."

42. Narciso G. Menocal, *Architecture as Nature: The Transcendentalist Idea of Louis Sullivan* (Madison: University of Wisconsin Press, 1981). Sullivan's position is related to Emerson's essay "Nature" (1836) and Viollet-le-Duc's *Histoire d'un dessinateur* (1879), in which there is the line "And if one really wishes to understand this word beauty as something else beyond a convention or canon, the only way for it lies in the observation of the manner in which nature operates, not in the reproduction of an eclectic type. The beautiful is nothing more than the harmony, the exact correspondence, between form and function."

43. Nicholas Pevsner, *Ruskin and Viollet-le-Duc: Englishness and Frenchness in the Apprecia-tion of Gothic Architecture* (London: Thames and Hudson, 1969).

44. Raymond Fitch, *The Poison Sky: Myth and Apocalypse in Ruskin* (Athens: Ohio University Press, 1982).

45. Klaus-Jürgen Sembach, *Henry van de Velde* (London: Thames and Hudson, 1989). Among the sources leading to the new abstraction of nature were Owen Jones's *Grammar of Or-nament* (1856).

46. Iain Boyd Whyte, *Bruno Taut and the Architecture of Activism* (Cambridge: MIT Press, 1982).

47. David Adams, "Rudolf Steiner's First Goetheanum as an Illustration of Organic Functional-ism," *JSAH* (Journal of the Society of Architectural Historians) 51 (June 1992): 182–204.

48. Ibid.

49. Wolfgang Pehnt, *Rudolf Steiner: Goetheanum, Dornach* (Berlin: Ernst & Son, 1991). Pehnt points out that the forms of the Goetheanum were not always integral to the structure.

50. Robert Beevers, *The Garden City Utopia: A Critical Biography of Ebenezer Howard* (Lon-don: Macmillan, 1988), p. 41.

51. Robert Fishman, *Urban Utopias in the Twentieth Century: Ebenezer Howard, Frank Lloyd Wright, and Le Corbusier* (Cambridge: MIT Press, 1982), pp. 64–75, describes the setbacks to cooperative life: "Despite Howard's hopes, the Garden City could not create its own oa-sis of social justice in an unjust society."

52. Mervin Miller, *Letchworth: The First Garden City* (Chichester, Sussex: Phillimore, 1989). Thomas Adams, the chief planner of the New York Regional Plan (1930), was the manager of works at Letchworth, and Patrick Geddes was a frequent participant.

53. Peter Kropotkin, *Fields, Factories and Workshops* (London: Sonnensschein, 1899).

54. Donald L. Miller, *Lewis Mumford, a Life* (New York: Weidenfeld and Nicholson, 1989), pp. 197–200. Mumford wrote "The Intolerable City" in 1926 and accused the Megalopolis of being unable to support itself as an organism, fostering ecological imbalance. The idealis-tic subdivision of Radburn, N.J., begun in 1929 on designs by Clarence Stein, was one of Mumford's pet causes for an American Garden City.

55. Marshall Stalley, ed., *Patrick Geddes: Spokesman for Man and the Environment* (New Bruns-wick, N.J.: Rutgers University Press, 1972). Geddes made the first plan for the Hebrew Uni-versity on Mount Scopus in Jerusalem. Although Geddes worked on the planning of Haifa and Tel Aviv in the early 1920s, the results were a serious compromise of the Garden City ideal. Eventually the lot sizes proved too large for a single urban house and too small for an apartment building. On the influx of radical Eastern Europeans, see Michael Levin, *White City: International Style Architecture in Israel* (Tel Aviv: Tel Aviv Museum, 1984), and Gilbert Herbert and Silvina Sosnovsky, *Bauhaus on the Carmel: The Coming of Mod-ern Architecture to Hadar HaCarmel, Haifa,* no. 8 (Haifa: Technion, 1985). The chief city plan-ner for the first twenty years of the kibbutz movement was a German architect, Richard Kauffmann, who had studied in Munich under Theodor Fischer in the same class with Erich Mendelsohn. Kauffmann's connection to the German Garden Cities movement was well established before his emigration to Palestine, and in 1921–22 he traveled with the di-rector of the Jewish Agency to Essen to observe the new town settlements serving the Krupp factories.

56. Richard Ingersoll, *Munio Gitai Weinraub: Bauhaus Architect in Eretz Israel* (Milan: Electa, 1994), pp. 83–104.

57. Joseph Blasi, *The Communal Experience of the Kibbutz* (New Brunswick, N.J.: Transaction Books, 1986). As of 1979 there were 270 kibbutzim with a total population of 120,000, or 3.66 percent of the population.

58. Victor Olgyay, *Design with Climate* (Princeton: Princeton University Press, 1963).

59. Roland Wiedenhoeft, *Berlin's Housing Revolution: German Reform in the 1920s* (Ann Ar-bor: University of Michigan Research Press, 1971).

60. Lembrecht Migge, *Die Wachsende Siedlung, nach biologischen Gesetzen* (Stuttgart:Franck-ische verlagshandlung, 1932).
61. Ludwig Hilberseimer, *The New City* (Chicago: Theobald, 1944). For a critique of Hilber-seimer's urbanism, see Albert Pope, *Ladders* (Rice University Press, forthcoming).
62. Fernández Galiano, *El fuego.*
63. Leland M. Roth, *America Builds: Source Documents in American Architecture and Plan-ning* (New York: Harper and Row, 1983), pp. 364–76; Stanislaus von Moos, *Le Corbusier: Elements of a Synthesis* (Cambridge: MIT Press, 1972).
64. Fishman, *Urban Utopias,* pp. 122–55, cites Wright's opinion of cities: "To look at the plan of any great city is to look at the cross-section of some fibrous tumor." His categories of housing in Broadacre City were based on the number of automobiles one owned, from one to five.
65. Tim Benton, ed., *Le Corbusier, Architect of the Century* (London: Arts Council of Great Britain, 1987), pp. 299–303.
66. Eduard Sekler and William Curtis, *Le Corbusier at Work: The Genesis of the Carpenter Cen-ter for the Visual Arts* (Cambridge: Harvard University Press, 1978).
67. Reyner Banham, "Frank Lloyd Wright as Environmentalist," *Arts and Architecture,* Sep-tember 1966, pp. 26–30. Banham analyzes the Prairie Houses as thermally well-planned structures.
68. John Sergeant, *Frank Lloyd Wright's Usonian Houses: The Case for Organic Architecture* (New York: Whitney Library of Design, 1976), pp. 15–30.
69. Donald W. Aitkin, "The Solar Hemicycle Revisited: It's Still Showing the Way," *Wisconsin Academic Review* 39, no. 1 (Winter 1992–93): 33; many thanks to Jeff Chusid for this source.
70. Brendan Gill, *Many Masks: A Life of Frank Lloyd Wright* (New York: Putnam, 1987), pp. 326–34.
71. Butti and Perlin, *Golden Thread,* pp. 200–217.
72. Thomas Hines, *Richard Neutra and the Search for Modern Architecture: A Biography and History* (New York: Oxford University Press, 1982). The Moore House in Ojai is perhaps the best example. Neutra's *Survival through Design* (New York: Oxford University Press, 1954) contained his "biorealist" position.
73. Richard Plunz, ed., *Design and the Public Good: Selected Writing, 1930–1980, by Serge Cher-mayeff* (Cambridge: MIT Press, 1982).
74. Christopher Alexander et al., *A Pattern Language* (New York: Oxford University Press, 1977).
75. Richard Ingersoll, "Utopia Limited: Houston's Ring around the Beltway," *Cite* 31 (Winter–Spring 1994): 10–17.
76. Richard Ingersoll, "Interview with Richard Stein," *Design Book Review* 20 (Spring 1991).
77. Sim van der Ryn and Peter Calthorpe, *Sustainable Communities* (San Francisco: Sierra Club Books, 1986), pp. 17–18.
78. Ibid., p. 39.
79. Don Canty, "Sea Ranch," *Progressive Architecture,* February 1993, pp. 84–92. The initial planning concept of Sea Ranch degenerated a few years after and is criticized by the origi-nal protagonists as "suburbanization."
80. Richard Ingersoll, "The Ecology Question," *Journal of Architectural Education* 45, no. 2 (February 1992): 125–27.
81. Manfredo Tafuri, *Vienna Rossa: La politica residenziale nella Vienna Socialista, 1919–1933* (Milan: Electa, 1980).
82. Barry Commoner, "Ending the War against the Earth," *Nation,* April 30, 1990, p. 589. This has been at the cost of over one trillion dollars.
83. Bramwell, *Ecology,* 195–208, reveals that the Nazis were the first radical environmentalists to achieve political authority at the state level. Somehow the world is still not ready to ac-cept that Dachau was not only the site of a notorious death camp but also of an experimen-tal organic farm, and ecologists will doubtlessly feel squeamish about this historical prece-

dent. Rudolf Hess, Hitler's deputy, and Walther Darré, the minister of agriculture, helped establish two thousand biodynamic farms, based on the organic principles of Rudolph Steiner. Nazi Germany was also the first European country to establish nature reserves. Nazi slogans such as "Blood and soil" and "A new era is upon us which will be the era of the peasant" made a tight fit with ecology. That both Hitler and Himmler were vegetarians and believed in animal rights also created a natural affinity.

84. Pippo Ciorra, *Peter Eisenman: Opere e progetti* (Milan: Electa, 1994), pp. 200–202. The project for Max Reinhardt Haus, Berlin (1992), for example, is based on a metaphorical application of "folding," in emulation of folding theory in physics.

85. Kenneth Frampton, "Critical Regionalism," in Hal Foster, ed., *The Anti-Aesthetic* (Port Townsend, Wash.: Bay Press, 1983). The term "critical regionalism" was originally coined by Alexander Tzonis and Liane Lefaivre.

86. S. Ishida and C. Garbato, *Renzo Piano: Buildings and Projects, 1971–1989* (New York: Rizzoli, 1989), pp. 92–119.

87. Michael Crosbie, *Green Architecture* (Washington, D.C.: AIA Press, 1994).

88. Charles Correa, *The New Landscape* (London: Butterworth Architecture, 1989).

89. Peter Calthorpe, *The Next American Metropolis* (New York: Princeton Architectural Press, 1993).

90. Peter Katz, *New Urbanism: Toward an Architecture of Community* (New York: McGraw-Hill, 1994).

91. Richard Register, *Ecocity Berkeley: Building Cities for a Healthy Future* (Berkeley: North Atlantic Books, 1987).

92. On Almere, see Richard Ingersoll, "L'Orizzonte perduto delle città nuove: The Woodlands e Almere nella vastità megalopolitana," *Casabella* 58, no. 614 (July–August 1994): 22–35; on Curitiba, see Kris Herbst, "Brazil's Model City: Is Curitiba Too Good to Be True?" *Planning,* September 1992, pp. 24–27.

CULTURAL STUDIES AND CRITICAL PEDAGOGY: CULTURAL PEDAGOGY AND ARCHITECTURE

INTRODUCTION: REVIVING "CRITICAL" AND AGENCY

The last fifteen to twenty years have witnessed extensive change in architectural expression and discourse. Architecture has exploded into a throng of aesthetic styles and preferences, each striving for visibility. Such distinguishes the postmodern in architecture, where the command of a visual dominant is neutralized by the sheer volume of competing fashions that simultaneously (and contradictorily) stand independent and incorporate each other. As Jim Collins puts it: "Post-Modernism departs from its predecessors in that as a textual practice it actually incorporates the heterogeneity of those conflicting styles, rather than simply asserting itself as the newest radical alternative seeking to render all conflicting modes of representation obsolete."[1] Hollywood supplies ready and sometimes startling examples of this. In Ridley Scott's *Blade Runner,* the dystopic future landscape of Los Angeles is one of massive corporate power towering over teeming masses, where gray, bleak wastelands are punctuated by the posh extravagance of neon and electronic billboards patrolling overhead, and where architectural imagery vibrates from the collision of Mayan, Chinese, Egyptian, Greek, and Roman revival styles side by side with modernist and futuristic representations. Architecture, invigorated by the rise of the postmodern condition, incorporates heterogeneity at a feverish pace, the likes of which we have never seen. This complexity and confusion I suspect make it difficult even for Charles Jencks to keep up.

An important question to ask amid this hemorrhage of change is whether there has been any progressive thinking about social accountability, about theorizing a critical architecture and what this may hold for architectural practice and design strategy. Not so long ago, questions of social justice and progressive politics were more central to architects' conceptualization of their professional responsibilities. Such a shift has been twenty or so years in the making, and by default, architecture has been complicitous in the larger cultural-political transformation of the postmodern age. In the late 1970s and early 1980s architecture centered around trends promoting a return to history and historical allusion, the analysis of precedent, the nostalgic paths of classicism and the lessons of Rome, and the use of parody and double coding. A more recent swing of the pendulum promotes strategies of disjunction, the poetics of desolation, the attempt for an architecture of the floating signifier, for an architecture that means nothing, and finally the propensity for an architecture to be undecidable and to deconstruct the discipline of architecture as a referent for a world that is indeterminate and confused.[2] As one might expect of an architectural media hungry to exploit trends by casting them into marketable fashions to sell magazines, these two loosely defined trends have been codified into the binary of "reconstruction" and "deconstruction." Whatever they may be called, I do not reject them summarily (for there are lessons to be learned from Rome, and strategies of disjunction can reveal new meanings through diverse juxtapositions), but my point is that their theoretical formation and application were constructed within conservative discourses. Reconstruction has to be understood within the context of "counter-revolution," (as critical theorist Herbert Marcuse put it),[3] that is, the thrust by corporations and other institutions of power to relegitimate their waning authority through the appropriation of historical style, after the sting of the 1960s. Deconstruction, understood somewhat parochially as a counterresponse to reconstruction's claim to establish coherent meaning in architecture, is remarkably similar to the economic practices that have gushed forth in the restructuring of capitalism from Fordism to flexible accumulation.

I realize the danger in collapsing architectural trends into another binary. What I find amusing, though, is that both positions proclaim social commitment. Historicists articulate the humanist project to restore certainty and authenticity through the revival of tradition, no matter how literal or abstract. The deconstructionists seek to promote the posthumanist project of the end of (take your pick) truth, history, subjectivity, theory, representation, the author. Espousing social responsibility, then, the historicists try to strike responsive chords to pacify a troubled world. Also espousing social responsibility, the deconstructionists try to disrupt frames of reference, manipulate meaning, and undermine convention as means to opening texts and experiences to alternative interpretations. But in the end both these tracks are reifications: neither offers constructive strategies for the transformation of society.[4] While the historicists try to provide direction in a confused world (precisely whose world?), couching their project in a universalist discourse that silences many in the name of tradition, the deconstructionists withdraw from social direction and wind up merely articulating that confusion.

An architecture of social responsibility (worthy of the name) resists dominant social trends in order to promote social justice and "radical democracy" and works toward liberation by helping groups achieve a spatial voice in new forms of community and solidarity, conceived within difference. This brings us closer to a better definition of "critical," arguably the most overused and hence meaningless word in architectural discourse today. If social responsibility and the social project are to advance, architects must recover this term "critical," as well as infuse it with progressive meanings appropriate to today's conditions. The definition I prefer aligns closely with the views of historian Bryan Palmer and feminist critic Nancy

Fraser. Palmer insists that "critical" is "not simply a question of the arbitrary and coercive espousal of premises, precepts, and categories, but rests instead on the kinds of coherent thought that can actually lead to the emancipation of humanity."[5] Fraser says something similar: "A critical social theory frames its research program and its conceptual framework with an eye to the aims and activities of those oppositional social movements with which it has a partisan, though not uncritical, identification. The questions it asks and the models it designs are informed by that identification and interest."[6] A better definition of "critical," then, works against the social construction of inequity and injustice and does not hesitate to name oppression. A better definition strives to demystify representations that construct reality for individuals. Demystification of this sort must be context specific, working through the representations of life of particular audiences as one comes to know how such audiences experience reality. In this vein demystification is empowering, creating the conditions whereby languages of critique and possibility develop, enabling people to reflect and take action. The following words of critical pedagogues Peter McLaren and Tomaz Tadeu da Silva are instructive for architects:

> The task . . . is to provide the conditions for individuals to acquire a language that will enable them to reflect upon and shape their own experiences and in certain instances transform such experiences in the interest of a larger project of social responsibility. This language is not the language of the metropolitan intellectual or the high-priests of the post-avant-garde, although it may borrow from their insights. It is a language that operates critically by promoting a deep affinity for the suffering of the oppressed and their struggle for liberation, by brushing commonsense experience against the grain, by interfering with the codes that bind cultural life shut and prevent its rehistoricization and politicization, by puncturing the authority of monumental culture and causing dominant representations to spill outside their prescribed and conventional limits.[7]

Not enough architects today heed the words of McLaren and da Silva. The project remains for architects to engage oppositional discourses that critique dominant trends and offer transformative possibilities with regard to ethics, cultural values, and new societal directions. This chapter contributes to this larger project by tracing developments that have emerged within the humanities and education, namely cultural studies and critical pedagogy. Prevalent among these two oppositional discourses is a concern for agency, that is, the attempt to understand how people value their world and act within it. If architecture lies at the intersection of culture, power, and representation and thus contributes to our identities and how we know the world, then a concern for agency would consciously probe that relationship between architecture and identity. This seems obvious and hardly worth

THOMAS A. DUTTON

mentioning except that with much postmodern theory, with its pervasive tone of nihilism and antiutopianism, human agency is drowning and now requires resuscitation. The insight that cultural studies and critical pedagogy bring to agency helps us recognize that making meaning and acting out choices are cultural and pedagogical processes, enveloped in experiences cut by race, class, gender, ethnicity, and so on. Within the frames of cultural studies and critical pedagogy, to take agency seriously is not merely to analyze or investigate social data. It is to structure experience and knowledge in ways that can lead to more transformative notions about how life might be lived, both theoretically and practically. This means, to cite Nancy Harstock, that cultural critics need "to expose and clarify theoretical bases for political alliance and solidarity" around "emancipatory accounts of subjectivity," as well as to effectuate those bases into material practices for transformative ends.[8]

For architects, then, their contribution to breathe life into agency can be to theorize, consciously and explicitly, the cultural production of identity and to develop processes that reveal how people make sense of their world and how they make meaning of buildings and community environments. But understanding such concrete meanings, hopes, and experiences is just the first step. The next one is to work *with* and work *on* such knowledge, weaving it into the wider project to alter the production of meaning in society (by making form, enabling program, structuring space) in the interests of social justice, solidarity, and democracy; in effect, to intend transformative meaning and experience (knowledge) through architecture. Knowledge, and most certainly transformative knowledge, can never be just something offered, or simply intended, by those who believe they possess it. Knowledge has to be produced. Just like the interaction among students and teachers engaged in the production of classroom knowledge, architects and publics (social movements) can collaborate to develop new knowledge for transformative ends. So, in sum, taking agency seriously means two things. First, it means that architects cannot step back from intending politically transformative meanings through the medium of their work, based upon the cultural capital of publics. Second, to weave transformative political content into architectural form and experience presupposes the need for architects to link organically with politically transformative movements, which, in turn, necessitates developing professional practices that ensure a mutual interaction between publics and architects. If architects embrace agency in this critical fashion, they can operate as "organic intellectuals," participating in social movements and encouraging citizens to act on their agency, opening the possibility for them to critique their lived experiences and to act upon those forces shaping their lives through their contribution to, and use and management of, buildings.

Issues of agency, process, and social action are not antithetical to beauty and good form. Often, social responsibility is equated with designing for the lowest common demoninator, appealing to mass interests unreflectively, without theory. As such, social responsibility is positioned against beauty and aesthetics as the negative other, a hindrance to be avoided because it compromises formal interest and investigation. This need not be the case, as richer form can come through social responsibility. We will see this in the work of Dolores Hayden, Lucien Kroll, and Gunter Behnisch and Partner.

To this end—a social project invigorated by "critical" and agency—this chapter examines the intersection of cultural studies and critical pedagogy and what this holds for redirecting architectural theory and practice in more progressive directions: cultural pedagogy.[9] As I will show, setting architecture at this intersection highlights ethics, identity, difference, and voice as central principles of both a transformative architecture and a larger struggle for critical democracy in social life. Cultural pedagogy helps reconstruct the social project in architecture.

CULTURAL STUDIES

Generally, what is now called cultural studies is a progressive, academic-based movement investigating the relationship between daily life and society. It concerns how social groups produce, constrain, and transform meaning in their struggle to place themselves within society and to contribute to their understanding of culture. Power is a key theoretical category of analysis here, in that in its social production and distribution, it establishes cultural asymmetries that both enable and disable individuals and social groups to define themselves and realize their needs. Another important category is signification and its cultural-political ramifications. Cultural studies examines literature, art, architecture, and media representation as signifying practices, probing what is and what is not "said" as these practices are taken up by particular social subjects. A decidedly popular cast, then, imbues the tradition of cultural studies. Much of the best work in the field has probed popular culture. Evolving strategies that have pioneered the production of theory as well as method, cultural critics reveal much about the experiences of everyday life, from the reception of television news and soap operas to the inner world of punk subcultures and life among working-class youths in high school. Cultural studies charts power, culture, and representation in their myriad interrelations to bring into focus the construction of personal and social identities; in short, the production of human subjectivities as they cut across different terrains.

"Customarily, cultural studies is seen to begin with the publication of Richard Hoggart's *The Uses of Literacy* (1957) and Raymond Williams's *Culture and Society 1780–1950* (1958) and *The Long Revolution* (1961)."[10] These words are from *British Cultural Studies* (1992), by cultural theorist Graeme Turner, a very useful book tracing the history, development, and contribution of cultural studies in Britain, especially as it took form in the Birmingham Centre for Contemporary Cultural

Studies (BCCCS), begun under Hoggart's directorship in 1964. Cultural critic Stuart Hall, deputy director of the Centre from 1966 to 1968 and director from 1969 to 1979 and a leading cultural studies theorist today, agrees with Turner as to cultural studies' foundations but adds E. P. Thompson's *The Making of the English Working Class* to the list of formative texts. These texts did not inaugurate outright a new, coherent disciplinary line of cultural research and critique. It was more that they provided a new insight for a different kind of cultural-political engagement. Each in their own way "brought disciplined thought to bear on the understanding of their own times."[11] These writers confronted new constellations of economic, political, and cultural forces that began to converge in postwar British society. Primary here were the revival of capitalist production, the advent of the cold war, and the establishment of the welfare state. Equally significant in this "re-narrativization of England" was the "historic rendezvous of the colonizer and colonized" within England itself as "colonized peoples chose to migrate to *their* home of England," which, as cultural critic Bill Schwarz puts it, replayed the "primal narratives of earlier 'encounters'" in such ways as to reracialize English society, and "white ethnicity" in particular.[12] This reconfiguring of English society contributed to profound economic and cultural transformations: shifts in class formations and consciousness, capitalist practices, and cultural representations. One of cultural studies' greatest contributions to intellectural criticism is that it problematizes this dialectic between the economic and the cultural. As E. P. Thompson remarked, "There is no such thing as economic growth which is not, at the same time, growth and change of a culture."[13]

In the same way that cultural studies was a product and producer of its cultural-political environment, the BCCCS found itself navigating within a particular intellectual-historical conjuncture. Cultural studies represents a convergence of the domains of literary studies and criticism, structuralism, semiotics, and Marxism. Although embroiled in their own traditions, cultural studies burrowed its way through these domains, engaging each singularly for purposes of reconstructing and recombining them collectively into a new integrative force for critical cultural theory and practice.

Literary Studies

Initially, literary studies and criticism was the dominant domain within the BCCCS. Working within the shadow of elitist definitions of culture — what was considered the best in art, literature, and thought — each of the texts mentioned above moved toward a fundamentally contrary conception of culture: "when we are at our most natural, our most everyday, we are also at our most cultural."[14] These texts advanced this contrary conception of culture in two ways. First, they responded to the deeply felt need within British society to take up the burgeoning cultural landscape exploding across all terrains—the proliferation of television, new forms of music, rock and roll, the Beatles of Liverpool, the jukebox, the cinema, the mass circulation of newspapers as well as crime and romance novels, and so on. Second, in the attempt to apply literary forms of analysis to these wider cultural products, the object of study was unabashedly the representations within working-class cultures. As Hall portrays Hoggart's *Uses of Literacy,* it deployed "literary criticism to 'read' the emblems, idioms, social arrangements, the lived cultures and 'languages' of working class life, as particular kinds of 'text.' "[15]

Structuralism

This new effort to connect texts and society—to link literary analysis with social inquiry—required new theoretical ground from which to comprehend this dialectic more deeply in its interrelations. The charge became, as Turner states, that "one was required to think about how culture was structured as a whole before one could examine its processes or its constitutive parts."[16] The Continental influence of structuralism, which studied the structural nature of language based upon Saussurean linguistics, provided a timely, useful framework. Thus originally organized around a theory of language rather than a theory of society or culture, the structuralist impulse nonetheless offered a theoretical frame that allowed for a theory of culture in ways that did not dissolve culture into language. Hall is instructive here: "Structuralism's main emphasis was on the specificity, the irreducibility, of the cultural. Culture no longer simply reflected other practices in the realm of ideas. It was itself a practice—a signifying practice—and had its own determinate product: meaning."[17]

Semiotics

The question of meaning—what texts mean, to whom, based on what—took a giant step forward in the late 1960s and early 1970s with the importation of semiotics into cultural studies. Although Hoggart, Williams, Hall, and others were engaged in reading social practices, cultural products, and even institutions as texts, the success of such attempts was limited by a reluctance to modify literary criticism's methods as well as the ideological assumptions upon which these methods were based. In essence, the effort to broaden the concept of text beyond the printed page to include the wider experiences, arrangements, and processes of everyday and working-class life, although exemplary, was thwarted by the lingering dominance of "literary-moral"[18] definitions of culture rather than anthropological ones. Semiotics supplied cultural studies with a vocabulary and theoretical frame that enabled the cultural analysis of nonlinguistic signs.[19] Not until semiotics became accessible through the works of Roland Barthes and Umberto Eco in the late sixties were the semiological and sociological — "the power of texts and the importance of social and political contexts"[20] — combined in ways that gave cultural studies its distinctive character.

Marxism

Cultural studies' links with Marxism took a crucial turn at this time. From the beginning cultural studies held an uneasy alliance with Marxism. As Hall says in his "Cultural Studies and Its Theoretical Legacies," "There never was a prior moment when cultural studies and Marxism represent[ed] a perfect theoretical fit."[21] But the fascination was clearly there, as Hall continues:

> Cultural studies [was] profoundly influenced by the questions that Marxism as a theoretical project put on the agenda: the power, the global reach and history-making capacities of capital; the question of class; the complex relationships between power... and exploitation; the question of a general theory which could... connect together in a critical reflection different domains of life, politics and theory, theory and practice, economic, political, ideological questions, and so on; the notion of critical knowledge itself and the production of critical knowledge as a practice. These important, central questions are what one meant by working within shouting distance of Marxism, working on Marxism, working against Marxism, working with it, working to try to develop Marxism.[22]

In essence, the adaptation of Marxism to cultural studies began as a critique and reconstruction of Marxism, in hopes of countering its orthodoxy. Orthodox Marxists displayed historical and theoretical insensitivity to the questions of culture and had "misconceived the very meaning and nature of culture, and as such had failed to develop adequate notions of consciousness, experience, or human agency."[23] Although traditional Marxism placed compelling questions on the agenda, their dialectical relations were often subordinated to a vulgar economism that devalued the significance of culture by positioning it as part of the superstructure of society, merely a reflex of the economic base.

It was the work of the French Marxist philosopher Louis Althusser that allowed cultural studies to insist that culture was not simply reflexive of economic relationships, nor was it independent of them, either. Not uncoincidentally, then, Althusser advocated a Marxism influenced by structuralism, wherein the "social formation" is regarded as a "decentered structure."[24] In other words, many determining forces — economic, cultural, and racial, for instance — compete and conflict with each other while maintaining some degree of autonomy within the complex mix we call society. Marxism, through the structuralist nuances of Althusser, helped cultural studies create a space for culture as a determining force in society and to envelop itself as a progressive, political project.

Although Althusserian Marxism was a vitally important icebreaker, opening the field and orienting structuralism to progressive investigations, it was the turn to the late Italian Marxist Antonio Gramsci that gave cultural studies its cutting edge, especially in theorizing ideology, human agency, and the role of intellectuals. In his *Gramsci's Marxism,* political scientist Carl Boggs notes that "throughout Gramsci's writings, the role of ideological struggle in the revolutionary process looms very large — an emphasis reflected in the concept of 'ideological hegemony,' the dominant and probably the most original construct in his work."[25] Boggs explains more of Gramsci's view of hegemony, that "domination is exercised as much through popular 'consensus' achieved in civil society as through physical coercion (or threat of it) by the state apparatus, especially in advanced capitalist societies where education, the media, law, mass culture, etc. take on a new role."[26] This notion of hegemony was a significant breakthrough in the debates about the role and function of ideology. Marxists have always had difficulty in theorizing and explaining Marx's dictum that the ruling ideas of society are the ideas of the ruling class. How do ruling ideas come to rule? How is it that some social meanings gain legitimacy while alternative and perhaps oppositional meanings are pushed away, repressed? Ideological compulsion?

Gramsci's ideological hegemony suggests that the social process by which meanings are produced, distributed, and signified is characterized by struggle and contestation, and that the meanings that come to be privileged are fought for, accomplished, consented to, won. In other words, hegemony is more than simply that dominant groups dominate. Dominant groups have to win over the subordinated. Hegemony manufactures consent. Turner puts it succinctly:

> The idea of hegemony does not suggest that domination is achieved by
> manipulating the worldview of the masses. Rather, it argues that in order
> for cultural leadership to be achieved, the dominant group has to engage in
> negotiations with opposing groups, classes, and values — and that these
> negotiations must result in some *genuine* accommodation. That is,
> hegemony is not maintained through the obliteration of the opposition but
> through the *articulation* of opposing interests into the political affiliations
> of the "hegemonic" group.[27]

This notion of ideological hegemony has tremendous, liberating implications for human agency. Because if hegemony is something "not automatically delivered by way of the class structure"[28] but secured through contestation and struggle, it means that ideological control and domination are never completely determined, closed, without resistance. It means that popular culture is a strategic battleground where dominating and oppositional forces clash for hegemonic power. Popular culture is contested terrain where the process of signification—what gets represented, by whom, and how—is what we call politics. In this view, popular culture can never be reduced simply to mass culture, supposedly congruent with dominant ideology, a view rendering human agents as mere props, or as the effects of determinants that preclude the possibility of resistance and transformation.

These insights begin to unravel the threads of the structuralist carpet and to reposition the human agent as a reflexive yet socially constructed subject that mediates the world. The drawback of structuralism, while initially strategic to cultural studies, was that it contained too much theoretical baggage that reduced the "importance of consciousness and experience as ... determinants in shaping history."[29] Educational critic Henry Giroux puts it this way: "The force of the structuralist argument rests in its rejection of consciousness ... and experience as adequate starting-points to understand how a society functions and reproduces itself. ... Put another way, it is the force of material practices and the constituting social relations they produce that, in this case, reduce human beings to props or supports of structurally determined roles."[30]

Gramsci's contribution to cultural studies provided the theoretical path to rescue the passivity of human agency from the grips of a disabling structuralism. Through Gramsci, the human subject (like ideology) cannot be understood as something delivered through given structures, the result of discourses and contexts that circumscribe a person. The turn to Gramsci affirms human agency as self-reflective and mediating, and counters structuralist accounts that exhaust the possibility of maneuverability, struggle, and transformation.

Gramsci's theory about the role of intellectuals—the "organic intellectual"—in capitalist society and its significance to cultural studies constitutes another seminal contribution. As Stuart Hall recalls the intention of the BCCCS, "There is no doubt in my mind that we were trying to find an institutional practice in cultural studies that might produce an organic intellectual. ... Gramsci's account still seems to me to come closest to expressing what it is I think we were trying to do."[31] Writing in the wake of the Bolshevik revolution, Gramsci evolved the concept of organic intellectuals as persons who, as Boggs writes, "must be an organic part of the community: they must articulate new values within the shared language and symbols of the larger culture."[32] Thus:

> New ideas would not be introduced or "propagandized" as extraneous inputs into mass politics but would be integrated into the very fabric of proletarian culture, life-styles, language, traditions, etc. by revolutionaries who themselves worked and lived within the same environment. Only this

could ensure the dialectical relationship between theory and practice, the intellectual and the spontaneous, the political and the social, which could lay the foundations of an authentic *Marxist* subjectivity in popular consciousness itself.[33]

As this charge was taken up by the BCCCS and gradually became its very heart as a cultural-political project, it became clear that organic, intellectual work had to address two fronts. Hall explains:

> On the one hand, we had to be at the very forefront of intellectual theoretical work because, as Gramsci says, it is the job of the organic intellectual to know more than the traditional intellectuals do: really know, not just pretend to know.... But the second aspect is just as critical: that the organic intellectual cannot absolve himself or herself from the responsibility of transmitting those ideas, that knowledge, through the intellectual function, to those who do not belong, professionally, in the intellectual class. And unless those two fronts are operating at the same time, or at least unless those two ambitions are part of the project of cultural studies, you can get enormous theoretical advance without any engagement at the level of the political project.[34]

Ethnography

Although constantly changing, the trajectory of cultural studies through the intellectual frames of literary studies, structuralism, semiotics, and Marxism resulted in a compelling blend of intellectual work spanning disciplines, practices, and theories. This convergence marks the reformulation of culture as a key, critical category for analyzing the social forms structuring human life: the processes by which humans gain consciousness, make choices, and sustain their identities.[35] Cultural studies remains a progressive cultural-political project directing analyses to popular culture, the life of the everyday, with the end to dissect society's structures of domination, that is, the connection between social relations and power. The object is to analyze the workings of power relations in such sites as the workplace, the school, youth subcultures, working-class housing, and even the home in the activity of watching television. Such analyses attempt to educate citizens so they can maneuver better to negotiate interests, to weigh options, and to act as responsible agents. Always theorizing how cultural domination and hegemony are sustained through the continual winning of consent, cultural studies constantly seeks to understand how consent is won and how negotiations are framed as first steps in forging an agency indispensable to countering hegemony.

Perhaps no better example of this search to analyze the workings of hegemony and counterhegemony exists than in the ethnographic work of the BCCCS. Emerging out of the general trend toward qualitative research, ethnography developed as a means to study concretely the production of cultural life. Ethnography is defined as that tradition in anthropology and sociology "that provides techniques for researchers to enter another culture, participate in it and observe it, and then describe the ways in which it makes sense for those within it,"[36] as well as those on the outside. If cultural critics are to understand how social groups take up everyday life, they will have to merge with those groups and develop methods that can describe those lives with some degree of accuracy, but in a manner that is also critical and self-reflexive on the part of the researcher.

Although not born of the BCCCS, ethnographic practice was modified and extended by the Centre and constitutes some of its best work. As professor Richard Quantz states, "The adoption of ethnography as a major approach to research at the Centre resulted from an interest in tying theory to reflected experience."[37] The concern was that if experience without theoretical grounding was in "danger of ideological distortion," theoretical developments outside experience only encouraged "myopic and irrelevant formalism."[38] In this way, ethnography became more than an empirical exercise that merely documented what was seen or experienced by the researcher. It became theoretical inquiry as well, offering "a practical model of theoretically informed empirical work."[39]

During the 1970s several fascinating studies were published by the BCCCS that concentrated on the subcultural instead of the dominant culture, on subordinant groups and their meanings rather than the dominant and its meanings. For example, Phil Cohen's seminal 1972 article, "Subcultural Conflict and Working Class Community," offers a penetrating account of how the construction of "housing estates" in East London after World War II actively participated in the destruction of working-class communities.[40] Dick Hebdige's *Subculture: The Meaning of Style,* published in 1979, takes the reader on a wild ride through the youth subcultures of postwar Britain: the Teddy boys, skinheads, mods and rockers, and punks.[41] Mostly interested in the political readings of subcultural style, those that seem to challenge hegemony or subvert dominant meanings, Hebdige provides a lucid semiological reading of the meanings surrounding dress, dance, music, and behavioral styles. But it is the work of Paul Willis in his *Learning to Labour: How Working Class Kids Get Working Class Jobs* (1977) that marks a high point in ethnographic research within cultural studies.[42] Conducted over a three-year period in the mid-1970s, Willis followed the lives of twelve closely tied working-class "lads" within their final years of school and in the workplace after graduation. As part of his research, Willis attended class with the boys, worked alongside them, and relied upon personal interviews with parents, teachers, shop managers, and employees. Group interviews, informal discussions, and diaries were also used. The study is not simply empirical, as Willis offers a larger political analysis of the workings of social power and ideology in working-class culture as a setting for the ethnographic evidence.

Willis examined the dynamics of the lads' school culture within the material relations of the broader society. And what he concludes through his analysis is startling. Willis found that the boys resisted school life at almost every turn. Willis began his project by questioning how working-class youths come to fill working-class jobs and what roles schools play in equipping them for later life. The answer apparently was that working-class kids chose such jobs because they saw them as serving their interests in defiance to the middle-class bias of most schoolwork. Seeing academic knowledge and the logic of the school as a great con, as negating their masculine-based subcultural codes, the youths resisted, setting up a "counter-school culture" where their contempt for education took some form in every aspect of school life: in their lack of attendance, their truancy, by avoiding homework, "by being in class and doing no work," by "roaming the corridors looking for excitement."[43] This is an odd resistance, not one that leads to new ideas about the reorganization of life or how consciousness might be politically transformed, but one that well prepares the youths "for the unskilled working class jobs in which they end up."[44] This is a resistance that works against their own emancipation. As Graeme Turner says, "A better example of the process of hegemony would be hard to find."[45]

Cultural Studies and the United States

Because of such compelling work as well as its publications, studies, and personnel, the BCCCS enjoys world fame. Not surprisingly, cultural studies can be found in some form the world over. This is certainly the case within the United States, where cultural studies has crested since its float across the Atlantic. As Cary Nelson, Paula Treichler, and Lawrence Grossberg announced in 1992, "Cultural studies is experiencing ... an unprecedented international boom. ... In the United States, where the boom is especially strong, many academic institutions — presses, journals, hiring committees, conferences, university curricula — have created significant investment opportunities in cultural studies."[46] The boom is not just geographical. Cultural studies constitutes an explosion across all cultural terrains. In April 1990, an important international conference — "Cultural Studies Now and in the Future" — was held in the American Midwest at the University of Illinois at Urbana-Champaign. The breadth of the subject matter was extensive: "the history of cultural studies, gender and sexuality, nationhood and national identity, colonialism and post-colonialism, race and ethnicity, popular culture and its audiences, science and ecology, identity politics, pedagogy, the politics of aesthetics, cultural institutions, the politics of disciplinarity, discourse and textuality, history, and global culture in a postmodern age."[47]

This explosion across terrains and the consequent blurring of their boundaries constitute genuine excitement by those seeking new practices forged by the interpenetration and crossing of intellectual borders, who draw from whatever fields necessary "to produce the knowledge required for a particular project."[48] In this sense, cultural studies is not just one discipline: it is interdisciplinary, and perhaps antidisciplinary.[49] It is a loose web encompassing multiple actions taking place in multiple sites. This may be cultural studies' greatest contribution to intellectual work. Social critic bell hooks judges cultural studies exciting and compelling because "it makes a space for dialogue between intellectuals, critical thinkers, etc. who may in the past have stayed within narrow disciplinary concerns. . . . And it is rapidly becoming one of the few locations in the academy where there is the possibility of inter-racial and cross-cultural discussion."[50] This is the potential for cultural studies, that it can forge a collectivity organized through a language of solidarity, engendering interrelationships of disciplines without minimalizing or depoliticizing their specificity. Cultural studies can address this task by providing a larger frame through which discourses, disciplines, and social movements can interconnect and give form to something larger than their separate causes.

It remains to be seen whether cultural studies can do this, a question we will examine later in this chapter in the form of a critique of cultural studies and its implications for architecture.

CRITICAL PEDAGOGY

Distinct from but complementary to cultural studies, critical pedagogy holds great theoretical and practical value for progressive cultural-political work. Relying upon the vast contribution and practice of world-reknowned educator Paulo Freire and other critical pedagogues who attempt to broaden the meaning of pedagogy, I suggest that critical pedagogy can be a vital intellectual frame for the practice of architecture.

The term "pedagogy" typically evokes educational environments. Schools, universities, and classrooms are commonly acknowledged as sites where pedagogy is institutionalized. Accordingly, pedagogy is something that teachers do. Often it is seen simply as teaching technique. This unfortunate definition robs the term of its more provocative and potentially liberating forms of human exchange. In our postmodern world, where now the production of meaning may be as important as the production of labor, such a definition needs broadening beyond its association with schools and classrooms and the mechanics of technique. A better definition equates pedagogy with the social production of meaning generally. In this sense, pedagogy refers to "all those practices that define what is important to know, how it is to be known, and how this production of knowledge helps to construct social identities."[51] Pedagogy is part of processes shaping what people know and how they come to know it, processes always inherent within institutions and other social forms. This definition of pedagogy establishes a useful theoretical tool to dissect and explain some of the confusion, spectacle, and dazzle of the postmodern age. It also describes a classroom. Classrooms are in fact sites where strategies and techniques are enacted to define what is important to know—say, biology—how it is to be known—say, dissection of frogs—and these realities certainly help to construct one's view of the world, one's values, one's attitudes: one's subjectivity. Hence, "any practice which intentionally tries to influence the production of meaning is a pedagogical practice."[52]

Pedagogy in this broader sense focuses on how people come to understand and articulate their subjectivities. It investigates the social distribution of meaning and knowledge, the institutional constraints of that distribution, and thus how people and groups construct meaning. It means, in essence, probing the links between knowledge and power, because like any commodity, "knowledge is a social construct, produced and distributed according to particular voices situated in relations of power for particular ends."[53]

If this constitutes an expanded conception of pedagogy, a *critical* pedagogy recognizes that all forms of learning are enveloped in political processes. As Roger Simon writes, "To propose a pedagogy is to propose a political vision,"[54] which can be turned around to say that proposing a political vision is also to propose a pedagogy. For example, schools in particular are never neutral sites or free spaces above the conflicts of society. Tangled within the infinite relations of society, they unavoidably produce, reproduce, and challenge political, social, cultural, and economic directions of society. Schools, like any institution, are places of ongoing struggle over meaning, truth claims, the organization of knowledge and interpersonal relations, classroom practices, and so on.

Recognizing the inherently political nature of teaching and learning, critical pedagogy gravitates toward those theories and practices advocating social transformation. There is a moral imperative here. In a world of needless pain and social suffering, critical pedagogy values social justice, democracy, equality, and emancipation. This is why critical pedagogy is critical. Deriving its project in part from the long history and tradition of critical theory, critical pedagogues such as Paulo Freire, Henry Giroux, Kathleen Weiler, Roger Simon, bell hooks, Peter McLaren, Michael Apple, and Stanley Aronowitz consistently interrogate the social construction of reality and the dominant interests and educational institutions instrumental in its reproduction. Their aim has been to name, penetrate, and break the forms of domination within all types of pedagogical practice that have accompanied the emerging forms of capitalism and late capitalism.

Paulo Freire

One compelling example of critical pedagogy rests with the work of Paulo Freire. Freire, a Brazilian, holds a worldwide reputation but (interestingly) is not so well known in the United States. His influence is extensive on two fronts. Geographically, as Peter McLaren and Peter Leonard point out in their tribute to him, *Paulo Freire: A Critical Encounter,* his work has been instrumental in "dozens of countries spanning four continents,"[55] including Nicaragua, Cuba, Chile, Tanzania, Angola, and Guina-Bissau. Intellectually, Freire's influence has been felt in education, social work, liberation theology, sociology, economics, and participatory research, to name a few. Not surprisingly, Freire is considered "a philosopher and revolutionary educator of pivotal significance to the project of liberation and social transformation."[56]

Freire currently is secretary of education of the city of Sao Paulo in Brazil, a remarkable testament given that he was forced into exile in 1964 after the military seized the national government. Up to that time, Freire was a professor at the University of Recife, working closely with peasant communities in northeast Brazil during the nation's literacy campaign.[57] He returned to his native land in 1980, one year after amnesty was granted.

Freire's project is literacy, helping people to read and write based upon the "conviction that every human being is capable of critically engaging the world in a dialogical encounter with others."[58] He believes learning to read and write are political acts and that gaining literacy is a "step toward political participation."[59] In this spirit Freire considers the pedagogical to be political and the political pedagogical. In turn, all educational theories are political theories, a conviction demanding that every "teacher must be fully cognizant of the political nature of his/her practice and assume responsibility for this rather than denying it."[60] Approached in this consciously political fashion, literacy is a form of cultural action helping people to respect their own agency, to see what it means to be a self and socially constituted agent. Hence the project for literacy can never be a mechanical transaction where reading is approached technically, as mere skill to be acquired. Opposed to what he calls "banking education"—where all-knowing treachers deposit knowledge into the unknowing minds of passive students—Freire's approach is context specific and characterized by dialogue and reciprocity. For Freire, learning to read and write must take place within a community, a specific place, where the teacher draws upon the concrete situations of people's lives to generate meaningful themes for learning. This is both strategically and politically indispensable, as Cynthia Brown makes clear:

> If nonreaders learn to read by writing and reading their own words and opinions, then they learn that their perceptions of reality are valid to others and can influence even those in authority. If, on the other hand, their teachers require them to learn the words and ideas in a primer that is donated by those in power, then the learners must accept that experience as more valid than their own. They must accept the concepts of social and

economic structure transmitted by the teacher—or decide not to learn to read.[61]

It is in this sense that Freire's adage—as one learns to read the word one also learns to read the world—becomes a possibility. This dialectic between word and world is Freire's guiding principle. As Freire conceives literacy in both theory and practice, its "true significance" is "a force to transform the world." Freire is worth quoting at length:

> From the beginning, we rejected the hypothesis of a purely mechanistic literacy program and considered the problem of teaching adults how to read in relation to the awakening of their consciousness. We wished to design a project in which we would attempt to move from naivete to a critical attitude at the same time we taught reading. We wanted a literacy program which would be an introduction to the democratization of culture, a program with men [*sic*] as its Subjects rather than as patient recipients, a program which itself would be an act of creation, capable of releasing other creative acts, one in which students would develop the impatience and vivacity which characterize search and invention.[62]

Freire put these goals into practice through the formation of "culture circles" within peasant communities. Consciously aligned with the oppressed in a manner not dissimilar to the ethnographic practices of cultural studies, Freire used a set of ten drawings to challenge nonliterates to think critically about their lives and the nexus of relations that produced them. Engaging the cultural circles through dialogue, Freire built upon the experiences of the peasants to generate those words central to their lives. Unlike other literacy programs where teachers usher forth content through standarized primers and workbooks, Freire collaborated with the circles to derive "generative words," words that led to a new understanding of social conditions and a transformed political consciousness through the act of reading. "Literacy makes sense only in these terms," Freire writes, "as the consequence of men's [*sic*] beginning to reflect about their own capacity for reflection, about the world, about their position in the world, about their work, about their power to transform the world, about the encounter of consciousness."[63] For Freire, learning to read and write has meaning only when it makes people discover that the world is dynamic and changing, and that part of being human is being an agent to make the world a better place.

CULTURAL STUDIES AND CRITICAL PEDAGOGY: CULTURAL PEDAGOGY

Much is similar between the separate discourses of cultural studies and critical pedagogy. In many ways they parallel one another, overlap, and pursue similar ends. Certainly the lexicon of each is parallel. Vocabulary within cultural studies includes identity, difference, and culture; within critical pedagogy there is voice, empowerment, and community. Both are concerned about the politics of signification: the question of how meaning is socially produced and challenged by constituencies that find themselves in specific material relations. Both are concerned with what has been called a politics of difference: recognizing that all institutions and social spheres are characterized by multiplicities that should be celebrated in the face of widespread universalizing social trends. Examples of such trends, in education for instance, include the push toward a national high school curriculum, standardized testing, and attacks on multiculturalism and bilingualism as threats to a (supposed) common American culture, all of which organize difference in repressive ways.[64] As an accompaniment to a politics of difference, a concern for voice is another important feature shared by cultural studies and critical pedagogy. To take voice seriously as a theoretical tool for cultural-political analysis is, as Henry Giroux says, to "address the wider issue of how people become either agents in the process of making history or how they function as subjects under the weight of oppression and exploitation within the various linguistic and institutional boundaries that produce dominant and subordinate cultures in any given society."[65] And finally, another similarity between cultural studies and critical pedagogy is their attempt to move beyond mere discursive struggle by practicing some form of ethnography, grounding analysis and action in particular places with particular others in ways allowing transformation to evolve from that context.

Although similar, this does not mean that cultural studies and critical pedagogy consciously interact, cross over, or fold into each other so as to establish a conjunction more potent than their individual domains. The task remains to create something more powerful through their intersection. That this is a desirable objective is starting to take hold within both arenas. Although professor David Sholle is correct in noting that "American cultural studies has omitted attention to the pedagogical,"[66] recent efforts are underfoot to correct this fault by linking the two fields together.[67] This is a little ironic, given the strategic importance of the field of education to the beginnings of cultural studies. As Sholle paraphrases Raymond Williams, "Cultural studies began as a specific educational project [that brought] the best in intellectual work to both confront and empower people to understand the pressures upon them."[68] Also citing Williams, Henry Giroux writes that the "deepest impulse [informing cultural studies] was the desire to make learning part of the process of social change itself."[69] Popular culture critic Lawrence Grossberg elaborates:

All of the founding figures of cultural studies (including Richard Hoggart, Raymond Williams, E. P. Thompson, and Stuart Hall) started their careers, and their intellectual projects, in the field of education, outside the university, in extramural departments and adult working-class courses. It was in such adult education classes that Raymond Williams first started to look at the idea of culture. Such pedagogical contexts, which existed outside the formal educational institutions of the state, served people (primarily women and members of the working class) who were deprived of any opportunities for, indeed actively "blocked from," any higher education.[70]

The trend to link cultural studies and critical pedagogy should continue. Both cultural studies and critical pedagogy would do well to consciously connect and thereby produce a union—cultural pedagogy—that can realize powerful new insights in framing cultural analysis as well as pioneer new practices for advancing social movement. This union can be conceived as the combination of strategy and tactics. In developing modes of analysis and criticism of concrete social practices and experiences, cultural studies' contribution to cultural pedagogy is principally strategic. That is, insofar as cultural studies is, as Grossberg describes, a "theory of contexts,"[71] it contextualizes knowledge and experience for the purposes of rigorously analyzing and understanding, deciphering and explaining how life is lived. It is mostly preoccupied with critique. Critical pedagogy certainly encompasses analysis and critique, but as a social practice that organizes learners and experiences to particular ends, critical pedagogy's contribution to cultural pedagogy is mostly tactical. That is, insofar as pedagogy is inherently about making some*thing,* about forming and constructing knowledge for specific purposes, it constitutes a tactical practice that extends the strategic character of cultural studies into the realm of producing culture. Critical pedagogy is more about possibility. In this vein, rather than being correctives for each other, cultural studies and critical pedagogy enhance one another by joining the languages of critique and possibility. And when oriented to recovering subjugated knowledges and deconstructing dominant histories in order to construct new identities, the intersection of cultural studies and critical pedagogy equips cultural pedagogy with a strategic and tactical arsenal to revive human agency in the project of social change.

CULTURAL-PEDAGOGICAL ROLES FOR ARCHITECTURE: THREE PROJECTS

I turn now to three architectural projects that I believe capture the spirit of cultural pedagogy. These projects are not new and they certainly are not flawless. But they do illustrate more than a language of critique by manifesting directions of possibility. The architects of these projects—Dolores Hayden, Lucien Kroll, and Behnsich and Partner—do not necessarily profess allegiance to either cultural studies or critical pedagogy as the basis of their work, although I doubt that they would disagree with my analysis. Selecting these projects as exemplary of cultural-pedagogical analysis and action is my choice; they deepen the possibility for a critical architecture because they take seriously issues of difference, voice, and agency conceived within an ethnographic-based project for social transformation. More to the point, the three projects understand architecture as pedagogy; that in its making and use, architecture is a pedagogical practice that frames the world, structures experience, shapes consciousness and identity, and reinforces assumptions about culture and politics. As C. Richard Hatch says, "Much of what we know of... institutions and their meanings we know from the large array of building types and styles we encounter."[72] Although perhaps less strong than other forms of representation, architecture still reifies social roles and makes three-dimensional statements about culture and power.

Any person promoting architecture today as a project for social justice and emancipation runs the risk of being positioned as a throwback to the sixties. But to put this project in postmodern terms, to take up concepts like "disruption," "subversion," and "deconstruction," architects need to extend these ideas beyond mere formal play and ground them in real social life as a strategy for societal transformation. To repeat a main point of this chapter, there is a need to challenge the preferred, often universalized meanings of society so that opportunities become available for the voiceless and powerless to construct counterhegemonic processes for social advancement. This is why cultural workers like Paul Willis and Paulo Freire align with the oppressed, and why architects should follow their example. Because when oppositional groups affirm their partiality—their traditions, histories, narratives—then the dominant culture is exposed as to its own specificity and partiality. As professor Iris Marion Young asserts, "When oppressed groups insist on the positive value of their specific culture and experience, it becomes increasingly difficult for dominant groups to parade their norms as neutral and universal."[73] This struggle, of course, is never equal. By virtue of their power, dominant groups have greater ability to legitimate their specific, partial perspectives as the preferred meanings around which society should be organized. And through that legitimation, such preferred meanings become naturalized and universalized, and in what amounts to a strange paradox, they become invisible while at the same time rendering oppositional meanings of the world invisible. Of course, dominant groups are never totally victorious in these contests, but nonetheless, they are far more successful in ordering society around an "imposed consensus that is organized around [their] own interests rather than develop[ing] one around points of consent negotiated among diverse interests."[74]

To promote diverse interests (to brush reality against the grain) is to construct other ways of knowing that can potentially disrupt the self-interested ways of knowing by which power blocs see themselves. It is in this vein that the projects of Hayden, Kroll, and Behnisch offer lessons toward transformative constructions of social meaning, motivated by the desire to encourage agency by organizing the design process in an ethnographic manner not too dissimilar to Freire's culture circles and the ethnographic work of cultural studies.

Power of Place: Los Angeles

In 1983, a group of architects, planners, preservationists, historians, and designers formed a nonprofit corporation to commemorate sites in Los Angeles indicative of the city's multiethnic history. Known as Power of Place,[75] the corporation was established by Dolores Hayden and sought to "help everyone recall and remember" the contributions made by ethnically diverse populations to the built and natural landscape of L.A.:

> Building on recent advances in American social history, and helped by a California inventory of historic resources for a multi-ethnic population, we have chosen sites here to represent the economic contributions of major ethnic and racial groups that have settled in this landscape: Native Americans, Mexican-Americans, Blacks, Japanese-Americans and Chinese-Americans, as well as Caucasians from different parts of the United States and Europe. These sites reflect the everyday lives and economic contributions of ordinary people in previous times. They speak to the experiences of laborers as well as bankers and business leaders, of women and children as well as men. As a group, these sites begin to tell the economic history of Los Angeles.[76]

Arranged into a self-guided tour not unlike the Freedom Trail in Boston, sites marking the contributions of women and ethnic and racial groups to the development of Los Angeles include fire stations, oil fields, citrus groves and vineyards, flower markets, and produce markets, as well as those places important in labor struggle and unionization. One example is Fire Station No. 30, which became an all-black fire company in 1923 and "provided a quarter century of service to the community around Central Avenue and Fourteenth Street, hub of Black activities in Los Angeles in the 1920s and 1930s."[77] Another example is the homestead of Biddy Mason. Born a slave in Georgia in 1818, Mason "litigated to win her freedom in a California court in 1856," went on to practice midwifery, and established Los Angeles' first day care center and orphanage. She was also "the first Black woman to own property in the city,"[78] and, out of her own home, she founded the first black church, the African Methodist Episcopal Church.

Power of Place offsets a cultural chauvinism already manifest in Los Angeles by the commemoration of historic-cultural monuments. In its analysis, Power of Place cataloged 299 existing landmarks. Out of this total, 97.7 percent celebrated Anglo-American history and 2.3 percent marked "Native American and ethnic minority history."[79] Only 4 percent of the total was associated with any aspect of women or women's history. As Hayden summarizes, "The landmark process has favored the history of a small minority of white, male landholders, bankers, business leaders, and their architects."[80]

Power of Place constitutes a vital counterhegemonic project. As it weaves together community groups, scholars, students, and alternative experiences of history, Power of Place attempts a re-representation of marginalized history in spatial and architectural terms: a rewriting of the spatial narrative. In this sense, Power of Place is more than recognizing plurality or multiplicity; it moves toward a transformative politics of difference and voice. It does this in four ways. First, Power of Place recovers repressed and unacknowledged voices of history. Second, this effort to recover the submerged stories of Los Angeles is crucial because it can lead to questioning the objectification of history generally; that is, why some stories are unacknowledged in the first place and remain so over time. Thus, Power of Place critiques conventional (hegemonic) processes through which history is written—processes that structure knowledge in such ways as to foreclose certain stories and cause certain voices to be suppressed. Third, Power of Place works to transform those processes, and thereby constitutes a critique and practice against supposedly objective, disinterested history writing, or put another way, it reveals the unavoidable partiality of all history writing. And finally, Power of Place is directed toward the present and future, and is not just looking backward toward the past. That is, to recover the past is for the purposes of rewriting the present and producing counterhegemonic identities for the future.

Together in these four ways, the cultural-pedagogical significance of Power of Place lies in its effort to link both history and future in one counterhegemonic project for popular audiences. This is significant. Power of Place is not about reifying or setting the record straight about the past. It is not just about validating that which has been suppressed. It is more about constructing new identities and communities in the interest of social justice, based upon new understandings of the past.

Catholic University of Louvain: Atelier Lucien Kroll

In 1969 an extraordinary experiment in architecture began under the leadership of Belgian architect Lucien Kroll. The Catholic University of Louvain in Belgium was expanding its medical school in the outskirts of Brussels. Kroll's entry into the project came one year after the university had already relocated some facilities. Constructed were a large hospital, support facilities, and residential buildings in an architectural style and spatial arrangement that were uncreative, rigid, and institutional: banal. After this initial phase the university administration consulted with the students (recall that this was just after the protests of May 1968), who promptly rejected these new buildings. Inspired by the events of the previous

Figure 4.1. Catholic University of Louvain, Brussels, Belgium, Atelier Lucien Kroll. (Photo by Thomas A. Dutton.)

year, medical students strongly questioned the role of medicine and health in society, conceptualized alternatives, and formed new ideas about medical practice. They did not like the buildings already constructed, seeing them representative of the institutional practices and values they were trying to overcome. The students put forth proposals of their own: that buildings should not be of single use; that whenever possible functions should be broken up and integrated with the fabric of the surrounding neighborhood; that proposals from community residents should be considered and acted upon. These proposals were rejected (of course), but interestingly the administration allowed the students to propose the architect. Lucien Kroll was hired.

What Kroll inherited was considerable: the program called for forty thousand square meters for studios, twenty apartments, two hundred rooms for single students, two hundred rooms for grouped apartment living, a theater, a restaurant, a nursery school and kindergarten, places for worship, a post office, a metro station, and offices for student services and administration. Although an extensive program, Kroll initiated a participatory design process. (Kroll will not take a commission unless he can work with those who are directly affected by the design.) Kroll spent months working with a large representative team of students, faculty, and administrators to develop the program and to initiate the design.

Figure 4.2. Catholic University of Louvain, Brussels, Belgium, Atelier Lucien Kroll. Symbolizing what the medical students were trying to overcome in conceiving new forms of medical practice, the rigid and banal style of the hospital (background) stands in stark contrast to the creative interplay of form, color, texture, and material of Kroll's contribution. (Photo by Thomas A. Dutton.)

From the very start, it was the group's intention, in Kroll's words, "to express the diversity of individuals and not the authority of institutions."[81] Everywhere in the final design this intention is manifest. Kroll states: "The building forms are not static. Walking through the site they change constantly, always in an unexpected fashion. The materials of the windows, their colors, curtains, balconies, and plants increase the sense of diversity. They reinforce the individuality and the autonomy of the occupants, and not the power of the central administration."[82] This richness of diversity is not merely on the surface. For example, Kroll spent considerable time convincing structural engineers to investigate structural design in more creative ways. For one building Kroll proposed "a plan of wandering columns,"[83] a system where columns were not arranged in the normal grid, either horizontally or vertically. Kroll felt that the regular grid of equal bays was too conformist, that it "risked producing unimaginative behavior."[84] In this way, Kroll attempted to build diversity right into the core of the building to guard against uniform space planning in any future renovations. Other examples abound, with the result that the entire complex is a living testimony of Kroll's urging construction workers to go beyond the norm, to be creative and inventive in their use of material and the organization of their work. Arguing the value of seeing the brushstokes of the painter, Kroll challenged mechanical engineers to make sculpture with their air ducts; carpenters to apply patterns and textures to concrete formwork through the use of plants and saplings; and masons to interchange wall material, to configure how buildings meet the ground, and to design ground sculptures that became the play stuctures for the nursery school. Participation also extended to the students. In the dormitories, partitions were designed to be movable, encouraging user involvement. In the upper sections of some buildings, three-story volumes were left open to allow students to design their own loft systems with a kit of parts designed by Kroll. As a result of participation extended to workers and students, the feel of the complex is one of individual initiative, changeability, facilitation, and involvement.

Beyond the mixtures of colors, textures, patterns, materials, and constructional systems, the message of diversity is also read (perhaps more deeply) through the organization of space. Kroll states, "No architectural volume can be said to be dominant (the composition is not hierarchical). There are many important places, many centers, each connected to and integrated into the others by an elaborate network of circulation."[85] For Kroll, the nonhierarchical composition of space and function offers an opportunity to comment on the connection of space and power. Understanding that power is nearly always reinforced by space, it is interesting how Kroll organizes space to effect a critique of power, to challenge it and redistribute it so as to empower the individual and those normally eclipsed from its sources. For example, the office of the director of the Medical School is directly across the hall from the nursery school, and when his window is open he will hear the children's

THOMAS A. DUTTON

voices as well as the sounds from the apartments for married students which are directly above. Which is to say, the nonhierarchical organization of space positions social roles, especially around authority, in a more egalitarian and democratic politics of difference.

Viewing the medical university buildings through the frame of cultural pedagogy reveals remarkable similarities between Kroll's participatory design process and the indices of agency, difference, and voice. Undoubtedly, Kroll understands architecture as a form of cultural politics and argues that architects should work for social transformation. As he states: "Ours is primarily a political project and not an aesthetic one. It is more or less ungeometrical, anti-authoritarian, anarchical (anarchitectural), that is to say, human — as organic as a family of plants, and as ecological."[86] Through the design process of participation Kroll encourages the multiplicity of voices that are always a part of any building to speak out and engage. But Kroll is not interested in just any talk. His guiding interest is critical democracy and emancipation. Kroll uses participation to empower, to change people, to have them engage the cultural, political, and economic conditions that circumscribe their lives in order to change those conditions. Kroll believes it possible that through the making of architecture, aesthetics, space, and construction can be organized (like difference) around a critical reading of ideology, culture, and power, to see how these practices work in society to limit and expand everyday experience. He is adamant about using the power of architecture — both in product and process — to alter consciousness and/or the social relations of power. But Kroll is not naive or an idealist. He is cautious:

> The role of the architect is far from neutral. Clearly, the architect's sketches are not going to change society, but, in a certain sense, they can serve as a detonator, an obstruction, an alibi, and can suddenly throw light on hidden mechanisms.... The sketch becomes as much an instrument of institutional analysis as the speech: there are sketches that stir things up and others which comfort, sketches which quietly encourage initiative among those who have lost the habit and others who are immobilized.[87]

Günter Behnisch and Partner

When possible, Dolores Hayden and Lucien Kroll work directly with community groups and future occupants as a cultural pedagogical strategy to assess processes of knowledge formation, encourage reflection about social life, and empower through participation. Günter Behnisch and Partner have similar goals. In the words of critics Richard Reid and Dieter Hauser, "Behnisch considers that the democratic process should involve users in the design and administration not only of their dwellings, but also of their immediate locality, their neighbourhood, workplace, company, and schools."[88] Although Behnisch and Partner hold these beliefs, they do not always engage participatory design processes; they elect other paths for such ends.

Behnisch originally formed his practice in 1952 and has enjoyed an extensive and prolific career. But it is only over the last decade or so that his firm has gained greater visibility in the international media. This is due largely to the construction and widespread publication of three projects: the Hysolar Institute at the University of Stuttgart-Vaihingen, the German Postal Museum in Frankfurt, and the Plenary Complex of the German Bundestag in Bonn. What must be acknowledged beyond these three projects are the firm's many social buildings: libraries, schools, sports halls, social service agencies, and housing for the elderly. This work, spanning the last ten to twelve years, I believe can be called *social formalism*.

That the work of Behnisch has ascended to visibility is telling in light of global changes in economics, politics, culture, nationality, and so on. "Turbulence" might be one term to describe these changes, with the rebellion in south central Los Angeles, the dismantling of the Berlin Wall, and ethnic strife in Bosnia, Haiti, and Rwanda qualifying as but a few examples. "Boundaries" might be another term, especially as they multiply and become hard-and-fast borders, often serving to separate and insulate rather than integrate and solidify. Behnisch's architecture has to be understood against this backdrop. His architecture is very much about social tension; it is both nourished by and commentating on issues of social concern, conflict, power, and representation. Behnisch's commentary is more than critique, however, and in this way he distinguishes himself from other architects and movements with which he shares similar formal vocabularies, compositions, and strategies. His architecture suggests progressive possibility. Through what critic Peter Blundell Jones calls "responsive irregularity," Behnisch seeks to articulate what could be, but grounded in a conscious critique of cultural and political trends and the problematic of democracy, with the intent to assert freedom and the power of the individual through form. In a world society teetering out of balance, or seeking to find a new one (a new world order?), Behnisch has not abandoned the attempt for intending shared, transformative meaning through the arrangement of program, form, and content. Jones puts it succinctly:

> The aim has not been disorder or the inspiration of despair. Rather a kind of idiosyncratic ordering has been sought in relation to the place and task, as opposed to the ready-made orders of type and technique. It has led to a new kind of architectural space, which is certainly related to our time and beliefs, but is neither primarily ironical nor negative in intention. Through and through, the emphasis has been not on empty form, but inhabited space: form and content only make sense in terms of one another.[89]

Several commonalities characterize the work of Behnisch, but no particular aesthetic or style is embraced by the firm. Behnisch is a modern, industrial architect.

THOMAS A. DUTTON

Figure 4.3. German Postal Museum, Frankfurt, Germany, Günter Behnisch and Partner. (Photo by Christian Kandzia. Used by permission.)

He maintains the modernist proclivity to express materials honestly and directly. Materials most used include steel, extensive glazing with individually operated external blinds, and other industrial cladding systems. The buildings have the compelling dichotomy of looking industrial while not overwhelmingly technological. In fact, the overall experience is optimistic, airy, with a strong sensitivity to detail that values the human scale.[90]

That Behnisch achieves a sensitivity to human character is supported by the absence of "rationalizing grids" or "orthogonal layouts." Like Kroll, Behnisch is motivated by diversity and expression of individuality over institutional power, thus shying away from central axes, symmetry, and other forms of organization suggestive of hierarchical relations of power. To these ends, forms are playful and skewed, individual parts take precedence over the whole, and spatial fluidity is preferred while functions receive special articulation. The entire composition reads as an "organic," embodied order and not as an imposed one.

Because of such design strategies, Behnisch is often positioned in relation to the German organic tradition, perhaps best exemplified by Hugo Haring (1882–1958) and Hans Scharoun (1893–1972). In an enlightening article that ties Behnisch to that tradition of German modernism, Jones highlights three principles of his firm's work: aggregative planning, geometric irregularity, and aperspectival space.[91] Aggregative planning is "the assembly of a building from a series of independent parts such that each retains its own identity and sense of place . . . while yet contributing to the whole."[92] Geometric irregularity "is necessary if the various parts are to develop according to their own requirements rather than being subordinated to a grid or a system of Neo-classical axes."[93] Aperspectival space grows out of the other two and carries the philosophical sensibility to subvert technological rationality. It attempts to break down hierarchical spatial organization and the standardization of modern technology. Whereas perspective implies orthogonal organization and the privileged position of a static viewpoint, aperspectivity asserts the experience of space from a changing position.

Because Behnisch's work exhibits such principles, he is sometimes linked with deconstructivism. For instance, the Hysolar Institute is prominently published in books and journals advocating deconstruction. This is a mistake. The end point of Behnisch's architecture is never just formal play or gesture, even when motivated to question the conventions of architectural representation (see Chapter 6 in this volume). A strong social ethic underscores his work. This is clearly evident in his buildings, as well as in his writings about those buildings. Behnisch links the social with the formal. The message is clear that spatial organization should question social organization, and that even the handling of building components becomes an opportunity to symbolically express social concerns. In a recent lecture, Christian Kandzia, a twenty-five-year veteran of the firm, elaborated on the firm's intention to link formal manipulations to social readings:

> We try to see the world in a differentiated way, to focus on diversity. This leads us to differentiate individual components of a building depending on their role. In the case of a steel girder the upper chord is subjected to compressive stress, and its geometry is therefore different from that of the lower chord, which is subjected to tensile stress. And for us, the midspan of a girder is different from its free end or the joint with another part of the building. . . . This is democratic architecture in that each component depends on the others. No part could be removed without disturbing the balance, and each part assumes its role in the context of the building as a whole. This may be regarded as symbolizing an ideal social order.[94]

THOMAS A. DUTTON

Behnisch argues that "the parts of a building should have some independence in the same way as individuals in a democracy."[95] Refreshing though they are, efforts to symbolize democratic intention through architecture are not necessarily progressive or radical. But there are times in Behnisch's writing when he declares the need for a more self-conscious, progressively political architecture, motivated by social justice. He writes:

> Interests which are indeed powerful, and often monumental, hardly need much promotion from us: their claims are powerfully represented by other parties. There are other considerations that are in urgent need of our commitment: ecology, for example, our fellow-men, children, people, working methods, communal living and many others.... We are in a position to enable hidden forces, neglected in the reality of our society, to find expression and to assume their visible form. The more such aspects we can identify, the more richness . . . and the greater the diversity of the resultant architectural form.[96]

The objective of progressive social intention and its expression becomes clearer when we compare Behnisch to the work of Bernard Tschumi at Parc de la Villette. I want to examine briefly how the notion of *autonomy,* as a concept and design strategy, is architecturally manifested by both designers. As I will discuss in greater detail shortly, at La Villette Tschumi superimposed grid, lines, and surfaces as a strategy to diffuse the power of the designer to control the composition and as a statement about the dispersal of meaning. As Tschumi said, "La Villette looks out on new social and historical circumstances: a dispersed and differentiated reality that marks an end to the utopia of unity."[97] In this way, Parc de la Villette attempted intertextuality, read through the collision of formal, autonomous systems of order such that the resulting indeterminacy frees individuals to make their own meanings and engage the text in new ways. A liberative impulse was intended here.

My critique of Parc de la Villette is that while superimposition implies socially positive goals of nonhierarchy, say, it does so regressively. That is, while intersecting formal systems do at times provide provocative juxtapositions that can lead one to pause and reflect, what is also present as a reading, and is in fact dominant, is that autonomy is all there is. Formal systems do not acknowledge or mediate their intersections in any way (which is precisely Tschumi's intention). Because nothing exists beyond autonomy, Parc de la Villette reads as a statement of conservatism: a banal brand of anarchy reifying rugged individualism — individuals without collectivity or relation.

By contrast, the tension between the collective and the individual is precisely what animates the architecture of Behnisch. While respectful of autonomy, the

Figure 4.4. Parc de la Villette, Paris, France, Bernard Tschumi. The concept of colliding formal systems is clearly evident in this photo. Mediation between the bridge, the upper walkway, and the folly is not attempted, or intended, reinforcing a social reading of rugged individualism, individuals without relations. (Photo by Thomas A. Dutton.)

reading is also clear that relationships matter. Behnisch achieves individuality and collectivity through varying forms of mediation. Take, as one instance, the design of railings and handrails. For Behnisch, in the effort to privilege individual parts to form the larger composition, the handrail is one part like any other. In the Frankfurt Postal Museum, for example, the design of the handrail is special at nearly every condition. As railings enclose both sides of an open staircase, the railing on each side is different. A balcony handrail is different from the balcony below it, although both front the same volume. Whenever a handrail changes direction, a new expression results. Even the corner receives special attention. But while special treatment of handrails upholds a reading of autonomy, also clear is a reading of integration. In other words, Behnisch's handrails are not just different for their own sake and left at that. Great concern is evident in how railings meet, intersect, and mediate each other, but in such ways where the collectivity formed is not violative of the parts. The overall reading is one of autonomy *and* relation.

This architecture of Behnisch constitutes a formal representation of difference. This is a reading I bring to bear on Behnisch's work, but it is encouraged by his drive to conceive of the geometry of architectural elements and the arrangement of space and program as opportunities to link autonomy with collectivity, parts

Figure 4.5. German Postal Museum, Frankfurt, Germany, Günter Behnisch and Partner. Through a mediation of all parts of a building—including railings and handrails—intersections are designed to privilege autonomy *and* collectivity. Parts are not compromised in their specificity, yet they interrelate and combine to form a larger whole. (Photo by Thomas A. Dutton.)

with wholes, in short, the social with the formal. As pedagogy, a Behnisch and Partner building is not the sum of the parts, or a superimposition, but is a conscious, interactive holistic construction valuing autonomy. It is a difficult whole — affirming the need to integrate and complement without sacrificing individuality. As a representation of difference, the work of Behnisch is significant, but it is also limited in that it engages the struggle for transformative futures not in the ethnographic manner of Kroll and Hayden, but principally in the realm of form. Hence my qualifier, social formalism. In this regard, Behnisch's work is formalist, but it is a formalism with self-conscious social intention, and in this historical moment, this is not to be discounted.

CULTURAL PEDAGOGY AS A PRACTICE OF CRITIQUE: RESISTING TEXTUALIZATION IN CULTURAL STUDIES AND FORMALISM IN ARCHITECTURE

The work of Dolores Hayden, Lucien Kroll, and Behnisch and Partner offer important lessons in the application of cultural pedagogy. In what they produce, in how they attempt to represent that production, and in their collaborative work with others, they engage a cultural pedagogy; that is, the values of difference, voice, and agency are conscious concerns of their design strategies. All three work toward oppositional meanings about history, building, culture, power, and the organization of sociocultural life, and how such knowledge might embolden people to question normalcy and ultimately to act. In this sense, Hayden, Kroll, and Behnisch are cultural pedagogues, attempting to revive agency and social transformation through architectural projects. They are similar to critical pedagogues of classroom settings. Only the sites are different.

The fact that Dolores Hayden, Lucien Kroll, and (when possible) Gunter Behnisch ground their practices in some form of ethnography — within the relations of material life — is no small achievement. This is especially so in light of a disturbing trend in recent architecture — coincident with some forms of postmodern theory — that is enveloped in a language of progressive fervor that stops well short of full material action; it is fervor only of the discursive realm. This trend is formalism. In this last section I critique this swelling trend of formalism, which pushes matters of social concern aside, or toys with them obscurely in high-end formal language games, in discursive realms not meant to be shared with those embroiled in daily struggle but who desperately need good, organic intellectual help. My critique will spring from cultural studies, but there is an irony here. Cultural studies is entangled in its own sweeping formalism, what some call "textualization." In essence, then, what *formalism* is to architecture, *textualization* is to cultural studies; two names for similar processes affecting both fields. However, one significant difference does exist between the fields. Textualization in cultural studies is a recent phenomenon, while formalism in architecture has a long history. I think this bodes well for cultural studies, because the specter of textualization has angered many, enough to enact counterstrategies. The longevity of formalism in architecture has angered fewer and ensures its future through complacency.

Postmodernism, Cultural Studies, and Textualization

Depending upon the intellectual domain, textualization is codified by a number of names. For example, historian Bryan Palmer warns of the "linguistic turn" in the writing of history. As he writes in *Descent into Discourse: The Reification of Language and the Writing of Social History,* language has become "the essential ground within which social life is embedded."[98] Palmer finds this problematic, arguing that language is reified and thus placed beyond social, economic, and political relations, which in turn displaces the materializing relations of "economy and culture, necessity and agency, structure and process"[99] to adjunct roles in conceiving history. Lynn Hunt, also a historian, examines in "History beyond Social Theory" the rise of "discursive models of culture." Arguing similarly to Palmer, she cautions about the "textualizing of context," which is the attempt to efface the distinction between text and context.[100] In a very useful book, *Post-Modernism and the Social Sciences,* political scientist Pauline Marie Rosenau talks of "skeptical postmodernism" (characterized most by French poststructuralists Jacques Derrida, Jean-François Lyotard, and Jean Baudrillard) as that brand which relinguishes the project of social transformation by withdrawing inward from the political and refusing "all responsibility for what goes on in the society."[101] "Retreating from the political," what then remains "for the skeptics is a social science that exhibits a passion for discourse, that serves as a means for self-exploration, self-reflection, and self-expression, but that is passive because it does not move beyond conversation."[102] Rosenau's skeptical postmodernism is akin to Teresa Ebert's "ludic postmodernism," in "which reality becomes a theater of simulation marked by the free play of images, disembodied signifiers, and the heterogeneity of differences."[103] For Ebert, ludic postmodernism is "rhetoric, isolated from social struggles and substituting for social contradictions.... Consequently, textual difference—the differing, deferring, dispersing play of unanchored signifiers—deprives the political of its connection to social relations and dismantles transformative politics."[104] In the end, ludic postmodernism is not "a subversion of reality as a reinscription of the status quo: it reduces history to a free-floating trace of textuality, and politics to rhetoric."[105] And finally Robert Scholes, looking at life within university departments of English and the humanities generally, points to the "deconstructive turn" in academic work—the "profound attraction" and "irresistible" appeal that deconstructive discourse has within the academy: "Its appeal is so strong because it allows a displacement of political activism into a textual world where anarchy can *become* the establishment without threatening the actual seats of political and economic power. Political radicalism may thus be drained off or sublimated into a textual radicalism that can happily theorize its own disconnection from unpleasant realities."[106]

What these examples characterize is a broad "reconceptualization of how we experience and explain the world around us."[107] Vast changes are underfoot in all intellectual fields, affecting both theory and practice. Textualization marks the ascendancy of what might be called discursive hegemony, which is the privileging of textual practices (like pastiche, parody, and fragmentation) in a manner (almost) completely removed from the material relations that produce them and are influenced by them. The concern captured by discursive hegemony is that intellectual work is in full-dress retreat from materialist interventions. It is as though, in Peter McLaren's words, "the social is sucked up and dissolved into the world of signs and electronic communication while depth of meaning is imploded into superficiality."[108] This is what Scholes means by textual radicalism coming to displace political radicalism, and what McLaren means by representation coming to displace the real.

The sad irony here is that cultural studies, it will be recalled, always had a sense of "political urgency," as Angela McRobbie puts it:[109] that cultural-political analysis *and* possibility based upon ethnographic methods never lost sight of the relation between text and context, or the semiological and the sociological, with the goal to revive agency and engage political strategies in order to change the institutions of cultural life. That cultural studies is losing that urgency through textualization is ominous. However, more than a few cries of alarm have sounded and critique is emerging. For Angela McRobbie, the detours through "literary and textual excursions" shake the foundations of cultural studies and throw into question the very purpose of its project.[110] Likewise, Stuart Hall fears that in American cultural studies, questions of power, history, and politics, which heretofore were central to cultural studies, will fall to the "deconstructive deluge" (instead of simply a "deconstructive turn") and be "formalized" out of existence: that social life will be textualized as a supplement of signification, or as the trace of textuality.[111] Hall makes clear this is not a problem of theory or theoretical adeptness, that is, he recognizes that American cultural studies does theorize "race, class, gender, subjugation, domination, exclusion, marginality, Otherness." But he continues: "There is hardly anything in cultural studies which isn't so theorized. And yet, there is the nagging doubt that this overwhelming textualization of cultural studies' own discourses somehow constitutes power and politics as exclusively matters of language and textuality itself."[112]

Architecture and Formalism

Architecture is enveloped in these larger, postmodern trends of textualization. Discursive hegemony has had theoretical and practical parallels within architecture. That is, in this time of regressive societal transformation that has produced despair, nihilism, and desparate need, the architectural mainstream has abandoned critical discourses and practices that can advance progressive cultural and political concerns. Within architecture, and certainly within society, the triumph of aesthetics has displaced ethics. As geographer Darrell Crilley notes, "While architects were previously lambasted for being too demonstrative, authoritative, and naively utopian in their aspiration to effect social transformation through architecture, the contemporary moment is disquieting for the opposite reason: resigned abandonment of social concern in the bid for professional status and individual recognition."[113] Crilley continues:

> Postmodern discourse, with its barely concealed agenda to resurrect
> architecture as a three-dimensional art form, the mode of practice with
> which it is associated, and main currents of criticism facilitate this shift
> from ethics to aesthetics. Such trends contrive to ghettoize architecture,
> narrowing the concerns "proper" to architectural discourse to the
> formalistic and symbolic. In such a context it becomes illegitimate to ask
> troubling questions about the social and political purposes of a venture....
> Who builds what, where and for whose benefit are all clearly external to
> the "meaning" of architecture.[114]

For Crilley, much contemporary architecture signifies "not the autonomy and freedom of the architectural creative act, but its unapologetic embrace of commodification."[115]

Just as textualization in cultural studies reduces material political struggle to that of language, writing, and academic work, architecture has come to negate politics in its real/material urgencies by privileging the linguistic, the formalistic, the aesthetic. Accordingly, this negation has two consequences: (1) It separates architects (as possible organic intellectuals) from the politics of social movements, but in whose interest such a politics is articulated, and (2) it persuades architects to confuse aesthetics with politics.

Consider the work of Leon Krier and Lebbeus Woods, two architects who profess the need for the transformation of social life, for new architectural expressions that can lead to new urban cultures. At first glance, their work is about as far apart on any spectrum one could imagine. Krier's project has been the reconstruction of the European city. He has argued consistently that architects should engage an "anti-industrial resistance" to help revive artisan culture and counter the destructive effects of zoning, the primacy of the automobile, and what he calls the Manhattanization of Europe. Accordingly, Krier advocates "traditional" urban values, and in a manner reminiscent of the best of Jane Jacobs's writing, his work emulates densely populated, mixed-use districts in the form of streets, squares, and quarters. The preindustrial city is his model. The tone animating his drawings and writings is what might be called The Great Return, revealed in his declaration, "Forward Comrades, We Must Go Back."[116]

In contrast, Woods's architectural proposals are marked by a plasticity of form and material. His work has an overpowering technological and machine-like presence, where the formal parts are highly articulated as though autonomous. His work evokes great industrial plants, but in smaller forms inserted within a traditional urban fabric. Woods's project is "experimental architecture" in the promotion of "heterarchy."[117] By "experimental" he means "work initiated with the purpose of gaining experience for its own sake,"[118] work that is self-consciously inventive and innovative, requiring the architect to be free of the constraints of clients, agencies, and authorities. By "heterarchy" he means a system that is the opposite of hierarchy, where autonomous parts are loosely arranged in a self-regulating whole that does not compromise those parts. How experimental architecture and heterarchy come together is not quite clear, but Woods portends: "The experimental architect of today is the precursor of the free and autonomous individual of a cultural heterarchy yet to come."[119]

While different in their formal prescriptions for urban form, Krier and Woods share much conceptually. Both exemplify an aestheticized politics. Both are basically drawing-room artists (who do draw very well). Both mourn a disfigured world and refigure it in solitude. They detach themselves from social movements that could benefit from their analyses and programs. I suspect that Krier distrusts social movements, fearing their ignorance will rule the day, and Woods hesitates to engage them because they would restrict his autonomy. Because of their disengagement, both cannot help but generalize and universalize their discourse, in other words, to speak *for* people instead of *with* them. In this regard Krier and Woods reproduce the "cardinal sin" of modernism, as Fredric Jameson puts it, which is "precisely to identify (or conflate) the political and the aesthetic, and to foresee a political and social transformation that is henceforth at one with the formal processes of architectural production itself."[120] Thus Krier and Woods end up advocating a position not unlike that of Le Corbusier, who it will be recalled, was not against political revolution per se but rather "saw the construction and the constitution of new space as the most revolutionary act, and one that could 're-place' the narrowly political revolution of the mere seizure of power."[121] But without the attempt to ground such vision in the body politic and the struggle of social movement and daily life, such work tends toward the world of idealism, where anything becomes possible by the stroke of the pen. Of course, this is not to argue that an idealist haven is an ungrounded position. It is more that the position is transcendent, a location that allows (and facilitates) intellectualizing without organic linkage. In this way, Krier and Woods perform an intellectual role without the organic one, which, as Stuart Hall argued, constitutes a failure of responsibility to carry through what it means to be an intellectual. This is how both come to constitute the architecture of formal aestheticism, where theory and formal experimentation, conceived in the private, sheltered, and detached shadows nurtured by discursive hegemony, act as substitutes for material engagement with political realities.[122] In essence, architecture becomes the content of architecture. Architecture merely looks at itself.

Consider, as another example of textualizing trends in architecture, a comparison between the competition entries of Leon Krier and Bernard Tschumi for La Villette Quarter in Paris, the competition Tschumi won with Parc de la Villette, now nearly completed. Krier did the expected. His scheme was composed around a major spine of public and civic buildings of monumental proportions, with the rest of the quarter arranged in a grid of small blocks with housing above first-floor commercial and professional uses. Tschumi's scheme is ever so different. Tschumi designed a park, but it is more an "open-air cultural center with separate buildings" arranged by the superimposition of three systems: grid, lines, and surfaces.[123] The follies establish the grid: those bright, fire-engine-red structures designed without regard to function and as such free to be appropriated for whatever uses. Currently in place are a café, a preschool, a video workshop, and a visitor's center. The lines are represented by allées of trees and the "cinematic promenade," which is a walkway that winds through the park and connects the individual gardens. The surfaces are the open green spaces as well as the prominent buildings that occupy the site, including the existing Grande Hall, the expansive Museum of Science and Industry, and the Conservatory of Music designed by recent (1994) Pritzker Prize winner Christian de Portzamparc. La Villette is not designed as a homogenized totality. As architectural critic Geoffrey Broadbent mentions, "The superimposition of his [Tschumi's] structures prevented any idea of a 'pre-established causality' between the programme, the architecture and its signification thus encouraging the 'intertextuality' he sought and the 'dispersion of meaning.'"[124]

Again, the comparison seems odd at first glance: the traditionalist and the deconstructivist. But I believe the two share a dialectical relationship with regard to notions of subjectivity, agency, and the social production of meaning. On one hand, Krier seems annoyed with that which has been lost in architecture and society. For him, the best time in architecture came and went. Lost is the permanence of architectural tradition, the continuity of meaning, and the authenticity of architecture to stabilize the human subject. Krier thus strives for certainty, but it is a vain search that forces him to withdraw into an idealist haven, the only place where certainty is possible. On the other hand, Tschumi's writings are chock-full of phrases about the multiplicity of impressions, the pure trace of language, and interpretive infinity. For him, architecture never had a best time, and nothing is lost because architectural tradition, meaning, and the human subject can never be fixed or certain. Tschumi thus strives for an architecture of undecidability and indeterminacy, of random signifiers at play: for an architecture, as he says, that "means nothing."[125] So, as Krier harks to some timeless and mythical past (to recover that which did not really exist) and bemoans the loss of some mythical humanist subject, Tschumi acknowledges the death of the humanist subject and seeks to represent the rise of the posthumanist subject. In other words, Krier looks for authenticity and desires to establish meaning forthwith. Tschumi understands the impossibility of fixing meaning, but opts out of intention all together: there is only the peaceful coexistence of semantic plurality. What they share, therefore, is a failure to take into account how meaning is produced in society. Both fail to acknowledge how politics and processes of power shape society and come to privilege the ability of some groups to make meaning, while marginalizing others. Who gets represented, who speaks, for whom, and by what power are questions seemingly unimportant to Tschumi and Krier. In this sense, both erase any sense of history and politics, because it is precisely in the concrete struggles over naming reality, of making meaning, that history and politics are made. Hence there is no agency. Theirs is an architecture conceived without agents. The project to help transform subjectivities in the interest of making a better world is absent. Immersed in a textual world where the play of signification is ungrounded materially, both Krier and Tschumi undermine the social project of renaming the world in the interest of social justice and democracy, of working toward progressive cultural-political meaning.

Conclusion: Reaffirming "Critical" and Agency

The recent architectural and postmodern trends toward textualization, or discursive hegemony, mark a numbing poverty in addressing the difficult issues of our time in ways that sustain a critical agency. Agency is the crucial factor here, because what engagement has occurred has been mainly through discursive practices, the evoking of languages as ends unto themselves without care as to how these languages stir action. Such is the architecture of aesthetic formalism: an architecture highly subjective but without a politics of subjectivity; an architecture that valorizes individualism, desire, and pleasure but without a politics of solidarity or community; an architecture portrayed as liberatory and resistant but that is couched only within language. Such an architecture cannot be considered critical. In this moment of late capitalism where worldwide forces daily subvert and silence people's voices, lives, and futures, architects must do more to enact modes of practice that engage people in a Freirean or ethnographic manner so that they can build upon those lives to subvert and possibly counter the forces of hegemony, or at least strive for symbolic meanings that work toward progressive readings of social transformation. These are the lessons of Dolores Hayden, Lucien Kroll, and Behnisch and Partner.

It is remarkably ironic that architecture pulled away from social concerns precisely when cultural studies forged ahead with ethnography and Paulo Freire gained an international reputation with his pedagogy of the oppressed. This chapter has argued it possible that architecture, as one cultural-political and artistic practice capable of influencing meaning, can question existing structures and work toward new social relations and new forms of politics, mobilized around oppositional meaning grounded in material relations. In such a struggle, the issue of meaning — what things mean, what they signify, how they are named — is paramount. How we name reality is crucial, which is why much postmodern talk privileging unanchored or floating signifiers is counterproductive; such talk does not "consider signifying practices to be an ensemble of material operations involved in economic and political relations."[126] People and the meanings they make are constituted not only discursively but materially as well. References to floating signifiers undermine the struggle for social change because they undermine the terrain on which that struggle is ultimately fought: the terrain of the signified. What "things" mean to people in the various circuits of their lives, within their communities, within their culture, is indispensable to any project for social transformation.

Architecture is one of those "things," a fact that architects must take far more seriously by establishing deeper bonds between architecture and countercultural movements. Without such bonds, architecture itself runs the risk of becoming a floating signifier, thereby retarding the development of enriching and transforming practices based upon the cultural capital of marginalized peoples. "It is when architecture becomes part of a community's tradition and enables people to see themselves in it that it acquires cultural significance," writes architect Stefani Ledewitz. "If architecture is part of a social context, then its task is not to embody a cultural critique but to become part of that culture's critique . . . not a formal representation of resistance, but an instrument of resistance."[127] To this end, architecture would do well to follow the leads of cultural studies and critical pedagogy.

Notes

1. Jim Collins, *Uncommon Cultures* (New York and London: Routledge, Chapman and Hall, 1989), pp. 114–15.
2. See Thomas A. Dutton, "Architectural Education, Postmodernism, and Critical Pedagogy," in Thomas A. Dutton, ed., *Voices in Architectural Education: Cultural Politics and Pedagogy* (New York: Bergin and Garvey, 1991).
3. Herbert Marcuse, *Counter-Revolution and Revolt* (Boston: Beacon Press, 1972).
4. See Dutton, "Architectural Education."
5. Bryan D. Palmer, *Descent into Discourse: The Reification of Language and the Writing of Social History* (Philadelphia: Temple University Press, 1990), p. xvi.

6. Nancy Fraser, *Unruly Practices: Power, Discourse and Gender in Contemporary Social Theory* (Minneapolis: University of Minnesota Press, 1989), p. 113.
7. Peter McLaren and Tomaz Tadeu da Silva, "Decentering Pedagogy: Critical Literacy, Resistance and the Politics of Memory," in Peter McLaren and Peter Leonard, eds., *Paulo Freire: A Critical Encounter* (London and New York: Routledge, 1993), p. 49.
8. Nancy Harstock, *Cultural Critique* 14 (Winter 1989–90): 24, 19.
9. The term "cultural pedagogy" is not mine, but my use of it is both similar and dissimilar to David Trend, *Cultural Pedagogy: Art/Education/Politics* (New York: Bergin and Garvey, 1992).
10. Graeme Turner, *British Cultural Studies: An Introduction* (New York and London: Routledge, Chapman and Hall, 1992), p. 12.
11. Stuart Hall, "Cultural Studies and the Centre: Some Problematics and Problems," in Stuart Hall, Dorothy Hobson, Andrew Lowe, and Paul Willis, eds., *Culture, Media, Language* (London: Hutchinson, 1980), p. 16.
12. Bill Schwarz, "Where Is Cultural Studies?" *Cultural Studies* 8, no. 3 (October 1994): 382.
13. Hall, "Cultural Studies and the Centre," p. 17.
14. Turner, *British Cultural Studies,* p. 2.
15. Hall, "Cultural Studies and the Centre," p. 18.
16. Turner, *British Cultural Studies,* p. 12.
17. Hall, "Cultural Studies and the Centre," p. 30.
18. Ibid., p. 19.
19. Turner, *British Cultural Studies,* p. 22.
20. Ibid., pp. 88–89.
21. Stuart Hall, "Cultural Studies and Its Theoretical Legacies," in Lawrence Grossberg, Cary Nelson, and Paula Treichler, eds., *Cultural Studies* (New York: Routledge, 1992), p. 279.
22. Ibid.
23. Henry Giroux, *Theory and Resistance in Education* (South Hadley, Mass.: Bergin and Garvey, 1983), p. 124.
24. Raman Selden, *A Reader's Guide to Contemporary Literary Theory* (Lexington: University Press of Kentucky, 1989), p. 39.
25. Carl Boggs, *Gramsci's Marxism* (London: Pluto Press, 1976), p. 17.
26. Ibid.
27. Turner, *British Cultural Studies,* pp. 211–12.
28. Ibid., p. 212.
29. Giroux, *Theory and Resistance in Education,* p. 129.
30. Ibid.
31. Stuart Hall, "Cultural Studies and Its Theoretical Legacies," p. 281.
32. Boggs, *Gramsci's Marxism,* p. 76.
33. Ibid., pp. 77–78.
34. Hall, "Cultural Studies and Its Theoretical Legacies," p. 281.
35. At the BCCCS this blend is far from unitary, and as time has passed, feminism and poststructuralism have left their indelible marks. Hall attributes to feminism a very special role: "The most profound challenge to any attempt to establish a Cultural Studies 'orthodoxy' has . . . arisen from the emergence of feminism within the Centre's work." See Hall, "Cultural Studies and the Centre," p. 38.
36. Turner, *British Cultural Studies,* p. 136.
37. Richard A. Quantz, "On Critical Ethnography (with Some Postmodern Considerations)," in Margaret D. Lecompte, Wendy L. Millroy, and Judith Preissle, eds., *The Handbook of Qualitative Research in Education* (San Diego, Calif.: Academic Press, 1992), p. 455.
38. Ibid.
39. Douglas E. Foley, *Learning Capitalist Culture* (Philadelphia: University of Pennsylvania Press, 1990), p. vii.
40. Phil Cohen, "Subcultural Conflict and Working Class Community," in Hall, Hobson, Lowe, and Willis, eds., *Culture, Media, Language.*

41. Dick Hebdige, *Subculture: The Meaning of Style* (London and New York: Methuen, 1979).
42. Paul Willis, *Learning to Labor: How Working Class Kids Get Working Class Jobs* (Lexington, Mass.: Heath, 1977).
43. Willis, *Learning to Labor,* quoted in Turner, *British Cultural Studies,* p. 175.
44. Turner, *British Cultural Studies,* p. 174.
45. Ibid., p. 176.
46. Cary Nelson, Paula A. Treichler, and Lawrence Grossberg, "Cultural Studies: An Introduction," in Grossberg, Nelson, and Treichler, eds., *Cultural Studies,* p. 1.
47. Ibid.
48. Ibid., p. 2.
49. Ibid.
50. Bell hooks, *Yearning: Race, Gender, and Cultural Politics* (Boston, Mass.: South End Press, 1990), p. 125.
51. David Sholle, "Authority on the Left: Critical Pedagogy, Postmodernism, and Vital Strategies," *Cultural Studies* 6, no. 2 (May 1992): 272–73.
52. Henry A. Giroux and Roger Simon, *Popular Culture, Schooling, and Everyday Life* (New York: Bergin and Garvey, 1989), p. 230.
53. Thomas A. Dutton, "The Hidden Curriculum and the Design Studio," in Dutton, ed., *Voices in Architectural Education,* p. 168.
54. Roger Simon, "Empowerment as a Pedagogy of Possibility," *Language Arts* 64, no. 4 (1987): 371.
55. Peter McLaren and Peter Leonard, "Absent Discourses: Paulo Freire and the Dangerous Memories of Liberation," in McLaren and Leonard, eds., *Paulo Freire: A Critical Encounter,* p. 2.
56. Ibid., p. 1.
57. Ibid.
58. Ibid.
59. Cynthia Brown, "Appendix: Literacy in 30 Hours: Paulo Freire's Process in Northeast Brazil," in Ira Shor, ed., *Freire for the Classroom* (Portsmouth, N.H.: Boynton/Cook, 1987), p. 215.
60. Paulo Freire, "Letter to North American Teachers," in Shor, ed., *Freire for the Classroom,* p. 221.
61. Brown, "Literacy in 30 Hours," p. 215.
62. Paulo Freire, *Education for Critical Consciousness* (New York: Seabury Press, 1973), p. 43.
63. Ibid., p. 81.
64. Henry A. Giroux, "Living Dangerously: Identity Politics and the New Cultural Racism," in Henry A. Giroux and Peter McLaren, eds., *Between Borders: Pedagogy and the Politics of Cultural Studies* (New York and London: Routledge, 1994), p. 39.
65. Henry A. Giroux, "Resisting Difference: Cultural Studies and the Discourse of Critical Pedagogy," in Grossberg, Nelson, and Treichler, *Cultural Studies,* p. 205.
66. Sholle, "Authority on the Left," p. 272.
67. See Giroux and McLaren, eds., *Between Borders.*
68. Sholle, "Authority on the Left," p. 272.
69. Henry A. Giroux, *Disturbing Pleasures* (New York and London: Routledge, 1994), p. 132.
70. Lawrence Grossberg, "Introduction: Bringin' It All Back Home — Pedagogy and Cultural Studies," in Giroux and McLaren, eds., *Between Borders,* p. 3.
71. Ibid., p. 5.
72. C. Richard Hatch, ed., *The Scope of Social Architecture* (New York: Van Nostrand Reinhold, 1984), p. 9.
73. Iris Marion Young, quoted in Peter McLaren, "Critical Pedagogy, Multiculturalism and the Politics of Risk and Resistance: A Response to Kelly and Portelli," *Journal of Education* 173, no. 3 (1991): 51.

74. John Fiske, *Power Plays, Power Works* (London and New York: Verso, 1993), p. 301.
75. Dolores Hayden, *The Power of Place: Urban Landscapes as Public History* (Cambridge: MIT Press, 1995).
76. Dolores Hayden, Gail Dubrow, and Carolyn Flynn, *Power of Place: Los Angeles,* map and tour guide text (Los Angeles: Power of Place, n.d.).
77. Ibid.
78. Ibid.
79. Dolores Hayden, "Placemaking, Preservation and Urban History," *Journal of Architectural Education* 41, no. 3 (Spring 1988): 46.
80. Ibid.
81. Lucien Kroll, "Anarchitecture," in Hatch, ed., *The Scope of Social Architecture,* p. 167.
82. Ibid., p. 171.
83. Ibid., p. 179.
84. Ibid.
85. Ibid., p. 171.
86. Ibid., p. 167.
87. Lucien Kroll, quoted by Tony Schuman, "Participation, Empowerment, and Urbanism: Design and Politics in the Revitalization of French Social Housing," *Journal of Architectural and Planning Research* 4, no. 4 (December 1987): 357.
88. Richard Reid and Dieter Hauser, "Towards A Democratic Architecture," *Architectural Review* 177 (June 1985): 51.
89. Peter Blundell Jones, "Responsive Irregularity," *Architectural Review* 190 (February 1992): 19.
90. Brian Carter, "A Trio of Airy Behnisch Buildings," *Architecture,* September 1989.
91. Peter Blundell Jones, "Guenter Behnisch and Partners: A Continuing Contribution to the Organic Tradition in German Modernism," *A + U,* no. 236 (May 1990).
92. Ibid., p. 114.
93. Ibid.
94. Christian Kandzia, "Gunter Behnisch and Partner: Recent Work," lecture in the Department of Architecture Lecture Series, Miami University, Oxford, Ohio, January 25, 1995.
95. Jones, "Guenter Behnisch and Partners."
96. Günter Behnisch, *Behnisch and Partners: Designs 1952–1987* (Stuttgart, 1987), p. 156.
97. Bernard Tschumi, *Cinegramme Folie: Le Parc de laVillette* (Paris: Champ-Vallons; Princeton, N.J.: Princeton University Press, 1987), p. viii.
98. Palmer, *Descent into Discourse,* p. 3.
99. Ibid., p. 5.
100. Lynn Hunt, "History beyond Social Theory," in David Carroll, ed., *States of Theory* (New York: Columbia University Press, 1990), p. 108.
101. Pauline Marie Rosenau, *Post-Modernism and the Social Sciences* (Princeton, N.J.: Princeton University Press, 1992), p. 141.
102. Ibid., p. 144.
103. Teresa L. Ebert, "Political Semiosis in/of American Cultural Studies," *American Journal of Semiotics* 8, no. 1/2 (1991): 115.
104. Ibid., p. 118.
105. Ibid., p. 115.
106. Robert Scholes, "Deconstruction and Communication," *Critical Inquiry* 14 (Winter 1988): 284–85.
107. Pauline Marie Rosenau, *Post-Modernism and the Social Sciences,* p. 4.
108. Peter McLaren, "Multiculturalism and the Post-Modern Critique: Towards a Pedagogy of Resistance and Transformation," in Giroux and McLaren, eds., *Between Borders,* p. 199.
109. Angela McRobbie, "Post-Marxism and Cultural Studies: A Postscript," in Grossberg, Nelson, and Treichler, eds., *Cultural Studies,* p. 720.
110. Ibid., p. 721.

111. Hall, "Cultural Studies and Its Theoretical Legacies," p. 286.
112. Ibid.
113. Darrell Crilley, "Megastructures and Urban Change: Aesthetics, Ideology, and Design," in Paul L. Knox, ed., *The Restless Urban Landscape* (Englewood Cliffs, N.J.: Prentice-Hall, 1993), p. 142.
114. Ibid.
115. Ibid.
116. For a critique of Leon Krier, see Thomas A. Dutton, "Cities, Cultures, and Resistance: Beyond Leon Krier and the Postmodern Condition," *Journal of Architectural Education* 42, no. 2 (Winter 1989).
117. Lebbeus Woods, "Experimental Architecture: A Commentary," *Avant Garde* 2 (Summer 1989), and "Zagreb-Free-Zone: Heterarchy of Urban Form and Architecture," *Avant Garde* 5 (Winter 1991).
118. Woods, "Experimental Architecture," p. 11.
119. Ibid., p. 18.
120. Fredric Jameson, "Architecture and the Critique of Ideology," in Joan Ockman, ed., *Architecture, Criticism, Ideology* (Princeton: Princeton Architectural Press, 1985), pp. 71–72.
121. Ibid., p. 71.
122. For an examination of Peter Eisenman in line with this critique, see Diane Ghirardo, "Eisenman's Bogus Avant-Garde," *Progressive Architecture,* November 1994, p. 73.
123. Geoffrey Broadbent, *Deconstruction: A Student Guide* (London: Academy Editions, 1991), p. 68.
124. Ibid., p. 70.
125. Tschumi, *Cinegramme folie,* p. viii.
126. Ebert, "Political Semiosis in/of American Cultural Studies," p. 117.
127. Stefani Ledewitz, review of Dutton, *Voices in Architectural Education: Cultural Politics and Pedagogy,* in *Design Book Review,* no. 25 (Summer 1992): 68.

ACCOMMODATION AND RESISTANCE: THE BUILT ENVIRONMENT AND THE AFRICAN AMERICAN EXPERIENCE

INTRODUCTION

American architecture, the design and planning of the environment, has rarely been studied through the lens of race, let alone its association with culture and class. "Race" has always remained invisible in environmental design. As with most aspects of our society, race and culture are in part architecturally constructed, just as architecture can be racially and culturally deconstructed. In his book *Race Matters,* cultural critic Cornel West examines how social conditions are intimately tied to race. He makes the point that race is, indeed, a fundamental feature of our history and society and that Black people are a major element of our life and history.

The powerful message of West's book can apply to architecture and planning. Race does matter in environmental design, just as race matters in the arts, business, humanities, science, and the rest of our society. Architecture, building, and planning are inherently racially constituted activities. Environmental design is very much an expression by people responding to cultural and social criteria, among many other forces. Architecture, in this context, cannot be "color-blind" or culturally neutral. Architecture, in theory as well as in practice, is inextricably tied to race as it is to class, economics, politics, and gender.

In U.S. society race is a powerful determinant affecting architecture education, architecture practice, architecture design and aesthetics, planning of neighborhoods, and the full realities of the built environment. The United States was built, in part, upon the subjugation of "people of color," which is translated into distinction and separation in our spatial and urban layout of the built environment. This chapter explores environmental design's relationship to race, especially to African Americans, as part of their continuous struggle with a strategy of accommodation and resistance in our society.

Three historical periods of African American participation in the design and construction of the physical environment are crucial to understanding environmental design's relationship to race: slavery, the Jim Crow period, and the Civil Rights era, this last era having a promise that remains unfulfilled, thus shaping the built environment we live with today. A consequence of this history is the invisibility of African American architects, the lack of documentation of their historic contributions, and the nearly complete absence of general knowledge about the centuries-old racist spatialization of U.S. society.

Many African Americans today are beginning to explore the ever-changing terrains of architectural practice and education, with an explicit theoretical focus on race as a central issue to the design of socially responsible physical environments. I utilize a framework forwarded by Cornel West in his important essay "The New Cultural Politics of Difference" to chart recent efforts by African American architects to be critical, resist appropriation, overcome invisibility, and alter the social relations that have produced spatial domination. Following this approach, I critique contemporary issues of architecture and race by exploring several culturally significant projects.

THREE HISTORICAL PERIODS

Slavery

The physical manifestation of racial separation and domination becomes an important starting point in understanding the African American experience and its relation to architecture. The architecture and the planning of slavery most clearly reveal racial impacts on our built environments. Looking at the system of slavery, we can see how attitudes toward racial differences generated opportunities and structured design ideas for artisan-slaves and those who stole their labor.

In a perverse way, the most active period of African American involvement in design and building was during the period of slavery. African craftsmen-slaves were the primary builders of the South, usually under the strict control of a "master," yet often in a role of "supervisor-designer-builder." Based on their superior skills, freed slaves also were involved in much building of the North during this period. Booker T. Washington noted in his autobiography *Up from Slavery* that "the slave system took the spirit of self-reliance and self-help out of white people."[1] Slave narratives tells us that slave builders were so prolific, efficient, and established that many of the plantation and slave owners did not know how to build and had to be taught after slavery ended.

Of course, independent and unique African-influenced design and creativity were limited because of the controlling, oppressive relationship of the "master" over his slaves despite their skill. Unlike the uniquely African American influence in gospel music and other personal arts developed within the slave experience, architecture was much too visible, public, and permanent to allow clear African motifs and references to be expressed. In fact, many subtle African and African American influences are often found in and around the plantations and urban areas of the Deep South. In "The Black Architectural Experience in America," architect and educator Richard K. Dozier cites how African skills in ironworking and woodcarving, as well as a "proficiency in the use of earth and stone," qualified the slave "as an architect alongside many other early-American craftsmen."[2]

According to Dozier, the extent to which such skills were applied stretched well beyond the design and construction of furniture, tools, bridges, and general maintenance on plantations. Slave artisans were responsible for numerous plantation houses themselves. As Dozier states, "Records and building technologies reveal slave involvement in most early plantation construction throughout Louisiana. A few notable examples include Oakland in Bermuda, Cherokee in Natchez, and Kate Chopin's house, now the Bayou Folk Museum, in Cloutierville."[3] Many slaves were hired out to other plantations because of their talent. And with such a direct hand in design and making, "architectural characteristics such as steep hip roofs, wide overhanging roofs, central fireplaces, porches, and earth and moss construction" suggest the influence of the African slave.[4] Even emulating stone buildings through wood detailing can be attributed to slave artisans.

Two decades ago professor Carl Anthony's research cleared the path for this investigation. In "The Big House and the Slave Quarters," a two-part series examining the architectural contributions of Africans in the New World, Anthony counters the pretense of "so many architectural historians, that the slaves played no important role in shaping the architectural traditions of the country during its formative years." Anthony refuses to believe "that millions of Africans would leave no trace of their architectural heritage on the New World they helped to colonize."[5] Anthony doesn't have to dig deep to make a convincing argument. Compiling evidence from archival material, paintings, books, narratives, and his own travels, Anthony offers numerous cases of African influence in the design and organization of the environment. For example, in the "tidewater plantations" of Virginia, Anthony is struck "by the number of modest eighteenth-century outbuildings behind the main house and its dependencies that seemed genuinely African in proportion, siting, or construction." In Williamsburg, Virginia, "several groups of outbuildings with their modest dimensions and pyramidal roofs create the visual effect of a piece of an African village with its multiplicity of dwelling units and granaries.... Undoubtedly the outbuildings of Williamsburg were often constructed by slaves and may have been their own design." In New Orleans, Anthony cites evidence that "the famous wrought iron balconies of that city were fabricated largely by blacks." Anthony sees historical precedent for the ironwork in its motifs: "I have seen iron standards used for sacred ancestral shrines in Dahomey very much like the garde de frise frequently used on balconies in the Vieux Carré."[6]

As another example, Anthony sheds light on the New World evolution of the now-ubiquitous front porch, countering the conventional view that "early English colonists invented it in response to new climatic requirements." Pointing out that the "veranda is widespread in the indigenous architecture of the West African rain forest,"[7] the front porch is not so much a matter of colonial invention as it is of colonial adaptation. This hypothesis is borne-out by the later work of John Michael Vlach, writing in Dell Upton's primer *America's Architectural Roots: Ethnic Groups That Built America*. Vlach states:

> No antecedent for the front porch, as it is commonly found in the South, can be found in England or elsewhere in northern Europe. The experience of tropical heat and humidity inspired such additions, and verandas are common to African house design. Soon after both slaves and their masters arrived in the New World, a cross-cultural encounter occurred, and generations of white builders adopted the custom of porch building. Although the Victorian period spawned galleries and verandas on houses all over the United States, for almost 250 years the southern front porch has owed its existence mainly to the adaptive genius of local carpenters acting on African notions of good architectural form.[8]

But it is Thomas Jefferson's home, Monticello, that serves, perhaps, as Anthony's best-known example of the unique collaboration between white master as designer and slave as designer-builder. Jefferson is credited as the designer, but Anthony suggests that his carefully selected and skilled slave craftsmen not only contributed greatly to the design, "*they* built Monticello."[9] Jefferson and his talented slaves were design partners, forming a type of antebellum design team. The members of this design team influenced each other in much of the design process, means, and methods of building Jefferson's domain.

Beyond illustrating the contributions made by African slaves to Monticello, Anthony presents a penetrating portrayal of the spatial distribution of the institution of slavery as it took form there, and George Washington's Mount Vernon, as well. Through a sharp analysis, Anthony shows how Jefferson's detailed handling of such architectural features as hidden stairs, specially designed doors, a two-tiered system of circulation, and land undulation and site layout all contrived to facilitate the daily functions of the plantation in a manner seemingly absent of slaves: "He effectively rendered the slaves invisible while integrating their activities into a single structure at one with the surrounding landscape."[10]

Similar involvement of slave builders-designers aided Benjamin Latrobe and James Hoban, the architects of record for the design and construction of the U.S. Capitol and the nation's White House, respectively.[11]

So it was that slaves and their master were precariously bound together. On the one hand, the spatiality of domestic slavery was clear and unmistakable, and it reinforced servitude on every level. But on the other hand, while the master had full control over the slave, slaves owned architectural knowledge and the skills to build. Unlike the owner-architect relationship we see today, the master's power was not only the result of financial position, but of the larger oppressive system, as well. That oppressive system also explains the concentrated activity to design and build with slaves. Under the system of slavery the client-designer relationship was necessary to effectively keep the process and status of both the master—whose social position discouraged the taint of "labor"—and servants—who labored for both. Slavery operated on the selection and exploitation of highly skilled African craftsmen who received no credit, compensation, or other means to promote their contributions.

The working plantations that slaves helped to build also became their homes and neighborhoods. Blacks, during this period, also lived in segregated areas of the cities or urban areas in the South as well as in the North.[12] But it was at the southern plantations where consistent and direct racial interplay was staged through the built environment. The slave homes or cabins (the Black environment) were often arranged in ordered clusters, away from but in view of the big house (the White environment). The slave cabins and related areas then became the first Black neighborhoods, with the counterparts in the cities becoming the first Black communities (ghettos). Slaves living and working together against the play of the "master" directing their lives gave great importance to the community over the individual cabins. This would be in direct contrast to the importance of the definition and design of the plantation big house. While the big house was the singular symbol of security and authority on the plantation, the slave cabin as a building was an architecture of confinement, dependence, and labor, an insecure containment. Instead, the collective spaces, the "neighborhood," including the fields in which they labored in relative freedom, were more important than the individual cabins. The collectivity of the neighborhoods and fields, along with the secret hiding places of the outdoors—like the communal living in West African villages—represented a scrap of independence and a place of communication for the slaves.

The impact of slave artisans on the plantations and the built environment was significant. Although artisans can be made visible for their role in building the plantations, they must also become visible for their history of resistance. Some historians of slavery, such as Eugene D. Genovese, have studied this complex relationship between accommodation and resistance to slavery.[13] According to Genovese, because skilled slave artisans and builders were often in close proximity to slave masters, many gained literacy or were taught to read in order to understand plans and blueprints. In addition, their close proximity to whites allowed them to "overhear" and learn of civic and political plans beyond the plantation. In this way, Genovese asserts, "accommodation itself breathed a critical spirit and disguised subversive actions and often embraced its apparent opposite—resistance."[14] Many times were slave artisans the leaders and organizers of that resistance. Resistance came in many forms, ranging from subtle or hidden African details and dimensions to planned construction flaws and to outright systematic arson—burning the very plantation buildings slaves had designed and built. The most significant slave rebellions were led by "invisible," literate, skilled slave artisans who had contributed to the "building" of the South under slavery, yet their most visible role resided as the architects of major slave insurgencies to tear down buildings and institutions and disrupt the slave economy. Gabriel Prosser, a skilled blacksmith, planned to seize Richmond, Virginia, in 1800. In 1822, Denmark Vesey, a freed carpenter who had traveled and learned of the uprisings in the Caribbean, planned to burn Charleston, South Carolina, then the sixth largest city in the nation, in order to instigate a general slave revolt. In 1831, Nat Turner, a plantation foreman and builder, led a rebellion in the town of Jerusalem, Virginia.

In reflecting on the period of slavery, then, the formative character of race in shaping the built environment assumes a dual role. This double-edged role of the slave artisan-builder—creator and builder of the South's many buildings and at the same time leader of the destruction of that infrastructure—illustrates the simultaneous accommodation and resistance to slavery on the part of the Black slave leadership.

Jim Crow Era

The end of slavery marked the beginning of the political effort to establish legal differences between the races. Following the Union victory in the Civil War, a brief period ensued in which freed slaves were given land, voted, elected Blacks to state government, and participated in a large upsurgence in mixed-race public education. Legal changes flourished: the Thirteenth Amendment outlawed slavery, the Fourteenth Amendment declared all persons born in the United States to be citizens, the Fifteenth Amendment guaranteed the right to vote regardless of race, and a Civil Rights Act of 1875 outlawed exclusion from public facilities. However, it was nearly immediately that all the advances made in this period known as Black Reconstruction were viciously attacked. "Jim Crow" racial discrimination laws erupted throughout the South and in the rest of the country, eclipsing this brief moment of Reconstruction. This racial discrimination, combined with European immigration, industrialization, professionalization of architecture, and other labor and economic forces marked the end of the great African American participation in the designing and building of the American environment. Constituting a major shift from the free and abundant labor of the slave economy to the paid labor of the postslavery period, the Jim Crow economy discriminated against and marginalized newly freed Black builders-designers—despite their skill and experience—in the new "open" labor market. The Jim Crow movement called for favoring of White labor despite its inexperience and limited availability. This period also transformed and defined the Black neighborhoods, or "ghettos" and townships, institutionalizing the new segregated environments of the United States.

The Freedman's Bureau and other institutions were created by the federal government, at the beginning of Black Reconstruction, to legislate and assist the masses of African Americans in resettlement to independent, segregated Black townships or "reservations," similar to the Bureau of Indian Affairs' relocation of Native Americans. Also during this period the major African American social, religious, and educational institutions began or expanded as a response to the continuing institutionalization of the segregated society. As the period of Black Reconstruction became replaced by greater racial segregation and discrimination laws, the major Black institutions, which consisted of Black churches, Black schools and colleges, Black fraternal organizations, and Black financial organizations such as insurance companies, became important components of the development, survival, and advancement of African American culture. These institutions formed to help mitigate the hostile segregated society and to offer support. These institutions were also the places in which African Americans could firmly practice their religion, seek education, support their community, develop financial advancement, and design, build, and practice architecture. The strict segregation of this period limited opportunities and development to Black institutions and townships, especially for the new generation of Black professionals who could not gain design or building commissions elsewhere. Yet within the confines of the Black townships and the many institutions they supported, Black professional education and greater opportunities for practice did develop.

Black churches and educational institutions not only constituted support and opportunities for the African American architect, they also emerged as the centers of African American intellectual development and political thought and action for these architects. The Black colleges were the birthplaces of the new professional class, as well as highly articulated and prolific debates about the direction and leadership of the Black community. These debates can be characterized as the contest between approaches emphasizing accommodation, gradualism, or conciliation versus strategies of resistance, opposition, or change in evaluating how Black culture and professional life ought to advance in that era of retrenched racism. These debates continue today, reflected in the education and politics of race, space, and the built environment.

Several Black colleges taught architecture and building design to large numbers of African American students. These schools included Hampton Institute in Virginia, Tuskegee Institute in Alabama, Howard University in Washington, D.C., and Morgan State University in Baltimore, Maryland. Tuskegee, along with the other schools, became a center of teaching and learning for the Black building industry. As Booker T. Washington, founder and leader of Tuskegee, recounted in his autobiography: "During the now nineteen years' existence of the Tuskegee school, the plan of having buildings erected by student labor has been adhered to. In this time forty buildings ... have been built.... As an additional result, hundreds of men are now scattered throughout the South who received their knowledge of mechanics while being taught how to erect these buildings."[15]

The few already trained African American architects and builders of this time positioned themselves within these institutions as a means to build and design through teaching and practice. Many of the early buildings of the major Black educational institutions were designed by the architecture division faculty and built by the architectural students under the supervision of the faculty. At Tuskegee, for example, Booker T. Washington believed in the importance of practical and vocational training as a way for Blacks to develop architectural, aesthetic, and theoretical skills. The students there designed, helped make the building materials for, and constructed needed classrooms and offices on the campuses. The limited access of the African American architect to wider opportunities gave great importance to the Black institutions as perhaps the only creative and professional outlet for the African American architect.

Robert R. Taylor, the first African American to receive a degree in architecture (MIT, 1892), worked for years teaching in the Department of Mechanical Industries and founded the first architecture division in the country to educate Black students at Tuskegee Institute. There he educated many of the next generation of African American professional architects such as John Lankford, Wallace Rayfield, and Vertner Tandy, who became a prominent church architect in the African American communities of Atlanta, Savannah, and Birmingham and of Chicago and other northern cities. Professor Taylor also designed and supervised the construction of many buildings on that campus, now a registered historic district. Taylor, like the rest of the small number of African American architects, depended greatly on the Black universities and other Black institutions as his clients, as a means of practicing architecture and as a means of exploring architectural aesthetic theories.

The Black churches, universities, businesses, and other organizations were essentially the sole client base, seeking a limited scope of building types for the small but emerging group of professional African American architects during the period that lasted from the late nineteenth century to the mid–twentieth century. There were certainly no opportunities for African American women to practice architecture anywhere during this period and virtually no work for the Black architects in the larger society. There were a few exceptions, however, including Julian Abel, a graduate from the University of Pennsylvania in 1902, who designed much of Duke University and the Philadelphia public library while working for Horace Trumbauer and Associates. Paul R. Williams, also a noted exception, graduated from the University of Southern California in 1919, and designed many homes for Hollywood stars and received numerous government and private commissions.[16] For the most part, however, the segregated environment of the larger society was reflected in the form of delivery of architectural services. Architecture was practiced within the isolation of the Black community with Black clients and Black users. The Black architect and builder had the skills and access to these special skills through the Black colleges and from the tradition of building during slavery. This isolation produced adjustments in business practices, design process, and, in more subtle ways, different theoretical and aesthetic considerations. This isolation and denial of participation of African American architects in the larger field of building clearly fostered an architecture that served the particular needs and aspirations of the Black community while not requiring the racist physical separation built into the Jim Crow aesthetic. Yet, the architecture of the Black community would rarely bring acceptance from the mainstream market.

The environmental design from the White society that evolved for official segregated living rarely dealt with the dignities or realities of the Black communities. The segregated social system required separate waiting areas, eating areas, seating areas, and sleeping areas in public and in many private buildings of the South and more subtle separate physical arrangements throughout the rest of the country. Architecture, planning, and environmental design efforts by Whites in the Black communities were characteristically inadequate, incomplete, and insensitive. The concealment of African American influences in the built environment combined with the mainstream architecture professional's role in the spatial manifestation of racial distinctions—from the micro scale of segregated drinking fountains and the duplication of public facilities such as schools, to the macro scale of segregated subdivisions and towns—led to racial segregation as a guiding principle of urban planning, environmental design, and professional training. The vast dimensions of racialization inscribed in the nation's landscape during the one-hundred-year period of Jim Crow contributes to the basis of the civil rights and environmental justice movements of the next period.

Civil Rights

The Civil Rights era brought about another shift in the evolution of race as an influence on environmental design. This period started during the 1950s, manifested major activism during the 1960s, and realized polices in the 1970s and 1980s. Numerous Black architects were educated and gained access to the architecture profession as a result of the Civil Rights movement. Norma Sklarek became the first African American female director of the California Council, American Institute of Architects (CCAIA) during this period. Harvey Gantt fought and won admission to Clemson as the first African American to attend that university. Taylor Culver was elected president of the American Institute of Architects Student Chapter (AIAS) in 1968. Robert Nash of Washington, D.C., was elected vice-president of the AIA in 1970, becoming the first Black architect to hold this national office. Several other examples of significant achievements of African American architects resulted from the Civil Rights movement. Although legal barriers to the active involvement of the African American architect in all segments of the profession and with all clients were lifted as a result of civil rights law, discriminatory practices existed, and hidden discriminatory practices are still part of the profession today. Just as constitutional protections gained after the Civil War failed to be enforced, similarly, the Civil Rights Act has only been as effective as its enforcement. Census and research conducted by the University of Cincinnati in 1995 established that there are approximately 1,060 registered African American architects in the United States, which represents approximately 1 percent of all registered architects. The same research identifies approximately 90 African American women registered architects, approximately one tenth of one percent of all architects.[17] The absence of African American architects, educators, and other environmental design professionals is one result of continued discriminatory practice, at least in part, in the profession and in the architectural schools.

This discrimination against and marginalization of African American architects helps explain the shift of the main client base and building type to the government and quasi-government institutions. Little direct research in this area is available, but several preliminary surveys indicate that the primary client base today for African American architects is the government, made possible by the gains of affirmative action policies in support of minority-owned businesses recognizing past discrimination. With few exceptions, government work represents over half of the commissions for African American architecture firms. The majority of African American architecture firms depend upon the government for 85 percent or more of their jobs. African American architects, educators, and advocates have noted the singularity of the government or public-sector client base among these architects. The New York City architect J. Max Bond Jr. asserts that there has never been a major architectural commission to a Black architect outside of Harlem in downtown New York City.[18] It is noted that the few architectural commissions awarded to African American architects in Harlem are exclusively from Black institutions or the government.

The threat to affirmative action policies, if successful, would eliminate work for Black architects, as many are tied solely to the government as their prime client base. The private market is virtually unwilling to commission African American architects. At the same time, traditional Black institutional clients have slipped away from African American architects, opening themselves up to larger mainstream architectural firms, with mainstream firms taking advantage of an increased, previously ignored, private market of Black institutions. Affirmative action policies enacted by the government have certainly increased this dependence of African American firms on the government as client, but most cite the architecture profession's and the private market's continued discrimination as the central problem.

As the promise of Civil Rights remains unfulfilled and Black unemployment reaches heights greater than at any time since the Great Depression, the position of Black professional life is again in question. The same debates about the direction to be taken to overcome structural racism—accommodation or resistance—arise in new forms.

THE INVISIBLE PRACTICING ARCHITECT

The character of the landowner seeking design, starting with the plantation master, moving to segregated Black institutions and, presently, to the government, has conspired to make the African American architect professionally invisible. The contributions of the slave builders are clearly hidden. The work by African American architects for the many Black institutions is little known, examined, or cited, leaving them invisible. The governmental projects, even the largest projects, are often considered purely utilitarian, aesthetically compromised and architecturally unimportant. The most prized governmental commissions rarely grant a Black architect the prime position, and when they are part of these projects the African American architect is often relegated a minor role as subarchitect collaborator. The affirmative action programs that are part of the government process for the selection of architects have always diminished the preeminence of the African American architect while usually not affecting the role or reputation of the White architect. Within the profession the government as client has the same effect of helping to render the African American architect invisible.

There have been and are today a few noted and established African American architects working in the mainstream of practice. In his inaugural Howard Hamilton Mackey Lecture in 1992, Harry G. Robinson III, dean of the School of Architecture and Planning at Howard University, makes the point that Black architects have been an important part of architectural practice:

> The contemporary African American architect has deep and mature roots in the culture of this nation. We have come to where we are on the shoulders of our predecessors—Robert Robinson Taylor, Julian Abel, John Lankford, Percy Eiffel, W. Sidney Pittman, Albert Cassell, Henry Livas, Howard H. Mackey, Hilyard Robinson, Paul Williams, et al. We are not "invisible" as some in the architectural press would suggest. The extent to which we are "endangered" is within our control.
>
> We practice, we teach, we write, we serve the profession and the community at-large, we are leaders, we are team players, we have philosophies and theories, we exist. Through our designs and teachings we transfer our knowledge and vision and bring joy and enlightenment to our clients, students, and society. We do not ask for special quarter and we expect none. We are architects! We design. We build.[19]

African American architects do exist, although, as we have seen, in relatively small numbers and often at the margins and overlooked. Robinson's need to declare the presence of African American architects indicates their very obscurity. Because of the historical context and the current system of practice, African American architects and their buildings have always been invisible. African American architects and their works are perceived and relegated to a substatus or a dubious role of invisibility. Buildings designed by African American architects are perceived as anonymous, with little or no recognition; they are often forgotten, yet usually have social relevance and responsibility in the cultural community or in the African American experience.

The African American architect, then, is caught between two worlds of architecture—the mainstream dominant formal and the invisible now forgotten—unable to enter the first world architecture as a fully recognized member. Ironically, for African American architects their mainstream formal work becomes anonymous and is made invisible. For example, the architecture practice of distinguished African American architect John Moutusseme was so invisible that even his design of the North Pier Towers was ignored in the architectural and planning community of Chicago. This forty-plus-story project is the largest tower next to Mies van der Rohe's Lake Shore Towers. In an architecturally sophisticated city, this seemingly controversial project received little attention, due in part, to the lack of attention afforded African American architects.

CHANGING TODAY'S PRACTICE

The African American architect has had to practice in an architectural profession that has succeeded in constricting full participation. The role of architectural education and the larger system of practice needs reevaluation. The challenges of designing in a multicultural society, especially African American culture, should become a part of any school's curriculum. The practice of architecture that makes hidden and anonymous the works of African American architects reduces the obvious positive influence to African American architectural students, but it is detrimental to all students. It is not surprising, then, to find polls suggesting that a relatively large percentage of African American architectural graduates are finding their way into alternative professional careers, such as facilities engineers, corporate representatives, and other related fields of employment. Unlike the traditional practicing architect, these related roles tend to elevate the visibility and credibility of the African American architectural professional.

While our society has become increasingly diverse, the architectural profession has not. Skills in marketing, design ability, and other business aptitudes are important to the success and visibility of the African American architect, as with all architects. Yet the historical and current status of African American architects and the nature of their ties to clients and the larger profession exert extra professional burdens. The structure of the system of architectural practice is as critical to the equal and balanced access for African American architects as is the professional development of the African American architect that is so often proposed. It is clear that in the uncertainties of the economy the African American architect cannot and should not have to depend solely on the government for commissions. At the same time they should be able to continue to work closely with Black institutions, not just for economic security or survival, but for tradition, identity, and cultural continuity. More important, they should have full access to all segments, clients, and locations of professional practice—an architecture for all.

When looking into the question of who is able to exploit and who is really being well served by our system of architectural practice, we find that the architectural field can shift, to make structural changes in its ability to accommodate all its members. Affirmative action is one means to push the system to ensure access to underrepresented architects. Affirmative action is now being vigorously attacked as obsolete and unfair, with some justification, but given the systematic exclusion of diverse cultural expressions, it remains necessary to move the system. The idea of moving the system rather than just changing the African American architect has important merit. Both should be done using an inclusionary approach, moving the field toward access and using an educational approach, changing the practice of the African American architect. This can lead to a transformation of the practice to respecting, accepting, and allowing fuller access and visibility of African American architects to the profession. The African American architect can use the traditional tactics of honoring the system and working twice as hard, focusing only on the Black institutions or working for the government to overcome race and culture, but that in the past has not always ensured great success and runs counter to breaking into the established exclusive White private-client market pool.

The corporate and mainstream private sector has been the elusive client for the African American architect except when forced together in the oppressive system of slavery. Without access to this mainstream client base, and by historical circumstances, the African American architect becomes an anomaly within the profession. The dilemma for the African American architect is how to thrive and even survive as a relatively hidden, marginal professional in a field that requires mainstream values, visibility, and friendship with private corporate clients for success.

The vital dialogue about aesthetic practices that critique White supremacy with its attendant racialization of space as well as promote an affirmative culture for diverse peoples is most advanced today, but a deeper and sharper conversation is still needed. Carrying forward the lessons learned from each position debated throughout African American history, critical practitioners today are faced with many more questions—and alternative paths—than simply the continuing struggle to survive our invisibility. We are now in positions to lead, both within our various local political institutions and the dominant institutions of the governing culture. Again, the struggle persists between the paths of assimilation within the mainstream and opposition to it (while, of course, no artist or critic can exist outside of that mainstream). This dilemma of surviving within the mainstream without sacrificing one's identity pertains to all artists or critics of color, and is thus not particular to African American architects or even architects of color. In his important essay, "The New Cultural Politics of Difference," critical theorist Cornel West—advocating a path of resistance—makes this precise point: that to thrive as a critic or an artist one must possess not only the pertinent skills for critical practice but must have the "self-confidence, discipline, and perseverance" to succeed without unduly relying upon the "mainstream for approval." For West, the widespread denial of "intelligence, ability, beauty and character of people of color puts a tremendous burden on critics and artists of color to 'prove' themselves in light of norms and models set by white elites whose own heritage devalued and dehumanized them." West continues:

> This is more a structural dilemma than a matter of personal attitudes. The profoundly racist and sexist heritage of the European Age has bequeathed to us a set of deeply-ingrained perceptions about people of color including, of course, the self-perceptions that people of color bring. It is not surprising that most intellectuals of color in the past exerted much of their energies and efforts to gain acceptance and approval by "white normative gazes." The new cultural politics of difference advises critics and artists of color to put aside this mode of mental bondage, thereby freeing themselves to both interrogate the ways in which they are bound to certain conventions and to learn from and build on these very norms and models.[20]

Recognizing that putting aside mental bondage is certainly easier said than done, West promotes what he terms "prophetic criticism," which is a mode of theoretical inquiry that bridges art, criticism, and politics and makes explicit its moral and political aims. Springing from "social structural analyses of empire, extremism, class, race, gender, nature, age, sexual orientation, nation and region," the prophetic critical task is to demystify the "complex dynamics of institutional and other related power structures in order to disclose options and alternatives for transformative praxis."[21] For West, this is not a call for essentialism, or as cultural critic bell hooks argues in a similar vein in "An Aesthetic of Blackness," not a call to mobilize black artistic practice and cultural production around black nationalism or any movement that tends toward separatism itself. Hooks is instructive here:

> Black artists concerned with producing work that embodies and reflects a liberation politic know that an important part of any decolonization process

is critical intervention and interrogation of existing repressive and dominating structures. African-American critics and/or artists who speak about our need to engage in ongoing dialogue with dominant discourses always risk being dismissed as assimilationist. There is a grave difference between that engagement with white culture which seeks to deconstruct, demystify, challenge, and transform and gestures of collaboration and complicity. We cannot participate in dialogue that is the mark of freedom and critical agency if we dismiss all work emerging from white western traditions.[22]

For West and hooks, it is precisely the relation between the marginal and the dominant that needs focused critique and deconstruction in order to form new links between art, architecture, criticism, and revolutionary politics. That this struggle, historically and presently, is treacherous and that critical work produced is often appropriated should come as no surprise, and points to the intense difficulty of African American architects and artists of color to persevere in the face of repressive, determining structures. West recounts and elaborates the four options by which people of color have attempted to survive and thrive within these conditions "as serious practitioners of their craft,"[23] challenging us to position our practice of architecture and environmental design.

The first option West calls "Booker T. Temptation," which, in critical allusion to Washington's symbolic position as conciliator, is characterized by "individual preoccupation with the mainstream and its legitimizing power." This is arguably the option of accommodation and the one of choice for most artists and critics of color; as West says, most try to "bite this bait." Although the lure is strong, the success rate in entering the mainstream and sustaining activity is very low. Even with the "pervasive professionalization of cultural practitioners of color in the past few years," West says, this "has not produced towering figures who reside within the established White patronage system." Still, West cautions, it remains "unrealistic for creative people of color to think they can sidestep the White patronage system."[24]

Efforts to sidestep often lead to the second option, what West terms the "Talented Tenth Seduction," which is the move toward group insularity. The value of this strategy is clear, "to preserve one's sanity and sense of self as one copes with the mainstream." But West warns against the more self-defeating fallout of this option: it "usually reinforces the very inferior complexes promoted by the subtly racist mainstream," and it "tends to revel in a parochialism and encourage a narrow racialist and chauvinistic outlook."[25]

The third option of West's taxonomy is the "Go-It-Alone" strategy. Understood as the resistance and the "extreme rejectionist perspective that shuns the mainstream and group insularity," it nevertheless holds virtue in that it "reflects the presence of independent, critical and skeptical sensibilities toward perceived constraints on one's creativity."[26] The drawback, of course, is the lack of a community that can nurture critical dialogue and integrate practitioners from differing fields.

What West considers the most desirable option is when artists of color become "critical organic catalysts." By this West means a person who "stays attuned to what the mainstream has to offer—its paradigms, viewpoints and methods—yet maintains a grounding in affirming and enabling subcultures of criticism." In this way, artists, architects, and critics simultaneously position themselves within the mainstream while remaining "clearly aligned with groups who vow to keep alive potent traditions of critique and resistance."[27] West points to such people as Louis Armstrong, W. E. B. Du Bois, Ella Baker, and Martin Luther King as exemplars of this option, who retained an openness to mainstream directions but did not become co-opted. The lesson here is that "group autonomy is not group insularity," and that the preconditions for a new cultural politics of difference are "communities, groups, organizations, institutions, subcultures and networks of people of color who cultivate critical sensibilities and personal accountability—without inhibiting individual expressions, curiosities, and idiosyncrasies."[28]

Cornel West is useful here because his four options provide a framework in which to evaluate the contemporary work of African American architects, architectural educators, and institutions concerned with black professional and cultural life in light of their attempt to overcome invisibility and to embrace critical practices. In other words, when applied specifically to the work of African American architects and educators as well as the practices of institutions resisting white supremacy, the taxonomy West provides reveals much about their success and failure in forging transformative directions and resisting appropriation and commodification. It is important to note that while West's categories are useful for analysis, the boundaries between them are fluid and some work may be exemplary of more than one option.

Mainstream Identity

The identity of the Black architect has always been forged in the context of White supremacy, or put differently, lack of a White client base in the context of the established field. Many Black architects, in negotiating this field, pursue West's Booker T. Temptation option of assuming a strong tie to and an assimilation with the mainstream of the architectural profession and its apparent ability to grant a valid identity. The act and ritual of becoming a registered architect—schooling, apprenticeship, passing the registration examination, and participating in professional practice—should allow Black architects to enter this mainstream. Yet many Black architects who choose to connect with mainstream practice are still marginalized within it. This is reflected in the extremely low numbers of licensed

Black architects, as stated earlier, and the correspondingly small number of private commissions awarded to Black architects, their minimal exposure in the architectural press, their low numbers as full-time professors in the schools of architecture (*fewer than 5 percent*), and their nonexistence as invited guests to lecture at architectural meetings, conventions, architecture schools, and other settings.[29] In looking at more than one hundred architecture schools' and museums' published lecture series for the 1992 through 1994 lecture season, only six African American presenters were listed out of more than six hundred lectures.[30]

As Harry Robinson III, dean of Howard University's College of Architecture, has already pointed out, there are noted and established Black architects, architecture educators, and scholars, but they constitute a tiny part of the mainstream. This tradition includes Paul Williams and Robert Kennard, the first and the oldest Black architectural firms in California, respectively, and the Black architects who practice within large offices.

Harvey Gantt, fellow of the AIA, is one example of active African American architects to have assumed a close connection to the mainstream of professional practice. His firm of Gantt Huberman Architects has built a notable practice in Charlotte, North Carolina, since 1971. Harvey Gantt is, perhaps, most known and distinguished as a politician, having been mayor of Charlotte from 1983 through 1987 and the surprising challenger in the 1990 race for the Senate seat in North Carolina, opposing Jessie Helms.

Gantt's mainstream status is well established through his political placement as well as his architectural practice. His election as mayor of a predominantly White city and his straightforward campaign for Senate mandate a strong preoccupation with the political mainstream, including the corporate and business community as well as basic middle-class voters. Few African Americans have become senators, and an African American architect has never occupied a major federal elected office; very few architects of any kind have been elected to federal office since Thomas Jefferson. Gantt is a talented architect with a strong sense of community design, and his architecture practice benefits and is more closely related to the mainstream because of his political endeavors. He says, "I have always believed in this profession, but I've always felt that it wasn't living up to its potential."[31]

As with many Black architects working within the mainstream, Gantt has endeavored to make the correct professional moves, "working twice as hard" and often breaking bold new ground in the process. He was the first African American to enter Clemson and to graduate in the architecture program, having been admitted only as the result of a lawsuit against school segregation. He was the first African American to become mayor of Charlotte. He was the first African American and architect to mount a major campaign for Senate in North Carolina. He is a member, a strong supporter, and a fellow of the American Institute of Architecture (AIA) and other professional organizations, including the National Organization of Minority Architects. His discipline, hard work, political astuteness, and architectural skills allow him to embrace and be accepted by the mainstream.

His commissions, therefore, reflect not only his design talents, but also his connection with the mainstream. His repertoire of building types includes housing, offices, places of worship, community centers, and educational facilities of both public and private concerns. Handsomely designed and competently detailed, his buildings are generally contextually appropriate and modernist in style with an enduring beauty. They are not noted for a culturally identified aesthetic, design philosophy, or style. While Gantt may have challenged the political monopoly with his run for Senate, his architecture tends not to be a loud challenge or to be critical of the mainstream system. His balance of private and public commissions, along with the architectural style of his designs, is a strong signal of his standing and professional identity in the mainstream of architectural practice.

It is ironic here that Gantt, along with others, had to challenge the mainstream and establish a strong political strategy of resistance and activism to achieve acceptance in the same mainstream of architectural practice. His accommodation to mainstream identity is not without struggle and not without continuing to question the most protective elements of the mainstream. For Gantt and many Black professionals, especially those who sought to enter the profession during the Civil Rights era, opposition to the mainstream was required to gain voice, visibility, and a connection to the mainstream. Gantt's entry to the mainstream of architecture practice, like his entry to politics, constitutes some change in the system.

GROUP INSULARITY

Another strategy for the black architect is what West defines as group insularity. In this approach, self-definition and self-understanding become important as one practices in the architecture mainstream. The National Organization of Minority Architects (NOMA), the Historic Black Colleges and Universities' (HBCUs) schools of architecture, and other "minority" and black professional groups operate, in part, as a collective self-empowering network.

NOMA's main function, for example, is keeping its membership of nearly three thousand African American and other "minority" professionals and fifteen hundred students informed of and active in current mainstream architectural issues, while networking and advocating issues important to African Americans and "minority" architectural practice and education.[32] As a professional organization it connects its many members who are at the margins of the architecture field to the center while simultaneously addressing the special concerns of being on the margins of the profession.

NOMA grew out of the AIA during the 1971 AIA National Convention in Detroit, Michigan. Several African American AIA members had become increasingly dissatisfied with the AIA and its lack of direct focus on the important urban design issues of the inner cities, as well as those issues related to African American professionals in their practice. A caucus of architects, which included Wendell Campbell of Gary, Indiana; Harry Overstreet of San Francisco, California; Robert Coles of Buffalo, New York; Charles McAfee of Wichita, Kansas; Harold Williams of Los Angeles, California; and seven others met to organize NOMA as a national professional organization to specifically address the concerns of African American and other "minority" architects. The stated purpose from the founders of NOMA is the following:

> We, the Minority Architects and Planners of this Nation, in order to bring the insights and concerns of architecture to the greatest number of people in the communities in which we live and in confrontation with today's world, do establish this organization on the common bonds of professional interest and personal concern which unites us all. Careful thought, good design and fresh ideas multiplied by the strength of numbers and reinforced by the minority experience in this country, can and will contribute to the solution of the problems confronting our environment. Our concern is that this contribution not be restricted by past and current barriers to equal participation in the mainstream of National Life.[33]

NOMA's specific goals are modeled, somewhat, after AIA goals and directions, with a particular eye to advancing African American and other "minority" architects and to examining the environmental health of African American neighborhoods.

Tension has been felt from the start around the question of how faithful NOMA should be to the AIA and its mainstream values, which so often neglect the immediate interest of NOMA members, as well as the question of how close the focus should be on the special issues of African American and "minority" architects. NOMA's successful relationship to the AIA can be measured by many occurrences, including the AIA National's establishment of an Annual Diversity Conference and the AIA California Council's Resolution upholding affirmative action.

While NOMA has been in the forefront of "minority" issues, it has been incomplete in embracing the concerns of African American women and other women architects of color. Cheryl McAfee, the daughter and partner of one of NOMA's founders, Charles McAfee, will finally become NOMA's first female leader in 1996. She and other active NOMA female members have been working to bring to NOMA a direction related to "minority" women in architecture.

The dual role of exposing the mainstream while at the same time focusing on special cultural experiences is one of the principal educational missions of the schools of architecture in the HBCUs. The five schools of Architecture and Environmental Design at the HBCUs have had long traditions of providing a culturally rich, technically sound, and pragmatically useful education. Their special mission of preparing young African American and other "minority" designers to enter the mainstream world while embracing their cultural identity keeps these institutions as important, viable, and popular alternatives.

The application of cultural design philosophy of interior design and classroom space can also be part of a process that addresses the ideas of the dual role of group insularity. In looking at the African Heritage Rooms of the Nationality Rooms at the University of Pittsburgh (see Figure 5.1), we find architectural design connected to educational ideals in ways that encourage voice and self-identity while satisfying the functional requirements of a classroom. The Nationality Rooms Program is a collection of active classrooms conceived and designed as an interpretation and recreation of environments from particular ethnic groups or nationalities. It is meant to be a physical statement about the diversity of cultural heritage, identity, and learning. The central purpose of the African Heritage classroom is to present the history and diversity of African culture and to encourage an African worldview as revealed through visual, physical design.[34]

The classroom's unifying concept is the eighteenth-century Asante temple courtyard. Throughout Africa, courtyards are the setting for family activities, ceremonial events, learning, and worship. The courtyard seems to be an important "trans-African" built environment. It is this idea of courtyard as a place for learning and for keeping traditions alive that evokes the idea of classroom. The classroom is organized with double-tiered seating or benches built into the back walls surrounding a small courtyard-like area, with traditional chieftain stools scattered around the center. Large bas-reliefs surround the room, with openwork window screens on the window walls, all referring to traditional African environments. The frieze symbols on the upper walls; relief carvings on the doors, seats, and chalkboard; and "furniture" all depict and communicate spiritual, historical, and religious elements of the African culture and landscape. The room was conceived to have the character of authentic representation. Colors, details, and symbols, although not always constructed of traditional materials, are correctly described and produced, giving the room a type of "living museum" quality.

As in the African tradition, all surfaces of the classroom are articulated and decorated not just for simple visual enjoyment but for the more profound reason of transmitting stories and ideas. Designs and details imbue the classroom with information and meaning. This synthesis of tradition, ideas, and utility in African culture equates to the Western concept of visual beauty. The design process and resulting room seek to establish an identity, surrounding African Americans with a story about environments for learning that connects them with an African cultural experience.

NOMA, the HBCUs, the African Heritage Rooms, and other related institutions and cultural designs act directly to preserve and reinforce the identity of African

Figure 5.1. The African Heritage Room at the University of Pittsburgh with authentic West African motifs, details, and furniture. (Photo used by permission.)

American architects while assisting to negotiate an interaction with the larger architecture practice system. There is a group cultural self-esteem associated with these institutions and designs. West notes that this important activity of reinforcing the group's identity through complete and direct cultural insulation is best as a temporary or transitory process toward full development and understanding of African American architects. A singular, complete, and permanent adherence to this option of cultural insulation is, as West says of other insular practices, "self-defeating in that it usually reinforces the very inferior complexes promoted by the subtly racist mainstream."[35] The Afrocentric nature of these institutions and designs can hold important alternative viewpoints, yet can also become self-contained and oppressive.

THE INDEPENDENT AFRICAN AMERICAN ARCHITECT

An idealistic strategy for identity is to locate the Black architect as a unique and independent individual. Here Black architects position themselves not as part of a larger professional insular group such as NOMA or as attached to the mainstream of practice, but as individuals, rejecting mainstream validating powers. The culture and tradition of the architectural profession promotes this independent persona; it is consistent, perhaps endemic, to the creative imperative of the architectural designer of any race. While it may allow for a degree of self-definition and independence, the low numbers of Black architects limit the ability of self-definition. The larger group will tend to place an identity on this very small group of architects.

There are several individuals trying to make their mark as independent Black designers. Architects Greg Williams and Joe Addo, an African American and an African, respectively, each with a small artistic practice in Southern California are examples. While they clearly identify with Black architects, they are strongly independent and unique architects, much in the concept of the idealized artistic master-builder. Their design work is conceptually strong and resonates in and out of the cultural bounds that tend to identify them or their work with Black culture, yet they are never really able to shed their ethnic identity by striving to be just unique and talented individual designers. The effort to dislocate the Black architect from the larger cultural group and to become an individual and independent artist can never quite fully take. The invisibility of African Americans shapes everyone of this group into a common form, a type of group stereotype. The invisibility of African American architects, indicated by low numbers and status, collects them into a common group and makes this strategy of unique talent difficult for the Black architects to influence greatly and to benefit from the larger architectural community.

ORGANIC CATALYSTS:
CULTURAL POLITICS OF DIFFERENCE

West's most desirable way to secure an appropriate yet critical identity for the Black architect is to position oneself in the area of "cultural politics of difference" and to locate in an "organic" middle ground.[36] One's practice becomes a critical place, with membership in the best of the mainstream and a close grounding with one's personal and cultural history and with African American architects. In this way, the Black architect is fluent with the mainstream yet is clearly sustained by the power of his or her ethnic identity, Black architectural experience, and history.

J. Max Bond Jr., formerly of Bond/Ryder and Associates and now partner with Davis Brody Associates of New York City, is one leading African American architect practicing today who, I believe, embodies the notion of a "cultural politics of difference" in his architecture. He views architecture as a dynamic cultural and social art that in turn is a means of social and community development. As he says, "I have always viewed architecture as a social art that is not only about form, content, function, and context, but about values, culture and power. Underlying my own design is a concern with 'social uplift.'"[37]

Bond positions his ideas and designs in the critical position of a close grounding in the modernist aesthetic tradition, but at the same time, aligns himself with strains of resistance and change. He understands the boundaries of the dynamic influences that are part of the social conditions and incorporates these issues as a catalyst to broaden the role of his architecture. His work, especially his design philosophy and process, is guided by his strong commitment to respond to aspirations of the users and the larger community, while not overlooking the mainstream context of architectural practice. He is viewed as a proactive critic, a responsive activist in the practice of architecture. He is always looking for the relationship between the familiar mainstream and the improvisational African American cultural condition. This is done with a strong connection to the social, popular, and economic context:

> People have to have some say about the buildings — about the creation of the buildings — and so inevitably they will express it either through the shape and the form of the building or through the context of the building. For example, in housing, it's really unlikely that if black people were building housing for themselves they would have the same kinds of divisions of homes that we find in — say, housing provided for them.[38]

Bond's recent example of working with this identity of the "organic middle ground" is his work on the Civil Rights Institute, located in the Birmingham Civil Rights District, Alabama (see Figure 5.2). The Birmingham Civil Rights District is important in its implications for environmental design and race related to Black experience. This comprehensive district, planned and designed by an ensemble of architects, includes a historic community of Black businesses, the restored sixteenth Street Baptist Church, the Alabama Jazz Hall of Fame, the Black Masonic Temple, the George Washington Carver Theatre, Kelly Ingram Park, and the New Civil Rights Institute. The New Civil Rights Institute designed by Bond along with John Brown and Associates was the catalyst and centerpiece for the whole district. The institute is a "state-of-the-art" facility housing exhibits that depict historical events from post–World War I racial segregation to present-day racial relations. The institute comprises 58,000 square feet, with archives, offices, galleries, meeting rooms, and a large museum space dedicated to the story of civil and human rights. The institute's accommodating scale has a prominence and power that is enhanced by its siting near the noted sixteenth Street Baptist Church (the site of the 1963 bombing that killed four Sunday School children), its location across the street from the new Kelly Ingram Park, and its proximity in the area of the redeveloped Historic Fourth Avenue Black Business District.

Bond's Civil Rights Institute embodies the idea of the "march" as community activism through the design of the long upward walk from the main gate to the building's main entry. One starts at street level and "marches" up through a rising exterior entry court to the main rotunda. Typical of Bond's cultural work, the entry rotunda is a symbolic monument, but it is not monumental in scale. The rotunda's

Figure 5.2. The rotunda of the Civil Rights Institute overlooking the Kelly Ingram Park in the foreground, Birmingham, Alabama. (Photo by Bradford C. Grant.)

roof form and geometry topped with copper relates to African or African American culture. The primary use of brick, the scale, and the roof forms of the institute clearly relate to the materials, scale, and roofs of the adjacent churches and residential buildings. This strong contextual response makes the new Civil Rights Institute at home and part of the community.

The Civil Rights District represents an effort to radically portray the African American environment as an important and connected part of Birmingham itself. With few exceptions the district and the individually redeveloped buildings were designed by African American architects and planners. Perhaps the largest planned redeveloped African American neighborhood by African American professionals outside of Harlem, the district is a functioning community of the African American experience, much like the Chinatowns and other ethnic places in North American cities. The area has been designed with wonderful and colorful unifying streetscapes, facade elements, and street furniture that distinguish the district, giving the street a vitality consistent with the active neighborhood. A regularly spaced, African-weave paving pattern of brick on the sidewalks helps to define the district while symbolizing the unity of the area and its history. A most appropriate addition to the area is the new Hugo Black Federal Courthouse (named for the former Supreme Court justice), which is just two blocks away from the institute, outside of but adjacent to the district. Given that civil rights successes were finalized by strategic federal legal actions and supreme court decisions, this new granite and glass federal building, symbolically, seems to be at home here.

Representational symbolism seems to be a key concept throughout the design of the district. The most clear symbols and messages are the sculptures in the new Kelly Ingram Park. This park was the site of the infamous water gunning and attacks by German shepherds on the nonviolent civil rights demonstrators. A sequence of sculptures in the park portrays the water cannons, the jailed children demonstrators, and the leaders of the Civil Rights movement kneeling in prayer. But it is the axis and view corridors from these sculptures to the entry of the Civil Rights Institute and to the Sixteenth Street Baptist Church that symbolically and visually connect the physical setting and buildings to the memory and history of the movement.

The representation of memory, of the collective cultural memory of the Birmingham African Americans and of the Civil Rights experience, is perhaps the greatest contribution of the district and its buildings. The Civil Rights District and its many components were laden with legal problems, political challenges, and questionable financial maneuverings typical of urban development of this nature. Resistance from some members of the White Birmingham community was significant. Whites who resisted the development apparently did not want this cultural memory expressed, exposed, and explained through the permanently designed built environment and interpreted through the writings, artwork, and exhibits of the area. The African American community felt the developed district was a powerful and empowering cultural element of experience and a means to mediate the two communities. The power of the district is that it is an extended urban area and not just one building or museum. The cultural symbols and messages leak out of the Civil Rights Institute into the park and streets, allowing the public to learn about the cultural and racial memory of a whole area and not just from the exhibit design of the institute.

Like the Civil Rights Institute and District, the Martin Luther King Center for Non-Violent Social Change (the King Center), located in the heart of one of Atlanta's National Historic Site and Preservation Districts, is a comprehensive environmental memorial (see Figure 5.3). The King Center, also designed by J. Max Bond Jr., is tied to the Black historic district as an urban institution. It contains the library and archives for the world's largest collection of primary source material on the Civil Rights movement. It is also the burial site of Dr. Martin Luther King Jr. The King Center opens up to Alburn Avenue, a major avenue through the Black neighborhood, to allow a view of the white marble crypt of Reverend King for all to see and experience. There are no architectural barriers to stop one from seeing or approaching the crypt from the street. This arrangement becomes a symbolic urban gesture of openness particularly appropriate and consistent with King's memorial: "The architecture of the Center reflects the non-violent nature

Figure 5.3. The crypt of Dr. Martin Luther King Jr. at the King Center for Non-Violent Social Change, Atlanta. (Photo by Bradford C. Grant.)

of Dr. King's work and the continuing civil and human rights movements. The formal organization of the spaces, the elegant proportions of the buildings, the introduction of a reflecting pool into the complex and carefully chosen materials each possess a spiritual, cultural, and in some cases economic relationship to the goals of the Center."[39]

Making important cultural items and memories an integral part of the urban environment is a feature of Bond's architecture of cultural significance. This aspect of his architecture and philosophy was first seen in the Schomburg Center of African American History and Research in Harlem, New York City, one of Bond's early major commissions. The Schomburg is also set in the midst of the vibrant and active Black urban setting of Harlem. Since it opens to the neighborhood on the first-level gallery through a screened window wall, one who is viewing displayed art also can see street life directly. The symbolic octagonal reading rooms allow the casual pedestrian outside to look into and down on these rooms. The people of Harlem can easily learn and understand the meaning and importance of the Schomburg from the outside because of Bond's effort in making the building part of the urban and social environment.

In his practice and designs, Bond works to balance cultural aesthetics with ideas of an ecology of economics. The Schomburg Center, the King Center, and his other culturally centered work reflect their specific context and certain African American influences, while using appropriate materials selected not only for their functional or aesthetic qualities, but also to help increase the use of local black labor and suppliers. The ecology of economics takes into consideration the local economy that is served by the specification and selection of materials and construction techniques. It allows Bond's buildings to become more than physical cultural monuments or institutions, and his architecture goes far in achieving greater community development of the African American local economy. His architecture uses the mainstream structure to promote and develop a critical cultural and economic catalyst.

Another noted individual of Cornel West's fourth strategy is Jack Travis of JTA, New York City. While Travis has a viable architecture and interior design practice, he is most known for his premiere book, *African American Architects in Current Practice,* published with much celebration in 1991. This book is the first ever about Black architects and one that locates their identity within the larger architectural system. The book is, in many ways, an outgrowth of Travis's professional involvement with the filmmaker Spike Lee in *Jungle Fever,* in which Wesley Snipes was cast in the lead role as an architect. Travis was his coach, as well as the architect who designed Lee's retail boutique and home and Snipes's several homes. It was Lee's influence (a "wake-up call") coupled with Travis's lack of role models that motivated Travis to research and document his fellow Black architects. In much the same way that Spike Lee markets T-shirts, "X" hats, and other consumer items, Travis has developed a series of T-shirts and calendars that list African American architects.

Travis has also developed and instituted a summer architecture program for "minority" high school students. Called the "Afri-Environments Studio," this six-week program is run out of his office and is intended to stir up interest, curiosity, and understanding of Afrocentricity in architecture and design to young African Americans and other underrepresented members of the design profession. He and other professionals volunteer their time during the summer program to provide workshops and lectures, called Tribe Vibes, for these youths. Through designing, writing, traveling, and research Travis introduces his students to different cultural sensibilities and traditions in hopes the students may learn to connect these sensibilities and to see aesthetic traditions more inclusively. This unique attention and commitment to expose these young people to the fields of architecture and design while at the same time running a busy architectural and interior design practice connect Travis to the cultural "politics of difference" option. It is clear that Travis works within several cultural and professional practice positions while never becoming disconnected from his African American experience. He uses the advances gained by earlier Black professionals and influences others to advance. Although his work, programs, and business directions are not confrontational to the establishment, they are, when taken together, critical of the profession while making progressive moves.

Sharon E. Sutton, a distinguished professor of architecture, also demonstrates the ideals of West's "cultural politics of difference" in environmental design and architectural education. Sutton holds advance degrees in architecture, psychology, and philosophy, and is a faculty member of the College of Architecture and Urban Planning at the University of Michigan. The only woman of color in the architecture program at Michigan and one of approximately ten African American women architecture professors in the country, she is further noted as the first and only African American woman full professor of architecture in the United States and the second to be a fellow of the AIA. Combining environmental research and teaching, Sutton activates a critical view of cultural identity and leadership within the architecture system. Education and research become powerful tools for Sutton to fuse an understanding of mainstream values with an active, creative, and critical response to those values.

Like Bond, Sutton focuses her professional energies on promoting an environmentally sustainable and socially just society, utilizing novel approaches to educational, research, and leadership issues. She is very aware of the social and political importance of education in our society: "Obviously, I do not accept the premise that education is value-free but rather believe that it is a powerful instrument for either reinforcing or changing social inequities."[40] For Sutton, teaching, research, and leadership skills are means of critically examining mainstream cultural identity.

The centerpiece of Sutton's own cultural politics of difference is her creation and development of the Urban Network. The Urban Network is an intensive, non-profit program in urban design for young people. It is meant to motivate children to learn about the built urban environment (see Figure 5.4). Participating in a variety of activities, children discover underlying principles of the built environment, but, most important, the quest is to empower them to aid in the renewal of our inner cities: "The Urban Network has also provided the impetus for understanding how the physical environment of socioeconomically diverse communities affects children's ability to envision themselves as empowered agents of change."[41] Urban Network instructional guides and periodicals are produced as pedagogical resources, networking opportunities, and portfolios of environmental education projects by children across the country. Sutton lectures and presents workshops for teachers and youth development workers around the country on the material she develops through the Urban Network. She uses the mechanism of the Urban Network to broaden her scholarly base, bring the ideas of environmental change to researchers outside her area of expertise, and communicate with practitioners and the politically powerless contingent of children. Children are the largest group in our society in poverty, according to the latest census report. By exposing children, especially African American and other marginalized children, to the making and changing of our built environment, Sutton directly fosters environmental

Figure 5.4. Environmental design project by children involved in the Urban Network Program.

understanding, justice, and agency but also connects children in a critical way to their mainstream environmental context.

CONCLUSION

The powerful determinant of race in affecting every aspect of the built environment has a long history. The spatialization of race relations — a social act of structural racism that rests at the core of the dominant culture's practice of planning and building — needs greater theoretical analysis combined with activist practice to overcome uneven development. Because the United States is built upon the genocide of the American Indian race as well as the forced relocation and enslavement of the African race, separation and dominion are primary categories that constitute the built environment, and they continue today. Too much of this history is taken for granted by the architectural profession. My hope is that critical architects of color, especially African American architects, would align with the most progressive social movements in place today in order to extend forms of resistance even as we accommodate (perhaps unavoidably so) the mainstream.

In addition to Bond, Travis, and Sutton, other professionals and organizations who represent progressive political ideas of cultural difference in architectural practice and education need mentioning. These include Architects and Designers Opening the Border Edge of Los Angeles (ADOBE LA), a Latino-based group of architects, artists, and designers documenting the Latino physical presence in the L.A. urban landscape and mobilizing resources for community participation in artistic work;[42] the artists and critics associated with Cultural Explainers, who are working collaboratively in the Los Angeles communities of Koreatown, Pico-Union, and South Central to promote through their art and sculpture cross-cultural understanding and explanation;[43] the Power of Place corporation, which is a group of architects, planners, historians, and community leaders in Los Angeles working to commemorate sites indicative of the city's suppressed, multiethnic history (see chapter 4 in this volume);[44] Cynthia Hamilton's sustained theoretical and activist work on environmental racism and spatial apartheid in the American city;[45] the work of architect Mabel O. Wilson and geography professor Heidi J. Nast, who, through comparing an affluent subdivision with two low-income housing projects in Kentucky, are weaving into one analysis an architectural investigation of the spatial organization of social practices, the linguistic construction of "heteropatriarchal law," and a feminist critique of house designs;[46] the work of editors Darell W. Fields, Kevin L. Fuller, and Milton S. F. Curry in their recently founded *Appendx*, a journal intending to construct a new space of resistance in architectural discourse through a rigorous critique of the intersections of race, class, ethnicity, gender, and sexuality in architecture;[47] and my own experimentation with pedagogical tactics to place students in the contexts of other subcultures, in the hope that this will lead to self-transformation based upon direct, social experience.[48] All these groups and individuals, like Bond, Travis, and Sutton, enjoy a reasonable degree of success operating in mainstream institutions, but they have not been co-opted or critically silenced by them. Their professional identity is enlarged by their openness to and understanding of the mainstream, while at the same time challenging it. Bond's practice of culturally significant buildings, especially relating to the African American cultural experience, helps to define and promote a multicultural architecture as an integral part of our built environment. Travis's understanding of the importance of establishing inclusive visibility through his picture books, calendars, T-shirts, and the teaching of young adults raises the level of resources needed to thrive and the Black cultural capital to continue to progress as Black architects. Sutton's strong research in multicultural environmental leadership and children's environmental education also positions multicultural under-standing as an integral part of environmental justice. Accommodation and resistance are the common threads that run through African American architecture identity throughout the history of Black involvement in the built environment.

Notes

1. Booker T. Washington, *Up from Slavery* (New York: Bantam, 1963), p. 18.
2. Richard K. Dozier, "The Black Architectural Experience in America," in Jack Travis, ed., *African American Architects in Current Practice* (New York: Princeton Architectural Press, 1991), p. 8.
3. Ibid.
4. Ibid.
5. Carl Anthony, "The Big House and the Slave Quarters: Part II, African Contributions to the New World," *Landscape* 21, no. 1 (Autumn 1976): 13, 14.
6. Ibid., pp. 11–12.
7. Ibid., pp. 12, 13.
8. John Michael Vlach, "Afro-Americans," in Dell Upton, ed., *America's Architectural Roots: Ethnic Groups That Built America* (Washington, D. C.: Preservation Press, 1986), p. 45.
9. Carl Anthony, "The Big House and the Slave Quarters: Part I, Prelude to New World Architecture," *Landscape* 20, no. 3 (Spring 1976): 14.
10. Ibid.
11. Robert J. Kapach, "Building Liberty's Capital: Black Labor and the New Federal City," *American Visions,* February/March 1995.
12. Gwendolyn Wright, *Building the Dream: A Social History of Housing in America* (New York: Pantheon, 1981), p. 53.
13. Eugene D. Genovese, *Roll, Jordan, Roll: The World the Slaves Made* (New York: Pantheon Books, 1974), esp. pp. 587–99.
14. Ibid., p. 599.
15. Washington, *Up from Slavery,* p. 105.
16. See Karen E. Hudson, *Paul R. Williams, Architect: A Legacy of Style* (New York: Rizzoli, 1993); also Karen E. Hudson, *The Will and the Way: Paul R. Williams, Architect* (New York: Rizzoli, 1994).
17. Bradford C. Grant and Dennis Mann, *Directory, African American Architects* (Cincinnati: University of Cincinnati, 1991, addendum 1995), p. 6.
18. David W. Dunlap, "Black Architects Struggling for Equity," *New York Times,* December 4, 1994, sec. 9, p. 8.
19. Howard G. Robinson III, "Preserving the Historic Trust of Architectural Education in Howard University" (Inaugural Howard Hamilton Mackey Lecture, Howard University, Washington, D.C., February 10, 1992).
20. Cornel West, "The New Cultural Politics of Difference," in Russell Ferguson, Martha Gever, Trinh T. Minh-ha, and Cornel West, eds., *Out There: Marginalization and Contemporary Cultures* (New York: New Museum of Contemporary Art, 1990), p. 32.
21. Ibid., p. 31.
22. Bell hooks, *Yearning: Race, Gender, and Cultural Politics* (Boston, Mass.: South End Press, 1990), p. 110.
23. West, "The New Cultural Politics of Difference," p. 32.
24. Ibid., p. 33.
25. Ibid.
26. Ibid.
27. Ibid.

28. Ibid., p. 34.
29. Grant and Mann, *Directory, African American Architects.*
30. Bradford C. Grant, Cal Poly State University (unpublished survey, 1995). (Six additional African American presenters were also noted from HBCUs.)
31. Harvey Gantt, "Breaking the ICE: Building New Leadership," *AIArchitect* 1 (October 1994); Stephanie Stubbs, "Architects Break ICE," ibid.
32. See Robert Easter, "Letter to Deans and Chairs of Programs of Architecture and Design," working paper, National Organization of Minority Architects, Richmond, Va., August 19, 1994.
33. *NOMA News* 21, no. 1 (First Quarter 1991): 2.
34. See Thomas A. Dutton and Bradford C. Grant, "Campus Design and Critical Pedagogy," *Academe* 77, no. 4 (July/August 1991).
35. West, "The New Cultural Politics of Difference," p. 33.
36. Ibid.
37. J. Max Bond Jr., quoted in Travis, ed., *African American Architects,* p. 22.
38. J. Max Bond Jr. and Carl Anthony, "Max Bond and Carl Anthony on Afro-American Architecture," in W. Lawson, ed., *The Yardbird Reader* 4 (1976): 13.
39. Davis Brody Associates, "FAIA Application to the AIA," Davis, Brody and Associates Architects, New York, September 26, 1994.
40. Sharon Sutton, "Promotion Statement," September 10, 1993.
41. Ibid.
42. See Margaret Crawford, "Mi casa es su casa: ADOBE LA," *Assemblage* 24 (August 1994), and ADOBE LA, "Saber es poder," a project in Russell Ferguson, ed., *Urban Revisions: Current Projects for the Public Realm* (Los Angeles: Museum of Contemporary Art, 1994).
43. See "Two Los Angeles Community-Based Projects," in Ferguson, ed., *Urban Revisions.*
44. See Dolores Hayden, *The Power of Place* (Cambridge, Mass.: MIT Press, 1995).
45. See Cynthia Hamilton, "Coping with Industrial Exploitation," in Robert D. Bullard, ed., *Confronting Environmental Racism: Voices from the Grassroots* (Boston, Mass.: South End Press, 1993); Cynthia Hamilton, "Environmental Consequences of Urban Growth and Blight," in Richard Hofrichter, ed., *Toxic Struggles: The Theory and Practice of Environmental Justice* (Philadelphia: New Society, 1993); Cynthia Hamilton, "Apartheid in an American City: The Case of the Black Community in Los Angeles" (Los Angeles: Labor/Community Strategy Center, 1992–93).
46. Heidi J. Nast and Mabel O. Wilson, "Lawful Transgressions: This Is the House That Jackie Built," *Assemblage* 24 (August 1994).
47. See *Appendx* 1 (1993) and *Appendx* 2 (1994).
48. Bradford C. Grant, "Cultural Invisibility: The African American Experience in Architectural Education," in Thomas A. Dutton, ed., *Voices in Architectural Education: Cultural Politics and Pedagogy* (New York: Bergin and Garvey, 1991).

DECONSTRUCTION AND ARCHITECTURE

INTRODUCTION

Four long city blocks from my house on Capitol Hill, the wide diagonal of Pennsylvania Avenue marks a supremely important American site: "Main Street, U.S.A.," the tour guides call it, reminding visitors of famous inaugural, funeral, and protest marches from the Capitol to the White House. Along with well-established monumental buildings like the National Gallery of Art, the Justice Department, and the IRS, Pennsylvania Avenue has more recently acquired a good number of modernist and (stretching the term) postmodern structures, and it is busy acquiring more. A group called the Pennsylvania Avenue Development Corporation (PADC) has been working to lend the avenue the architectural density and significance it has long lacked, and the result is a kind of laboratory of new American architecture. These buildings, the PADC hopes, will replace the agoraphobic feel of present-day Pennsylvania Avenue with a rich urban intensity.

Among the recently completed commissions, a mixed-use project on a prominent corner exemplifies many of the problems inherent in the theory and practice of design. As you approach from my neighborhood, you notice first, on the corner of Pennsylvania and Sixth Street, the salvaged facade of an older building on the site; rising from this sandstone front is a new setback front of limestone. Continuing on the avenue, you encounter yet a third, also new, facade. The retail space behind this third facade stood empty for months; then an uninviting jewelry store rented some of it and quickly went out of business. You are vaguely aware that the building stretches back quite a bit down Sixth; and although you cannot see much from Pennsylvania, you may peer over to discover that the project is in fact composed of two almost matching buildings, separated from one another by a garden so deeply hidden and of such uncertain access that you cannot imagine crowds gathering there. The effect of the building on an observer receptive to new architecture, bored by modernist boxes like the Labor Department two blocks back, is disappointing. In theory, this "postmodern" blend of styles and materials represents precisely what you are looking for, yet here you confront an incoherence suggesting pragmatics rather than vision, cobbled-together compromise rather than eclecticism.

The work's principal architect, Jaquelin Robertson, defends this office, hotel, and retail space in *The Chicago Tapes,* transcripts of a 1986 symposium of influential architects who offered recent projects for discussion and critique by their peers.[1] Robertson begins apologetically, admitting his own unhappiness with a project that says more about the way "the constraints of the larger order of the city tend to dilute personal vision and control" than about architecture itself.[2] He distinguishes between "urban design" and "architecture," arguing that this project was essentially, given PADC specifications, an exercise in the former rather than the latter: "I think I succeeded in designing the building from an urban design point of view. I think architecturally it has a number of problems."[3] Robertson views urban design as a task of technical competence and civic responsibility, and architecture as the communication of a personal vision of the built environment. "Architects are urban designers first," he insists, and later asserts, "You can't build good streets by doing individual buildings that are good."[4]

While some architects in the audience (among them Cesar Pelli and Paul Rudolph) support Robertson's attempt to mediate between innovative vision and city fabric, a significant contingent doesn't buy it. "Well," remarks Bruce Graham, "I think the Bible reads, 'first there was architecture and then urban design.' It seems to me that there are many examples of buildings between buildings that are fantastic. They don't have to be banal. Certainly Gaudi's buildings in Barcelona are a very good example."[5] Urban design, says Mario Gandelsonas, an architect and theorist associated with the *Tel Quel* group in the seventies, "belongs to economics and business administration. The other thing is the idea of the city as a referent for architecture, a point where we can practice architecture."[6] By "practicing architecture," Gandelsonas means persisting in individual expression even while acknowledging civic as well as contextual constraints. (Of course, "contextual" may mean only an ironic nod in the direction of a building's surroundings.)

Yet while these dissenting responses to Robertson still accept his primary distinction between urban design and architecture, other participants at the Chicago meeting (Frank Gehry, Rem Koolhaas, and Peter Eisenman) go some distance toward repudiating contextualism and constraint altogether. Blurring the distinction between architecture and art, building and sculpture, Gehry shows the Chicago group his sketches for a restaurant in Japan that will be a seventy-five-foot fish: "It's made almost exactly like the Statue of Liberty, which has a central shaft and has spokes going out that catch the outside."[7] Gehry also proposes a fish skyscraper for New York, while Koolhaas designs a surrealistic, forties-style villa in the midst of nineteenth-century houses in the Paris suburb of Saint-Cloud. Finally, Eisenman announces that, in a world itself so surreal as to be in fact without context, architecture has no business seeking to establish or strengthen context; it ought rather to draw attention to the condition of drift and alienation at the heart of modern placelessness. His plans for an acontextual museum in Long Beach baffle the architects examining them; the sketches are so vague, themselves so lacking context in the language of architecture, that their observers cannot interpret them.

Tensions of this sort between artistic gesture and plan, individual commentary and committee compromise, and personal creative statement and corporate power pervade modern architectural practice and discourse. Indeed an important source of architecture's fascination as art and science lies in the dialectic between the coerciveness and density of the socioeconomic realm within which the architect moves and the seductive ethereality of the realm of architectural theory, drawing, and modeling. Yet what is new in architecture is not only a dramatic intensification of this conflict (to the point where more and more architects fall rather easily into the realms of architect-sculptor, corporate insider, pure theorist, weak contextualist, and so forth), but also the emergence within the architectural establishment of an effort to subvert the range of symbolic values long considered implicit in every act of building. That is, not only can one discern a trend toward various forms of acontextualism among contemporary architects; one can also discern a related, more radical effort toward creating a *deconstructive* architecture that would undo the very notion of the building as a solid physical emplacement carrying certain embedded cultural meanings. If acontextualism removes the building from relatedness with other buildings, deconstructive architecture removes the building from relatedness with itself.

Like deconstructive literary theory, deconstructive architecture is about differences *within*. Architects influenced by the poststructuralist theory of Jacques Derrida and Michel Foucault (whose assertion of the nonontological, nonfoundational nature of reality stresses the unstable, socially constructed status of all human phenomena) create *displaced* buildings with disseminated meanings, buildings that no longer express, say, shelter, domesticity, industrial productivity, beauty, truth, or social value, but instead do violence to the entire range of traditional values associated with architectural manifestations. If the coherent and culturally reassuring literary text is the object of critique for literary deconstructionists, the "finished" building communicating univocal meaning is the object of critique by architectural deconstructionists. Architects like Eisenman, Daniel Libeskind, Zaha Hadid, and Bernard Tschumi produce plans and buildings that communicate incoherence, fragility, drift, disorientation. Their work seems to argue that the catastrophes of our recent past (holocaust, nuclear attack, global warfare, totalitarian dictatorship), as well as the perceptually bewildering reality of our present life within multinational capitalist economies, belie the structural integrity of the values and meanings cherished by Western European culture. Architects, like other artists with this new form of awareness, must now confront us with the emergent unsettling truths of our time, so as to enable us to live in the world lucidly and without aggression. For it is, say deconstructivist thinkers, the aggressive and deluded defense of those false values that has brought civilization to the brink of destruction.

I want in this chapter to clarify deconstructive architecture by approaching the subject in three ways: I'll first discuss its intellectual antecedents in deconstructive theory and practice in the humanities and the ways in which deconstructive thought has entered architecture; I'll then focus briefly on the work and writing of some representative deconstructive architects; and, finally, I will attempt to describe what a socially critical architecture for our time might look like. My main contention throughout is that while deconstructive architecture is formally inventive, it is socially useless because it conveys a rejection of all traditional warrants for political action.

THE ORIGINS AND LIMITATIONS OF DECONSTRUCTIVE DISCOURSE

In the late seventies in America and Europe, literary theorists, and then intellectuals from other disciplines in the humanities and social sciences, became intrigued with the process of reading texts not as coherent narratives or arguments, but as intrinsically incoherent, inevitably failed, efforts at signification. Underlying this new interest in plural and contingent meaning was the great epistemological shift of the nineteenth century, in which the departure of common religious faith and shared cultural values left people intellectually and morally adrift. Nietzsche's description of this new human condition, in which, all conceptual and spiritual foundations having been shattered, modern individuals were confronted with the task of recognizing the absurdity of the universe and attempting to create a new world, constitutes one of the most important sources of deconstructive thought.

Deconstructive theorists like Jacques Derrida, relying not merely on Nietzsche's evocation of contingency but also on Sigmund Freud's portrayal of the human personality as intrinsically fragmented and strange to itself, traced a history of disintegrating human agency within which the sort of premeditation and intentionality that would allow for the creation of coherent philosophical theories and aesthetic masterworks, for instance, was now impossible. In this new understanding, the act of *interpreting* arguments and creations shifted from one of reconstructing a unified design, a controlled structure, to the playful business of discovering the elements in texts that undermined the texts' pretensions to univocality. Likewise, the *description* of the act of creation shifted from that of the imposition of a stable personal view upon the world to that of the fashioning of dislocated, disembodied artifacts.

Deconstructive literary critics, who long dominated deconstructive thought in the United States, exhibited a distinct preference for those texts, like *Tristram Shandy* and *Finnegans Wake,* that seemed already to acknowledge the impossibility of integrated expression in their ludic and disseminated form; but they also deconstructed traditional novels like *Middlemarch* and *Jane Eyre,* reading in them a submerged tension between the writer's desire to found meaning and value and language's tendency to float free of the writer's authority. In many cases, decon-

struction's *own* theory of value underlay these subversions of traditional and ideologically coercive meaning and value in the text; deconstructionists implicitly or
explicitly argued that one needed to surrender one's will to power over one's self,
other people, and texts, so as to deal less invasively with the world. The recognition that human identity is always unstable and that meaning is always plural should
at the very least, they argued, produce tolerance for differences in ideology and
style of life. At the very *most,* these deconstructive attitudes could take one beyond the tame liberalism implicit in this tolerance toward so powerful a subversion of established categories of understanding, so sharpened a perception and
appreciation of "otherness," as to enable revolutionary social change. In destabilizing our perceptions of institutional reality, deconstructive analysis and aesthetics have ultimately sought (without being very precise about *how*) to destabilize
the institutions of capitalism. Within this deconstructive movement, deconstructive *architecture* has constituted an attempt to critique the ideology of foundationalism in the most "founded" creative sphere—that of building.

The convergence between deconstructive critical theory and architecture—
part of a larger expansion of theory into the fields of literature, art history, anthropology, psychoanalysis, history, and so forth—is embodied in the collaboration
on a variety of written and built projects between Eisenman, the most intellectually ambitious contemporary American architect, and Jacques Derrida. In a recent
interview, Derrida recounted how he and Eisenman were brought together by
Bernard Tschumi, the architect of the Parisian Parc de la Villette follies (which
I'll discuss later): "Once I had a phone call from Bernard Tschumi, who[m] I didn't
know at the time, except by reputation. Tschumi told me: 'Some architects are interested in your work and would you be interested in working with some of them,
or one of them, on a project in La Villette?"[8] The architect whom Tschumi had in
mind, Eisenman, had long been fascinated by Derrida's writing, discovering in
deconstruction a rationale for his own "dislocating" architecture.

Derrida confesses in his interview to an initial skepticism about the possibility
of any connection between the stolidly foundational reality of architecture and the
free play of deconstruction:

> Well, I don't know... I must say, when I first met, I won't say
> "Deconstructive architecture," but the Deconstructive discourse on
> architecture, I was rather puzzled and suspicious. I thought at first that this
> was an analogy, a displaced discourse, and something more analogical than
> rigorous. And then... I realised that on the contrary, the most efficient way
> of putting Deconstruction to work was by going through art and
> architecture. As you know, Deconstruction is not simply a matter of
> discourse or a matter of displacing the semantic content of the discourse,
> its conceptual structure or whatever. Deconstruction goes *through* certain

social and political structures, meeting with resistance and displacing institutions as it does so. I think that in these forms of art, and in any architecture, to deconstruct traditional sanctions — theoretical, philosophical, cultural — effectively, you have to displace . . . I would say "solid" structures, not only in the sense of material structures, but "solid" in the sense of cultural, pedagogical, political, economic structures.[9]

Derrida thus comes to understand architecture as a field within which deconstructive undoing can be enacted in the material world, in which deconstruction can be efficiently "put to work." Even buildings, seemingly the most declamatory and determined of objects, can be made to oscillate with the manifold significations of the deconstructed text; deconstruction can "displac[e] institutions."

But there are serious problems with the claim that deconstruction can truly undermine institutional foundations; indeed, Derrida would have done well to hold to his initial skepticism about deconstructive architecture being more than an analogy or suggestive set of metaphors, for an examination of deconstructive architectural analysis, and of deconstructive buildings, reveals it to be far more about form and attitude than action. There is, I will argue, nothing authentically politically progressive, or even social, about deconstruction; on the contrary, its politics, to the extent that these can be discerned, are usually far removed from reality, despite the fact of deconstruction's sometimes heated political rhetoric. The ultimate effect of deconstruction is to reinforce our culture's already strong tendency toward political quietism.

Before I consider some deconstructive buildings, let me make clearer the philosophical and political claims of architectural deconstruction, and the serious weaknesses of those claims, by looking at the arguments of two representative writers in this vein: Jennifer Bloomer and Mark Wigley. In *Architecture and the Text: The (S)crypts of Joyce and Piranesi,* Bloomer continues in the now well-established tradition of feminist deconstructive writing, in which a "postmodern" mélange of personal and theoretical remarks in a mode of intellectual obscurity and punning whimsy seeks to demolish the masculine, Enlightenment tradition of rationality, coherence, clarity, and seriousness. Architecture, Bloomer argues, is a central element of this modernist, technocratic tradition: "Western architecture, is, by its nature, a phallocentric discourse, containing, ordering, and representing through firmness, commodity, and beauty: consisting of orders, entablature, and architrave; base, shaft, and capital; nave, choir, and apse; father, son, and spirit, world without end amen."[10] Deconstructive discourse and architecture reveal the suppressed incoherence, instability, disorder, infirmity, and dis-ease within this monumentality; it is a feminine operation of subversion, uncovering an inherent, fecund, messy vitality. It is that unsettling deconstructive vitality, that unrepressed nonphallic energy, which will liberate architecture from its alliance with imperialist, patriarchal power structures. Bloomer's own mocking prose, with its sexual boldness and wit ("base, shaft...") and its rambling, illogical progressions (from architectural form in general to elements of church interiors to the Christian Trinity to a satirically rendered quotation from Scripture), seeks to trivialize and disintegrate all claims to cultural legitimacy any element of the Western tradition might make.

Other features of Bloomer's approach, again familiar from established feminist deconstructive method, involve repeated self-flattering claims to be doing something risky (hers is a "revolutionary architectural criticism, a 'criticism from within' that goes deeply into the within, into the conventions of architecture's collusion with mechanisms of power"), irrelevant autobiographical remarks ("Laura Barrett [Bloomer's daughter] sees Baby-in-the-Mirror and wiggles and laughs and reaches out for her, calling, 'baba,baba!'"), and anguish over the fact that despite being marginal in the sense of being a woman in a phallocentric world, Bloomer is not as marginal as people who are more marginal than she ("How can I, a white, bourgeois, academic, woman, sitting smack as a woman can in the center, presume to identify with those in the margins?").[11] Much of this is either uninteresting or untrue; I will concentrate on the untrue.

Bloomer's approach to architecture is not revolutionary; it adopts as its theoretical justification a philosophy (Derridean poststructuralism) so paralyzed by internal contradiction as to enter the political arena dead on arrival. Derrida is notorious for never having, in his long career, been able to decide whether deconstruction *does* anything to the world, whether it makes any difference. As the earlier quotation from him suggests, he has been known to get excited about things like architecture and decide that no, deconstruction is *not,* despite all that he has previously said, only a matter of discourse; but then, just as quickly, he will retreat to the well-known rhetoric of conceptual evasiveness and jaunty nihilism that has marked deconstruction from its inception. Like Derrida, Bloomer mistakes linguistic assertion for worldly activity; she is one of many deconstructive writers who, as Jürgen Habermas complains, have "textualized" socially critical discourse, reducing oppositional practice to verbal play.

A similar conflation of political language with politics disables Mark Wigley's book, *The Architecture of Deconstruction.* Wigley initially insists that deconstruction is impossible to define; it is that which undermines all definition, an "ongoing structural event, a continuous displacement of structure that cannot be evaluated in traditional terms because it is the very frustration of those terms."[12] "It is important to remember," Wigley writes, "that deconstruction is not a method, a critique, an analysis, or a source of legitimation. It is not strategic. It has no prescribed aim, which is not to say that it is aimless. It moves very precisely, but not to some defined end."[13] Because of its enigmatic and exceptional nature, deconstruction can never be grasped as a concept; more important, however, one cannot attack Wigley's argument, since in order to attack it one would have to use the language of definition that deconstruction has neutralized, the language to which deconstruction has declared itself impervious.

Having ruled any critique of his position an impossibility, Wigley next suggests that in fact deconstruction is itself a critique, except that its critique takes place only metaphorically. Or does it? Shortly thereafter, Wigley claims that deconstruction sometimes does have actual political effects. Yet he cannot say precisely how these effects occur, or what they are. Nonetheless, he reiterates forcefully, it is absolutely true that architecture itself is politics and deconstruction is political. But what *is* "politics"? Wigley nevers says. He says only that deconstructive architectural analysis is political because "institutions are understood as buildings that can be displaced only by rethinking architecture.... The questioning of the very idea of building is aligned with a questioning of institutional authority. It is the rethinking of architecture that defines the politics of deconstruction."[14] (Note how Wigley has himself fallen into the language of "definition" here.)

But what is the quality of this rethinking? When Wigley cites Derrida's deconstruction of the French university system as exemplary for deconstructions of American academic institutions, he seems indifferent to the fact that the sprawling, open American university bears virtually no resemblance to the concentrated, hierarchical French system. He notes that the university is "a system that describes itself as a kind of building and organizes itself according to a rhetoric of ground, footing, foundation, structure, space, architectonics, and so on."[15] He then quotes Derrida, who argues that "the properly architectonic or architectural figure of the institution, as a founded and structured edifice, constructed like an artifact" means that "one cannot think of the university institution, as an institution of reason ... without this role of architectonics. There is no university architecture without architectonics."[16]

Yet Derrida's assertion ignores phenomena like the Polish "Flying University," established during World War II as an underground educational institution that held regularly scheduled classes in private homes during those years, and was then reactivated during martial law in the eighties. This university, dispenser of reason, defender of Enlightenment values against political regimes of absurdity and cruelty, was a key element in the organization and morale of the Solidarity free-trade movement. It made material contributions to the overthrow of tyranny; it helped passive and cynical people believe they could effect revolutionary political change. It had no architecture, no material existence beyond people gathering in rooms with books and papers, and yet it was a true university.

Derrida and Wigley are only able to envision the university as one sort of thing — a hierarchical, rigid sort of thing ripe for liberation by deconstruction. They are unable to imagine the possibility of a university without any foundation beyond a naive and pragmatic belief in progress, for this sort of phenomenon is outside of the deconstructive world, with its need to posit universal repression in order always to have something to deconstruct, and with its postmodern conviction of the total illegitimacy of all Enlightenment metanarratives. The deconstructive stance, according to which all politics is polluted by metaphysics (one obscure result of which is that deconstructive critics cannot condemn Paul de Man for his fascism and anti-Semitism), glamorizes political inaction as intellectually sophisticated.

Wigley's general argument, then, looks something like this: deconstruction teaches that we can never disentangle metaphor from reality in our writing. Everything is text, so the world doesn't exist. Or, yes, the world does exist, but before we can do anything about what's wrong with it we have to produce a lot of discourse disentangling the relationship between discursive metaphor and institutional self-justification. Thus does deconstruction begin and end in the pages of a book—and, in the cases of Wigley and Bloomer, not even politically critical books that would yield insights clarifying the nature of social injustice. For deconstruction is disarmed politically from the start by its having made illegitimate *all* concepts inherited from the Enlightenment, among them concepts of tyranny and democracy, freedom and enslavement. In a recent review of Bloomer's book, Vincent Pecora notes that deconstruction has become "a rhetorical prison blind to its own conventions and numbing in its routines."[17] I would go one step further: deconstruction ignores those places in the world where real political change has occurred and continues to occur; it discounts, negates, and is blind to the reality that while people like Wigley elaborate their "increasingly urgent" rereadings of Heidegger, other people are learning from the liberal tradition of dissent how to change the world. Unfortunately, the numbing work of deconstruction takes place in already profoundly benumbed and depressed advanced Western nations whose own traditions of liberal Enlightenment, an inspiration to millions of suppressed people, ironically remain obscured.

DECONSTRUCTIVE ARCHITECTURE

What do buildings informed by deconstructive thought actually look like? They are typically fragile, unstable, quirky artifacts—they tilt, their walls have holes in them from which bricks tumble onto the ground, their edges don't meet cleanly. They are either excessively finished, with too much ornament and too many architectural features, or obviously uncompleted. They stand precariously, in pieces, with jarringly dissimilar architectural styles flush against one another, and with various elements—columns, walls, towers—simply stuck here and there, pointless and without function. The feel of a deconstructive building may be playful, celebratory, even infantile; on the other hand, the building may evoke melancholy and anxiety in its communication of vague unfulfillment or verge-of-collapse. But its true deconstructive nature will derive from its expression of a cold, hard acceptance of the failure of intellectual and moral supports in the contemporary world.

"While a house today must still shelter," writes Peter Eisenman, "it does not need to symbolise or romanticise its sheltering function; to the contrary such symbols are today meaningless and merely nostalgic."[18] If this sentence were written in the 1920s, by a committed modernist, we would expect the writer to go on to urge upon us the adoption of certain meaningful and fully "present" symbolizations of our own time—new sources and embodiments of vitality, renewal, and cultural community that we might be able to see and experience through experimental art. But Eisenman's critique is a Beckettian end game: "I don't believe that words can contain the same mythology and meaning that they did in the classical period because in the present, which I see as having no future, all we can do is make empty words."[19]

In the absence of any revolutionary or restorative vision, Eisenman's work subsists within a sort of concretized irony, embodying again and again the fact of cultural dissolution. His and other deconstructive architecture thus tends to be performative or rhetorical, rather than ameliorative or transformative; its distrust of any progressive "metanarrative" in which human life on earth may undergo significant improvement (the term "metanarrative" was made famous by Jean-François Lyotard, a major postmodernist theorist, and a contributor to La Villette) means that it will always back off from assertion and from feeling.

Deconstructive architecture regards itself as uncompromising in its commitment to lucidity about the nihilistic nature of our lives; it positions itself as a kind of purgative, freeing us from every trace of nostalgia, regret, and passion. Its ideal user is the contemporary type whom Charles Jencks characterizes as "the Empty Man, the nomadic 'man without qualities' who can weave his way through all hierarchies showing them to be temporary and nonsensical."[20] Although it may sometimes look like the purely playful postmodernism of Frank Gehry and Michael Graves, deconstructive work, as I've suggested before, is informed by a quite serious rejection of metaphysical certainties, and its practitioners tend to see people like Gehry as expressing either nostalgia for a lost unity or a kind of dissolute pleasure at the meaninglessness of life. As Eisenman says in an interview with Jencks, "Deconstruction has nothing to do with style; it has to do with ideology. What is wrong with Post-Modernism [of the Gehry sort] is that it is anti-ideology."[21]

Although Eisenman goes on to tell Jencks, "Deconstruction is not ultimately visible. It is about building unbuildable ideas. I do not think any multi-national corporation is going to build deconstruction," deconstructive buildings have in fact been built as well as sketched.[22] One of Eisenman's own projects, the Guardiola House in Spain, attempts above all to make architecture *move,* to unsettle the seemingly inescapable stability of the constructed artifact.[23] A stack of tangential L-shapes that interweave in a suggestively fluid manner constitutes the structure of the house. Eisenman likes the L-shape not only because in certain arrangements it suggests a rotating movement but also because it deconstructs the binary opposition between "frame" and "figure." That is, we are accustomed to thinking hierarchically about a house and its structural supports, just as we would think about a picture and its frame, with the frame secondary in significance to the image itself. But the L-shape here is both structural support and house itself.

The Guardiola house, Eisenman writes, "has the qualities of a controlled accident, of a line once put down which cannot be erased, but in whose linearity is the density of unpredictable reverberations."[24] In other words, each "line" of this house is thick with signifying possibilities; although each line is "permanent," in the sense that it "cannot be erased," it is also fluctuating because it is part of a structure that does all that it can to deconstruct "structure." All lines, whether architectural or literary or painterly (as in the work of Cy Twombley), designate not singular but proliferating meaning, "unpredictable reverberations." This "textured," multiply signifying line is also apparent in Eisenman's project for the Long Beach museum, in which "the forms do not come from any given natural vocabulary of architecture, but rather from what can be called a superposition of present, past, and future forms."[25]

Eisenman further discusses this notion of superposition in an essay entitled "Architecture as a Second Language." Here he analyzes the David Lynch film *Blue Velvet* as an exemplary "text of between," in which a "complex and intentional tissue of superpositions of future and past create a temporal dislocation."[26] Lynch's film, set in the fifties, uses a version of the title song recorded in 1963, gives its hero a 1968 Oldsmobile to drive, places an earring in a male character's ear, and shows the locals drinking Heineken in a southern bar (an impossibility, according to Eisenman, before the late fifties). Yet the general "feel" of the film *is* that of the fifties; the audience registers these dislocating details in a subliminal way, and this experience of being "between" the natural and the conventional, the past and the present, accounts for the pleasurably uncanny quality of Lynch's work (also displayed in the television series *Twin Peaks*). Similarly, writes Eisenman, dislocating buildings "refuse any single authoritative reading. They do not appeal to the logic of grammar or the reason of truth. Their 'truth' is constantly in flux. [Dislocating architecture] does not symbolize use, shelter or structure. Its aesthetic and history are other. Its dislocation takes place between the conventional and natural. Thus, what is being violated is the maintenance of the system as a whole."[27]

Perhaps the best-known deconstructive architectural work is neither a private home nor an office building, but Tschumi's Parisian Parc de la Villette project (1982), a gallery of architectural follies interspersed with the cinematic promenade, in a large, multipurpose park on the Seine. Together these gridded fire-engine red constructions compose what Tschumi calls "the largest discontinuous building in the world, and the first *built* work specifically exploring [the] concepts of superimposition and dissociation."[28] It's true enough that by isolating in each folly certain architectural elements, La Villette reviews and neutralizes the history of built forms, but it's debatable whether what Tschumi has done at La Villette itself amounts to building rather than sculpture. One of his constructions is a café, but the café differs physically from most of the other follies in having greater size, obvious function, and interiority. Most of Tschumi's objects, as one walks around La Villette, look and feel like elaborate playground climbing equipment.

In part this effect is due to context—La Villette is, after all, a park, with (when I visited) young boys playing soccer around the follies and children scrambling about on all sorts of slides and swings. The brilliant colors and the Lego-like fun of the follies (heightened by contrast with the distinctly un-Parisian grimness of the part of Paris that adjoins La Villette) make them not, as Tschumi would have it, "mechanical operations that systematically produce dissociation" in the viewer, but rather objects of whimsy that can be passively enough enjoyed.[29] Indeed, although Tschumi announces, "La Villette is anti-contextual. It has no relation to its surroundings," one does feel there the oppositional tension between the rigidly didactic and socially ambitious modernism of the local midrise office buildings and apartments on the periphery of the park and the playful, asocial postmodernism of not only Tschumi's work, but also the work of others scattered at La Villette.

La Villette, Tschumi has written, "aims at an architecture that *means nothing, an architecture of the signifier rather than signified*—one that is pure trace or play of language."[30] The effect of that trace, Tschumi hopes, will be to reveal the "repressed" texts of architecture—the disunity and precariousness of life that traditional buildings deny—in order to unsettle nothing less than the history of architecture itself and our perceptions of built reality. Yet can the dissolution of meaning and the decentering of structure in fact help shape a socially radicalizing consciousness, as Derrida, Eisenman, Wigley, and Tschumi argue? What happens to historical self-consciousness in a context of "errant" signification, free association, drift, the negligent gesture? What happens to social analysis, to political resistance, in a context of pure specularity? As an interviewer of Lyotard once asked him, "How is it possible to keep 'in control' the strategy of an indeterminate system, a system which is supposed to develop organically around dissent and the creative potential of difference?"[31] Since postmodern subjectivity is "weak," she writes (adopting the terminology of Gianni Vattimo), since it "does not assume any *a priori* world vision, aesthetic project, or predeterminate moral stance," how are we to proceed to understand each other, to build any particular sort of world?

In his response to these questions, Lyotard insists that we respond to the dissolution of metanarratives by cultivating a "thought of non-control," an "inattentive meditation" that "lets itself emerge from things, from ideas, from associations, from those images which can look odd, dangerously disquieting, but which are the true resources of thought. I see our task in being 'present,' which means pointing out that there is something 'other' and someone 'other.'"[32]

Yet it seems to me that this condition of openness to drifting signification, while a necessary component of a postmodern sensibility, is not in itself an adequate response to the world. Indeed, the problem I and others have with the theoretical stance of Eisenman, Derrida, Lyotard, and Tschumi in relation to architecture is that, while it is easy to say how it is defamiliarizing (it isolates distorted objects, for instance, in order to allow creator and audience to define the contemporary consciousness), it is hard to say how it is *critical.* The condition of "wandering restlessly in the labyrinth of multivalent images," as Manfredo Tafuri, a Marxist architect and theorist, describes it, may yield some intriguing, even illuminating, "intensities," but the effects are too transient, inchoate, and private for much analytical use.[33] It is not that these effects, as critics like Fredric Jameson and Terry Eagleton worry, necessarily induce a kind of passive madness; you can enjoy postmodern flux and dislocation without losing the ability to count your fingers and toes. Rather, it is that the experience of deconstructive postmodernism in architecture, the visual arts, and literature makes you aware only of the instability of institutions and their objectifications; it has nothing to do with which cultural formations we might want to salvage or which particular sorts of institutions we might prefer over others.

The salvage operation I have in mind is neither the retention of unremarkable facades in a sentimental gesture toward some past, nor the attempt to regain a cultural state of grace by worshipping at the relics of Athenian democracy; it is simply the effort to isolate certain beliefs that most of us continue to want to hold onto, bringing whatever mix of playfulness and seriousness we might now want to bring to the expression of those beliefs. The editors of *Architecture, Criticism, Ideology* and *ArchitectureReproduction* attack the "value-free play and unbridled celebration of meaning's dissolution" of some deconstructive architecture because they recognize that, without some form of foundationalism (even an uncertain and ironical foundationalism), people have no location from which to criticize the conditions of their lives.[34] What we need, writes Sharon Willis in "Spectacular Topographies: *Amerique*'s Post Modern Spaces," is "to theorize and inhabit a mobile, shifting analytical perspective—a series of positions that always temporarily fix or install a relation and a reference, out of which analysis emerges."[35]

The contributors to *Architecture, Criticism, Ideology* and *ArchitectureReproduction* direct one important polemic, for instance, against "conservative institutional interests" that use the latest architecture as "legitimation of existing power structures." Diane Ghirardo, in a 1984 essay titled "Past or Post Modern in Architectural Fashion," mounts a similar attack against the purely stylistic, nostalgic postmodernism of someone like Robert Stern, who caters to the aristocratic desires of nouveau riche clients by giving them houses that look like eighteenth-century British estates.[36] Left theorists regard this superficial, commercial eclecticism of historical styles as an effort to "evaporate history," Willis writes in her essay on French postmodernist Jean Baudrillard. The "utopia of nonreferentiality," she remarks, "looks suspiciously like a dream of escaping history altogether by refusing to acknowledge its specific effects."[37] In this regard, both the intellectually rigorous deconstruction of Eisenman and the cynical revivalism of Stern constitute forms of the evasion of historical specificity. If they are not so blatantly evasive as the Disneylands Gehry and Graves create, they are nonetheless evasive, since they miss the actual quotidian experience of being in a dislocating world, or they deliberately remove a building's users from that scene of dislocation, or they merely mark dislocation, often in an inaccessible, unintelligible way.

This is not to say that formally deconstructed architecture cannot ever be critical. Among completed deconstructive commissions, I find the Hysolar Institute building (1987) on the campus of the University of Stuttgart, a project of Behnisch and Partners, one of the most effective (see Figure 6.1).[38] This small building houses laboratories for the study of solar energy. The structure's dramatic fragmentation into seemingly chaotic bits of construction instantly marks it as a deconstructed artifact; its tilted walls, projecting beams, and randomly placed windows, portholes, and panels make it appear a fragile survivor of some natural calamity, or perhaps some gradual process of desuetude, like the sagging, splintering old barns one speeds by on rural highways. Unlike the muted tones of the weathered barns, however, the building's pleasing colors, combining various shades of blue with a jolt of red provided by a long horizontal beam, give its surface a shiny newness. Solar panels leaning skyward atop miniature scaffolding and steel tubing snaking around a corner of the structure suggest a touch of high-tech purity amid the general mess.

And yet, if it is undeniably a mess, a ragtag stitching together of architectural odds and ends, the Hysolar Institute building has a couple of things going for it. First of all, it is emotionally and intellectually diverting in the way new and complex objects tend to be: one enjoys the initial shock one feels looking at it, as well as the slow analysis of its parts. A funny building—nonaggressive, with a sweet, shabby integrity—it has an all-too-human domesticity that deconstructs the cold, pompous, computeroid architectural language typical of technological buildings. Indeed, here one begins to entertain a possible reading of the building. Solar power represents the antithesis of sleek, scary, unrepresentable nuclear power; it presents itself as the homey, natural, simple option to that arcane, unnatural, complex alternative. While anybody can hoist a few solar panels, it is difficult to imagine nuclear power plants for the home. Thus, the do-it-yourself feel of the Hysolar building seems appropriate to a technology at once new and familiar.

The Hysolar building's other advantage is its interior, a surprisingly clean and functional space given the tumbledown exterior (see Figure 6.2). In a tiny version of I. M. Pei's East Wing of the National Gallery of Art, triangular skylights account for much of the roof and, with the addition of the many windows, produce a brilliantly sunny interior space. To be sure, a certain incoherence of walkways and

Figure 6.1. Exterior, Hysolar Institute, University of Stuttgart, Germany, Behnisch and Partners. (Photo by Christian Kandzia. Used by permission.)

panels marks the central public area of the building, but one feels confident that behind the doors that surround this space one will discover conventional laboratories. Altogether, the building seems both a plausible place to pursue research and a canny assault upon traditional objectifications of technology. The monumental eternality high-tech buildings want to give themselves and the foundational solidity most buildings want to give themselves undergo deconstruction in the careening, unsteady Hysolar Institute; the little sunhouse undoes what Jeffrey Kipnis describes in *Restructuring Architectural Theory* as "the futile pursuit of permanence—in materiality, in aesthetics, in history, in the relation of building to the dream of a permanent and entirely self-aware 'man.'"[39] But the building departs from deconstructive ideology in its sponsorship of *some* cherished cultural values, chief among them a faith in some forms of progress. The Hysolar building says,

Figure 6.2. Interior, Hysolar Institute, University of Stuttgart, Germany, Behnisch and Partners. (Photo by Christian Kandzia. Used by permission.)

most simply, what proponents of solar energy say: we should change our ways. And the building participates in the larger culture of progressive postmodernity by articulating localism, the return to the pragmatic, the limited, the ordinary, in the failure of modernism's grand designs. What I like about this building, in short, is its ability to be both deconstructive and reconstructive. It does not content itself with dislocating traditional architecture in an act of playful negativity; it suggests something beyond the negligent gesture of a Barthesian aesthetic.

HOW CAN ARCHITECTURE BE CRITICAL?

Deconstruction's decline from its peak in the mid-eighties to its enfeeblement today can be accounted for in both large cultural and small personal terms. No movement, first of all, has much of a life span among advanced consumer capitalists, who demand constant changes in intellectual as in any other fashion. As deconstructive technique became increasingly popular, uninspired as well as inspired practitioners took it up, with mediocre results. Increasing self-contradiction within the movement, coupled with a refusal to develop an intelligible core argument, meant that deconstruction became more a narrow technique than a destabilizing view of the world. Thus, while poststructuralist philosophy (or antiphilosophy) remains strong today, especially in the provocative work of Richard Rorty, the deconstructive method of undoing a text, even if done well, has become, as Pecora suggested, predictable, and readers have turned away from it in boredom.

At the same time, efforts to integrate deconstructive insights into resonating social critique failed because, as Habermas has argued, the end of epistemological legitimation means the end of consensus. The corps of deconstruction-inspired scholars has been unable to agree upon even the most basic claims about human dignity and freedom and has therefore fragmented into various shifting "identity politics" camps, which have been known to trade among one another charges of sexism, homophobia, racism, and elitism. In a recent issue of the *Village Voice,* the author of an article titled "Why They Won: The Left Lost Touch" writes in the wake of the devastating 1994 congressional elections that the "left... is finished" because it "paid too much attention to its tiny narcissisms and too little attention to the needs of most Americans."[40] The one-upmanship deconstructive intellectuals display among themselves is a small version of a larger problem among left thinkers in America today. Ordinary Americans, the *Voice* writer notes, are "more complicated human beings than the reactionary, racist, sexist, and homophobic buffoons that the left too often paints them in caricature to be. [Those on the left employ] a system of political ranking by which all who [do] not subscribe to the newest and trendiest and most subversive... policy positions... [are] immediately written off as enemies of 'progressivism.'"[41] The writer concludes that the Left will remain a loser until it realizes that "every new and superficially radical idea is not good, [and] second, that every old — dare I say it, traditional, idea is not bad, and, last, that some combination of the two can constitute a real progressive vision."[42]

Deconstruction's real deathblow arguably came, however, from precisely the human personality upon whose dissolution it has insisted. Paul de Man's personal history of fascism, anti-Semitism, and bigamy, coupled with his followers' refusal or inability to condemn these things, damaged deconstruction more than anything de Man ever wrote about the end of Romanticism. (In *The Condition of Postmodernity,* David Harvey notes that J. Hillis Miller's defense of de Man is based exclusively on concepts drawn from the Enlightenment tradition, whose tenets Hillis Miller has aggressively deconstructed in other writers.)[43] As for Derrida, his recent petulant defense of his intellectual property rights is so at odds with his earlier abuse of people like John Searle for copyrighting their articles that he begins to look both hypocritical and humorless.

A final human problem within deconstruction has had to do with what might be called the fate of performativity within an intellectual movement that implodes all claims to expressive substance. Radical skepticism about the legitimacy and stability of any intellectual position and about the existence of anything approaching a coherent human personality has made many deconstructive intellectuals obscure on the page and vapidly theatrical on the podium. "Obsessed with 'difference' and 'demystification,' deconstruction has never managed to halt its swirling patterns of negation," writes William E. Cain, a literary critic; "it is a formidable weapon for undermining other methods, positions and beliefs, yet seems unable to furnish positive terms of its own. It is in the very nature of deconstruction to turn upon and undercut its moments of apparent stability, and thus it cannot substantiate or solidify the reasons for political choice or even justify an act of choice in the first place."[44] David Harvey goes further: "In challenging all consensual standards of truth and justice, of ethics, and meaning, and in pursuing the dissolution of all narratives and meta-theories into a diffuse universe of language games, deconstructionism ended up, in spite of the best intentions of its more radical practitioners, by reducing knowledge and meaning to a rubble of signifiers. It thereby produced a condition of nihilism that prepared the ground for the re-emergence of a charismatic politics."[45]

While Harvey has in mind the charismatic politics of Reaganism, it is equally intriguing to consider the emergence within institutionalized deconstruction itself of charismatic intellectuals who perform rather than argue, dramatize rather than articulate. Indeed the most visible deconstructionists today are those who have acted out, as it were, the deconstructive attitude of proliferating identities and playful significations, and whose public behavior tends to be precisely the sort of thing that outrages the ordinary Americans whom the *Village Voice* writer correctly notes have become completely alienated from the academic culture of the Left—Gayatri Spivak (who recently signed a petition defending the Shining Path Brigade), Jane Gallop (whose whorish dress at academic conferences intends to deconstruct gender roles), Eve Sedgwick (whose contribution to a recent issue of *Assemblage* was a reminiscence about how much she masturbated as a young girl in her parents' house), and Judith Butler (who is wont to dance on conference tables).[46] In architecture, Eisenman plays something like this role, verbally abusing his colleagues, discussing his psychological problems, and boasting of his indifference to intellectual clarity and moral accountability.

Yet rather than liberating, these performances tend to feel coercive; they remind one that intense forms of individualism, especially individualism unfounded upon comprehensibility, have a tendency to shade into authoritarianism. One can understand how there is an obvious link between this behavior and the deconstructive ethos I discussed earlier, according to which one recognizes one's own disseminated identity; one can grant, that is, that this behavior aims to provoke in others a recognition of disseminated personal and institutional identity. In practice, however, these performances can seem manifestations of subcultures rather than expressions of constitutive communities. Charismatic performativity within deconstruction has both moved the focus of audiences from the content of deconstructive argument to the personality of particular deconstructionists, and sustained privatized subcultures rather than public communities.

Deconstruction, then, has a limited, provocative role to play in progressive architectural building and theory. By assuming a formal and philosophical extremity, it allows others to clarify certain flexible boundaries of meaning and beauty and value; it helps others to understand the grounds for cultural articulation. Christopher Norris has written that deconstructive work seeks to achieve much more than this, that it wants to be "a dislocating force, an energy of style."[47] But given its unswerving attack upon passional Romantic or transformative modernist values and its unwillingness to allow itself the emotionality that comes of commitment to a point of view or set of moral beliefs, *energy* is precisely what deconstruction lacks.

How, then, can one talk about a truly critical architecture? First, no form of cultural expression can be critical if it is merely negative. In a recent essay titled "The Joyless Polity: Contributions of Democratic Processes to Ill-Being," Robert E. Lane, a political scientist, examines links between life in liberal democracies and high rates of depression.[48] At one point in his essay, Lane distinguishes between "criticality" as an attitude and "negativity." The critical disposition observes the troubled world lucidly, but grants the existence of some encouraging events amid the disasters and therefore believes that the world can in various ways be improved. The attitude of negativity, writes Lane, amounts to "a pervasive tendency to respond toward the world in terms of critical, deprecatory, and even hostile opinions."[49]

Peter Eisenman's deconstructive architecture cannot be critical because it is negative in precisely this sense. Let me be more precise about its negative character by considering Eisenman's account of a project he once headed. In 1982, Eisenman discussed a plan for social housing for Berlin with colleagues at a conference at the University of Virginia.[50] The site was along the Berlin Wall, at Checkpoint Charlie, and Eisenman reported having found "abhorrent" the thought of putting a housing project by the wall: "I would never want to raise a child there."[51] Yet the German government insisted that this remain the nature of the project, and Eisenman complied, fashioning a design that, Eisenman proudly announced, refused to "erase" the disastrous history of Berlin, since this would be a dishonest gesture. Berlin exemplifies the obvious truth that "we cannot be optimistic about the future; we live in a futureless present in which buildings have lost their traditional meaning. The meaning of this building stems from its own internal process. . . . Let others [have] nostalgia for the past, hope for the future. All I am saying is that if it is possible to make words empty of meaning, I'd like to try."[52]

The dismantling of the Berlin Wall in 1989, across from what might have been a critically deconstructive project, must have stunned Eisenman, on whom the existence of millions of Poles, Czechs, Hungarians, Germans, and Russians whose belief in a better future caused the wall to come down still seems not to have registered. These people, by and large, were not paralyzed either by Eisenman's nihilism or by reactionary nostalgia, although of course they were nostalgic and in part rightly so, since almost anything must have looked better than the particularly grotesque tyranny under which they lived. They simply had a set of convictions about reality that enabled them to believe that difficult and risky subversive activity was worthwhile.

Despite his relentless characterization by many architects and theorists as reactionary and despite his relative professional inactivity, I believe Leon Krier to be among the most promising and progressive of current working and writing architects. While certainly vulnerable to the charge of textualism (see chapter 4 in this volume), Krier nonetheless has undeniable power as an intellectual provocateur, and he defends forcefully and eloquently the critical postmodern values of localism, communicability, populism, and some forms of tradition.

Krier is one of the few voices confident and smart enough to take on Eisenman, as he did in an exchange at a meeting in Chicago in 1989.[53] Eisenman begins the exchange by announcing that his essential standard of value in architecture is "presentness" — to what extent does a building continue to strike its viewers with a startled sense of the immediacy and relevance of its design? To what extent does it resist "the inexorable force of history" and continue to live? Eisenman cannot be much more precise about presentness than this, as he admits: "I think it's different for each individual. I went to see Rem Koolhaas' Dance Theatre in the Hague and I was struck by its presentness. There was something about it that moved me. I don't know what it was."[54]

Eisenman continues that since culture undergoes constant drastic revision, the best architecture most drastically expresses the revisionary nature of its own time. Eisenman thus complains that Ronchamp, Le Corbusier's famous church, already no longer moves him; like the Parthenon, its presentness has been eroded by history.

In reply, Krier points out that such standards as presentness, as Eisenman himself has already suggested, are notoriously subjective: "There are many, many people out there for whom [the Parthenon] is absolutely present."[55] The founders of the American republic knew, he reminds Eisenman, that "different conceptions of the world can exist side by side, respectfully, and that the inexorable forces of history are not just on one line, moving in one direction, but that they change around."[56] Krier's own preference is for buildings that, far from freeze-framing their cultural moment, rely on transhistorical symbols to gain "everlastingness." His projects—often master plans for the reconstruction of entire cities or parts of cities—feature immediately legible buildings, incorporating arches, towers, columns, gates, spires, and all other culturally articulate forms of architecture: "The fundamental types of spaces and construction," he explains to Eisenman, "have been known for a long while. They remain relevant exactly because they are time-less."[57] Krier's towns are built on a human scale; no skyscrapers, and indeed no buildings of more than a walkable number of stories, appear in his plans. He typically divides cities into self-sufficient *arrondissements,* and everything a person might need—groceries, church, public transportation, libraries, government services, and entertainment—lies within easy walking distance.

Krier counters Eisenman with a bracing acceptance of some obvious truths. First of all, he says, everyone, including Eisenman, knows that the old cities so lacking in presence for him "are in fact the most desirable places to live." There are reasons why cities like Rome and Paris sit squarely in the middle of a nearly universal fantasy of American suburbanites, and they have little to do with ignorant nostalgia and a great deal to do with the glorious reality of daily life in richly textured, humanly alive, walkable cities. Indeed, while Eisenman's focus remains on the isolated aesthetic object and his own experience of presentness, Krier's eye scans the collectivity of the town: "The problem is not the way the home looks or the way it is organised," he remarks. "That problem is largely solved. The problem is how most homes relate or don't relate to the town."[58]

Krier's signature house at Seaside, a planned town in Florida, features a Roman temple open to sun and sea views on its roof; room has been left for a balcony off the temple. The larger house it sits on is a simple white cube with small windows on each side. Krier's mixing of the grandiloquent temple with the domestic house is shocking enough, but his bold elevation of the temple high into the air is amazing. This house proudly asserts both the contemporaneity and the fitness of ancient forms of shelter and worship. Other houses at Seaside are less dramatic, but are also immediately legible as houses and nothing else: pitched roofs, soft weathered colors, spacious porches, and a quality of distinctive lived identity in each construction combine to express settled and joyous domesticity. Yet there is nothing unhealthily private and withdrawn about this domesticity; houses stand very close to one another on narrow streets, open not only to sun and ocean but to people.[59]

Given his small output and his all too easy assimilation by unreflective traditionalists, Krier in no way represents the answer to the problem of architecture's trivialization and privatization in late modern culture. But his anger, his *passion,* is instructive and exemplary for those who would radically reenvision architecture.

CONCLUSION

The act of reading deconstructive writing these days is rather like reading William Faulkner's novel, *Absalom, Absalom!*, in which each chapter begins in the present moment and then quickly submerges into the deep and deeper past, drowning people and events in pain and incomprehensibility. Our cultural and historical inheritance, this writing insists, continues to dissolve any effort at rational communication, much less concerted political action. And so today we have the bizarre, much-remarked spectacle of affluent Western intellectuals who live within governments that grant them, by any real measure, enormous personal freedom along with quite a lot of personal security, wearily demonstrating the impossibility of human agency; while in other, poorer, more dangerous, more traditional, less intellectually advanced parts of the world, like central and eastern Europe, people accomplish nothing less than the overthrow of state terror. Samuel Huntington, an American political scientist, has written of a "third wave" of democratization in the world today, beginning with Spain, Portugal, and Greece, moving through Latin America (Argentina and Chile, in particular), and most lately manifesting itself in central and eastern Europe (Poland, the Czech Republic, Slovakia, Hungary, Slovenia, and the Baltic States), and of course in South Africa.[60] All of this is encouraging, and should be occasion for some tentative satisfaction and grounds for further hope. And yet here is the voice typical of the oppositional American academics: "A citation from Antonio Gramsci enjoys a kind of underground cultural status today: 'The old is dying, and the new cannot be born.' In this interregnum there arises a great diversity of morbid symptoms. The Modernist revolution is all but dead in our Northern climes, there is no alternate culture visibly taking shape on our horizon, and literary academe now forms part of our gloomy interregnum."[61]

If we are, as the editors of this volume of essays on "architecture's social project" write, committed to helping create the conditions for "greater democracy in public life," if we want to end the profound privatization in contemporary America (a privatization, as I have tried to suggest, dramatically exemplified by the "charismatic" fate of deconstructive academics), one thing we ought to do is recognize that the phenomenon we designate "deconstruction" is a branch of late modernism, with its irrationality, elitism, obscurantism, and incorrigible melancholy. The total political failure of left oppositionality in American society (and in most other societies) should prompt intense reflection upon the fervent late modernist commitment to shock, innovation, and scandal as politically and aesthetically useful tools; it should lead to a sympathetic investigation of established beliefs and forms of conduct for too long dismissed as "bourgeois" — so that we can begin to understand the precise details of our local history and environment and begin to fashion a "postmodern" architecture that replaces an alienation effect with an effect of critical self-recognition: a reconstruction.

Critical architecture, like the Hysolar building, and critical architectural discourse, like Leon Krier's, knows that, as Charles Jencks writes, "the tradition of the new made such a fetish of discontinuity that now a radical work of quality is likely to have a shock of the old."[62] The critical architect must look hard at the way people actually live now and must then search the past for building types and urban plans that reflect the most practical, humane, and hopeful tendencies within us. She should not duplicate those models, but rather should admiringly reinterpret them for a technological world, as Behnisch does with the sunhouse. She should ignore people who, because she does not uncritically accept the necessity of novelty, call her nostalgic; she should persist in her defense of the proposition that history is not a nightmare from which we are unable to awake, but rather a mixed picture of catastrophe and enlightened change, of brutality and nobility.

Notes

1. "Jaquelin Robertson," in University of Illinois at Chicago, *The Chicago Tapes* (New York: Rizzoli International, 1987), p. 116.
2. Ibid., p. 122.
3. Ibid., p. 120.
4. Ibid.
5. Ibid., p. 122.
6. Ibid.
7. Ibid., p. 101.
8. "Jacques Derrida in Discussion with Christopher Norris," in Andreas C. Papadakis, ed., *Deconstruction II* (London: Academy Editions, 1989), p. 8.
9. Ibid., pp. 7–8.
10. Jennifer Bloomer, *Architecture and the Text: The (S)crypts of Joyce and Piranesi* (New Haven: Yale University Press, 1993), p. 166.
11. Ibid., pp. 174, 181.
12. Mark Wigley, *The Architecture of Deconstruction: Derrida's Haunt* (Cambridge: MIT Press, 1993), p. 29.
13. Ibid.
14. Ibid., p. 47.
15. Ibid., p. 48.
16. Ibid.
17. Vincent P. Pecora, book review, *Journal of Architectural Education* 48, no. 4 (May 1995).
18. Peter Eisenman, *House of Cards* (New York: Oxford University Press, 1987), pp. 182–83.
19. Ibid., p. 17.
20. Charles Jencks, "Deconstruction: The Pleasures of Absence," in Andreas C. Papadakis, ed., *Deconstruction in Architecture* (London: Academy Editions, 1988), p. 25.
21. Ibid., p. 57.
22. Ibid., p. 60.
23. Peter Eisenman, "Guardiola House, Santa Maria del Mar," in Papadakis, ed., *Deconstruction II*, pp. 56–62.
24. Ibid., p. 59.
25. "Peter Eisenman," in *The Chicago Tapes*, p. 184.

26. Marco Diani and Catherine Ingraham, eds., *Restructuring Architectural Theory* (Evanston, Ill.: Northwestern University Press, 1989), pp. 69–73.
27. Ibid., p. 71.
28. Bernard Tschumi, "Parc de la Villette, Paris," in Papadakis, ed., *Deconstruction in Architecture,* p. 38.
29. Ibid., p. 39.
30. Ibid.
31. Giovanna Borradori, "Towards an Architecture of Exile: A Conversation with Jean-François Lyotard," in Diani and Ingraham, eds., *Restructuring Architectural Theory,* p. 16.
32. Ibid.
33. Manfredo Tafuri, *Architecture and Utopia: Design and Capitalist Development,* trans. Barbara Luigia La Penta (Cambridge: MIT Press, 1980), p. 137.
34. Joan Ockman, ed., *Architecture, Criticism, Ideology* (Princeton: Princeton Architectural Press, 1985); Beatriz Colomina, ed., *ArchitectureReproduction* (Princeton: Princeton Architectural Press, 1988).
35. Sharon Willis, "Spectacular Topographies: *Amerique*'s Post Modern Spaces," in Diani and Ingraham, eds., *Restructuring Architectural Theory,* p. 67.
36. Diane Ghirardo, "Past or Post Modern in Architectural Fashion," *Telos* 62 (1984): 187–95.
37. Willis, "Spectacular Topographies," p. 65.
38. Behnisch and Partners, "Hysolar Institute, University of Stuttgart," in Papadakis, ed., *Deconstruction II,* pp. 82–87.
39. Jeffrey Kipnis, "Though to My Knowledge," in Diani and Ingraham, eds., *Restructuring Architectural Theory,* p. 110.
40. Michael Tomasky, "Why They Won: The Left Lost Touch," *Village Voice,* November 22, 1994.
41. Ibid.
42. Ibid.
43. David Harvey, *The Condition of Postmodernity: An Enquiry into the Origins of Cultural Change* (Cambridge: Blackwell, 1992), p. 357.
44. William Cain, "English in America Reconsidered: Theory, Criticism, Marxism, and Social Change," in Gerald Graff and Reginald Gibbons, eds., *Criticism in the University* (Evanston, Ill.: Northwestern University Press, 1985), p. 91.
45. Harvey, *Condition of Postmodernity,* p. 350.
46. Eve Sedgwick, "Queers in (Single-Family) Space: Michael Moon and Eve Kosofsky Sedgwick," *Assemblage* 24 (August 1994): 30–37.
47. Christopher Norris, "Jacques Derrida," in Papadakis, ed., *Deconstruction II,* p. 9.
48. Robert E. Lane, "The Joyless Polity: Contributions of Democratic Processes to Ill-Being," draft for Conference on Citizenship Competence sponsored by Committee on the Political Economy of the Good Society, University of Maryland, February 10–11, 1995.
49. Ibid., p. 7.
50. "Peter Eisenman," in University of Virginia, *The Charlottesville Tapes* (New York: Rizzoli International, 1985), pp. 140–45.
51. Ibid., p. 140.
52. Ibid., p. 145.
53. Peter Eisenman and Leon Krier, "My Ideology Is Better than Yours," in Andreas Papadakis, ed., *Reconstruction/Deconstruction* (London: Academy Editions, 1989), pp. 7–18.
54. Ibid., p. 15.
55. Ibid.
56. Ibid., p. 9.
57. Ibid., p. 13.
58. Ibid., p. 15.
59. Leon Krier, "Projects in Florida and Amiens," in Andreas Papadakis, ed., *Imitation and Innovation* (London: Academy Editions, 1988), pp. 50–59.

60. Samuel P. Huntington, *The Third Wave: Democratization in the Late Twentieth Century* (Norman: University of Oklahoma Press, 1991).

61. Gene H. Bell-Villada, "Criticism and the State (Political and Otherwise) of the Americas," in Graff and Gibbons, eds., *Criticism in the University,* p. 143.

62. Charles Jencks, *What Is Post-Modernism?* (London: Academy Editions, 1986), p. 43.

SUBVERTING THE AVANT-GARDE:
CRITICAL THEORY'S REAL STRATEGY

> Utopia is at one end of town. Maybe not. At the other end is
> Fashion. They slowly approach one another. It is high noon and
> their guns are loaded. In the four minutes in which they have
> been facing one another, weapons raised, Fashion has changed
> outfits eight times. He is threatening Utopia, telling her he has
> promises to keep and moments to guarantee. He says that he
> wants her and must deliver her to his followers by sundown.
> —Barbara Kruger, *Remote Control*[1]

As fascist ideology moves once again from veiled menace to bold contender throughout a newly recapitalized Europe and across the United States, as Mafia henchmen rule the streets of Moscow, as the People's Republic of China offers neither democracy nor socialism, the reexamination of European Marxist theory is one productive study to undertake as it impacts present debates about architecture and the built environment.[2] I say *one* because, by its own self-critical definition, critical social theory as identified with European Marxism has many limits: it has not integrated the significant contributions of Third World–centered revolutionary theory from Du Bois to Fanon to Mao; it has not adequately addressed gender and, in particular, women's oppression; it has bypassed the growing ecological debate through which the entire paradigm of built environment conquering nature has been critiqued and rejected; and even where it has broached state power it has not solved the problems of redistributing built environment resources. Nonetheless, the great theoretical debates about totality and heterogeneity, realistic representation and abstract experimentation, and counterhegemony and the unending capacity of capitalist and state socialist culture to suppress and simultaneously co-opt critical cultural practices are of great value to social theorists and culture practitioners, from Bombay to East Los Angeles. The association of this tradition of social theory and socialist practice with a Western, white, male set of thinkers need not lead to a rejection of lessons to be learned from the significant debates that have impassioned the architects of buildings and of revolutions throughout the world.

Can critical practices of architecture contribute to the production of left oppositional cultures and, what's more, the social transformation of society? The prominent critical theorist of the post–Vietnam War era, Italian Marxist Manfredo Tafuri, has spent his life examining the realities of architecture production and the production of architecture ideology and argues "No": "Bound to 'build' — because by definition the architect cannot just give voice to his protest, dissent, or nausea — but with no trust in the structures that condition their planning, in the society that will use their architecture, in the independence of their specific instruments, those architects who are more aware find themselves in an ambiguous, contorted, almost ridiculous situation."[3] Tafuri's materialist "operative" criticism has moved an entire generation of would-be architects into the ranks of professional critics.

Alternately, leftist practitioners wedded to their call to "build" have rejected the established institutional frameworks of architecture, hoping to sidestep its ideological allegiances in a valiant struggle to alter the relations of architecture production, that is, to redistribute shelter resources to those in need by every means possible.[4] Architects choosing this approach have allied with neighborhood developers throughout the United States to assist a movement demanding shelter as a human right. Operating outside of the discourse of architecture, this politically driven motion has not attempted to influence architecture institutions, yet warrants serious consideration by historians, critics, and practitioners of architecture. I myself advanced my Marxist thesis — *Building Shelter in a Corporate Society,* which analyzes the political and economic relations of production in the architecture building industry[5] — by leaving the "profession" to pursue more direct political practice through factory organizing, affirmed as I felt by Tafuri's conviction.

This chapter, however, focuses on the significant number of practicing architects who — taking the dissent of critics as constructive and the practice of socially responsible shelter advocates as challenging — approach architecture as a critical cultural practice that attempts to challenge bourgeois cultural hegemony. Loosely aligned with cultural criticism and constructive practices as theorized by leading U.S. Marxist scholar Fredric Jameson, they refuse the closure implied by critics such as Tafuri and do not allow their politics to remove them from the chance to generate material culture criticism, as have many shelter advocates. These practitioners hear Tafuri's acknowledgment that "the question marks left pending by... the ambiguous relation between art and revolution set by twentieth-century avant-gardes are not themes exhausted and resolved . . . : they are, on the contrary, problems still open, urgently in need of a solution."[6] Theorists themselves, these cultural producers seek "the possibility of inserting, within reality, a fragment of utopia," as Tafuri allows and Jameson encourages.

For theoretical orientation these practitioners borrow from the tenets of Marxism and posthumanism that are woven into the critical theory that has fueled theoretical debate in the fields of sociology, history, and art. Likewise, their practice is motivated by lessons drawn from the political crises of Soviet socialism, European social democracy, and the post–Vietnam War era right-wing reaction in the United States. *This theoretical framework of explanation makes the problems of society (and the critique of bourgeois culture) the ground-plane from which a critical practice of architecture is theorized.* Looking at culture as socially constituted, these practitioners "affiliate" to varying degrees with the political Left's challenge to the unyielding force of the Right. The questions that orient these practitioners result from debates about the characterization of social totality and the development of strategies of *critical realism.* Through debates on these questions, the contradictions between the social production of culture and the leftist project of societal transformation have been framed. This essay explores the historical contexts that have produced this theoretical approach, then presents and critiques a variety of tactical operations for generating critical cultural practices in the present period of global capitalist assault.

AVANT-GARDE MEETS THE VANGUARD: THE REALISM DEBATES

> Only that historian will have the gift of fanning the spark of
> hope in the past who is firmly convinced that even the
> dead will not be safe from the enemy if he wins.
> —Walter Benjamin, "Thesis on the Philosophy of History"[7]

The social or, better, socialist, camp in architecture began as, and continues to be, an effort to produce *material criticism* of capitalism's crimes and punishments: capitalism's requirements to maximize profits and constantly expand; its drive toward the immiseration of workers, toward racism and war; its commodification of human relations; and its use of technological development to destroy nature and generate a culture industry that can enforce its various but interrelated ideological apparatuses of domination, be they religious, educational, governmental, or military. In the twentieth century, however, the victories of the first workers' government in the Soviet Union and the growing power of socialist and communist parties throughout the world—especially in the immediate post–World War II and post-Soviet victory period—created new challenges as socialist theory moved from strategies of opposition to practices of governance. At that moment, a set of debates that had been submerged became central, and socialism had to maintain two contradictory but interrelated theoretical activities: on the one hand, *ongoing criticism of a resilient and constantly permutating advanced capitalism* and, on the other hand, *critical engagement with the comprehensive and liberating theory yet totalitarian practice of nascent socialism.*

The Politics of Culture: Revolutionary Change

> Photomontage appeared on the "left" front of art at the time
> when non-objectivity lost its meaning. For agit-art one needed
> realistic representation.... Formalist montage ... had no
> influence on the formation of political montage.
> — Gustav Klutsis, "Photomontage as a New Kind
> of Agitational Art"[8]

The modern avant-garde, centered around the various art institutions within the new Soviet Union and Germany, and the modern Marxist social critics, centered around the Frankfurt Institute for Social Research, critiqued capitalism and bourgeois individualism, as well as the alienating, fragmenting, and reifying operations of culture production within the period of developing fascism and monopoly capitalism. They each sought alternative strategies for producing critical and liberatory cultural works. Each had their specificity: the avant-garde artists foregrounded the production of culture, and the social researchers brought the critique of cultural production to the fore. But together they approached culture through the lens of social analysis and in one way or another struggled to understand the social totality, the "reality" of their time. And debate over the relationship between artistic avant-gardes and political vanguards allied with mass social movements has shaped critical strategies for architecture ever since, with renewed intensity since the collapse of European socialism.

In a brief moment in time, a Bolshevik-led communist revolution formed the Union of Soviet Socialist Republics in 1917, and a Social Democratic–led socialist movement foreclosed revolution by forming the Weimar Republic in 1918. These new governments—opposed to each other—shared the common goal, in their respective countries and internationally: the construction of socialism. Each fostered socialized production and the development of strategies for the ideological reeducation of a liberated populace and the production of a new culture.[9]

Architects have rarely identified themselves as political revolutionaries, but in the interwar period, the utopian impulses of the avant-garde in the arts—utilizing a cross section of oppositional strategies that mixed art forms, including painting, music, architecture, theater, and literature—were excited to merge art with life by the fervor of a political vanguard seeking a new society. And as fascism rose—annihilating the Weimar experiment in socialized capitalism and threatening the survival of the socialist Soviet Union—a purposeful fusion of aesthetic practice with social movements reached unprecedented heights.

Political revolutionaries struggled, at times to their death, over differing interpretations of the relationship of the material "base" of the mode of production to the ideological "superstructure" that Marx contended corresponded to it. Cultural workers produced projects that attempted to "reflect" the "totality" of society while simultaneously "demystifying" and "rupturing" bourgeois artistic practices that tended to "naturalize" or "reify" capitalist social relations. The challenge of constructing an entirely new social system based on completely reversed relations of production and political power called for new cultural institutions and strategies of artistic production capable of the ideological transformation of mass consciousness — establishing the cognitive as well as the material basis for "liberated objects," a "new socialist man," and a new "socialist reality." Social critics were transformed overnight into social constructors, and they attempted to harness the power of all means of "agitation and propaganda" in the service of socialist construction. As German dadaists George Grosz and Weiland Herzfelde wrote in 1922, the diverse cross section of artists and professional intellectuals who were drawn into political battle as "conscious producers" were "either siding . . . with the army . . . which develops the forces of industry and exploits the world; or showing the face of our time, representing it and criticizing it, as a propagandist and defender of the revolutionary idea and of its supporters."[10]

The Politics of Culture and the Construction of Socialism: The Soviet Union. In the newly unified USSR, the talents of the avant-garde were initially unleashed for the much-needed agitational work.[11] Artists and architects allied with the theoretical Institute of Artistic Culture (INKhUK), which was initiated by Wassily Kandinsky under the leadership of Nadezhda Krupskaya (head of the Chief Committee for Political Education *Glavpolitprosvet* and wife of Bolshevik leader Vladimir Ilyich Lenin). They assisted with technological modernization, built material culture institutions, and worked with the Bolshevik party's cultural counterpart, *Proletkult* (formed initally as a "third force" *educational institution* to help build working-class culture, thereby balancing the party and the trade unions). Under the leadership of Vladimir Tatlin, they participated in the implementation of Lenin's Plan for Monumental Propaganda. Journals such as *LEF* engaged the avant-garde in political debate.

In 1922 when the first Congress of Soviets of the USSR met in Moscow, Communist Party leader Sergei Kirov addressed the convocation, professing a central role for architecture in a cultural revolution: "Many say of us that we are erasing from the face of the earth all the palaces of bankers, landlords and tsars with the speed of lightning. This is true. Let us erect in their places a new palace of workers and laboring peasants . . . Comrades! Maybe this will give the needed nudge to the European proletariat, for the most part still slumbering, still unconvinced of the triumph of the Revolution, still doubting in the correctness of the tactic of the Communist Party, so that at the sight of that magic palace of workers and peasants they will realize that we have arrived seriously and forever."[12]

The nature and degree of actual political party affiliation varied greatly among prosocialist avante-garde artists. Architects Aleksandr Rodchenko and Vladimir

Tatlin had direct affiliations with the Bolshevik Communist Party of the Soviet Union (CPSUB), as did constructivist theorist Aleksei Gan, master of political photomontage Gustav Klutsis, and cinematographer Sergei Eisenstein; Kazimir Malevich was an anarchist who formed the art institution UNOVIS and with El Lissitzky advocated it as a political party.[13] Each of these individuals was greatly influenced by their contact with vital social forces and, in turn, applied their experimental approaches to the dismantling of the bourgeois institutions of art, to the critique of realistic representation in art, and to the advancement of an ideological revolution in the realm of material culture commensurate with the political transformation of Soviet society.

Malevich, experimenting with cubism and futurism in 1915, had launched abstract suprematism, calling it "the new Painterly Realism" in contradistinction to traditional representational painting. Sculptor Naum Gabo introduced the "constructive technique" in the 1920 *Realist Manifesto,* saying later that it was named such because "we were convinced that what we were doing represented a new 'reality.'"[14] Gan's 1922 principles of constructivism convey the attitude of the First Working Group of Constructivists toward the link between this realistic constructive technique and their political project. "Dialectical materialism is, for Constructivism, a compass that indicates the paths and distant objectives of the future... all [Constructivism's] essential ideas are to be found in communism."[15] Further, "*Construction* must be understood as the coordinating function of Constructivism. If the tectonic unites the ideological and formal, and as a result provides unity of conception, and the *fakture* is the condition of the material, then the construction reveals the actual process of structuring. Thus we have the third discipline, the discipline of the formation of the conception through the use of worked material." Constructivists sought to displace the painterly tradition of prerevolutionary realism, which they viewed as a bourgeois aesthetic strategy that falsely pretended to create "reflections" of "reality." The constructivists sharpened the attack on realism, calling it reactionary, and criticized any communist who condescended to the backward taste of a population whose consciousness had been formed by the ideological mechanisms of czarist oppression. Accordingly, while rejecting painterly realism as an approach that froze the mass cultural consciousness in a reactionary state, constructivism focused on actually constructing the projected reality of socialist production, thereby contributing to the mass ideological remolding necessary for socialist construction—the sublation of art into life through mass production.

Based on the fundamental Marxist premise that "it is not the consciousness of men that determines their being, but on the contrary it is their social being that determines their consciousness,"[16] such ideas supported cultural production strategies that would yield a material culture filled with everyday objects that had been cleansed of prior bourgeois subjective taste. Again rooted in Marxist philosophy, designs for socialized production could "objectivate," that is, generalize or abstract, individual experience into collective knowledge or ideals and then "objectify" the ideals by pressing them into model types to be reproduced as concrete objects. For Marx, this socialized process of cognitive transformation was essential to capitalism: transactions among people became the abstraction, "exchange," objectified in its concrete representation "money."[17] The Russian avant-garde absorbed the concept and combined all artistic diciplines in a comprehensive transformation of the built and experienced environment, a socialist constructivist utopia.

Sergei Eisenstein applied this strategy to film production in "The Problem of the Materialist Approach to Form." "*Revolutionary form is the product of correctly ascertained technical methods for the concretization of a new attitude and approach to objects and phenomena* — of a new class ideology — of the true renewal not just of the *social significance but also of the material-technical essence of cinema,* disclosed in what we call 'our content.' "[18]

Material culture designer Tatlin characterized this in his article "The Problem of Correlating Man and the Object."[19] "Confronted with the task of creating a specific everyday object with a defined function, the culture of materials artist studies all the properties of appropriate materials and their interrelations, the organic form (man), for which the object in question is being made, and finally the social aspect — this man is a worker and will use the object in question whilst leading a working life.... This produces a completely exceptional result — an original object which radically differs from the objects of the West and America.... as our way of life is built on completely different principles." During this time the avant-garde extended their prerevolutionary dadaist, cubist, and futurist experiments into the revolutionary political arena through a multitude of projects. Tatlin designed the influential utopian Monument to the Third International founded in 1919. Klutsis designed agitation and propaganda apparatuses for street organizing. Konstantine Melnikov designed numerous worker palaces, as well as many varieties of vendors' stalls, kiosks, and agitprop stands, and Lenin's sarcophagus upon his death. Iakov Chernikhov designed industrial buildings. Lyubov Popova designed many constructivist stage sets for the revolutionary theater. Nevertheless, leftist proponents of documentary, representational easel painting abounded and contended, under the banner of "socialist realism" and with the favor of Krupskaya, for influence over the aesthetic production of the new socialist state.

In 1922, the second year of the Soviet New Economic Program, Soviet artists and architects exhibited in Berlin under the initiative of Wassily Kandinsky, and constructivism was embraced by Berlin dadaists such as László Moholy-Nagy and architects like Walter Gropius as consistent with their practice of a *neue Sachlichkeit,* mixing practicality, objectivity, and sobriety. Ironically, as the Western avant-garde embraced the East, Soviet Minister of Enlightenment Anatoly Lunacharsky, interpreting the abstract forms as co-optable by bourgeois culture, found agreement with Western humanist art critics when he declared in response to the

Berlin exhibition: "I too believe that the new generation now educated in our schools is capable of mirroring the revolution in forms far richer and more immediate than those employed by leftist extremists, excellent men all, and often sincere friends of the revolution, but nonetheless influenced by the bourgeois leftist art of the Parisian *bohème*."[20]

This critique grew in form as the founders of the Association of the Artists of Revolutionary Russia (AKhRR) declared that constructivists were reactionary for promoting what AKhRR considered to be dehumanized, nihilistic formalist experimentation. AKhRR advanced socialist realism by advocating the appropriation of the equally bourgeois set of techniques of representational art for the revolution, defending the premise that they best rendered the social totality in a manner immediately accessible to the masses. "Artists in our society must depict accurately in painting and sculpture the events of the Revolution, they must portray its leaders and participants, and illustrate the role of the People—the simple toilers—the workers and peasants."[21] AKhRR's first exhibition of work concentrated on the social subject matter of art rather than its formal or technological aspects and carried the slogan "The revolutionary day, the revolutionary moment, is an heroic day, an heroic moment, and we must now in the monumental forms of heroic realism reveal our artistic experience." On the one hand, the Comintern's early popularization of proletarian realism fueled a period of international communist cultural production exemplified by the volume of work generated by prolific Black communist artists (members and sympathizers of the Communist Party of the United States [CPUSA])—in the realist tradition—in Harlem and Chicago in the 1920s. On the other hand, doctrinaire CPSUB and Comintern policies then censored much of the work produced, such that the "nationalist" label was placed on the Black artists' "bricolage" of Party ideology, African American collective memory, and lived experience.[22]

This did not stop the Soviets under Lenin's New Economic Plan from borrowing, and often uncritically assimilating, technological knowledge from the West to aid in the socialization of production, action that inevitably reinforced an industrial aesthetic. But by 1928, socialist realism had become the official Party approach to culture production, and constructivists, still refusing to propagate what they believed to be portraits of false unities albeit socialist, nonetheless had moved to embrace the power of photographic representation central to the new realism. Party members Gan and Klutsis began to incorporate "fragments of reality" through the montage tactics of "factography," adapted from German dadaist photomontage and French surrealist techniques of illusion.[23] Similarly, Eisenstein developed his film theory—"montage of attractions"—to incorporate "real" footage that would attract the audience through popular cultural forms and the Party through revolutionary subject matter, but he always placed this realism in a factographic critical construction that could not be easily absorbed as "truth." For architecture, this political consolidation yielded a period of work by Melnikov during which he revived his early flirtation with *architecture parlante* by exaggerating the scale of "real" everyday objects so that they became hyperrealist monumental buildings celebrating the cultural revolution. But by and large, this shift in aesthetic favor meant a separation between the miles of factory-produced buildings that carried the aesthetic of mass production but had lost the ideological charge of constructivism and the official monumental realism being built to signify Party institutions.

While Leninist "democracy" can be overstated, there was significant interparty debate in the brief Leninist era, in which the battle between socialist realism and constructivism, if just for a brief historical moment, could be understood by the Party as a constructive contradiction. As Stalin consolidated his hold on the Party, the movement toward the "end of contradictions among the people"—all artistic and cultural difference even within the Party was seen as a class struggle between the proletariat and bourgeoisie—led to suppression of all nonrepresentational forms of art and architecture as counterrevolutionary. The 1932 CPSUB decree made realistic depiction of revolutionary acts the official ideology of culture production, which, given the international membership of the Comintern, had enormous ideological influence over worldwide communist culture production. Thus, with Stalin in power and the ideology of socialist realism having supplanted bourgeois realism, avant-gardists Gabo and Kandinsky went to Western Europe; Lissitzky and Rodchenko became successful graphic artists; Tatlin and Malevich returned to figurative painting; Melnikov was officially purged from the practice of architecture in 1937 for refusing to critique his own inability to grasp "Soviet reality";[24] and Gan and Klutsis—the stalwart communists—died in prison camps.

The Production of Culture and the Critique of Capitalism: Germany.

The culture "workers" who congregated in Germany, from Berlin to Frankfurt, addressed the same questions regarding *culture's "reflection" of economic change and the role of art in "representing" social life,* as did the theorists in the Soviet Union.[25] The Social Democratic Party (SPD) nominally ran the liberal capitalist Weimar Republic formed after World War I, and artists were embraced as catalysts for development of a new postwar production mechanism, with a concomitant culture based on German excellence. Simultaneously, the German Communist Party (KPD) of Rosa Luxemburg and Karl Liebknecht—which included originating member-artists George Grosz, Weiland Herzfelde, John Heartfield, and Erwin Piscator—challenged the Weimar regime and drew support from the USSR, even while it critiqued Soviet bureaucratization, for a more thoroughgoing socialist revolution in Germany. The defeat of the Berlin uprising and murder of Luxemburg and Liebknecht in early 1919 both clarified and consolidated the political direction of the Weimar coalition government.

Within this very contradictory culture of the political Left, avant-garde artists coalesced. The Working Council for Art (Arbeitsrat für Kunst) included Bruno Taut and Walter Gropius, who also organized a secret correspondence of visionary architects — Die gläserne Kette (the Crystal Chain) — committed to stimulating their imaginations in preparation for the revolution to come. Gropius, interested to start a new German school for design according to modern principles of socialized production, obtained the INKhUK program for art education in the Soviet Union from Kandinsky in 1920. The dramatists Piscator and Bertolt Brecht joined the Soldiers' Soviets. *Die Aktion* and Berlin dada, from an antibureaucratic posture of criticism of the Soviet culture industry as well as that of the bourgeoisie, aspired to stimulate revolutionary sentiment by tactics such as Hannah Höch's insistence on "representing" the New Woman in photomontages that used ironic humor to counterpose present-day activities with utopian fantasies.[26]

In 1919 the young Walter Gropius received authorization from the socialist coalition in Thuringia to take over Henry van de Velde's Applied Art School in Weimar as a new State Bauhaus (Staatliche Bauhaus), early criticized by local reactionary nationalists for welcoming "foreigners" and ultimately closed because of its supposed support for Communist agitators. Gropius's vision for the Bauhaus was to unite art and technology by preparing artists to design for mass production. Influenced by German expressionism and the aesthetic theories of dada and the antecedents of Russian constructivism, Gropius believed the empathic artist could breath soul into the lifeless product, and (whether for socialist or capitalist construction) his students would learn to abstract the essence of the new culture and the requirements of production and imbed that essence into "type-forms" for concrete everyday objects — breathe soul into lifeless products: "A thing that is technically excellent in all respects must be impregnated with an intellectual idea — with form — in order to secure preference among the large quantity of products of the same kind."[27] As to Gropius's political persuasion, he was exceedingly pragmatic and attempted to avoid explicit affiliation. He saw the necessity of the new social program for the evolution of a "new architecture," a *neue Sachlichkeit* (thing-like-ness). He initiated a fraternal relationship with Kandinsky and the Moscow Vkhutemas. (Later, after constructivism began to lose favor in the Soviet Union but gained in Germany, Kandinsky arrived to teach at the Bauhaus.) The practical architectural work in partnership with Martin Wagner, a member of the German Socialist Party nominally in power, brought Gropius into the SPD circle in Weimar dedicated to mass production in housing. In 1920, in spite of his lack of affiliation and admonition of student support for a nationwide strike of resistance to the Kapp Putsch (a thwarted right-wing military coup), Gropius was commissioned by the Trades Council to design the monument to the nine worker victims killed. The Weimar Republic's attempt to construct a new socialized if not socialist society having failed by 1925 and the Bauhaus having been forced out, Gropius moved the school to Dessau with the goal of furthering the design of industrial-ized products and establishing a proper department of architecture, as far re-moved as possible from German political developments. After his flurry of design for the Dessau Bauhaus buildings, Gropius concentrated further on architecture practice and left the Bauhaus in 1928 to go to Berlin.

Under the directorship of architect Hannes Meyer, a more committed leftist who had agreed for the sake of the school to withhold explicit political statements, the Bauhaus, nevertheless, was moved to emphasize not only architecture but type-form product design—the development of the needs of the human collective (and the infusion of a collective consciousness) over any expression of individual human subjectivities. Éva Forgás records Meyer's assertion that "the creative opus [is] an 'autonomous entity,' as *l'art pour l'art* is dead: our communal conscience will not tolerate any individualistic disruption of order."[28] Thus, along with his as-sociates in the left circle surrounding the Swiss architecture periodical *ABC* and in propaganda theater, Meyer's commissions were largely for collective institu-tions, such as cooperatives, labor unions, and the League of Nations, which awarded him first prize in its palace competition in Geneva. Meyer believed with the Russ-ian constructivists that "Architecture as 'an emotional act of the artist' has no jus-tification.... [The] functional, biological interpretation of architecture as giving shape to the functions of life logically leads to pure construction: this world of constructive forms knows no native country. It is the expression of an interna-tional attitude in architecture . . . pure construction is the basis and the character-istic of the new world of forms."[29]

While the artistic institutions debated objective versus subjective approaches to fusing art and society, a group of independent, primarily academic Marxists co-alesced, who—critical of both the moderate socialism of the Weimar Republic and of the Bolshevik-inspired KPD—set about to reexamine Marxism itself and its articulation of the relationships between theory and practice and between so-cial transformation and the transformation of ideology—the "base/superstruc-ture" relationship that Marx had theorized and Lenin had tested in practice.[30] Birthed in what they called the "first Marxist Week" in 1922 in Thuringia—spon-sored by Felix Weil (a patron of KPD artists Grosz, Piscator, and Hertzfeld), with the participation of Hungarian philosopher Georg Lukács (who was serving as deputy commissioner of education of the Budapest Soviet), Karl Korsch (the Com-munist justice minister in the Thuringian SPD-KPD Coalition government), and Friedrich Pollock (a Marxist economist)—and nurtured through the plans of Weil, Pollock, and the philosopher Max Horkheimer, the politically independent Frank-furt Institute für Sozialforschung set about in 1923 to develop the Marxian frame-work for a critical theory of society, human subjectivity, and mass culture. What has come to be called "Critical Theory" as a proper name began here as a critical retheorizing of the Marxian inheritance based on the premise that materialist analysis to date had flattened the complexity of culture and, thereby, had weakened socialist theory's ability to transform mass consciousness. Weil, the link between the political vanguard, artistic avant-garde, and social theorists, commissioned Franz Röckle to design the building for the new institute in the style of the *neue Sachlichkeit* being developed in circles around the Bauhaus. Engaging in the same debates over how best to construct the relationship between art and politics, Horkheimer led a critique of Weil, Röckle, and the building itself for *sachlichkeit* rejection of human subjectivity.[31]

In 1923, as the Weimar Republic faltered, philosopher Walter Benjamin and the musician Theodor Adorno met in Frankfurt in circles around the socialist studies institute. They shared an interest in Marxism and aesthetics. While in Vienna over the next few years studying the music of Schönberg, Adorno's circle included artist Franz Werfel and Alma Mahler (who was visited there by Gropius, the father of her daughter). By 1928, as German fascism was rising, Benjamin, Adorno, Ernst Bloch, and Siegfried Kracauer centered in Berlin—where avant-garde art and left political theory converged—and there interlinked circles with Benjamin's friend dramatist Bertolt Brecht, as well as communist dramatist Erwin Piscator, composers Hanns Eisler and Kurt Weill, and artist Moholy-Nagy and architect Gropius, both having left the Bauhaus. A member of the Berlin Ring of Ten, Gropius worked to establish the cultural basis for a new architecture in practice and was elected to the directorate of the National Association of German Architects (BDA).[32] In this context he enthusiastically designed for Piscator the unrealized "Total Theater," planned to house two thousand proletarians seeking the new culture, as Moholy-Nagy designed stage sets.[33] By 1929 Felix Weil was also in Berlin bailing out the financially strapped leftist publishing house Malik Verlag and working with Piscator's theater, while Horkheimer ran the Frankfurt Institute. The German counterpart to Eisenstein, Piscator struggled to move Berlin Dada contributions into service of the KPD, to invent a proletarian form of theater, incorporating architecture and stage sets that would jolt the audience out of taken-for-granted understandings of class society and their role in it.[34] In this setting, many debates occurred about the relationship between artistic practices and political revolution in the context of technological and social transformations in production. Focus for avant-garde culture work was placed on what Brecht called "refunctioning" the aesthetic techniques of the avant-garde into revolutionary tools.[35]

As fascism gained power, suffice it to say that an informal alliance occurred between committed Marxist theorists working to "reform" the theory and avant-garde cultural practitioners eager for guideposts in an oppositional practice but unable or unwilling to work within the confines of doctrinaire Marxism or Party constraints. While there was general agreement in the earlier period that art should enable a greater understanding of social reality, and Berlin was a center of gaiety as well as intellectual fervor, once Nazism came to power, large numbers of professional intellectuals were forced into exile. Weil went to work with the Soviet Communist Party. The Bauhaus had closed and Hannes Meyer and his students went to the Soviet Union; Gropius and Moholy-Nagy went to the United States (both via England) to Harvard and the New Bauhaus in Chicago, respectively. And Marcuse, Adorno, and Horkheimer went to New York, where they reestablished the Institute for Social Research in exile. Yet as National Socialist fascism seized the consciousness of so many working-class people that it grew to become a worldwide threat, the debates intensified about strategies of resistance; serious reflection began on lessons learned from the practical experience testing the theoretical relationship between base and superstructure, the strategies for ideological remolding of mass consciousness, and the nature of "reality" and "social totality"; and struggles over the effect of diverse aesthetic strategies, now already defeated, reemerged.

The Theorization of Realism: In Exile. By 1934 Georg Lukács—from the position of exile in the USSR (and under severe constraint from censorship due to his commitment to maintain Party membership)—attacked directly in publication the ideological effect of modernist "expressionism," which he asserted to be making itself vulnerable to fascism and, thereby, sharpened the debate among the conscious dissidents over forms of organization, forms of struggle, and the role of culture. For Lukács, conceptual clarity was key in intellectual and artistic work because both abstract and subjective forms lent themselves to appropriation. Lukács was particularly critical of the German philosophical tradition, which he believed had effaced the interrelationships between economics and ideology—preventing the understanding of imperialism—and he saw artistic expressionism (particularly in literature) as contributing to that effacement. He viewed the German expressionists (even with their opposition to imperialist war) as guilty of indulging a subjectivism that undermined understanding of the totality of capitalist society, its social production of individual subjectivity, and the place of the individual within it—all necessary ingredients for revolutionary consciousness. For Lukács the function of art was "to portray objective reality,"[36] and artistic excellence could only be achieved through a practice of "critical Realism." Lukács worked to show that the individual experience of fragmentation belied the underlying order of capitalist relations of production. He sought art that portrayed the real characteristics of the society as a social whole and made it accessible to the masses of working people. Based on his understanding of fascism's explicit glorification of the emotional and irrational, he charged that the disruptive character of "modernist" techniques—those incorporating partial aspects of reality like "reportage" or "monologue" or "montage"—introduced irrationalism into a context in which rationality was key. Lukács charged the avant-garde experiment of "breaking up" with the crime of reflecting the state of social decay rather than critiquing it or presenting alternatives. His procedures called for the construction of "ideal types" (as the link between the social and the individual) that could be collectively judged. Strangely similar in argument to the logic used by the adversaries of realism, the constructivists, his critical realism advanced the strategy for conscious culture producers of objectivating subjective experience, that is, "forming reality" through the abstraction of particular real people into the category of the typical to function as collective models. This similar strategic goal of cultivating a new collective culture by the development of type-forms, be they forms designed by the material processes of industrial production or types (graphic, literary, or monumental) constructed by the political processes of social engineering, was argued for by both perspectives in contradistinction to the bourgeois subjectivity of expressionism. Yet Lukács clearly intended a narrative representation of the ideal and rejected the notion that the formal abstraction of Constructivism was objective. Georg Lukács called the entire process of abstraction of the relations between people into relations among objects "reification," which he saw as a precondition to modern production that needed to be made visible under capitalism and transformed under socialism.[37]

Ernst Bloch, a friend of Benjamin—now in exile in Prague—who was a committed sympathizer but not a member of the KPD, rebutted Lukács's attack. Witnessing the disorientation of a transitional epoch, Bloch was deeply concerned with the tendency of totalizing theory to become totalitarian in practice, not just within the Soviet parties that held state power, but in the practical mechanisms of democratic centralism and the international Comintern structures that governed democratic party life in communist formations around the world. Theorizing the alignment occurring between totalitarian state socialist culture and fascist state capitalist culture, Bloch upheld the revolutionary essence of subjective expressionism and its related modernist movements of dada, surrealism, and *neue Sachlichkeit* as he, like Lukács, associated their actual practice. Constructivism and *neue Sachlichkeit* were here viewed as avant-garde kinds of expressionism, despite their explicit rejection of subjectivity, because they employed the subjectivity of the artist as key to the process of objectivation by which they expressed the "reality of social production" in designed objects. He credited them with standing in actual opposition to the bourgeoisie. He heralded their residual humanistic character as positive in the face of the dehumanizing processes of capitalism and of the American Frederick Taylor's model of industrial production that severed mental from manual labor, a model being followed in the Soviet Union as well as in the West.[38]

Most significantly with regard to the development of critical social theory, he rejected Lukács's insistence on the very existence of the "real," which art was supposed to "reflect." Bloch understood all "representations" to be social constructions of an extant but unknowable social totality far too complex to begin to be seen. Thus, Bloch rejected the reductions that resulted from practices of codifying ideal models. Stressing, as did Lukács, the importance of a new culture of socialists capable of comprehending the idea of a totality more complex than that perceived by their direct experience, he challenged Lukács's confidence in the socialist reality he sought to reflect and his reliance on the potential of a new class consciousness that would transform in alignment with transition to a new economic base. Arguing for the cultivation of new socialist subjectivities to replace bourgeois subjectivities, Bloch focused on the utopian function of the new cultural practices, advocating development of what he called the *Novum,* "the startling and unpredictable new... always at the forefront of human experience," indicating "the qualitative reutilization of the cultural heritage."[39] Bloch stressed that in order for art to contribute to ideological transformation — to teach — it needed to bring to consciousness an understanding of the critical power of subjective hope for something yet to come as a driving force for change. He used the metaphor of "colportage," a traveling caravan selling a variety of cheap items that symbolize the dreams and wishes of the lower classes.[40]

Bertolt Brecht wrote a number of essays in response to Lukács's challenge, which were not published during his lifetime. He stressed that "true Realism" needed to change with the changing times, that such realism was not an aesthetic based on ideal types deduced from stilted tradition but a political vision based on real struggles in contemporary daily life with which the masses would identify. Therefore, in order to achieve this ever-changing focus on a changing world, experimentation was essential in the arts (particularly in the socialist movement); new and changing aesthetic devices were desired (as was the acceptance that such artistic freedom embraced the potential for failure). All varieties of technique and shifting valence could be useful in an effort to convey "reality." The purpose was not to "tell truths" to a passive audience but rather "to provide structured possibilities for reflection on the nature of capitalist (and socialist) relations and the place of the spectator within them."[41] Experimentation in art was a way of merging critical knowing with constructive action, so that the teaching function of art introduced pleasure in learning. A central mechanism for this was the production of the so-called "estrangement effect" (*Verfremdung*), that is, the presentation of a phenomena such that its taken-for-granted "natural" status is unveiled as appearance and the historical forces of its production are revealed as it is regrounded. The modernist concept of perceptual renewal was thus historicized and made to serve revolutionary ends, and knowing became a source of delight.

Walter Benjamin, a close friend of Brecht's and of Bloch's, was also close to the German Communist Party. Benjamin focused on ridding art of the aesthetic "aura" of bourgeois culture and looked directly to technology and its potential for the reproduction of aesthetic works to destroy this aura.[42] For Benjamin, the *production process* was the objectivating force leading to collective culture, not the artist: "Rather than ask, 'what is the *attitude* of a work to the relations of production of its time?'... ask, 'What is its *position* in them?'" He had an affinity for mass-produced art, which he believed to be inherently liberating in its attack on the aura of individual works and the institutions of high art. He placed value on what he called "distraction," with a theory about the powerful effects of the ubiquitous presence of architecture and its reception as opposed to audience-focused art.

In some aspects returning to Lukács's insistence on clear exposition of theoretical discourse, Theodor Adorno (with no party affiliations) critiqued both Brecht and Benjamin for celebration of the particular and fragmentary as well as the elevation of *techniques* of production over analysis of the *determinants* of artistic production. He upheld the ability of "high" avant-garde art to be "critical," believing in the power of "concentration" rather than distraction. Adorno questioned the relationship between avant-garde and mass-produced, that is, commercial, art under the conditions of late capitalism, critiquing what he considered to be Benjamin's naive acceptance of reproduction without understanding the capitalist purpose to which cultural reproduction—modeled after the United States, as all socialized production was, even in the Soviet Union—would be pledged. He framed the problem of cultural innovation (given constant appropriation of new styles and techniques) under yet-to-come global capitalism. And he asserted the critical place of the interrelationship between workers and intellectuals in the production of revolutionary art. While appreciating Lukács's theoretical rigor in contradistinction to the approaches of Brecht and Benjamin, Adorno again critiqued Lukács for defending a simple reflection theory of art—that is, art as an imitation of reality—and for a lack of understanding of how people actually come to "know" the contradictions of capitalism (which he believed could not occur through the didacticism of traditional realism). Adorno was particularly concerned with the epistemological problem of artistic reception: how would the subject develop an understanding of the objective or real world that exists outside of their perception?

According to Adorno, the task of art was, thus, to reveal the "real" by standing in distinction to it, critiquing it. In agreement with Brecht, the task was to "jolt signification."[43] In this sense he upheld the important *critical autonomy* of modern art and professed a modernist Marxism. Like Benjamin, Adorno was concerned with the radical potential of the process of artistic production, not with the artist's intent or with the real content of the work. But the negation of the normalizing character of bourgeois culture was a guiding principle. It is through the revelation of disharmony that the contradictions of capitalist society would be revealed and its invisible totality of strategic operations brought into view. Thus various operations could be employed to reveal the contradictions inherent in the apparent harmony of bourgeois culture. This negative would then evoke the utopian. Adorno understood the problem of the bourgeois culture industry's ability to co-opt fragmented experience, and he believed that the success of a work of art rested in its ability to manifest contradiction and resist its resolution: "The crucial difference is whether the negation of meaning in art works is meaningful or whether it represents an adaption to the status quo; whether the crisis of meaning is reflected by the work or whether it is immediate and bypasses the subject."[44] Synthesizing Lukács's commitment to revelation of a social totality with Bloch's and Benjamin's attention to the contradictory character of the historically specific aspects of such a whole, Adorno was able to bring focus to the cognitive capacity of art and the problem of how to produce an understanding of the imperceptible contradictory totality of capitalist society: "A successful work . . . is not one which resolves objective contradictions in a spurious harmony, but one which expresses the ideas of harmony negatively by embodying the contradictions, pure and uncompromised, in its innermost structure."[45] Further, "Beauty today can have no other measure except the depth to which a work resolves contradictions. A work must cut through the contradictions and overcome them, not by covering them up, but by pursuing them."[46]

In a detailed critique of the capitalist forces operating in the culture industry, protagonists of the Frankfurt Institute brought critical theory to bear in analyses of so-called affirmative culture, the culture of the bourgeois epoch that separated the mental world from the material one. As Herbert Marcuse wrote in 1937, "[The] decisive characteristic [of affirmative culture] is the assertion of a universally obligatory, eternally better and more valuable world that must be unconditionally affirmed: a world essentially different from the factual world of the daily struggle for existence, yet realizable by every individual for himself 'from within,' without any transformation of the state of fact."[47] Marcuse, like Adorno and Horkheimer, saw the goal of revolutionary art to be the negation of this bourgeois affirmative culture. This was not meant to debase all culture — since it was deemed possible, at least in theory, to advance a culture that "signifies the totality of social life in a given period, insofar as both the areas of ideational reproduction and of material reproduction form a historically distinguishable and comprehensible unity."[48]

As this tradition developed through twists and turns in the Soviet and German experiments, the key cultural analysts who affiliated with the Frankfurt Institute continued to develop a Marxian analysis of culture that foregrounded the formation of ideology, that is, group human subjectivities, epistemology, and the role of cultural practice in effecting social transformation. Continuing to surmise lessons from the problems of socialist construction and the rise of fascism, which had been the founding problems for research at the Institute, these theorists worked to root out idealism, positivism, and doctrinaire Marxist notions that the transformation of the mode of production by seizing state power would inevitably produce changes in the superstructure, yielding the hoped-for "new socialist man."

As historical events unfolded and fascism consumed Europe and the German Nazi government invaded the Soviet Union, many of the early strategies for using culture (and its instrument, technology) to liberate humankind were transformed into or exchanged for totalitarian versions of alienated socialized production, whether for purposes of attack or defense. Many Weimar artists who fled to the USSR were forced to repudiate their work when it became critiqued as "utopian humanism" and rejected by Stalin as not contributing to the organization of workers; others who fled to the United States to embrace Taylor's research assimilated the capitalist goals of industrialized production and the subordination of the workers to time and motion objectives. A handful strived to sell modern architecture to the fascists. World War II ensued, and while fascism was eventually, if temporarily, defeated, so were the nascent experiments in socialist construction.

In this context, the work of the Congrès Internationaux d'Architecture Moderne (CIAM) in institutionalizing the remaining threads of avant-garde initiative into an "International Style" facilitated the widespread appropriation of a critical experiment into the ubiquitous and hegemonic cultural background of capitalism, private or state. As Manfredo Tafuri points out, through the complex trajectories of the avant-garde, the proletarian international architecture that had been generated out of a theorization of a new democratic objectivity — initially symbolizing a revolutionary charge — soon came to represent the most oppressive and repressive aspects of corporate internationalism and its hegemonic inhumane ideology. Similarly, the claim of a cognitive function for realism was both its power and its pitfall. And, *built* realism further intensified this cognitive intervention, making architecture all the more compelling as a medium with which to produce cultural work, yet all the more dangerous when a Brechtian "experiment" yields the undesired result, cautioned by Lukács, of actually contributing to the embedding of dominant ideology into the consciousness of the mass movements. Thus, the emphasis, both essential and yet (in retrospect) also naive, of the Bauhauslers on technology to free the masses led Hannes Meyer to exile in the Soviet Union and Gropius to the United States, both still seeking the opportunity to "realize" their dreams.

Reflecting further on the very reality that the modern avant-garde sought to render articulate, it is useful to reiterate what Bloch had anticipated, that the growing authoritarianism of the socialist experiments and the growing isolation of critical social theories from optimistic social movements is partially rooted in the very mass production technologies that capitalism perfected and socialism sought to emulate. All the experimentation of the period had not sufficiently grasped Marx's elementary dictum: the relations of buying and selling determine all others. The capitalist Weimar Germany was only too rapidly transformed into the capitalist fascist German state — Volkswagen provided mass production for the Nazi masses, while the Nazi Party's murder factories from Buchenwald to Auschwitz employed unique and innovative forms of industrial organization to achieve the mass production of death for Jews, Gypsies, and communists. Accordingly, while the deep authoritarian and repressive policies of the CPSUB have been traced to both despotic feudal roots and the "class war" structures of a single party that proclaimed itself to be the defender of the proletariat, it was the supporters of Western capitalist technology — including then-ambassador to England Joe Kennedy — who urged Hitler to invade the Soviet Union, with the resultant deaths of twenty-eight million people, an entire generation of young people who were both heroes and victims on the front lines of fascism's defeat.

With another seven million dead in Hitler's killing camps, the postwar triumphalism of the West and the East made the debate about artistic and architectural representation increasingly urgent — if pursued with the goal of creating one of many fronts of reinterpreting the carnage — or increasingly irrelevant — if pursued with the goal of escaping from it. Any innocence once held about the direct, supportive relationship between artists and social movements and their path to progress was lost, and the high level of discourse generated by those involved was either never recorded, not widely disseminated or translated, or simply laid to rest as the Cold War began.

The Smoldering Ashes of Critical Theory and "Critical Realism"

> Authority is carried historically and circumstantially from the
> centers of power down to the actual workings of culture,
> through the network of agencies and intellectuals, operating *by
> rational consent* to maintain and elaborate some prior idea, to
> perpetuate some world view. *Authority is maintained by
> cultural consensus as well as repression.*
> — K. Michael Hays, "Photomontage and Its Audiences,
> Berlin, Circa 1922"[49]

Much of the work since the German intellectual diaspora has been theoretical, but aspects of it were taken up by the New Left around the world in the 1960s and 1970s. Louis Althusser in France, Antonio Gramsci in Italy, Raymond Williams in England, Joe Slovo in South Africa, Frantz Fanon in Algiers, Paulo Freire in Brazil: each has addressed the role of artists and intellectuals in relationship to social movements. While it is not clear what of the early Marxian artistic practices remained in the memory of the artistic movement after the world wars, it is clear that the rise of transnational capitalism, the Vietnam War, the growth of the culture industry presaged by Adorno and Marcuse, and the coincident translation into English of many of the earlier texts of the Frankfurt Institute theorists such as Adorno, Benjamin, and Bloch and cultural practitioners such as Brecht (primarily through the publications of New Left Books) established the conditions for a rebirth of this "critical theory" approach to political culture production. With U.S. cities exploding in crisis during the sixties — as the long-suppressed slave revolt finally took center stage and the "liberalism at home and fascism abroad" policies of Western imperialism were exposed by the Vietnamese revolution — faith in the inevitability of "progress" proffered by Enlightenment philosophers cum Kennedy-esque liberals finally came to an end. This cultural shift was supported by the increasing consolidation of the socialist governments around totalitarian political operations and state capitalist economics, which disillusioned many fellow travelers of the international communist movement.

The translation, publication, and rereading of the now-famous realism debates carried the questions about the aims and conditions of artistic practice from the 1920s and 1930s into the 1960s and 1970s. As resistance to the Vietnam War grew and sympathy with the Soviet state-capitalist model of "socialism" dwindled, artists and architects in many cities began once again to ally with political movements and to seek precedents for this relationship. Lessons from the theory and practice of the socialist experiments became a focal point of interest. The Great Proletarian Cultural Revolution in China furthered this trend, and Cuban revolutionary culture drew notice; work in theater and the arts flowered as part of these revolutionary movements for jobs and freedom — "bread and roses," the call.

The New Left in Europe and the United States — influenced by the movements of women and people of color, which both challenged and enriched theories of class struggle — began to study culture and ideology and to explore cultural criticism and the production of cultural works as part of the debate about what types of struggles to carry out within the heart of capitalism. American and European students crossed the Atlantic, exchanging ideas, experiences, and work. Not surprisingly, all of the earlier trends reemerged. Some people joined "new" Marxist-Leninist parties and studied Lenin's theories of agitation and propaganda, Althusser, and Gramsci; others joined anti-Leninist organizations and read the European Marxists Marcuse and Adorno; still others formed cultural nationalist organizations and focused on the inheritance of indigenous arts, while others sought opportunities through academe to support the special constituencies of women, peoples of color, and the working class. While the INKhUK and Bauhaus documents were still frozen behind the Iron Curtain, the Institute for Social Research was revived in Frankfurt, and writers, musicians, artists, and architects flocked there to study Critical Theory. Some students focused on "objectivity," "realism," and social practice among the masses; others studied "subjectivity," challenged "representation," and (in contempt of "naive" practice) focused on theory construction and the development of journals.

The blossoming conceptual art movement critiqued object-focused formalist aesthetic strategies that sought to link art with its audience. Similarly, performance art, particularly feminist performance art, worked to break the disciplinary boundaries within the arts, to challenge traditional institutional sites for artistic practice, and to bring personal subjective lived experience into the realm of public discourse. Political art brought the strategies of agitprop into new use in opposition to imperialism around the world.

The publication of Jane Jacobs's *The Death and Life of Great American Cities* in 1961 placed social analysis in front of the discourse on modern architecture and urbanism for many who adhered to the social project of architecture but lamented the installation of late modernist theories into the urban built environment. Some activists focused on direct aid to the oppressed and, after the Columbia University student strike of 1968, formed groups like Architects Renewal Committee in Harlem (ARCH). They learned from the international revolutionary movements how to wage effective struggles for housing and public institutional facilities. They traveled to Cuba, China, Nicaragua, Africa, and the Soviet Union studying socialist housing strategies and giving direct aid in the construction of new towns throughout the third world. Young architects took Peace Corps assignments all over the globe. In U.S. cities, storefronts opened to offer design and construction services to communities in need.

Others focused specifically on the semiotic and structural linguistic character of architecture as a language of "signs." Growing out of the American CIAM-like Conference of Architects for the Study of the Environment (CASE) and sparked by the vitality of the sixties, the Institute for Architecture and Urbanism (IAU) in New York was formed in 1967 with the journal *Oppositions* (1973) to directly import French, German, and English developments in literary critical theory into the discourse on architecture, urbanism, and the arts in the United States.

Convinced of the reactionary politics embedded in architecture's inherent attachment to bourgeois property relations, and influenced by my sympathies for the Civil Rights movement in the U.S. South, I focused my study of the task of architecture and design (begun in 1965 in the College of Environmental Design at University of California, Berkeley) on the fight for free speech, opposition to the Vietnam War, support for the Black Panther movement, and my own fight for women's rights.[50] I am a product of the circle that gathered around Marxist theorist-painter Jesse Reichek, who cultivated and consolidated the left inclinations of many architecture students at Berkeley into an internationalist, antiracist, class-based politics. In 1974, upon completion of my thesis "Building Shelters in a Corporate Society: Toward a Political Economy of Architectural Practice in the United States," I left Berkeley to work in industrial production and study Marxism-Leninism (that was never broached in the university) and its critique of European social democracy (in particular Adorno's resistance to the French student movement and Marcuse's ambivalent relationship with Students for a Democratic Society and the new Party Building Movement in the United States). Meanwhile, Ivy League architects who were sympathetic to the French structural Marxism of Althusser were meeting at Princeton for a "Practice, Theory, and Politics in Architecture" conference.[51]

Within the field of architecture in the United States, circles have coalesced around certain "independent" institutional forms (the Institute for Architecture and Urbanism in New York; in California, the Reichek Symposium at Berkeley and the Southern California Institute for Architecture in Los Angeles; and, nationally, Architects, Designers, and Planners for Social Responsibility [ADPSR]) and publications (*Oppositions, October, Assemblage,* and *Journal of Architectural Education*). The publication *Architecture, Criticism, Ideology,* which resulted from the IAU symposium of 1982, intentionally brought European debates about architecture and politics to the United States under the leadership of Tafuri and introduced Jameson to an architecture readership. While not trained in architecture, Jameson has been the central figure asserting — at the risk of considerable counterattack — the notion that there is more to the problem of social architecture than the just distribution of shelter and that a critical cultural practice is possible in architecture under conditions of capitalism. This is no small role, as it has drawn me back into the discourse.

The complexity of these problems makes the historic debates significant today. These questions have generated a large body of work. Certainly, the theoretical work of Tafuri and Jameson, while responding to other Marxist theorists such as Antonio Gramsci, is grounded in their knowledge and continuing participation in these now-called "realism debates." Commenting on these historic debates, Jameson argues that the problems of realism are unique among aesthetic forms, in that a cognitive function is attributed to an aesthetic experience that is constituted by its relationship to "the real." [52] This is unlike artistic forms that, able to remain separated from the subject of reality, strive for autonomy or for illusion. "It is extremely difficult to do justice to both of these properties of realism simultaneously. In practice, an overemphasis on its cognitive function often leads to a naïve denial of the necessarily fictive character of artistic discourse. . . . At the other pole of this conceptual tension, the emphasis . . . on the 'techniques' whereby 'illusion' of reality . . . is achieved tends surreptitiously to transform the 'reality' of realism into appearance."[53]

Yet, given the saturation of global culture with the aesthetic of novelty, Jameson challenges culture producers who follow the postmodern cultural logic of late capitalism to reject the seduction of floating signifiers and attach a work to a referent. "In these circumstances, indeed, there is some question whether the ultimate renewal of modernism, the final dialectical subversion of the now automatized conventions of an aesthetics of perceptual renewal, might not simply be realism itself!

LIAN HURST MANN

For when modernism and its accompanying techniques of 'estrangement' have become the dominant style whereby the consumer is reconciled with capitalism, the habit of fragmentation itself needs to be 'estranged' and corrected by a more totalizing way of viewing phenomena."[54]

Many variations of theories and artistic strategies have been advanced throughout this interim period, but in their complexity they constitute a *critical theory* approach to reconstructing the social project of architecture. Therefore, I distinguish modernism's humanist objective of achieving transcendental autonomy for the individual bourgeois subject (however novel its forms and estranging its tactics) from the historical avant-garde's project of decentering bourgeois subjectivity while undermining the institutional frameworks of art and culture production themselves. Due to the contradictory nature of modernism itself, characterized by the uneven development that marks capitalism, many of the avant-garde experiments (however seemingly historically limited) are far from exhausted and warrant further investigation under the contemporary conditions. Accordingly, while most commonly we think of CIAM and the Internationalist Style in architecture as the institutional originator of the theoretical drive for a modern "social architecture," it is the political avant-garde's approach to architecture as a component in ideological remolding for a new society—a marginalized subaltern aspect of early modernism and postmodernism—that I want to claim as the inheritance and carry forth.

Various architects, such as myself, who have participated in these historical and contemporary experiences as they have unfolded were thus already involved with the critique of humanism and the problems of hegemony in the culture industry long before Charles Jencks declared modern architecture dead. For this group, the sharp distinction between modern and postmodern never existed. Thus, while historical conditions have radically changed, the problem continues to be: *how can the medium of architecture participate in, and be used for, undermining or realigning political forces in the production of culture and social life?* This is very complex theoretical terrain. The historical debates are hardly part of common parlance for those who currently practice under conditions of capitalist domination, and where they are common knowledge, the difficulty of translating them from the context of socialist construction and the struggle against fascism under monopoly capitalism to the context of the failure of the socialist experiments and the rise, once again, of national chauvinism and fascism under late global capitalism becomes so great that theorists of the Tafuri school continue to insist with considerable credibility that it is not possible.

Jameson enters the discussion again here because of his understanding of architecture not as an isolated discipline but as central to the transformations occurring in culture in general, an arena of contestation that he believes can and must be a center of not just politics but political struggle: "Tafuri's account, finally, of the increasing closure of late capitalism (beginning in 1931, and intensifying dialectically after World War II) by systematically shutting off one aesthetic possibility after another, ends up conveying a paralyzing and asphyxiating sense of the futility of any architectural or urbanistic innovation on this side of that equally inconceivable watershed, a total social revolution."[55] He has continued to articulate his views on the cultural place of architecture not only because he, like others, sees architecture as having signaled in such explicit terms the transformations going on under late capitalism, but specifically because as the global power map changes the crisis unfolds in a particularly spatial manner. "Theories about this current situation, whether they have to do with its culture or its politics, must now pass through the code of the spatial in order to match their object of analysis."[56] Jameson, thus, looks at architecture to map what he calls the "constraints of the postmodern."[57]

K. Michael Hays, the leading contemporary historian of critical theory's practitioners within architecture, focuses attention on the socialized nature of production and the objectification of meaning in architectural works, associating the theoretics of Benjamin and Adorno from the Frankfurt Institute with the *neue Sachlichkeit* of the constructivists and the extreme objectivity of Hannes Meyer. Invoking Lukács's analysis of the concepts of "totality" and "realism," Hays analyzes the "interactive relation of form, subjectivity, and mode of production, in an openly political art."[58] Yet Jameson, the unwavering contemporary Marxist, adds the component of affiliation with actual social movements in struggle. Jameson well understands the place of space/terrain/place/property/scene/event/architecture in what has come over many years of revolutionary struggle to be called "a war of position."[59] A war of position takes place between capitalism and anticapitalism in which both the ideological and spatial must be reflected in a prerevolutionary period that may go on for decades or even centuries—that is, the concept of revolutionary reforms.

The co-optive nature of capitalist culture is by now legendary—yesterday's striker is today's happily consuming worker, yesterday's demand for Black studies is today's Black bourgeois studies curriculum designed by college administrators, and yes, yesterday's counterhegemonic proletarian built environment is today reified as a prop as we witness the Black Panther cardboard cutout in *Forrest Gump*. But efforts at understanding the dialectic between resistance and co-optation as a permanent condition allow and demand of organizers and activists in all fields the responsibility to create a moving target—to create "reforms" that expand the terrain of debate, engage with capitalist forms of domination, and teach people the difficult job of seeing their own ideas in physical expression—whether in a picket line or a picket fence, which in turn can be evaluated, critiqued, and either used or discarded in the now more fully apprehended, virtually endless revolutionary and counterrevolutionary war.

LIAN HURST MANN

"Specters of Marx": Contemporary Practices in Critical Realism

> [The] dominating discourse often has the manic, jubilatory,
> and incantatory form... [that] proclaims: Marx is dead,
> communism is dead, very dead, and along with it its hopes, its
> discourse, its theories, and its practices. It says: long live
> capitalism, long live the market, here's to the survival of
> economic and political liberalism!
> If this hegemony is attempting to install its dogmatic orchestration
> in suspect and paradoxical conditions, it is first of all because
> this triumphant conjuration is striving in truth to disavow, and
> therefore to hide from, the fact that never, never in history, has
> the horizon of the thing whose survival is being celebrated
> (namely, all the old models of the capitalist and liberal world)
> been as dark, threatening, and threatened.
> —Jacques Derrida, *Specters of Marx*[60]

While architects hover over Berlin in hopes of commissions now that the wall is down and the built product of capitalist economic development is going up, Jacques Derrida publishes his first interrogation of Karl Marx and the "messianic eschatology" of Marxism, accompanied by a scathing indictment of late-twentieth-century capitalism. Yet for some years now, Derrida's writings and Derrida himself have been imported into the field of architecture to be used by a sector of theorists and practitioners primarily interested in a critical interrogation of architectural language toward the "project" of disturbing modernist architecture's Enlightenment project. The erasure of Derrida's undeniable debt to Marxism and to critical theory by those who have made vulgar appropriations of his work, particularly in importing his methods of philosophical deconstruction into the United States and transposing them into some correlation with deconstructivism in architecture, accounts for the instant popularity of these novel works as commodities to be reproduced and collected within the growing postmodernism theory industry aimed at architecture dilettantes.

During the late 1960s and 1970s, due to the resonance between the strains of critical theory focused primarily on language and those focused on society, many of the terms introduced and certain aspects of the techniques, such as negation and estrangement, are embraced by both and are therefore found manifest in the practice of architects who have been most influenced by literary theory. These practitioners would include, most significantly, the disseminators of the theoretics of the *Tel Quel* journal within architectural circles, that is, Bernard Tschumi and the *AA Files* and Peter Eisenman and *Oppositions*. While the intent to challenge the hegemony of received architectural languages is clear among these architects, it is not through extending the use of critical theory of *society* but of *language* and its influence. The architects and artists I discuss here either intend to apply the principles and procedures initiated out of a *critical theory of society* (whether or not they incorporate aspects of the discussion of language) or, regardless of expressed intent, do—in the interpretation of Hays, Jameson, or myself—embody such practices.

Few, if any, of these theorist-practitioners identify themselves as Marxists or even leftists, as would Tafuri, Jameson, or I, and this, I will contend, bears on the degree to which they are able to amplify the gains of their undeniably innovative aesthetic work. Nonetheless, a variety of architects are working within the strategy of *critical realism,* and each tactical approach is worth recognition and further development by these architects and others. What is needed is a "comradely" exchange about the relative merits of different approaches, as well as a more "enlightened" discourse about the actual historical circumstances in which we find ourselves, the ways in which we choose to engage them (or not), and the effects produced by our work.

In an effort to render this practical work within the terms of this essay and to imagine its more explicitly valent possibilities, I have arranged the approaches into four categories with examples of each: the categories are difficult to distinguish, and certainly the practitioners' work is highly varied and often incorporates multiple tactics and techniques. Nonetheless, there is some value in distinguishing between them:

> *Objectivated Realism: Negation of the Centered Bourgeois Subject*
> One approach focuses on the socialized nature of production, the negation of affirmative bourgeois culture, and the objectivation of meaning and reformation of alternate affirmations following, on one hand, constructivists like Moholy-Nagy, Rodchenko, and Meyer and, on the other hand, cultural theorists Lukács, Benjamin, and Marcuse. This is exemplified by the *unprecedented realism* of Rodolfo Machado and Jorge Silvetti.

> *New Realism: Decentered Subject Experiences Totality*
> A second approach seeks a new realism that negates bourgeois subjectivity, posits a collective alternative, and attempts to use architecture to "think" the totality of society following from Lukács to Bloch to Adorno, Lenin to Mao, and Grosz, Brecht, Melnikov, Meyer, Eisenstein, and Klutsis. The *dirty realism* of the Office of Metropolitan Architecture models this approach.

> *Hyperrealism: Remontage of Attractions in a New Subjectivity*
> A third approach specifically utilizes theatrical effects such as "estrangement," "gesture," and "montage of attractions" to unsettle taken-

for-granted ideologies and "stage" sites for affirmative, alternative events, following in the tracks of Eisenstein, Piscator, Brecht, Marcuse, and alternately Moholy-Nagy and Klutsis. The *virtual realism* of Diller + Scofidio is the example here.

Activist Realism: Agitprop Reorients the Subject within the Social
The fourth approach attempts to subvert the contemporary avant-garde's retreat from responsibility to social movements. Appropriating every technique employed by the other approaches, this group of artists acts in a current history in the making. The *subversive realism* of my own collective AgitProps is the example here.

Out of respect for each approach as experimental, I present them largely from their own point of view. In conclusion, I offer critique and proposals for further work. In each case the pedagogical or cognitive function of art is embraced, as well as an understanding of the unending power of the culture industry, and encultured consenting subjects, to appropriate and incorporate whatever "new" operation appears on the culture horizon. These tactics seek not novelty but an unprecedented new of genuine possibility that exceeds the limits of the bourgeois society, the *Novum* advocated by Bloch.[61] Thus, the varieties of critical realism that are advanced here benefit from the history of the "realism debates" and the understanding that historical conditions have changed. They attempt to incorporate simultaneously the dismantling of bourgeois affirmative culture and the constructive anticipation of alternative concrete utopias. They accept Adorno's criteria to expose contradictions rather than resolve them; they also accept Bloch's criteria to engage the danger surrounding the articulation that "something's missing." By means of a variety of tactics and techniques they seek an effect that stimulates a generative cognitive response through which a new reality comes into view and a reorientation of human subjectivity can occur. They each attempt to revisit the avant-garde aesthetic operations that gave birth to their critical potential. Their common premises are based on the inheritance of critical theory and its legacy of material criticism.

Objectivated Realism: Negation of the Centered Bourgeois Subject

The bourgeois humanist conception of the creating or viewing subject is one of a free, active, autonomous, and unified personality appropriate for the freedoms of an emergent capitalist society; and the formal ideologies of humanism reinforce this self-created signification. But industrial capitalism also engenders acute anxieties deriving from the

chaotic metropolitan experience, and these challenge the
viability of such a conception. In order to criticize and
dismantle the humanist subject and its mode of artistic
reception, the avant-garde draws upon certain negative aspects
of the actual experience of such subjects in industrial society
and injects into bourgeois humanist normality the alienating
dissonance and contradictions that characterize rapid
industrialization in tension with the persistent but now
anachronistic ideals of unity and homology. Industrial
production is in this sense constitutively involved in the
avant-garde's practice of negation.
—K. Michael Hays, "Reproduction and Negation"[62]

Using Walter Benjamin's strategy of undermining the bourgeois artistic aura of cultural works by focusing on the socialized character of production and the standardization and reproduction of the work such that the author is superseded by the process, this approach attempts to transpose individual subjectivity into collective forms generating a lived experience free of sedimented meanings from the past. The object itself is no longer precious yet stands as a material "type-form." It critiques the homology the modernist avant-garde unwittingly produced between the object as material embodiment of objectivated collective consciousness and the object as abstract reification of the totality of human social relations into objects for exchange. The sociological and pedagogical process of a society through which human subjectivity is constructed—that is, the social construction of human cognition and therefore knowledge—can now be placed on display. Likewise, the ideation of characteristically subjective experience such as desire, longing, hope—more often registered in the factographic work of the revolutionary graphic artists and in the imaginary constructions of the Crystal Chain architects than in the productivist currents of *Sachlichkeit* architecture—produces as yet unknown possibilities.

As key spokesperson for this strategy of negation, Hays says, "There is a material congruence between the building system and the signification of the work.... the work is a trace or rather direct registration of those materials and procedures of reproduction from which it is constructed. It remains external to subjective aesthetic comprehension, acting only as an index of meaning."[63] The basis of this indexicality is the process of reproduction, through which the architect acts simply as a switching mechanism. Hays calls this "factural indexicality," bringing out its association to the Soviet constructivists' use of *factura* as materiality and, further, the factographic work that the Soviets counterposed to German expressionist photomontage.[64] However, today we no longer expect standardization, repetition, and reproduction—in and of themselves—to effect egalitarianism or even loss of aura or author. Rather, while bourgeois subjectivity may be successfully negated, these industrial processes more often affect a loss of *any* human potential. Therefore, other techniques come into play to temper the actual alienation experienced through the objectivation process: superimposition of indexes, cross-programming, and montage of pieces of detached signs may combine to negate taken-for-granted truths of bourgeois culture and codes of architectural composition.

Hays's pick among contemporary practitioners is the partnership of Machado and Silvetti, whose *unprecedented realism* merges further the tectonic indexicality that is intended to rid a project of received meanings with the overabundance of subjectivity—a hypersensuality—that recreates the possibility of new subjectivities:

> "Unprecedented realism" [is] interested in the production of an alternate reality, in a critique of reality, in a semantic manipulation.... [T]his unprecedented realism could be said to be interested in a "blurred recognizability" (or a partial recognizability, piece by piece but not of the whole), in a kind of incongruity or incommensurability, in a contempt for unity and for established syntax...; it may be interested in the possible ubiquity of things or in the simultaneity of events, in spite of the technical difficulties the realization of this may bring.[65]

Hays advances the work of Machado and Silvetti under the belief that their peculiar mixture of structuralism and social engagement constitutes the formal and social sources of a "realism" that is anticipatory and affirmative, presenting extant realities while "imagining the presently impossible." Critical of the contemporary socialist formalist avant-garde, Machado and Silvetti look for the *interaction* between architecture and politics rather than any inherent political charge of a particular form. Seeking a critical practice that is not cynical, they accept and pursue the notion of *engagement*. Hays links this strategy to those of Georg Lukács and Bertolt Brecht:

> In that seemingly paradoxical conjunction—autonomy of architecture and architecture's enactments of human possibilities—the paradigm is entirely consistent with traditional Marxian realisms, which seek to unite the experience of daily social life with certain "scientific" techniques, as well as tend to spatialize their constituent parts in narrative structures. But the "unprecedented" component of this new paradigm also seeks an architecture unbound by conventional formal and programmatic constraints, an architecture without a preceding instance or case that can fully account for its formal and social movement. Unprecedented realism posits that, as long as architecture keeps open the possibility of unforeseen connections among its formal and programmatic elements, it fulfills its vocation of linking up to and expanding, without necessarily negating, the

sociocultural context into which it erupts. It seeks, in short, to produce or constitute a figural and social space whose very conceptualization did not exist before the architecture that represented it.[66]

Hays is quick to clarify, lest we disbelieve the promise from the start, that the material practice of Machado and Silvetti does not constitute the material production of utopias but rather the production of the *concept* of such, as "properly utopian figures and anticipations, against and beyond the limits of our present way of life and modes of production."[67] The concept of utopia draws on Althusser's notion of the "imaginary" and Ernst Bloch's "concrete utopia," which reject any representation of the "natural" as anything other than a socially produced vision of reality through which the dominant culture has established consent. Thus, the imaginary is used to estrange the representation of reality in order to reveal its ideological character. As Machado explains, "Unprecedented realism is a critical operation concerned with demonstrating that a built reality other than the existing ones is possible."[68]

While the buildings utilize repetition and reproduction to achieve an objectivation, the concept of "verisimilitude" is employed to generate the effect of reality. Allowing an aspect of propaganda that represents reality rather than being it, the operation itself is foregrounded with an excess of "apparent" truth, making the plausibility obvious but nonetheless put into question. This excess of concrete detail renders the possibility of a public monumentality, again recalling Soviet monumental realism. Silvetti explains: "Thus, the old egalitarian 'reality' that modern architecture represented in its grand schemes has been transformed by the new understanding of democracy: either the realities of the market of this society, which stubbornly did not wither away and which are idealized through architecture, or the renewed, hopeful, yet always tragic representation of exemplary civic life in its passage from ideal principles to the empirical reality."[69]

In addition to utilizing Benjamin's notions of loss of aura through reproducibility, Machado and Silvetti experiment with Benjamin's notion of allegory as a superimposition of exaggerated meanings — or exaggeration of aura — in hopes of disturbing the cognitive tendency to receive monumentality as the delight of a humanist subject. Rather, like an Escher drawing, the iteration of monumentality puts its very role in question, while the remaining experience of delight is projected into an *anticipatory illumination.*

Jorge Silvetti's Four Public Squares (Leonforte, Sicily, Italy, 1983; see Figure 7.1) takes a "net of interrelated axes and nodes" on which are placed "counterpoints" or "echoes" to existing public squares and monuments that comment on what exists while facilitating a reorientation in the mind of the populace. This effect culminates in the Tower of Leonforte in the modern district that counterposes itself to the watering hole/view-framing wall of La Gran Fonte in the historic center: it

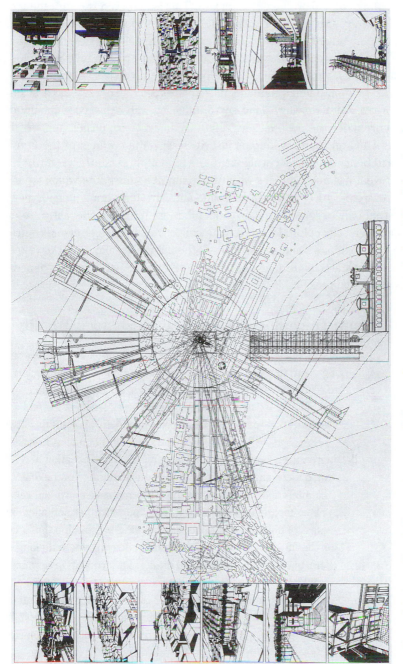

Figure 7.1. Jorge Silvetti, Tower of Leonforte, Sicily, Italy. (Image courtesy of Machado and Silvetti Associates.)

forces vision toward unexpected views, which are framed so as to exaggerate the role of "monument," to produce it in excess. This is achieved through the technically generated repeat use of "ready-made" optical devices projected on targeted views of monuments or event-spaces, which can be updated as new devices or targets evolve. Only by ascending the stair does the viewer become freed to look at the town anew. Employing again the tediously repetitive spiral stair and endless stonework, the monument simultaneously references its source, La Gran Fonte: the stair arrives at a viewing island surrounded by water that occasionally overflows and drenches the main facade; simultaneously, the opposite face, precisely as high as La Gran Fonte is long, is inscribed with the outlines of the Fonte facade. "As in Benjamin's 'dialectical image'—a kind of threshold/screen where the picture of what has been collides with the dream of a future into which we might cross—the architectural visions of Machado and Silvetti separate themselves from their referent only to reinvent a more hopeful, more multiple, alternative referent in a more specifically cultural form.... The collective fantasies, dreams, confrontations, and consolations stand across from ... the material realities that enable their production, but stand *against,* as unprecedented enlargements of experience, the limits of our actual present."[70]

New Realism: Decentered Subject Experiences Totality

> Under these circumstances, the function of a *new realism* would be clear: to resist the power of reification in consumer society and to reinvent that category of totality which, systematically undermined by existential fragmentation on all levels of life and social organization today, can alone project structural relations between classes as well as class struggles in other countries, in what has increasingly become a world system. Such a conception of realism would incorporate what was always most concrete in the dialectical counterconcept of modernism—its emphasis on violent renewal of perception in a world in which experience has solidified into a mass of habits and automatisms. Yet the habituation that it could be the function of the new aesthetic to disrupt would no longer be thematised in the conventional modernist terms of desacralized or dehumanizing reason, of mass society and the industrial city or technology in general, but rather as a function of the commodity system and the reifying structure of late capitalism.
> —Fredric Jameson, "Conclusion"[71]

Jameson's pick of practitioners is Rem Koolhaas of the Office of Metropolitan Architecture (OMA). Jameson calls Koolhaas's work *dirty realism,* an approach that incorporates a critique of bourgeois reality while refusing a representation of it. This is accomplished through a forced engagement with the social totality produced by the cross-programming and staging of events. For Jameson, the work of OMA offers insight into the problems and the potential of resistance in "Post-Civil Society."[72] The OMA work is based on understanding that the distinctions between public and private are collapsing, as public space and previously uncultivated nature are rapidly becoming privately controlled. OMA designs large "envelopes" for unprogrammed but differentiated activities. Not simply a romantic pluralist, Koolhaas places this random freedom for activities within an exaggeratedly rigid, inhuman, nonreferential form, something meaningless in which the meaning of activities will evolve. Concerning the problem of alienation and appropriation, Jameson credits OMA with both "registering" current culture and "making a statement about it."[73] Koolhaas himself accepts the mandate to produce a public architecture that is politically charged:

> One of the most important things to understand in terms of the present
> developments in Europe is that architecture has suddenly acquired a
> genuine, even political, importance, and that for the first time the
> powerlessness of the architect has been reversed: after two decades of
> deep unpopularity, there is now a very strong public, political expectation
> that the architect will be involved and will be able to articulate the self-
> inflicted, sometimes cosmetic surgery.... It is painfully clear that many of
> the architectural conceptions and most of the avant-garde architectural
> theories that were elaborated in the 1970s and '80s will be found wanting in
> the face of these strong expectations.[74]

Jameson believes that the grand envelopes of OMA can no longer be identified with either corporations or the state, but instead are revelations of the social totality achieved through a mimesis of urban totality. Sanford Kwinter considers OMA to be "virtually alone within today's avant-garde architectural milieu ... in venturing into ... the space of the sociotechnical formation of collective subjectivity, in other words, the politics of metropolitan 'delirium.'"[75] OMA rhetorically gestures toward heightened understanding of the artifice of architecture and the spatialization of society in the city with a variety of totalizing process-structures: *The Berlin Wall as Architecture* (1971), a city within a city in the exaggerated image of *The City of the Captive Globe* (1972), *Exodus, or the Voluntary Prisoners of Architecture* (1972), and *The Urban Strip as a City within a City: No-Man's-Land along the Berlin Wall* (1988). The theme of life constrained but unleashed within "walls" has focused OMA's procedure, remembering Adorno, of highlighting (or miming) the inherent contradictions in an endless irresolution. Koolhaas's focus on development of the retroactive concept was used in the 1980–81 competition for the Kochstrasse/ Friedrichstrasse project, sponsored by the International Building Exhibition, in which the unfulfilled potential of modernism's project to "rescue art from history, without having history disappear from art," was put on display by making the unbuilt utopias of Erich Mendelsohn, Ludwig Hilberseimer, and Mies van der Rohe the landmarks defining the streetscape.[76]

OMA's "culture of congestion," in Jameson's view, "is almost a political paradigm in the sense that the combination of formal requirements of a certain order without content permits all kinds of forms of freedom or disorder within the interstices."[77] Jameson continues, "Koolhaas's buildings seem to wish to stand as a mimesis of the whole microcosm itself. . . . [That's why] these buildings can carry certain political messages, or can include . . . political and social models, because they do have the ambition to grapple with the totality of the social itself."[78] The combination of law and freedom mimics the current time. As Koolhaas says, "Only through a revolutionary process of erasure and the establishment of free zones, conceptual Nevadas where laws of architecture are suspended, will some of the inherent tortures of urban life—the friction between program and containment—be suspended."[79] This leads to the cultivation of a void in "Architecture" that can be filled by the events of life; this void is not a formal one but a physical one: "Instead of . . . inventing special elements and articulating these special elements [of the program] as unique, maybe we could simply generate them by *not* building the building. In other words, if there was a sufficient density of program, a simple *absence* of building within the building could in itself, in a more refined and higher way, deal with the expectations of public life and public events." The expectation is that the mimesis (that is, "mime") inherent in the gigantic process-structures (which constitute the resultant "architecture" in the terms I have accepted) is so exaggerated as to maintain a critical edge. Thus, exaggerated scale, such that the exterior bears no relation to the interior, and the structure ("the irrevocable frontier of architecture") and mechanical (rather than architectural) systems such as elevators determine the collective and objective "indexical" determinants of the building form.

Carrying forward themes already explored in the built project in The Hague—Netherlands Dance Theater (1980–87)—OMA's so-called Big Buildings capture the relationship between event and built form, unlike the immense planning projects that could legitimately discard "Architecture," and they are therefore of more interest here (see Figure 7.2).[80] In each case, the procedure is essentially the same, a *process-structure* is formed that, in being uncontrollable, is unknowable and therefore unco-optable. What comes into being is not OMA's design but rather what Koolhaas calls "a precarious entity"—recalling for us Adorno's challenge to avoid false harmony and reveal contradiction fully and Jameson's call for totality—not a unity "to organize in a single building the coexistence of these autonomous elements without doing any injustice to their specificity or their programmatic delicacy."[81]

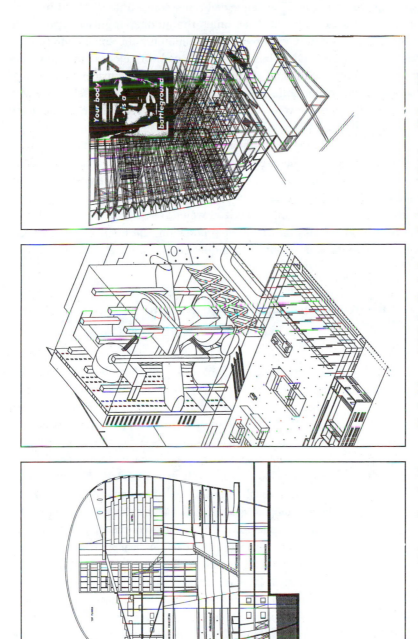

Figure 7.2. Office of Metropolitan Architecture, Big Buildings of 1989: Sea Trade Center, Zeebrugge, Belgium; National Library of France, Paris; and Center for Art and Media Technology, Karlsruhe, Germany.

The winning project for the Bibliotèque de France competition (1989), which was to accommodate the activities of three times the number regularly visiting the Centre Pompidou in Paris, is ordered around nine elevator shafts connecting a huge variety of programs. OMA believes that, "faced with electronic automation, the latest function of architecture will be to create symbolic spaces that respond to the persistent desire for collectivity."[82] In the design for the Zeebrugge Maritime Terminal (1989), the envelope becomes so huge in scale there is no outside. As a transnational point of human exchange and tourism, the terminal refuses to be appropriated by any national culture or any global capitalist hegemony because, regardless of whether it may be strewn with the gestures of McDonald's or Warner Brothers, the activity of the unprecedented mixture of populations establishes the realism of a social totality that can only be made conscious as an event. Like the "class consciousness" that Lukács theorized would result from the subjective positions of the working class in socialized production, the display of human cultural exchange and the transactions of the new Europe will yield a consciousness as yet unknown.

Hyperrealism: Remontage of Attractions in a New Subjectivity

> The other synthetic whole is the always-unachieved and hypothetical dynamic of a societal whole made up of social fragmentation and class contradiction in their specific historical forms. It turns on the interrelatedness of disparate elements in the process of social formation, and it is a product of the articulation of distinctions and differences rather than similarity and correspondence. It is a whole which sees "fragmentation as the reality of appearance," as Jameson says. It is also the whole of collective social desire. It is not an idealist utopian vision that constructs this synthesis but rather a utopian anticipation that employs concrete historical analysis and strategy in a struggle for political power in a battle over cultural hegemony. While this whole embodies the same dynamics of closure and exclusion, it is the resistance to this closure and the shared experience of otherness that mobilize an oppositional set of social forces to historical effectivity.
> —Lian Hurst Mann, *Structures for Knowledge for Change*[83]

My pick—from among the contemporary avant-garde architects—is Diller + Scofidio. Working within a much more explicit political interrogation of gender, body, subjectivity, mass media, popular culture, and the counterplay between appropriation and subversion, Elizabeth Diller and Ricardo Scofidio challenge the boundaries of architecture and place the cognitive function of art at the center of their understanding of the potential of architecture in a *virtual realism*. They utilize alternate subjectivities, multiple subjectivities, and the critique of bourgeois subjectivities to foreground the very denial of resistant and oppositional subjects. Operating in the tradition of political montage championed by Brecht, Eisenstein, and Klutsis, Diller + Scofidio use all variety of media to comment on bourgeois social norms, institutional investments, and architecture's complicity in not only registering but enabling ideological pedagogical domination by consent. Tactics of estrangement are endlessly employed in a performance architecture that creates scenarios in which complex, interrelated, and contradictory gestures challenge extant media consciousness while never falling into cynicism or closure, always incorporating elements of circus, play, and humor, which register the hope of a populace enculturated by a sophisticated advertising propaganda machine.

The tactic of estrangement has been broadly appropriated. Its applications range from the basic modernist precept to renew perception to the position now articulated by Tschumi, that is, to "celebrate fragmentation" as "a clear tool" in resisting architecture's general tendency to be "homely."[84] Diller + Scofidio's use of performance architecture to fragment and alter everyday activity, however, does not leave us disoriented. Constructing and deconstructing ritualistic activities, the installation *with Drawing Room* (San Francisco, 1987) looks at the rituals of property, etiquette, intimacy, and narcissism. In the installation, they set up an environment of destabilization. The property line cuts right through the house and the furniture, the double bed splits in two and rotates so that there is no stable space or function, and all the behavioral cues dictated by architecture are actively subverted. Their work treats the body as a corpse free to attract social relationships, but it is not a self. They are seeking an experience of a world beyond logic, language, architecture, or self. But it is not ultimately a new architecture, rather a new world. Again, following Bloch's hope, Diller + Scofidio use architecture itself to imagine a liberated subjectivity: "Architecture typically enters into a role of complicity, to sustain cultural conventions. However, architecture can be put into the role of interrogator. Given the technological and political re-configurations of the contemporary body, spatial conventions may be called into question by architecture. Architecture can be used as a kind of surgical instrument to operate on itself (in small increments)."[85]

In talking about their nearly built project *Slow House,* they say, "Posing is like turning your body, in advance, into an image." Vacation house, home away from home? They use the "real" practical commission for a vacation home — a "home away from home" — in the Hamptons to probe the notion of vacation, to focus an eye on vacation. Their intention is "to examine and reconfigure relations between the body and the conventions of domestic space with particular emphasis on the issue of what is leisure. They use the automobile windshield, the TV screen, and the picture window as apertures through which to make their investigation of connections to and escape from culture." The car windshield frames the transition between "civilized" culture and the arrival at nature. The house is shaped like a cone of vision, except it is distorted so that no central focal point is possible, no unified subject can control the house. The house is thus a series of events always changing. The view is not revealed until turning the arc on the one-hundred-foot-long wall. Diller + Scofidio hope that the house will produce frustration and function as "a mechanism of optical arousal." The picture window commodifies nature and extends beyond property lines to define the value of the property. The television screen captures a virtual nature. The forty-foot-high video camera is then projected on a monitor screen cantilevered in front of the picture window. The project attempts to bring to life leisure and nature and their "reality" as cultural constructs. In an irony that surpasses that of the design itself, their practical project remains half-constructed on its way to becoming a ruin, because this "leisure" is no longer viable under the current economic conditions.

In the Forty-second Street installation *Soft Sell* (New York, 1994), the merger of tourism, voyeurism, and desire with commodity consumption links their interrogation of visualization to the joining of pleasure with surveillance (see Figure 7.3). The project participates in the resistance to the "renewal" of the Forty-second Street district. Punctuating the commodification of the corpse, a sensuous voice stages itself as an "object of desire" and barks seductive slogans to passersby, with the motion of giant red lips that appear from behind the glazed entrance, beckoning the street walker — body or booty — to come in: "Hey you, wanna buy a one-way ticket outta here? Hey you, wanna buy a hot tip? Hey you, wanna buy the latest sensation? Hey you, wanna buy a set of encyclopedias with a four-color atlas? Hey you, wanna buy a new body? Hey you, wanna buy some fatherly advice? Hey you, wanna buy a building permit? Hey you, wanna buy a piece of the American Dream?..."[86] George Teyssot places the work of Diller + Scofidio among a group interrogating a "new subjectivity," and further links them to the tradition begun by Valerian Muriaviev and Melnikov in the 1920s, not based on stylistics but on their interest in the mechanical alteration of the human body.[87] The installation *Bad Press* heightens this approach with the celebration of the woman's work of ironing a dozen varieties of men's shirts. And the interactive video installation *Indigestion* uses a limited set of choices of stereotypical gender roles (represented by the detailed gestures of hands across a dinner table) as a tactic to explore "situated subjectivity." One virtual subject reaches across the table with aggressive gestures that challenge the passive subjectivity of the voyeuristic viewer, using the accompanying narrative: "I have been watching you. Everything points toward you, signifies you. You are the real. You are more than real."

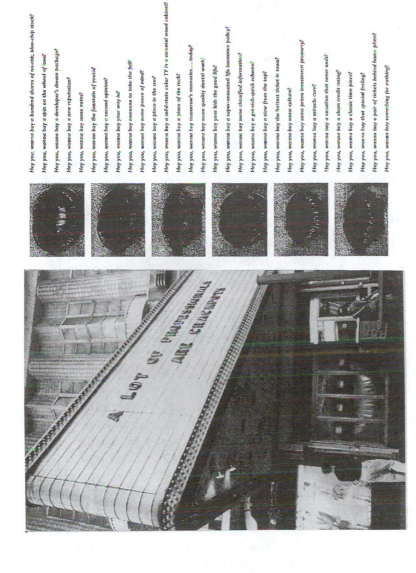

Hey you, wanna buy a hundred shares of no-risk, blue-chip stock?

Hey you, wanna buy a spin on the wheel of love?

Hey you, wanna buy a developer's dream package?

Hey you, wanna buy a new reputation?

Hey you, wanna buy some votes?

Hey you, wanna buy the fountain of youth?

Hey you, wanna buy a second opinion?

Hey you, wanna buy your way in?

Hey you, wanna buy someone to take the fall?

Hey you, wanna buy some peace of mind?

Hey you, wanna buy a place in the sun?

Hey you, wanna buy a solid-state color TV in a colonial wood cabinet?

Hey you, wanna buy a piece of the rock?

Hey you, wanna buy tomorrow's memories... today?

Hey you, wanna buy some quality dental work?

Hey you, wanna buy your kids the good life?

Hey you, wanna buy a super-annuated life insurance policy?

Hey you, wanna buy some classified information?

Hey you, wanna buy a get-rich-quick scheme?

Hey you, wanna buy a view from the top?

Hey you, wanna buy the hottest ticket in town?

Hey you, wanna buy some culture?

Hey you, wanna buy some prime investment property?

Hey you, wanna buy a miracle cure?

Hey you, wanna buy a vacation that never ends?

Hey you, wanna buy a clean credit rating?

Hey you, wanna buy a classic time piece?

Hey you, wanna buy that special feeling?

Hey you, wanna buy a pair of tickets behind home plate?

Hey you, wanna buy something for nothing?

Figure 7.3. Diller + Scofidio, *Soft Sell*, New York City. (Image and text from *Flesh*, courtesy of Princeton Architectural Press.)

Their monograph *Flesh* itself is an architectural remontage that equals the impact of many of the individual pieces it includes. Incorporating a critique of vanity publication, Diller's and Scofidio's hands are all over this piece. Not a formal disintegration — like so many that render the monograph incomprehensible — the book nonetheless refuses to simply re-present or "document" their work: it *is* their work. Through the contemporary art of factographic remontage — Bloch's colportage — their many influences are registered and multiple meanings inflected while still taking full and clear responsibility for their agency. This is no attempt to erase the evidence of authorship, but rather to place authorship on the stage for examination. "Deviants, by definition, cross lines,"[88] and Diller + Scofidio, despite their distance from the equally daring social movements of the resistance to global capital and bourgeois culture in the 1990s, offer a political valence that is neither deniable nor co-optable, as they put the museum on display inside itself, the rich vacationeer in question in his own backyard, and the vagrant, pimp, theater buff, and tourist under scrutiny in a mirrored space they cannot stand to know they share.

Activist Realism: Agitprop Reorients the Subject Within the Social Real

> [The practices of activist art] do not ... represent an evolution
> in "public art," but rather an exciting and unique
> synthesis of democratizing impulses linking the
> art world and the world of political activism.
> — Nina Felshin, *But Is It Art? The Spirit of Art as Activism*[89]

Nina Felshin distinguishes activist art practices from their related antecedents, conceptualism and public art, with the same fervor with which Benjamin challenged us to examine the place of critical work in the relations of production rather than for its ostensible meaning. Accordingly, the fourth approach follows the path of those producers of material culture who allied closely with political organizations and social movements by attempting to use critical construction to educate, to organize directly so as to actualize an effect on reality.[90] Contemporary practitioners of this approach are fully aware of the haunting problems of socialist democracy, in particular the tensions between artists fostering a culture of critical dissent and the political Left struggling for some level of reoriented consensus; they choose to engage the conundrum and to actualize social change as well as their work. Incorporating techniques from each of the other approaches, their main focus is political organizing. Strongly identified with the activist art movement, this approach to critical realism has developed among the ranks of practical historians, political organizers, performance artists, muralists, graphic designers, and architects who accept Tafuri's analysis of the constraints of contemporary anticapitalist practice and seek material cultural engagements of a more tactical, temporal, or gestural kind. Making no pretense of traditional architecture practice, the practitioners within this approach nonetheless take space and the built environment as subject matter and attempt to create counterspace in a contested terrain in the company of political movements. They presume the kind of interrelationship between the different artistic disciplines that characterized the historical avant-garde's practices of agitation and propaganda and employ all variety of media in order to harness not the fluid "soft" ideology of new multimedia technologies but the collective social potential of new modes of production—from people's monuments to photo-projections on extant buildings to the orchestrated production of evidentiary documents in bourgeois media.

A wide variety of work fits this category, starting with technniques that are didactic, even humanist. Focusing of the political urgency of *reorientation* in the face of bourgeois hegemony, some practitioners attempt to bring the voices of working-class subjects into the public domain. They often focus on restoring the erased memory of oppositional practices that have come before. A sort of *people's realism* that recalls the socialist realism strategies of the early socialist countries, these agitprop projects retell forgotten stories in the built environment. Sheila Levrant de Bretteville's wall mural, *Biddy Mason: Time and Place* (1989), part of the Power of Place project in Biddy Mason Park, Los Angeles, recounts the story of a Black slave who, in the late nineteenth century, won her freedom in court based on California's antislavery constitution and proceeded to build a homestead for her family and a movement for Black leadership in the building of the city.[91] Longtime feminist Levrant de Bretteville's work on the sidewalk in Little Tokyo commemorates the properties stolen from the Japanese during their internment in U.S. concentration camps. These two projects involve extensive research and active participation with community organizations. And, in the end, a heavy dose of authorial political agency—a feminist investment in tactility that, not unlike that of Machado and Silvetti, merges the tactics of indexicality and allegory—renders the environmental installation of these people's monuments most difficult to co-opt, despite the commercial enterprises that surround them.

Similarly, the ReStore project in Manhattan, in a simple urban infill gesture, hangs storefront signs that record historic events of cultural and political significance in the ethnic communities of the city. The Great Wall of Los Angeles and Neighborhood Pride programs, executed under the artistic directorship of Judith Baca and Gustavo LeClerc of the Social and Public Art Resource Center (SPARC) in Los Angeles, exhibit exemplary aspects of critical realism in their combination of visualization of an eclipsed history of both oppression and resistance and complete fusion of public artists with the members of affected communities. Their pedagogical process gives voice to the subjectivities of the working class and communities of color and simultaneously transforms these subjectivities through engagement, struggle, and reorientation based upon the potential relationship between cultural producers and community needs. This approach is extended internationally through Baca's *The World Wall: A Vision of the Future without Fear* (1986 and continuing), which brings together fourteen movable murals from international artists and moves them around the world, installing them in a potentially unlimited number of locations.[92]

The public environmental art of Krzysztof Wodiczko over the years has called into question many bourgeois institutions, codes, and cultural conventions through a series of "gestures," such as facade projections and material agitational interventions into the common daily discourse of street life. His recent Alien Staff project brings the burning social issue of immigration and xenophobia into common sidewalk talk.[93] The Alien Staff—a pole gadget carried by street organizers—uses an everyday colportage of devices such as video, storytelling, collection of sentimental tidbits, and the habit of making conversation with strangers to directly engage an "audience," challenging and transforming human subjective orientations on an individual yet public basis, thereby putting lived experience on stage.

In the former Soviet Union, there has been a flurry of art and architectural works that subvert and appropriate the tradition of realist monumental propoganda. Bringing this work to a U.S. audience, the Storefront for Art and Architecture in New York exhibited the projects of Vitaly Komar and Alexander Melamid (see Figure 7.4). Their work, like Wodiczko's, uses extant architectural elements superimposed with contemporary projections, ornaments, or events to disturb the now taken-for-granted anti-Communist, market-driven culture of the new Russia—*Between War and Peace* (1995)—just as they had dared to critique (with others of the Soviet paper architecture movement) the offenses of totalitarian Communism in *Double Self-Portrait as Young Pioneers* (1983).[94]

Many of the adherents to this strategy can be found within the Activist Public Art movement. Group Material in New York considers activism itself to be a work of art, claiming public space as a terrain in which to install agitprops such as posters in buses and murals on construction barricades. Opening a storefront with the manifesto "Caution! Alternative Space!" they defined space that "resembled a 'real' gallery" in order to enter the terrain of contestation over political power in Manhattan.[95] Similarly, Taller de Arte Fronterizo (Border Art Workshop) in San Diego takes Chicano activism to new heights with work like *Border Sutures* (1990), which laced together both sides of the border over a three-week program of performance art critical of U.S. immigration policy. This work has been continually amplified as California immigration policy leads the nation in its xenophobic aggression.

More explicit yet in its fusion of the strategic leadership of the artistic avant-gardes and political vanguards with the class consciousness of workers and community

Figure 7.4. Komar & Melamid, *Double Self-Portrait as Young Pioneers* (1983) *and Between War and Peace* (1995), Moscow, Russia.

activists is the work of the cultural collaborative AgitProps, produced out of the political campaigns of the Labor Community Strategy Center in Los Angeles, with which I am affiliated. AgitProps returns explicitly to the realism debates in their full political charge with the slogan "Reality Bites!" Collaborators seek to directly confront corporate power and contest bourgeois ideology, all the while questioning the historic tendencies of left organizations to limit agitprop work to the supporting tasks of arousing oppositional sentiment and glorifying struggles of resistance. Rather than attaching culture to politics, the loosely coalesced group seeks to define a politics and a practice of culture production. In this context, critical theory engages Latino teatro, African American jazz, Japanese performance art, and postcolonial feminist film, and the generally disparaged genre of agitprop is interrogated for a contemporary practice of subversive realism. As artist-theorist Martha Rosler has asserted, "Only crude works of agitation and propoganda are crude, and only those that offend our ideological precepts are dismissed out of hand."[96]

The current work of the Labor Community Strategy Center's AgitProps collective involves the construction of agitational and progaganda "props" for the staging, enabling, and enhancing of organizational and political engagement; these props are objects designed to assist political organizers in framing counterspaces and making spontaneous events out of their everyday practices of engaging people in the workplace, on the sidewalks, in the parks, riding the buses. A combination of all three previously mentioned tactical approaches—investment in the indexical characteristics of technology, estrangement from traditional formal languages, and the reorienting potential of event-structures—are deployed. Staging political action, AgitProps collaborators experiment with the cognitive power of material culture as a vehicle for experiential learning to enhance political struggles against Texaco Corporation, the Western States Petroleum Association, the Southern California Air Quality Management District (AQMD), the Metropolitan Transit Authority (MTA), and the Los Angeles County Board of Supervisors, with a distinct goal of contending for the control of physical space, however momentary it might be. In homage to Lenin's Agit Train (1918), the Theater of the People (1918), Gustav Klutsis's propaganda kiosks (1922), the antifascist (if not socialist and communist) legacy of the Bauhaus, and the New York Bread and Puppet Theater and the San Francisco Mime Troupe of the 1960s and 1970s, theories of negation and affirmation are employed in an explicit practice of agitation and propaganda. A description of several projects will bring focus to my objective in constructing the narrative of this entire essay as the context informing this practice.

AgitProps' action piece, *L.A.'s Lethal Air Kills the Dada-Puppen* (1993; artistic direction, Bianca Kovar),[97] makes reference to Hannah Höch's 1920 dada dolls, Walter Benjamin's charge to ask the position of a work within the relations of production and unhinge its bourgeois aura through its technical reproduction, and the longtime Mexican costuming tradition of *cadávera* (dressing up like the living skeleton that honors the memory of the dead), in an action montage of one hundred demonstrators carrying one hundred collectively assembled ready-made dead dolls donning the shriveled-lung bodies and faces of child cadavers (challenging the humanist presumption that dolls are alive). At a board meeting of the Air Quality Management District, during which the board voted on how many cancers per million they would allow in the Latino Wilmington community (a community surrounded by five oil refineries), the corpses were piled in a mass "grave" before the board in an act of collective rage and public mourning through civil disobedience. As board members left the podium and the community activists seized the board seats, claiming community control of the "space" until being removed from the room by the county sheriffs, the AQMD audiovisual personnel repeatedly flashed on the big-screen video monitor the "representation" of the board's consent to the "allowable cancer deaths"—that is, the presentation of the corpses and the camera panning the death and focusing in close frame on the individual faces of the amassed dead dolls (see Figure 7.5).

This challenge to the political hegemony of space extends to the "design" of event spaces, invention of props for field organizing, and continual efforts to take space, such as the Bus Riders Union/Sindicato de Pasajeros (BRU/SDP) "Trojan horse–style" takeover of the mike at the MTA community party at the Atlas jazz club—*Reality Bites* (1994; artistic direction, Eric Mann)—resulting in hundreds of signatures supporting the BRU/SDP civil rights class action suit against the MTA, as well as an *LA Times* Food Section report of the demonstration alongside the recipe for hors d'oeuvres enjoyed by all (no small accomplishment, given the systematic news blackout on the court case by the *Times*).

Under the institutional venue of the Strategy Center, AgitProps has produced performances of the San Francisco Mime Troupe, given institutional support to individual artists producing *fotonovelas* illustrating the lived experience of janitors leading the Justice for Janitors campaign, and staged an annual political "montage of attractions." Recently, beneath a flurry of mobile protest signs, the space of celebration—the local Upstage Restaurant (which has since lost its lease to the franchise that previously bought Sambo's and is now best known for its discrimination against Black customers, that is, Denny's)—was framed by carnival games like dart throwing at images of MTA board members, a donation contest to support the "Billions for Buses" campaign, and life-size cartoon representations of families waiting, and waiting, for buses (1995, Bus Riders Union Art Committee; artistic direction, Della Bonner and Sue Beilenberg).

For six months until we also lost our lease, the Strategy Center held COUNTERFRONT (1995, Bus Riders Union Visuals Committee; Kikanza Ramsey, artistic direction) at the intersection of Wilshire and Western Boulevards (where the MTA Redline station that is "urban removing" the area will open in 1997). Operating out of a small storefront previously occupied by the MTA itself and since by

Figure 7.5. AgitProps, *L.A.'s Lethal Air Kills the Dada-Puppen* (Bianca Kovar, artistic director), Los Angeles.

the rental agency seeking new vitality for the area with businesses like Denny's, Ralphs (the grocery chain recently judged in violation of antitrust law), and Blockbuster (the video franchise that has literally busted independent video vendors block by block in the Los Angeles region), the project sought to challenge the MTA–Chamber of Commerce hegemony over the intersection. Beneath the deteriorating neon of the MTA's old sign, the storefront windows framed full-size photocopied reproductions of the faces of Bus Rider Union members, and mobiles putting the demographic evidence of the MTA's racist transportation policies on display hung inside to entice the gaze of passersby. The ambiguous identity of the "back stage" storefront was clarified by organizers who formed a "counterfront" extending throughout the intersection and the adjacent MTA plaza — a major transit hub where all races and creeds of people in Los Angeles pass one another and make political gestures with a nod, a stare, an outstretched hand, a request for change, a ritual toast with the morning's paper cup of caffeine, or a conversation about the tortures of life lived on the MTA's declining bus system: individual experience became collective as random strangers joined the Bus Riders Union and became plaintiffs in the class action law suit. Currently, AgitProps billboard project *Make History* (1996; Kikanza Ramsey, artistic direction) is making counterspaces out of bus shelters throughout South Los Angeles, in preparation for the civil rights lawsuit againt the MTA. And the corresponding *Make History* journalwriting project is recording the diverse perspectives of the disparate peoples that constitute this "class." These projects were launched from a mass meeting of two hundred bus riders, left organizers, and their allies. Again, for a symposium on the lawsuit, the *Make History* project called for simple and temporary means of defining space and establishing the presence of the plaintiff class. Borrowing the adjacent moral authority of a parish hall, giant paper pillars (announcing the union's demands) framed the speakers asserting the majesty of the disenfranchised and marginalized social movement on the verge of explosion throughout the transportation system in the city.

Correspondingly, Strategy Center Publications draws on the factographic tradition of Soviet and German revolutionary artists such as Heartsfield and Moholy-Nagy, the remontage techniques of contemporary critical graphic artists as exemplified by Diller + Scofidio in *Flesh* and by the digital imperatives of graphic design journals such as *Emigre,* and a variety of cultural exemplars of multilingual agitational broadsheets. This approach has generated the *Bus Riders Union News,* a popular bilingual biweekly newsleaflet distributed by organizers on the buses updating the "class" on action in the lawsuit; propaganda booklets such as *Derechos humanos para los inmigrantes/Immigrant Rights, and Wrongs,* which merges images with Spanish and English text to teach the history of immigration and xenophobic policy; agitational *folletos* such as *A History of Transportation Racism in Los Angeles*; and the bilingual political quarterly *AhoraNow.* [98]

Fusion: Society Cannot Be Designed

> Before we can unite, and in order that we may unite, we must
> first of all draw firm and definite lines of demarcation.
> —V. I. Lenin, *What Is to Be Done?*[99]

Let me review the premises I established as a basis for reevaluating contemporary works that have inherited the specters of Marx, that is, the challenge to apply the strategy of critical realism to contemporary conditions: the work must strive for the simultaneous dismantling of bourgeois affirmative culture with the constructive anticipation of alternative concrete utopias, and through its effects expose the specific contradictions that unmask a present social totality and a future charged with hope. It must resist appropriation by the global bourgeois culture apparatuses. And it must anticipate an effect that engages its "audience" in a self-generating learning experience.

The architects in the four categories detailed profess admirable social intent and experiment with an engaging variety of tactics that employ contemporary interpretations of the strategy of critical realism. While some traditionally architectural critique is certainly possible and warranted (and questions regarding the problems of co-optation persist), my purpose here is to emphasize the limits of their thoughtful work when examined in terms of the effect it has on social change.

Thus, returning to the problem of theorists, Hays, suffering from what he has called "vestigial Marxism," employs the theoretical inheritance of Marxist critical theory to minimize the rigor and challenge of anticapitalist organizing. Hays avoids the social movements his theoretical sources would demand that he engage: "Realism makes the connections between the actual workings of a society and its appearances. And so, even though the achievement of a realized totality may remain absent from modern life, it can nevertheless be reasserted on the representational plan of artistic form."[100] While he mines Lukács for his understanding of "the interactive relation of form, subjectivity, and mode of production, in an openly political art," in order to discuss Hannes Meyer's Co-op Vitrine, he cannot relate to Lukács lifetime theoretical and practical struggle to actually *fuse* artistic practice with the practice of making revolution.

Hays's legitimation of Machado and Silvetti is brilliant. But Machado and Silvetti's own truly realist practice, making no pretense of the political intent Hays claims, in fact supersedes him. If not very radical, it is nonetheless honest in its commitment to a symbolic resolution of material contradictions. Hays apparently does not give priority to the actual world his sources studied and his chosen contemporary realists address. Instead, Hays has positioned himself as a safe critic, distorting Benjamin and Adorno for a whole generation of practitioners with his emasculating attention. As all Marxists who study various philosophical interpretations of what is going on in the world know, "the point is to *change* it."[101] If Hays would accept this point, the pages of *Assemblage* could be filled with factographic history in the making, stretching way beyond the bounds of interdisciplinary academic discourse.

Yet Hays takes his lead in this typically architectonic ideation from Jameson himself, who — out of valiant effort — has placed symbolic practices within their historic role as tactics in a strategy that must operate under conditions of such repression that no other action is possible. Jameson, therefore, examines Lukács's turn to the theorization of literary texts as a means of continuing his work under the conditions of a totalitarian form of party democratic centralism, and he examines Benjamin's treatment of the Paris arcades while awaiting the escape from Nazi persecution that would cause him to take his own life. However, these conditions cannot be used to excuse Gropius or Mies from offering the new architecture of the International Style to the Third Reich.[102] And the present conditions of bourgeois democratic freedoms that allow a level of right-wing organization unknown since the world wars present us with a momentary opportunity, and urgency, for a very different strategy — action (action that harnesses all the potential of our contemporary knowledge of the culture industry and its power representations in a new critical realism), not aesthetic formal symbolization.

Jameson, unlike Hays, is a rigorous opponent of capitalism grasping for some Gramscian reflection of his own ideas in the built environment or anywhere else. He is an intellectual organizer without perhaps being fully conscious of that role; he attempts, in the case of Koolhaas, to put a spin on realism that can both validate his own instincts and raise OMA's practice to the level of his theory. Jameson's tense synthesis of theoretical assumptions informs the assumptions underlying my own work as well as Hays's. Although I would challenge certain of his formulations on particular theoretical points, I have found no better contemporary framework for explanation of the interdependence of socioeconomic processes and lived experience in the generation of knowledge. Jameson accepts the materialist analysis of Ernest Mandel that describes the present historical stage as late multinational capitalism and, also, Alfred Sohn-Rethel's epistemological critique of "the traditional theories of science and cognition."[103] Jameson's notion of a *political unconscious* provides the methodological frame for examining the dynamic interdependency of social structure and subjective experience as a necessarily pedagogical relationship. Jameson tolerates the distortions and deviations of narrow and local interpretive methods and divergent frameworks of explanation in exchange for the profitability of mining their fields and appropriating their wealth and weapons. While investigating the oppositional possibilities of "socially symbolic acts," he strains, but strives, to claim these riches without faltering, promising never to forget that "there is nothing that is not social and historical—indeed, that everything is 'in the last analysis' political."[104]

By opposing the reliance on negative dialectic as a source of strategies for social transformation and articulating clearly the limits of a strategy of dialectical shock under the conditions of late capitalism's continual commodification of cultural products and practices, Jameson's perspective advances the teaching capacity of cultural work as appropriate and necessary. "A pedagogical culture which seeks to endow the individual subject with some new heightened sense of its place in the global system . . . will necessarily have to respect this now enormously complex representational dialectic and to invent radically new forms in order to do it justice."[105] Thus, for the examination of the concrete cultural practices of architectural design and the teaching of design located within a set of social forces that are presently forming the future of the architecture profession, this approach is particularly well suited. It allows for an *interested* critical practice of inquiry. It assumes that all intellectual work is strategic. It is able to explain the dynamic interaction of the forces of social formation, focusing on actually *seeing the structure through its effects.*

Yet, Jameson also struggles with the inheritance of the very Hegelian idealism Marx and Engels deconstructed in *The German Ideology.* In order to bring us critical theory, he has single-handedly fought a ghost greater than Marx, that is, Hegel, not always successfully. The current period being a time of tremendous disorientation, it is hard to fault his leadership.[106] He himself recognizes that the practical importance of his theoretical efforts to reassert the existence of a social totality rests in the disarray of left political organization, the attacks on social movements, and the great need for cognitive reorientation in a "whole new global system that can modify the values of any of its components. . . . We don't know how to represent this. We can only observe it from various forms of cataclysm. We are waiting to envision new maps. . . . The supposed new world of freedom and social difference [seen in Eastern Europe] is predicated on a standardization of human life. . . . Difference and identity are the same."[107] But he does not yet follow his own subaltern mandate. In a 1981 *footnote,* he asserts, "The privileged form in which the American Left can develop today must therefore necessarily be that of an *alliance politics*; and such a politics is the strict practical equivalent of the concept of totalization on the theoretical level."[108] Where is he to be found in this much-needed fusion of the avant-garde with the political movements? He is hanging out with the avant-garde in architecture who extend his infatuation with cognitive spatial maps.

Not a product himself of architecture discourse's pedagogical "effect," Jameson offers a much-needed outsider's analysis of architecture, but in so doing he falls under architecture's spell. Beginning with his selection of William Porter's Hyatt Regency Hotel in Los Angeles as the symbol of postmodernism—"the cultural logic of late capitalism"—Jameson has uncritically embraced the architectonic "mapping" metaphor that has "built the foundations" of the very bourgeois humanist philosophy he seeks to undermine, an operation executed in order to "frame" his strategy of reorientation through New Realism.[109]

As I have argued elsewhere in setting the stage for a new pedagogical theoretics based on interrogation and actualization as a bound antinomy, "*Architectonic cognition, as a means of reordering a social totality or visualizing a new utopia, is ruptured at the start. It is in the interrogation of this rupture that the pedagogy of *dis*orientation converges with the pedagogy of *re*orientation, each contributing to the possibility of resistant differentiation.*"[110]

It is in this light that I attempt self-critique of my treatment of the hyperrealism of Diller + Scofidio and the subversive realism of AgitProps. Like all theorists, I read the work around me in an act of theorizing. Thus, like Hays (who has suffered wrongly the criticism that he is "interested" in the validity of his argument rather than that his argument may not be successful), my intentionality and investment, my affiliations and my subjective biography may indeed distort my argument. Yet, I am eager for criticism that accepts my premises and advances my work accordingly. To date, response to my renderings comes in three distinct forms.

First, contemporary avant-garde practitioners respond that while they may choose to politically align "as citizens," they are in the last analysis architects; their unique practice binds them to the relatively autonomous architectural code system and specific sets of institutional affiliations and relations of production. An eloquent version of this is crafted by Jorge Silvetti in his "After Words" at the Tulane forum on the politics of architectural discourse: "With respect to politics, architecture is a weak device for sociopolitical criticism. This is partly because its mode of expressing such dimensions is weak, but also, and more importantly, because it is an inefficient mode for effecting change when compared to literature or painting or film, and particularly so when compared to real political action—an option open to all of us as citizens but rarely used by architects."[111] This was understood well in the early 1970s, which is why I left architecture to become a professional political organizer. This is also why I am particularly interested in the work of Diller + Scofidio. While clearly making a living through traditional affiliations with architecture, art, and publications institutions and withdrawing at the mention of social movements, they do not define their practice within traditional disciplinary bounds. They conjure fierce political statements. They create clients. They open work to explicitly social interaction. And, for my particular purposes, they generate rich dereification experiments challenging the ideological taken-for-granted within the ever-refreshing-itself dominant culture industry. Their willingness to deal directly with semantic substance hedges against the tendency for their art to be too quickly embraced. Given Silvetti's insistence that architecture and its discourse is "always and necessarily implicated in the representation of power,"[112] it is critical yet affirmative practices like theirs combined with theories like Jameson's about the cognitive power of art that hold my attention in architecture and foster my "crossover dreams," in this instance dreams of fusion between cultural producers and political movements such as that which fueled the creativity of the historical avant-garde. Talented practitioners are invited to join the ranks of the subversive realists and challenge those theorists who are presently courting the charge — pandering to the decadance of late capitalist practice!

This leads to the second criticism of my work: my undying love of architecture and particular attachment to the avant-garde. "After all," some say, "haven't we been saying all the time that they are a major part of the problem?" Historian of theory Margaret Crawford writes, "The narrowing of architectural practice has been balanced by an expanding architectural avant-garde, who, opposing the corruption of architecture as a business, take on roles closer to that of the artist.... The gap created by the absence of building has been filled by complex theoretical constructs that render architecture untouchable by the demands of modern life."[113] Yes, that is why, as a result of struggle over this point, I adopt the notion suggested by Tony Schuman, that my objective is subversion of the avant-garde, not recuperation of it. Yet there is, in my mind, no denying the power of the critical adventuresome imagination to decenter the bourgeois humanist subjectivity that remains frozen in the heart of both the mature capitalist and the nascent socialist cultures of our era. For me, the problem of shelter in the world is not architectural (which is why my personal response to my political economy of shelter was to work outside of architecture). The potential radical contribution of trained architects per se lies not, then, in leading a political struggle for redistribution of shelter resources (although they must not obstruct those who will lead such struggles). Rather, the unique contribution is to understand the social stage of the built environment and to appropriate it for the creation of antihegemonic counterspaces. This need not be "built" space, but neither need it be mere symbolic resolution. It is a subversive realism. The focus of my work is specifically in the possibility of fusion — the fusion I seek to effect is not a joint venture, not a merger, not a momentary indulgence, but a mutual transformation, in which the new capabilities produced are ones never before known, possibly even unimagined.

The intended subversion of the avant-garde in order to inform a new understanding of critical realism for contemporary social movements corresponds to that of its antecedents, so well described by art historian Paul Wood in his account of the interwar period: one "concept performed an important intentional function in cutting across the divide of social realist and avant-garde views.... This is the concept of 'proletarian culture.'"[114] Within AgitProps, individual visual artists, theater artists, writers, and architects recall the struggles of Lukács and Eisenstein, Mexican muralist Diego Rivera, African American writer Richard Wright, and South African journalist Ruth First, as well as contemporary artists such as Black American poet Amiri Baraka, Puerto Rican painter Elizam Escobar, and White middle-class sculptor John Ahearn, to commit to political organizational affiliations—despite the wrenching of the artistic temperament required and the tendency (or necessity) of left organizations engaged in direct political confrontation to advance master narratives—to understand and accept the revolutionary necessity of collective organization as the only vehicle capable of focusing individual resistance.[115] This brings into current reexamination many of the challenges to Party democracy that plagued the historical avant-garde and that are essential to pursue in the current period of crisis in the international Left. In the words of AgitProps painter Bianca Kovar, "It is a constant challenge to keep my head and heart on the same track as my words."[116] Thus, *the theoretical relationship between dissent and consensus, between interrogation and actualization of critical cultural work are central to the collective experiments.*[117] It is this challenge of fusion, and more, institutional affiliation that shapes my commitment to subverting the avant-garde.

The third criticism comes from the fellow political activists with whom I work. "Aren't you in danger when you represent what we are doing? Aren't you writing our history so that it is thus made?" Then, in the voice of some "empowerment" professionals, "You are 'manipulating' the political experience of the masses." Absolutely, and our experience together shapes us mutually. A representation coexistent with a practice is a theory, embodied. The pressures inherent in mass organizing work—"the suck cycle"—often produce an anti-intellectual culture among activists. And disassociation from the failures of advanced revolutionary movements can leave seasoned activists impotent, pursuing a lifestyle of "doing good works" rather than pressing to engage the "burning questions of our day." There are immense challenges to this work, and learning from the relative success or failure of projects is part of the pleasure. Agitprop work, by definition, involves affiliation and at best, fusion, with social movements. The theorist of such work—like any political leader—is definitely a designer of history: that is the very point, "to change it."

REALITY BITES! TAKE ACTION

> Historical materialism has good cause here to set itself off
> sharply from the bourgeois cast of mind;
> its basic principle is not progress, but actualization.
> —Walter Benjamin, "N[Theoretics of Knowledge]"[118]

The discourse within architecture has tended to appropriate the symbols and techniques of the historical avant-garde without regard to the moments and contexts in which it was moved to produce, and even more shocking, without regard for the political juncture that presently confronts us. From the vantage point of architecture, the tumbling of the Berlin Wall signals new design competitions and a flurry of commissions for an international coterie of architects. But isn't this perspective backwards? *The tradition of critical theory uses the analysis of society to set the terms* for a then "relatively autonomous," specifically architectural interrogation. Are the hordes of architects working in Berlin in 1996 engaging in the cultural battle over the contemporary reuse of Schinkel's NeueWache masterpiece, meeting with the *Autonomen*, working with the new Socialist Party, joining antifascist formations such as Museums against Xenophobia?

The question for left architects, from the point of view of critical theory, is, What is our ability to engage this historical moment and what are our mechanisms of accountability to any social movements, much less left organizations? Given the recent history of bitter experience among Eastern European artists, who, carrying forward the interwar avant-garde tradition, attempted to engage and transform their various socialisms from within, there are few artists anywhere seeking to align left. And given the very low level of the social movements and capitalism's colonization of the minds of most "grassroots activists," there is little social action that is explicitly oppositional. Is it unfair to challenge a petit bourgeois professional strata—dominated as it is economically by a transnational bourgeoisie and hardly pushed at all from below by a not-yet-self-conscious, newly reconceptualized international Left—to initiate explicit acts of resistance in one of the most powerfully dominated arenas, the built environment, an arena that involves by its very nature a large amount of capital (either public or private) under bourgeois control to a degree never before even comprehended, and more, to make political alliances with left organizations? This, after all, is not the time of the Progressive Party run by the LaFollette brothers that enlisted F. L. Wright or of the WPA, under whose umbrella government funds were understood to generate a certain level of radical or even revolutionary culture that was accepted as helpful to both the U.S. antifascist united front and the reestablishment (through Eleanor Roosevelt, Frances Perkins, and Harold Ickes) of a left-wing Democratic Party capitalism. Nor is this a period for federal Democratic Party programs like Lyndon Johnson's Operation Breakthrough. This is the period of Newt Gingrich, attacks on the NEA, cuts in cultural funding on all fronts, the rise of right-wing militias, international deregulation, and rampant, vicious nationalism, xenophobia, and racism. Maud Lavin's 1990 description of the crisis of reunified Germany, however, challenges us: "Tensions between the dream and the reality of one Germany have stirred debates about the country's public policies. . . . Now the silence has been broken, and at issue once more is the uneasy mix of hard-core capitalism and German democratic socialism. . . . Germany's current political debates about economic and social issues are strangely reminiscent of tensions during the Weimar Republic."[119]

Not only is the historic moment compelling for reasons other than an ambulance-chasing opportunity for architects, but also from the point of view of critical theory. There are certain standards of intellectual honesty and integrity that architects who would be intellectuals must hold for themselves, without the realities of corporate domination or weak social movements as an excuse. This involves an attempt to engage and be understood by some audience or constituency other than career social critics who operate in a closed loop of interpretation, attempting to resist the codes of a not only limited but also naive and simultaneously decadent discourse. Any material criticism living under the specters of Marx must expect an audience of oppressed people and left activists whose political activity would presumably inform the work, who would be moved by the work and make some use of it, and would, therefore, offer some transformative critique.

The Left requires a coalition culture, a voluntary unity of those who know from life experience the difference between the undeniable fragmentation and contradiction actually constituting the false whole and the appearance or *style* of fragmentation masking the concrete totality of history. Thus, criticism of the tendency toward false totality can be coupled with dialectical historical realization of the inevitable constructive nature of human activity as strategy. And, continuing to experiment with material critical realism, it is this constructive activity that can fuse the aesthetic contributions of the avant-garde with the undying hope of left political movements.

Notes

1. Barbara Kruger, *Remote Control: Power, Cultures, and the World of Appearances* (Cambridge: MIT Press, 1993), p. 214.
2. Critical theory in its more general sense includes a vast body of work evolved since the time of Plato (see Hazard Adams's two-volume edited edition of primary texts, *Critical Theory since Plato* (1971; New York: Harcourt Brace Jovanovich, 1992). However, "critical theory" as used here refers to the body of critical social theory that has guided and criticized the production of culture in the European socialist and communist movements originating between the two world wars.
3. Manfredo Tafuri, *Theories and History of Architecture,* trans. Giorgio Verrecchia (1976; New York: Harper and Row, 1980), pp. 235–36.
4. This approach to practice is exemplified by many projects, such as the Architects Renewal Committee in Harlem (ARCH) in the 1960s, the Rural Assistance League in the California Central Valley in the 1970s, the Architects and Planners in Support of Nicaragua (APSNica) in the 1980s, and People's Housing in the 1990s, all initiated by the practical visionary Stephen Kerpin.
5. Lian Hurst, "Building Shelters in a Corporate Society: Toward a Political Economy of Architectural Practice" (unpublished thesis, New York, UMI, 1969).
6. Rafael Moneo's translation of Tafuri's comments in *Theorie e storia dell architettura* (Bari-Laterza, 1968), p. 241, cited in Moneo's in "The 'Ricerca' as Legacy," *Casabella* 619/620 (January/February 1995).
7. Walter Benjamin, "Thesis on the Philosophy of History," in *Illuminations,* trans. Harry Zohn (1938; New York: Schocken Books, 1969), p. 255.
8. Gustav Klutsis, "Photomontage as a New Kind of Agitational Art," in *Izofront,* "Klasso-

vaya borda na fronte prostranstvennykh iskusstv" (Class struggle on the front of visual arts), 1931, p. 126, as cited by Margarita Tupitsyn in "From the Politics of Montage to the Montage of Politics: Soviet Practice 1919 through 1937," in Matthew Teitelbaum, ed., *Montage and Modern Life, 1919–1942* (Cambridge: MIT Press, 1992), p. 84.

9. These moments have also occurred in China, Cuba, Nicaragua, and other countries, and the potential for exploration of this work is great; but they thus far have been less widely discussed and have had less influence on the Western discourse in architecture.

10. George Grosz and Wieland Herzfelde, "Die Kunst ist in Gefahr" (Berlin, 1925), as cited in Manfredo Tafuri, "USSR—Berlin, 1922: From Populism to Constructivist International," in Joan Ockman, ed., *Architecture, Criticism, Ideology* (Princeton: Princeton Architectural Press, 1985), p. 123. Reprinted in Manfredo Tafuri, *The Sphere and the Labyrinth: Avant-Gardes and Architecture from Piranesi to the 1970s,* trans. Pellegrino d'Aciern and Robert Connolly (1980; Cambridge: MIT Press, 1987).

11. Christina Lodder, *Russian Constructivism* (New Haven: Yale University Press, 1983), details the history of Russian constructivism. See also Victor Erlich, *Russian Formalism: History, Doctrine* (The Hague: Mouton, 1965); Catherine Cooke, ed., *Russian Avant-Garde: Art and Architecture* (London: Academy Editions, 1983); Vladimir Tolstoy et al., eds., *Street Art of the Revolution: Festivals and Celebrations in Russia 1918–33,* trans. Frances Longman et al. (1984; New York: Vendome Press, 1990); Tafuri, *The Sphere and the Labyrinth*; Central Committee of the CPSUB, ed., *History of the Communist Party of the Soviet Union (Bolsheviks)* (1938; Calcutta: National Book Agency, 1968).

12. S. M. Kirov, *Izbrannye stati i rechi 1912–1934* (Moscow, 1957), p. 150, as quoted in S. Frederick Starr, *Melnikov: Solo Architect in a Mass Society* (Princeton: Princeton University Press, 1978), p. 73.

13. *El Lizzitsky: Architect, Painter, Photographer, Typographer, 1890–1941* (Eindhoven: Municipal Van Abbemuseum, 1990).

14. Naum Gabo, *Gabo: Constructions, Sculpture, Paintings, Drawings, Engravings* (London: Tate Gallery, 1957), p. 158.

15. Gan, "Konstruktivizm," as quoted in Lodder, *Russian Constructivism,* p. 99. Lodder indicates that large sections of Gan's text appear in English translation in S. Bann, ed., *The Tradition of Constructivism* (London, 1974), Thames and Hudson, pp. 33–42.

16. Karl Marx, "Preface," *A Contribution to the Critique of Political Economy, Karl Marx and Frederick Engels: Selected Works in One Volume* (New York: International, 1970), p. 18.

17. Karl Marx, *Grundrisse: Introduction to the Critique of Political Economy,* trans. Martin Nicolaus (New York: Vintage Books, 1973).

18. Sergei Eisenstein, "The Problem of the Materialist Approach to Form, 1925," in Richard Taylor, ed. and trans., *S. M. Eisenstein: Selected Works, vol. 1, Writings, 1922–34* (London: BFI, 1988), p. 60 (original emphasis).

19. V. Tatlin, as quoted in Lodder, *Russian Constructivism,* p. 211.

20. As cited in Manfredo Tafuri, "USSR," p. 158.

21. Slogan as reprinted in Lodder, *Russian Constructivism,* p. 184.

22. Robin D. G. Kelley, "Africa's Sons with Banner Red," in his *Race Rebels: Culture, Politics, and the Black Working Class* (New York: Free Press, 1994). See also Michael Brown et al., *New Studies in the Politics and Culture of U.S. Communism* (New York: Monthly Review Press, 1993).

23. Tupitsyn, "Politics of Montage."

24. Starr, *Melnikov,* pp. 220–27.

25. Many excellent studies address the relationship between art and politics during the Weimar period in Germany. John Willet, *Art and Politics in the Weimar Period: The New Sobriety, 1917–1933* (New York: Pantheon Books, 1978). Willet discusses all aspects of social, political, and artistic life in this provocative book. See also Barbara Miller Lane, *Architecture and Politics in Germany, 1918–1945* (Cambridge: Harvard University Press, 1968, 1985); Francesco Dal Co, *Figures of Architecture and Thought: German Architecture*

Culture, 1880–1920 (New York: Rizzoli International, 1990); Éva Forgács, *The Bauhaus Idea and Bauhaus Politics,* trans. John Bátki (1991; New York: Central European University Press, 1995); Tafuri, *Sphere and Labyrinth.*

26. Maud Lavin, *Cut with the Kitchen Knife: The Weimar Photomontages of Hannah Höch* (New Haven: Yale University Press, 1993).

27. Walter Gropius, "Recommendations for the Founding of an Educational Institution as an Artistic Counseling Service for Industry, the Trades, and the Crafts" (1916), in Hans M. Wingler, *The Bauhaus: Weimar, Dessau, Berlin, Chicago,* trans. Wolfgang Jabs and Basil Gilbert (1962; Cambridge: MIT Press, 1969), p. 23.

28. Hannes Meyer, "Die neue Welt," in *Das Werk* (Zurich, 1926/27), reprinted in Lena Meyer-Bergner, ed., *Hannes Meyer: Bauen und Gesellschaft. Schiften, Briefe, Projekte* (Dresden: VEB Verlag der Kunst, 1980), p. 31, as quoted in Forgács, *The Bauhaus Idea,* p. 163.

29. Hannes Meyer, "Building," in Wingler, *The Bauhaus,* p. 153.

30. See Martin Jay, *The Dialectical Imagination: A History of the Frankfurt School and the Institute of Social Research, 1923–1950* (Boston: Little, Brown, 1973); Susan Buck-Morss, *The Origin of Negative Dialectics: Theodor W. Adorno, Walter Benjamin, and the Frankfurt Institute* (New York: Free Press, 1977); Albert S. Lindemann, *A History of European Socialism* (New Haven: Yale University Press, 1983).

31. Heinrich Regius (pseudonym for Max Horkheimer), "Die neue Sachlichkeit," in *Dämmerung* (Zurich, 1934).

32. Winfried Nerdinger, *Walter Gropius* (Berlin: Bauhaus Archiv, 1985).

33. Richard Kostelanetz, ed., *Moholy-Nagy, an Anthology* (New York: Da Capo Press, 1970).

34. Erwin Piscator, *The Political Theatre* (1929; New York: Avon, 1978).

35. Walter Benjamin, *Understanding Brecht,* trans. Anna Bostock (London: New Left Books, 1973), p. 93.

36. Ernst Bloch et al., *Aesthetics and Politics,* trans. and ed. Ronald Taylor (1977; London: Verso, 1980), p. 14.

37. Georg Lukács, *History and Class Consciousness,* trans. Rodney Livingstone (1968; Cambridge: MIT Press, 1988).

38. Frederick Winslow Taylor, *The Principles of Scientific Management* (1911; New York: Norton, 1967).

39. Ernst Bloch, *The Utopian Function of Art and Literature,* trans. Jack Zipes and Frank Mecklenburg (Cambridge: MIT Press, 1988), p. xxxvii.

40. Ibid.

41. Bloch, *Aesthetics and Politics,* p. 148.

42. Walter Benjamin, "Art in the Age of Mechanical Reproduction," in *Illuminations.*

43. Lambert Zuidervaart, *Adorno's Aesthetic Theory: The Redemption of Illusion* (Cambridge: MIT Press, 1991).

44. Theodor Adorno, *Aesthetic Theory* (London: Routledge and Kegan Paul, 1986), p. 221.

45. Theodor Adorno, *Prisms* (London: 1967), p. 32.

46. Theodor Adorno, "Functionalism," *Oppositions* 17 (Summer 1979): 41.

47. Herbert Marcuse, "Affirmative Character of Culture," in *Negations: Essays in Critical Theory* (1937; London: Free Association Books, 1988), p. 95.

48. Ibid., p. 94.

49. K. Michael Hays, "Photomontage and Its Audiences, Berlin, circa 1922," *Harvard Architectural Review* 6, special issue, *Patronage* (1987): 29 (original emphasis).

50. Architecture students actively participated in "Women of Wurster" and fought the administration for a "space of our own" in Wurster Hall. As a trained architect (B.Arch., M.Arch., Berkeley), having just completed a Marxist political economic analysis of the architecture profession ("Building Shelters in a Corporate Society") and challenging the racism of the progressive women's movement (writing the infamous "Socialist Feminism Is Bourgeois Feminism"), I joined the Maoist League of Revolutionary Struggle (merger of the Chicano Nation's Marxist-Leninist August 29th Movement, the Chinese-in-form Communist orga-

nization that had fought to save the International Hotel in San Francisco's Chinatown I Wor Kuen, and the Black Revolutionary Workers League). I became a factory organizer. Life into art, art into life: I followed Gropius's mandate to complete the master's training with apprenticeship in industrial production and Lenin's mandate to bring revolutionary ideas to the working class in the basic industries. I studied the theory of agitation and propaganda that had guided German and Soviet artists and applied it in forming a workers' shop paper, *The Remolder,* and contributing to the revolutionary newspaper *Unity.*

Steeled in my understanding of both the ways in which Gropius's thread linking mental and manual work was being broken in the Taylorized factory and the ways in which Lenin's revolutionary factory cells were being isolated through sectarian practices and Mao's theory of contradiction was allowing the complete flip-flopping of political lines, I left the factory to return to the university with the intent of pursuing both the study of ideology and the practice of cultural organizing.

51. See Hays's discussion of the significance of this Princeton event, organized by Diane Agrest, for the future of structuralist and poststructuralist theory construction among circles on the East Coast; Tafuri's attraction to Althusser is central here.
52. Jameson, "Reflections in Conclusion," in Bloch, *Aesthetics and Politics,* p. 197.
53. Ibid., p. 198.
54. Ibid., p. 211.
55. Fredric Jameson, "Architecture and the Critique of Ideology," in Ockman, ed., *Architecture, Criticism, Ideology,* p. 58.
56. Fredric Jameson, "Envelopes and Enclaves: The Space of Post-Civil Society," in *Assemblage* 17 (April 1994): 37.
57. Fredric Jameson, *The Seeds of Time* (New York: Columbia University Press, 1994).
58. K. Michael Hays, *Modernism and the Posthumanist Subject: The Architecture of Hannes Meyer and Ludwig Hilberseimer* (Cambridge: MIT Press, 1992), p. 52.
59. Antonio Gramsci, *Selections from Prison Notebooks,* ed. and trans. Quintin Hoare and Geoffrey Nowell-Smith (New York: International, 1971).
60. Jacques Derrida, *Specters of Marx: The State of the Debt, the Work of Mourning, and the New International,* trans. Peggy Kamuf (New York: Routledge, 1994), p. 52.
61. Ernst Bloch, *The Utopian Function of Art and Literature,* trans. Jack Zipes and Frank Mecklenburg (Cambridge: MIT Press, 1988), p. xxxvii.
62. K. Michael Hays, "Reproduction and Negation," in Beatriz Colomina, ed., *Architecture-production* (Princeton: Princeton Architectural Press, 1988), pp. 153–54.
63. K. Michael Hays, *Unprecedented Realism: The Architecture of Machado and Silvetti* (New York: Princeton Architectural Press, 1995).
64. In addition to Hays, see Benjamin Buchloh, "From Faktura to Factography," *October* 30 (Fall 1984), and Tupitsyn, "From the Politics of Montage."
65. Rodolfo Machado, "Floridian Follies, 1986," in Hays, *Unprecedented Realism,* p. 14.
66. Hays, *Unprecedented Realism,* p. 14.
67. Ibid., p. 17.
68. Rodolpho Machado, "A Project for the City of Este, Italy, 1985," in Hays, *Unprecedented Realism,* p. 65.
69. Jorge Silvetti, "On Realism in Architecture," in Hays, *Unprecedented Realism,* p. 30.
70. Hays, *Unprecedented Realism,* p. 114.
71. Jameson, "Reflections in Conclusion," pp. 212–13.
72. Jameson, "Envelopes and Enclaves," pp. 31–37.
73. Ibid., p. 35.
74. Rem Koolhaas, "Precarious Identity," in *ANYone* (New York: Rizzoli International, 1991), p. 149.
75. Sanford Kwinter's remarks in the introduction of Rem Koolhaas, "Urbanism after Innocence: Four Projects," in *Assemblage* 18 (August 1994): 84.
76. Fritz Neumeyer, "OMA's Berlin: The Polemic Island in the City," *Assemblage* 11 (April

1992): 49. Neumeyer is referring to Nietzsche's dictum here.

77. Jameson, "Envelopes and Enclaves," p. 33.

78. Ibid., p. 37.

79. Koolhaas, "Precarious," pp. 151–52.

80. Rem Koolhaas and Bruce Mau, *S, M, L, XL* (Rome: Monacelli, 1995).

81. Koolhaas, "Precarious," p. 156.

82. Rem Koolhaas, in Jacques Lucan, *OMA–Rem Koolhaas: Architecture 1970–1990* (1990; New York: Princeton Architectural Press, 1991), p. 132.

83. Lian Hurst Mann, "Structures for Knowledge for Change" (unpublished dissertation, New York, UMI, 1990). See also Martin Jay, *Marxism and Totality: The Adventures of a Concept from Lukacs to Habermas* (Berkeley: University of California Press, 1984); Louis Althusser, "Contradiction and Overdetermination," in *For Marx,* trans. Ben Brewster (1965; London: Verso Press, 1977); Stuart Hall, "Marx's Notes on Method: A Reading of the *1857 Introduction,*" *Working Papers in Cultural Studies* 6 (1975); Ernst Bloch, *The Principle of Hope,* trans. Neville Plaice, Stephen Plaice, and Paul Knight (Cambridge: MIT Press, 1986).

84. Bernard Tschumi, "Bernard Tschumi: Six Concepts," *Columbia Documents of Architecture and Theory* 2 (1993).

85. Elizabeth Diller and Ricardo Scofidio, keynote address at the National Technology Conference, Phoenix, Arizona, January 29, 1993, as quoted in George Teyssot, "The Mutant Body of Architecture," in Elizabeth Diller and Ricardo Scofidio, *Flesh: Architectural Probes* (Princeton: Princeton Architectural Press, 1994), p. 9.

86. Diller and Scofidio, *Flesh,* p. 254.

87. Teyssot, "The Mutant Body of Architecture," pp. 3–37.

88. Diller and Scofidio, *Flesh,* p. 36.

89. Nina Felshin, ed., *But Is It Art? The Spirit of Art as Activism* (Seattle: Bay Press, 1995), p. 22.

90. See also Mary Jane Jacob et al., *Culture in Action: A Public Art Program of Sculpture Chicago* (Seattle: Bay Press, 1995); Baz Kershaw, *The Politics of Performance: Radical Theater as a Cultural Intervention* (New York: Routledge, 1992); Carol Becker, ed., *The Subversive Imagination: Artists, Society and Social Responsibility* (New York: Routledge, 1994); Douglas Kellner, *Media Culture: Cultural Studies, Identity and Politics between the Modern and the Postmodern* (London: Routledge, 1995).

91. Dolores Hayden, *Power of Place: Urban Landscapes as Public History* (Cambridge: MIT Press, 1995).

92. Judy Baca, "Whose Monument Where? Public Art in a Many-Cultured Society," in Suzanne Lacy, ed., *Mapping the Terrain: New Genre Public Art* (Seattle: Bay Press, 1995), pp. 131–38. See also Richard Carp et al., *Saber es Poder: Interventions* (Los Angeles: ADOBE LA, 1994).

93. Krzysztof Wodiczko, "Alien Staff," in *Assemblage* 23 (April 1994): 6–27.

94. Komar & Malemid, instigators, *Monumental Progaganda* (New York: ICI International Associates, 1993); Alexey Yurasovsky and Sophic Ovenden, eds., *Post-Soviet Art and Architecture* (London: Academy Editions, 1994). See also Joe Slovo, *Has Socialism Failed?* (South Africa: Umsebenzi Discussion Pamphlet, January 1990); Robin Blackburn, ed., *After the Fall: The Failure of Communism and the Future of Socialism* (London: Verso, 1991); *Socialism in Transition: Documents and Discussion,* a special edition of *Socialism and Democracy* 8, nos. 2–3 (1992); and Antonio Callari and Stephen Cullenberg, eds., *Marxism in the Postmodern Age: Confronting the New World Order* (New York: Guilford, 1994).

95. Jan Avgikos, "Group Material Time: Activism as a Work of Art," in Felshin, ed., *But Is It Art?* pp. 85–116.

96. Martha Rosler, "Lockers, Buyers, Dealers," in Brian Wilson, ed., *Art after Modernism: Rethinking Representation* (New York: New Museum of Contemporary Art, 1984), p. 322.

97. Based on Eric Mann et al., *L.A.'s Lethal Air: New Strategies for Policy, Organizing, and Action/El aero muerto* (Los Angeles: Labor Community Strategy Center, 1991).

98. Urban Strategies Group, *Derechos humanos para los inmigrantes/Immigrant Rights and*

Wrongs (Los Angeles: Labor Community Strategy Center, 1994).

99. V. I. Lenin, *What Is to Be Done? Burning Questions of Our Movement* (1902; Peking: Foreign Language Press, 1973), p. 136.

100. Hays, *Modernism,* p. 54.

101. Karl Marx, "Theses on Feuerbach," in Robert Tucker, ed., *The Marx-Engels Reader* (New York: Norton, 1978), p. 145.

102. Elaine S. Hochman, *Architects of Fortune: Mies van der Rohe and the Third Reich* (New York: Weidenfeld and Nicolson, 1989).

103. Ernest Mandel, *Late Capitalism,* trans. Joris De Bres (1972; New York: Verso Press, 1978); Mandel, *Power and Money* (London: Verso Press, 1993); Alfred Sohn-Rethel, *Intellectual and Manual Labor: A Critique of Epistemology,* trans. Martin Sohn-Rethel (London: Macmillan Press, 1978).

104. Fredric Jameson, *The Political Unconscious: Narrative as a Socially Symbolic Act* (Ithaca: Cornell University Press, 1981), p. 20.

105. Fredric Jameson, "Postmodernism, or the Cultural Logic of Late Capitalism," *New Left Review* 146 (1984). Reprinted in Fredric Jameson, *Postmodernism: The Cultural Logic of Late Capitalism* (Durham: Duke University Press, 1991).

106. See Douglas Kellner, ed., *Postmodernism/Jameson/Critique* (Washington, D.C.: Maisonneauve Press, 1989).

107. Fredric Jameson, "Varieties of Historicism," Conference of the Humanities Research Institute, University of California, Irvine (February 3, 1990).

108. Jameson, *Political Unconscious,* p. 54.

109. This critique is elaborated in Mann, "Structures for Knowledge for Change."

110. Lian Hurst Mann, "Crossover Dream: A *Parti(r),* Structures for Knowledge of Difference," in Thomas A. Dutton, ed., *Voices in Architectural Education: Cultural Politics and Pedagogy,* Critical Studies in Education Series (New York: Bergin and Garvey, 1991).

111. Jorge Silvetti, "After Words," *Assemblage* 27 (August 1995): 77.

112. Ibid.

113. Margaret Crawford, "Can Architects Be Socially Responsible?" in Diane Ghirardo, ed., *Out of Site: A Social Criticism of Architecture* (Seattle: Bay Press, 1991), p. 42.

114. Paul Wood, "Realisms and Realities," in Briony Fer, David Batchelor, and Paul Wood, *Realism, Rationalism, Surrealism: Art between the Wars* (New Haven, Conn.: Yale University Press, 1993), p. 270.

115. See discussion of Rivera's political attitude in Wood, ibid., pp. 251–331; struggles of Wright in Margaret Walker, *Richard Wright: Demonic Genius* (New York: Amistad, 1988); First's prison account in Ruth First, *117 Days* (New York: Monthly Review Press, 1989); Elizam Escobar, "The Heuristic Power of Art," in Carol Becker, ed., *The Subversive Power of Art* (New York: Routledge, 1994), pp. 35–54. On John Ahearn, see Jane Kramer, *Whose Art Is It?* (Durham, N.C.: Public Planet Books and Duke University Press, 1994).

116. Bianca Kovar, "Another Frigging Manifesto," from "I Pray You Find Me in the Wreckage" at World Wide Web site http://burn.ucsd.edu/kovar1.htm.

117. See discussion of this relationship in Mann, "Crossover Dream."

118. Walter Benjamin, "N[Theoretics of Knowledge; Theory of Progress]" [N2, 2], trans. Leigh Hafrey and Richard Sieburth, *Philosophical Forum* 15, nos. 1–2 (Fall–Winter 1983–84): 5.

119. Maud Lavin, "Photomontage, Mass Culture, and Modernity: Utopianism in the Circle of New Advertising Designers," in Teitelbaum, ed., *Montage and Modern Life,* p. 37.

Sherry Ahrentzen is professor of architecture at the University of Wisconsin–Milwaukee. Her research, focusing on new forms of housing to better address the social and economic diversity in the United States, has been published extensively in journals, magazines, and monographs. With Karen A. Franck of New Jersey Institute of Technology, she edited *New Households, New Housing*. In conjunction with Linda Groat at the University of Michigan, and with Kathryn Anthony at the University of Illinois at Urbana-Champaign, she has written articles and conducted studies identifying the social contexts and pedagogies of architectural education that enhance or hinder development of a diverse student and faculty population. A past member of the board of directors of the Environmental Design Research Association, she is currently associate editor for book reviews for the *Journal of Architectural and Planning Research*.

Thomas A. Dutton is an architect and professor of architecture at Miami University. He is editor of *Voices in Architectural Education: Cultural Politics and Pedagogy*. As a member of the editorial board of the *Journal of Architectural Education* since 1989 he has helped guest edit special editions on critical pedagogy, postmodern pedagogy, and housing and architecture. He now serves as the journal's associate editor for book reviews. Dutton was the 1990 recipient of the Creative Achievement Award of the Association of Collegiate Schools of Architecture for his contributions to architectural education and his creative use of the design studio.

Bradford C. Grant is professor of architecture at the California Polytechnic State University, San Luis Obispo. He received the American Institute of Architects Education Honors Award for his course "Images, Patterns, and Aesthetics of Subcultural Environments," and he received the New Faculty Teaching Award of the Association of Collegiate Schools of Architecture in recognition of his efforts to diversify the architectural curriculum. A past president of the National Organization of Minority Architects, his research focuses on cultural and social factors in environmental design related to African American architectural practice.

Richard Ingersoll is associate professor at Rice University, teaching courses in architectural history and urbanism. He is editor of *Design Book Review* and author of *Le Corbusier: A Marriage of Contours* and *Mumi'o Gitai: Weinraub, Bauhaus Architect in Eretz Israel.*

Lian Hurst Mann is an architect, theorist, and political organizer. She is a coauthor of *Reconstructing Los Angeles from the Bottom Up.* A founding member of the Labor/Community Strategy Center in Los Angeles, she is editor of its bilingual quarterly *AhoraNow.* She is artistic director of the culture collaborative AgitProps and editor of the AIA journal *Architecture California.*

Margaret Soltan is associate professor of human sciences and English at George Washington University. Her most recent essay, "In Warsaw," appeared in last winter's *Salmagundi.* The essay is part of a larger work in progress entitled *New World Street: The Aesthetics of Reconstruction.*

Anthony Ward was born and educated in Britain. After graduating from Birmingham University in 1965, he worked with Christopher Alexander and Barry Poyner in London before moving to Portsmouth, where in 1967 he initiated and organized the Portsmouth Symposium on Design Methods in Architecture. He is a founder-member of the Enviromental Design Research Association (EDRA). From 1969 to 1977 he taught at University of California, Berkeley. He now lives, teaches, and practices in New Zealand, doing work with the Maori and Pacific Island communities. His writing and teaching have won international awards, and he has lectured throughout Britain, Europe, Scandinavia, Australasia, and the United States. He is currently completing his Ph.D. on critical pedagogy in architectural education.

Berman, Marshall, 127
Bernini, Gianlorenzo, 29
Best, Steven, 9
Birmingham Centre for Contemporary
Cultural Studies (BCCCS), 162–70. *See
also* cultural studies
black colleges: Hampton Institute, 208;
Howard University, 208; Morgan State
University, 208; Tuskegee Institute, 208,
209, 210
Black Panthers, 44, 279, 282. *See also* race
Black Reconstruction, 207–8
Black Workers' Congress, 44
Bloch, Ernst, 7, 270, 273, 274, 276, 277, 284,
285, 288, 295, 298
Bloomer, Jennifer, 22, 24, 77, 242; critique of,
239–40; Statue of Liberty Competition with
Durham Crout and Robert Segrest, 93
Bofill, Ricardo, 57
Boggs, Carl, 166, 167
Bond, J. Max, Jr., 23, 211, 229, 231; Civil
Rights Institute, 223–26; Martin Luther
King Center for Non-Violent Social
Change, 226–27; Schomburg Center of
African American History and Research,
227–28
Bondi, Liz, 92
Bonner, Della, 303
Bourdieu, Pierre, 75
Bradshaw, Francis, 96
Brasilia: Lúcio Costa and Oscar Niemeyer, 39
Braudel, Fernand, 123
Brecht, Bertolt, 268, 270, 273, 274, 276, 277,
284, 287, 295
Broadbent, Geoffrey, 195
Brown, Cynthia, 173–74
Brown, Denise Scott, 75–76, 80; *Learning from
Las Vegas,* 52–53
Bunch, Charlotte, 95–96
Burger, Peter, 8
Bus Riders Union/Sindicato de Pasajeros,
303–5
Butler, Judith, 251

Cain, William, 251
Calthorpe, Peter, 23; comparison to Garden
Cities, 147; Laguna Ranch, 149, *151; The
Next American Metropolis,* 147; pedestrian
pocket, 147
Carmichael, Stokely, 43
Carson, Rachel: *The Silent Spring,* 138
Cassel, Albert, 212
Chermayeff, Serge, 139

Chernikhov, Iakov, 265
China, People's Republic of, 259, 278, 279
Choay, Françoise, 123
Chodorow, Nancy, 87, 89–90
Churchman, Arza, 96
City College Architectural Center (CCAC), 56
cognition, 265, 275, 276
Cohen, Phil, 169
Collins, Jim, 158
Collins, Patricia Hill, 90–91
Colomina, Beatriz, 82
Comintern, 266, 267, 272
Communist Party, Germany (KPD), 267, 269,
270, 272, 273
Communist Party of the Soviet Union
(Bolshevik), 265, 270, 272, 276
Communist Party, USA, 44
Community Design Collaborative, 58
Community Design Studio (New Zealand),
59–65; Otara Town Center project, 62–65;
Te Kura Tuarua o Hoani Waititi Marae
project, 61–62
Congrès Internationaux d'Architecture
Moderne (CIAM), 35, 37, 276, 281
constructivism, 8, 52, 264–68, 269, 282, 286
co-optation, 282, 292, 306
Corbett, Judy and Michael: Village Homes,
141
Correa, Charles: Belpur project, 147, *150*
Crawford, Margaret, 92
Crilley, Darrell, 193
critical pedagogy, 23, 158, 162, 171–78,
196–97. *See also* critical theory; pedagogy
critical theory, 21, 24, 259–318; in relation to
critical pedagogy, 171
Croxton Collaborative: National Audubon
Society Building, 147, *148*; National
Resources Defense Foundation Building,
147
Crystal Chain (Die gläserne Kette), 268
Cuba, 278, 279
cubism, 264, 265
Cuff, Dana, 55, 74
Culbertson Jacobs & Milling Architects, 103
Cultural Explainers, 231
cultural pedagogy, 23, 162–97
cultural studies, 23, 174–78; and the
Birmingham Centre for Contemporary
Cultural Studies (BCCCS), 162–71; and the
problem of textualization, 190–97
Culver, Taylor, 210
Curitiba, Brazil, 151. *See also* New Urbanism
Curry, Milton S. F., 231

Fuller, R. Buckminster, 122
fusion of cultural practitioners with social movements, 262, 300, 306. *See also* organic intellectuals
futurism, 264, 265

Gabo, Naum, 267
Gallop, Jane, 251
Gan, Aleksai, 264, 266
Gandelsonas, Mario, 235
Gantt, Harvey, 23, 210; and Gantt Huberman Architects, 218–19
Geddes, Patrick, 123
Gehry, Frank, 77, 235, 243, 247
gender: gendering architecture, 72–84; in the work of Diller + Scofidio, 294–98
Genovese, Eugene D., 206–7
Ghirardo, Diane, 53, 57, 77, 246
Giroux, Henry, 65, 167, 172, 175
Goethe, Johann Wolfgang von, 128
Goodman, Paul, 41, 43
Goodman, Robert, 46, 95
Gordon, Suzanne, 87
Graham, Bruce, 235
Gramsci, Antonio, 255, 277, 280, 307; and hegemony, 166–68
Graves, Michael, 243, 247
Gray, Eileen, 88
Greenan, Gary, 59
Gropius, Walter, 33–34, 36, 134, 265, 268, 270, 271, 276, 307
Grossberg, Lawrence, 10, 170, 175–76
Grosz, Elizabeth, 73
Grosz, George, 263, 267, 269, 284
Guattari, Félix, 6, 105
Guimard, Hector: Paris Metro Stations, 130
Günter Behnisch & Partner, 23, 24, 162, 176–77, 183–90, 197; German Postal Museum, 184, *185,* 188–90, *189*; Hysolar Solar Institute, 137–38, 184, 186, 247–49, *248, 249,* 256
Gutman, Robert, 76

Habermas, Jürgen, 240, 250
Hadid, Zaha, 77, 236
Haeckel, Ernst, 129, 131
Hall, Stuart, 4, 5, 23, 175, 192, 194: and the Birmingham Centre for Contemporary Cultural Studies (BCCCS), 163–68
Halprin, Lawrence: Sea Ranch, 142
Hamilton, Cynthia, 231
Haraway, Donna, 107
Harding, Sandra, 85

Haring, Hugo, 186
Harstock, Nancy, 161
Harvey, David, 5, 54, 56, 177
Hatch, C. Richard, 28, 54, 56, 177
Hauser, Dieter, 183
Hayden, Dolores, 23, 57, 83, 88, 101, 162, 176–77, 190, 197; Power of Place project, 178–79
Hays, K. Michael, 16, 24, 282, 306–7; on Machado & Silvetti, 285–90
Heartfield, John, 267, 305
Hebdige, Dick: *Subculture: The Meaning of Style,* 169
Hegel, Georg, 131
hegemony, 11, 16, 17, 18, 42, 50, 64, 65, 170, 276, 281, 294, 295; counterhegemony, 9, 20, 168, 259, 282, 310; discursive hegemony (textualization), 192–93, 196; by disorientation, 19–21; and Antonio Gramsci, 166–67
Heidegger, Martin, 242
Herzfelde, Weiland, 263, 267, 269
Heynen, Hilde, 8
Hilberseimer, Ludwig, 134–35, 292
Historic Black Colleges and Universities (HBCU), 219–21
Hitchcock, Henry-Russell, 35
Höch, Hannah, 302; New Woman photomontages, 268
Hockney, David, 42, 46
Hoggart, Richard, 23, 162, 163, 164, 175
hooks, bell, 86–87, 93, 94, 107, 172, 215; on cultural studies, 171
Horkheimer, Max, 269, 271
Horta, Victor: Maison du Peuple, 130
Howard, Ebenezer: Garden Cities, 132–32, 147; relationship to Leonardo da Vinci and Thomas More, 132
humanism, 7, 8, 14, 19, 20, 196, 276, 281, 285, 288
Hunt, Lynn, 191
Huntington, Samuel, 255

indexicality, 286–90, 292, 299
Ingraham, Catherine, 77
Institute of Artistic Culture (INKhUK), 263, 268, 278
Irigaray, Luce, 106
Ishikawa, Sara, 46

Jackson, George, 44
Jacobs, Jane: *The Death and Life of Great American Cities,* 38, 279

Pollock, Friedrich, 269
Pollock, Griselda, 98, 99
Popova, Lyubov, 265
positivism, 7, 35–36, 39–41, 275
post-Fordism, 4, 5
posthumanism, 3, 7, 8, 24, 196, 260
postmodernism: cultural logic, 280, 282, 308; historical condition, 2, 3, 172; postmodern Left, 8–11; postmodernism theory, 2, 6, 7, 172, 281, 283
poststructuralism, 21, 23, 236, 240
Power of Place project (Dolores Hayden, Gail Dubrow, Carolyn Flynn), 23, 101, 231; *Biddy Mason* mural, 178–79, 299. *See also* de Bretteville, Sheila Levrant
Poyner, Barry, 39
Pratt Institute Center for Community and Environmental Development (PICCED), 56, 58
proletariat, 263, 277, 310
Prosser, Gabriel, 207
Pyatok, Michael, 58–59

Quantz, Richard, 169

race: 85; Bus Riders Union civil rights lawsuit, 305; Civil Rights movement, 202, 210–12; and cultural feminism, 90; and cultural studies, 171; environmental justice, 143, 210; in post–World War II England, 163; racism and Social Darwinism, 129; social movements of people of color, 278, 300, 302; and suburban development, 101; and white solipsism, 91. *See also* Black Panthers
Ramsey, Kikanza, 303, 305
Rapoport, Amos, 40
Rayfield, Wallace, 209
realism: bourgeois, 267; cognitive function of, 276, 280; critical, 261, 284, 306; debates, 271–77, 280, 285; dirty realism, 284, 290–94; heroic, 266; hyperrealism, 267, 284, 294–98; monumental, 267; new, 266, 284, 309; painterly, 264; proletarian, 266; objectivated realism, 284–90; socialist, 265, 266; subversive realism, 285, 298–313; unprecedented realism, 284–90; virtual realism, 285, 294–98
reflection theory, 263, 264, 267, 272, 274, 275
Register, Richard: theory of ecocities, 150
Reich, Lilly, 88
Reichek, Jesse, 278–80
Reid, Richard, 183

reification, 187, 191, 263, 272, 282, 286, 290, 309
Remy, John, 80
Reynolds, Michael: earthships, 122
Rich, Adrienne, 91, 93
Rietveld, Gerrit, 80
Ritzdorf, Marsha, 101
Rivera, Diego, 310
Robertson, Jacquelin, 234–35
Robinson, Harry, III, 23, 212, 213, 218
Robinson, Hilyard, 212
Roche and Dinkeloo: Ford Foundation Building, 139; Oakland Museum, 139
Röckle, Franz, 270
Rorty, Richard, 92, 94, 250
Rosenau, Pauline Marie, 191
Rosener, Judy, 83–84
Rosler, Martha, 302
Rossi, Aldo, 145
Rousseau, Jean-Jacques, 127
Rowe, Colin, 145
Royal Institute of British Architects (RIBA), 28, 46
Rudofsky, Bernard, 41
Ruskin, John, 129–30, 135, 137, 139
Rutherford, Jonathan, 9
Rykwert, Joseph, 127

Sadan, Elisheva, 96
Sanoff, Henry, 45
Sartre, Jean-Paul, 40
Scharoun, Hans, 186
Schneekloth, Lynda, 107
Scholes, Robert, 191–92
Scholle, David, 175
Schön, Donald, 80
Schröder, Truus, 80
Schumacher, E. F., 121
Schuman, Tony, 45, 57, 310
Schurtz, Heinrich, 80
Sedgwick, Eve, 251
Segal, Walter, 46
semiotics, 23, 163, 164–65, 168
Silverstein, Murray, 46
Silvetti, Jorge, 284, 288, *289,* 309; Four Public Squares project, 288–90. *See also* Machado & Silvetti Associates
Simon, Roger, 172
Sklarek, Norma, 210
Social and Public Art Resource Center (SPARC), 24, 299
social architecture, 21–65
social formalism, 23, 184–90

social project of architecture, 1, 2, 3, 7, 17, 18, 20, 162, 255
social totality, 259, 261, 263, 271, 272, 275, 282, 286; in the work of Rem Koolhaas (OMA), 290–94
Soleri, Paolo, 23; Arcosanti, 122, 140
Solomon, Barbara Bryant, 96
Spelman, Elizabeth, 91
Spivak, Gayatri Chakravorty, 251
Sprague, Joan Forrester, 22; *More Than Housing: Lifeboats for Women and Children,* 97
Stalin, Joseph, 267, 276
Stein, Richard: *Architecture and Energy,* 140
Steiner, Rudolf, 23; First Goetheanum, 131, 139
Stern, Robert A. M., 246–47
Stichting Architecten Research (SAR): John Habraken, 41
Storefront for Art and Architecture, 300
structuralism, 7, 8, 23, 163–64, 287; and Marxism, 165–68
Stubbins, Hugh: Citycorp Building, 141
Sullivan, Louis, 23, 129
suprematism, 264
surrealism, 266, 272
Sutton, Sharon, 23, 231: Urban Network, 229–30; Urban Network and contextual feminism, 102–3
Sygar, Janet, 103
Szasz, Thomas, 41

Tafuri, Manfredo, 17, 48, 246, 260, 276, 280–82, 284
Taller de Arte Fronterizo (Border Art Workshop): *Border Sutures* project, 300
Tandy, Vertner, 209
Tatlin, Vladimir, 263, 265, 267
Taut, Bruno, 134, 139, 268; Glass Pavilion, 130
Taylor, Frederick, 272, 276
Taylor, Robert R., 209, 212
Team X: Giancarlo deCarlo, Alison and Peter Smithson, Aldo van Eyck, 37
textualization (discursive hegemony), 196; and cultural studies, 190–93; and feminism, 92–93
Teyssot, George, 296
Thompson, E. P., 163, 175
Thoreau, Henry David, 129
Torre, Susana, 79; fire station in Columbus, Indiana, 88; *Women in Architecture* exhibit, 88

Travis, Jack, 23, 231; Afri-Environments Studio, 228
Treichler, Paula, 170
Tschumi, Bernard, 23, 24, 52, 236, 246, 283; critique of Parc de la Villette, 187–88, 195–96, 238, 244–45
Tuan, Yi-Fu, 108
Turner, Graeme, 162, 163, 164, 166, 170
Turner, John F. C., 41, 46
Turner, Nat, 207
Tyng, Anne Griswold, 80
type-forms, 268, 269, 271, 286
Tzonis, Alexander, 139

Union of Soviet Socialist Republics (USSR), 261, 262, 263, 267, 271, 279
UNOVIS, 264
Unwin, Raymond: Letchworth, 132
Upton, Dell, 23, 99, 203
Urry, John, 4
utopia, 19, 20, 259, 260, 262, 265, 268, 273, 274, 276, 285, 288, 294, 306–11

Vale, Brenda and Robert: *Green Architecture,* 141
van der Rohe, Ludwig Mies, 33–34, 213
van der Ryn, Sim, 23; Integral Urban House, 140–41; Bateson Building, 141
van de Velde, Henry, 130, 268
vanguard, political, 262
Van Slyck, Abigail A., 97–98
Venturi, Robert, 13, 22, 80, 145; critique of, 51–56; *Learning from Las Vegas,* 52–53
Vesey, Denmark, 207
Vietnam War, 260, 261, 278, 279
Viollet-de-Duc, Eugène-Emmanuel, 129–30
Vitruvius, 12, 23; on nature, 123–24
Vkhutemas, 268
Vlach, John Michael, 203

Wagner, Martin, 134, 268
Wallace, William E., 74–75
Wallerstein, Immanuel, 5
Washington, Booker T., 203, 208, 209, 216
Weathermen: Students for a Democratic Society (SDS), 43–44
Weil, Felix, 269, 270
Weiler, Kathleen, 172
Weill, Kurt, 270
Weimar Republic, 262, 267, 268, 269, 276, 312
Weisman, Leslie Kanes, 73; *Discrimination by Design: A Feminist Critique of the Man-Made Environment,* 81–82

West, Cornel, 3, 6, 202; on cultural politics of
difference, 203, 215–30; prophetic
pragmatism, 108
Wigley, Mark, 24, 239, 245; critique of, 240–42
Williams, Greg, 223
Williams, Paul R., 209, 212, 218
Williams, Raymond, 23, 162, 164, 175–76, 277
Willis, Paul, 177; *Learning to Labour: How
Working Class Kids Get Working Class Jobs,*
169–70
Willis, Sharon, 246–47
Wilson, Mabel O., 231

Wodiczko, Krzysztof: Alien Staff project, 300
Woods, Lebbeus, 23; critique of, 193–96
Working Council for Art (Arbeitsrat für
Kunst), 268
Wright, Frank Lloyd, 23, 71, 140; Broadacre
City, 135–36; on climate control, 136–37;
Hollyhock House, 100
Wright, Gwendolyn, 77, 98
Wright, Richard, 310

Yoshida, Joanne, 103
Young, Iris Marion, 177

7/20/02-3c